LITERACY *ESSENTIALS*

Engagement, Excellence, and Equity for *All* Learners

REGIE ROUTMAN

Stenhouse Publishers

Portland, Maine

Stenhouse Publishers
www.stenhouse.com

Credits

pp. 63–66: "10 Lessons Learned About Teaching and Living from Taking Up Tennis" originally published as "10 Lessons About Life, Literacy and Learning.'" *Middleweb: All About the Middle Grades*. July 10, 2016. Used with permission.

p. 138: Optimal Learning Model adapted from *Read, Write, Lead: Breakthrough Strategies for Schoolwide Literacy Success* by Regie Routman, copyright © 2014. Reproduced with the permission of ASCD. ASCD.org.

pp. 147–148: "Making Fruit Tarts" originally published on *Regie's Blog*, http://www.regieroutman.org/blog/making-fruit-tarts/. March 18, 2012. Used with permission.

pp. 198–199: "Becoming a Reader" originally published in *Open a World of Possible*, edited by Lois Bridges, copyright © Scholastic, Inc (2014). Used with permission.

pp. 199–201: "Read Aloud Every Day" includes reworked excerpts from my original draft, "A Necessary Pleasure: Building a Sense of Agency Through Reading Aloud," abridged version published in *Reading Today*, May/June 2015, pp. 28–29. Reprinted by permission.

pp. 204–209: "Make Independent Reading a First Priority" first appeared in Fall 2016 in *The California Reader*, Vol.50. No.1, pp. 26–30. Reprinted by permission of the editor, Paul Boyd-Batstone.

pp. 303–304: "Twelve Essential Actions to Help English Language Learners Succeed" originally published in "Response: Teach English-Language Learners by Meeting Them 'Where They Are.'" Classroom Q & A with Larry Ferlazzo, *Education Week TEACHER*, October 24, 2015. Used with permission.

p. 345: Portions of text originally published in "Response: Provide 'Voice' and 'Choice' When Students Set Goals." Classroom Q & A with Larry Ferlazzo, *Education Week TEACHER*, January 17, 2017. Used with permission.

p. A13: "Talk Moves to Support Classroom Discussions" from *Intentional Talk: How to Structure and Lead Productive Mathematical Discussions* by Elham Kazemi and Allison Hintz, copyright © 2014, reproduced with permission of Stenhouse Publishers. www.stenhouse.com.

pp. A15–A16: "12 Writing Essentials for All Grade Levels" adapted from *Writing Essentials: Raising Expectations and Results While Simplifying Teaching* by Regie Routman. Copyright © 2005 by Regie Routman. Published by Heinemann, Portsmouth, NH. Reprinted by permission of the publisher.

Library of Congress Cataloging-in-Publication Data

Names: Routman, Regie, author.
Title: Literacy essentials : engagement, excellence, and equity for all learners / Regie Routman.
Other titles: Literacy and learning lessons from a longtime teacher
Description: Second Edition. | Portland, Maine : Stenhouse Publishers, [2017] |
    First edition published: Newark, Delaware : International Reading Association, 2012, under titleLiteracy and learning lessons from a longtime teacher. | Includes bibliographical references.
Identifiers: LCCN 2017016996 (print) | LCCN 2017030315 (ebook) | ISBN 9781571109408 (ebook) | ISBN 9781625310378 (paperback : alk. paper)
Subjects: LCSH: Language arts. | Effective teaching. | Motivation in education.
Classification: LCC LB1576 (ebook) | LCC LB1576 .R75835 2017 (print) | DDC 372.6--dc23
LC record available at https://lccn.loc.gov/2017016996

Cover design, interior design, and typesetting by Lucian Burg. LU Design Studios, Portland, ME www.ludesignstudios.com

Manufactured in the United States of America

 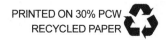

For my son, Peter
with love and gratitude

Contents

Contents with sections

Contents with sections

Contents with sections

Contents with sections

Stories Overview

ENGAGEMENT

EXCELLENCE

EQUITY

A Note About Notes and Other Resources

To keep the text clean and unencumbered, all references to research, ideas, authors, and quotations requiring explanation or further discussion are notated by a superscript in the text and listed in a Notes section beginning on page N1 in the end matter. The notes are divided by section (Engagement, Excellence, and Equity) and sequenced consecutively in each section and chapter. Many notes include bibliographic information to help you find referenced material easily. Simple reference citations not requiring annotation are contained in the References and Resources section beginning on page R1. Any statement or concept not attributed is based on my own teacher-research, observations, and more than forty-five years of teaching and leading experience.

Accompanying Website for *Literacy Essentials*

sten.pub/literacyessentials

- Study Guide

- Appendices

- *Literacy Essentials* References and Resources: for easy access through URLs

- Lesson Plan: framework, detailed daily plans, teacher and student reflections, anchor charts, examples of student work, and much more

- Class-authored, published nonfiction book: *Polar Bears Are King of the North*, by second and third graders, 48 pages

- Class-authored, published book: *Dreams: Listen to Our Stories*, by fifth graders
  - Follow-up comments by students as high school seniors

Acknowledgments

To you, my readers—the audience that keeps me writing—deepest thanks for your continuing support and affirmation over many years. I write because of you—fellow teachers and leaders who work tirelessly each day to do right by your students and colleagues. I write because it's the best way I know to figure out and share what I've learned, questioned, researched, and concluded after years of study and practice in diverse schools and districts. I write because I care so much about the state of education and what each of us might do to make a worthy difference for all students. Always, dear reader, you are by my side, pushing me to greater clarity and practicality.

I owe so much to so many. This book builds on what I have learned over several decades from ongoing collaboration with a multitude of talented educators and mentors. Sincerest appreciation goes to these educators, named and unnamed, for making the content of this book stronger. Related to the specific information in this text, thanks go, in alphabetical order, to colleagues whose interactions around literacy and learning contributed to the honesty, integrity, and information in this text:

Rod Berger (for encouraging me to write my education story), Randal Bychuk (for his enthusiasm and talent for beautifully connecting music with literacy), Harriet Cooper (for being my dearest, lifelong friend and for helping me keep a healthy life-balance and sense of humor), Nell Duke (for her essential literacy research and for reviewing my literacy research section), Larry Ferlazzo (for support of my work and for permission to reprint excerpts from former *Education Week* blog posts), Barb Ide (for her laser focus on doing what's right and best for students and for being a lifelong advocate for students as well as my dear colleague and friend), Marilyn Jerde (for her stories, humor, and treasured friendship and collegiality), Lori Johnson (for her honesty, courage, and firm commitment to underserved students), Mary Beth Nicklaus (for her contribution and feedback on stamina, the importance of failure, and our discussions regarding her important teacher-research), Daria Orloff (for being a stellar educator, dedicated collaborator, and generous contributor to this text), Matt Renwick (for his ongoing tech savvy, his feedback on all things educational—not just tech—and his generosity and friendship), the Twitter community (for all the informative blogs, research, websites, and affirmations, and to Rachel V. Small for getting me started), MaryEllen Vogt (for her insightful comments on the Optimal Learning Model), Judy Wallis (for keeping me in the loop in so many important professional and personal ways), and Angela Watson (for her permission to use "8 Ways Teachers Can Talk Less and Get Kids Talking More"). Thanks also to Cheri

Banks, Heather McKay, John Norton, Tree Swenson, Stacey Wester, and Nancy Wright for their important input and support.

Winnipeg colleague Trish Richardson requires singular recognition. I have had the great privilege to teach, coach, and lead alongside her at Strathmillan School and to witness her expert teaching, her generosity with peers, and her crucial role on her school's leadership team. Most significantly, Trish has been the extraordinarily thoughtful and expert reader-responder to this entire text. She has been my collaborator in the truest sense; her voice is woven into the text through her wise suggestions and reflections, her additions to the Take Action sections, her outstanding, comprehensive lesson plan on a real-world issue, and her Technology Tools appendix. Deepest thanks for her valued feedback, patience, and friendship.

I am also exceptionally grateful to Winnipeg, Manitoba, schools and colleagues for our joyful collaboration, since 2008, to improve and sustain the teaching of writing in many ethnically diverse schools. Our partnership has been the most gratifying and significant work of my career. First of all, this ongoing literacy project would not have been possible without the steadfast commitment of superb professional development coordinator and literacy expert Allyson Matczuk, in collaboration with three other outstanding visionary leaders: Jason Drysdale (assistant superintendent in River East Transcona School Division), Celia Caetano-Gomes (superintendent in Winnipeg School Division), and Tanis Pshebniski (assistant superintendent in St. James-Assiniboia School Division), who was also ably supported by Candace Borger and Michelle Clarke. It is noteworthy and unusual—and critical to our success—that the three above-named superintendents devoted themselves not only to steadfastly supporting principals and teachers in their own division but also to working together as a unified team across divisions. As well, heartfelt thanks go to all the dedicated Winnipeg principals, teachers, coaches, and students involved in our ongoing literacy work.

In particular, I want to highlight the contributions of Winnipeg's Strathmillan School, where I conducted residencies over four years. Exceptional and visionary principal Sue Marlatt and her staff established an intellectual, trusting, and joyful school culture, which made high writing achievement possible. Thanks to Sherri Steuart, Melissa Kirkland, Blythe Lodwick, Morgan Manns, Susan Maclean-Pilot, and other staff members for their contributions to this book. I am forever grateful to Sue Marlatt and the entire staff, all of whom have an enduring place of affection and admiration in my heart. Many of the ideas in this book evolved from our gratifying collaboration.

The Winnipeg work would not have been possible or sustainable without the contributions of my brilliant colleagues Nancy McLean and Sandra Figueroa, who also conducted residencies in Winnipeg over many years. I am enormously grateful for our marvelous collaboration and deep friendship. Nancy McLean's coaching skills are the best I've ever seen. She combines deep knowledge, sensitivity to people's needs, and abiding kindness and gentleness to all the students, teachers, and principals she works with. Sandra Figueroa is one of the most gifted educators I have ever had the privilege to work with. She knows and applies principled K–12 literacy and leadership practices better than anyone I know, and she endears herself to all who are fortunate enough to work with her. I am thankful, too, that she has been one of my dearest, most supportive friends for many years.

Working once again with beloved editor Toby Gordon has been an enormously gratifying experience. Toby understood and championed all I set out to do with this book by unconditionally and respectfully supporting me with honest and useful feedback. As well, it has been my good fortune over many years to have her as dear friend, admired colleague, and book soulmate. I am also indebted to the entire Stenhouse Publishers crew for their excellent contributions, flexibility, and kindnesses: Dan Tobin, president (for his warm welcome to the company), Chris Downey (for her meticulous editorial production skills), Grace Makley (for her adept production assistance), Kathleen Florio (for her superb, meticulous copyediting skills and for maintaining my voice), Jay Kilburn (for art direction), Lucian Burg (for our beautiful cover and book design), Deanna Butler (for the index), Chuck Lerch, Zsofia McMullin, Nate Butler, and Jacqueline Carr (for marketing content, planning, and outreach), Chandra Lowe (for coordinating author events), and Andrew Yemm (for overseeing sales).

To my precious family, I depend on you always. To my sister, Amy, and her husband, Earl, I am grateful for your love and support in all things. Thanks to my delightful granddaughters, Katie and Brooke, for their inspiration, love, and "coffee" and conversation "dates." To my son, Peter, and my daughter-in-law, Claudine, thanks for being ever present and loving in my life. And, finally, all my books are for Frank, without whom I would not be a writer. His unwavering love, support, and generosity continue to make all things possible.

Letter to My Colleagues

Dear Colleagues,

    You, my dear readers, are the reason I write. I wrote *Literacy Essentials* because I saw a need to simplify teaching, raise expectations, and make expert teaching possible for all of us. I saw a need to emphasize how a school culture of kindness, trust, respect, and curiosity is essential to any lasting achievement. I saw a need to demonstrate and discuss how and why the beliefs, actions, and knowledge we hold determine the potential for many of our students. Equal opportunity to learn depends on a culture of engagement and equity, which underlies a relentless pursuit of excellence.

Everyone talks about what a difficult, exhausting time it is to be a teacher, but that narrative has been true for as long as I've been teaching. Keeping up with all the planning, mandates, and assessment can be crushing; class sizes are large and challenging; required curriculum and standards are demanding; testing is out of control. How do we rise to the challenge of providing an engaging, excellent, equitable education for all learners—including those from high-poverty, underserved schools? In spite of all the obstacles we face—politically, professionally, personally—we teachers matter more than ever.

At my core, I am a teacher. My most joyful work—and when I feel most at one with myself—is when I am working with students. I experience a renewed sense of possibility, hope, and rejuvenation every time I go into a classroom and teach. I believe we have to love our work if we are to expend the necessary effort teaching requires. To love it, we have to savor the teaching process while leading full and encompassing lives. To love it, we have to be passionate and knowledgeable. If you've lost that love, this book is for you, to help you reclaim joyful teaching and pass on to your students an enduring desire for curiosity and a love of learning.

This is a long book. Knowing how busy and complicated life can be, I struggled with that length. However, at the same time I wanted to provide the tools, information, and inspiration you need to make your teaching and learning lives more authentic and vigorous. The book is organized for deep reading or for dipping in and out of the many issues. The text is not meant to be all encompassing; at the same time, many important aspects of teaching and learning are dealt with in depth. Use the detailed table of contents to help pinpoint your current concerns. Although I recommend starting at the beginning of the book, you can begin anywhere. The book's three sections—Engagement, Excellence, and Equity—are interconnected with one another, all focusing on a thriving school culture where every learner can succeed and feel empowered. How and why we must do better for all students is the overriding theme of this book and, I believe, the core civil rights issue of our time.

Stories, both personal and professional, are also an integral part of this book and are woven into each section. I believe we need to bring our stories and experiences into the classroom. Doing so means teaching as our truest selves. Stories connect us, sustain us, and add meaning to our lives. For our students, hearing and validating their stories affirms and celebrates who they are. Stories inspire hope, and hope is often in short supply these days. Yet, hope is what keeps our students and us showing up and giving our best selves to learning and teaching each and every day.

Literacy Essentials grew out of a first edition, *Literacy and Learning Lessons from a Longtime Teacher* (2012). The majority of this second edition is new and rethought with a much fuller and deeper picture of literacy and learning. This book includes additional materials online at sten.pub/literacyessentials, where you can easily access and print out the book's study guide and appendices, and retrieve the extensive references and resources that support the text and also make for excellent professional reading. You will find comprehensive, detailed lesson plans on a real-world topic studied in depth, a related and beautiful class-authored nonfiction book, and a class-authored book of students' dreams for their future.

Finally, this is not a book about teacher-as-technician, dutifully following a script, program, or rigid data results. It is for teacher-as-thinker, who responsibly takes the lead from her students as well as from curriculum and standards. How can we raise citizens who think for themselves if we ourselves do not wonder, imagine, seek to know more, and do better? *Literacy Essentials* is intended to give you more flexibility, knowledge, confidence, and opportunity to try new ideas, take new actions, think more deeply, and raise important questions. This book is also a call to action—to be our best selves and do all we can to make an excellent education an actuality for every student.

Expert teaching has always demanded not just content knowledge but also courage, compassion, and common sense. Never underestimate that time and patience can pay off, that change is possible, and that you—one caring and knowledgeable teacher—can make an enduring difference in a child's life.

Become a teacher of conscience; listen to your inner voice; hear all the voices of those you work with. Powerlessness is our enemy; perseverance is our strength. Hold onto your determination to do right by your students. Don't get frustrated; get focused! Think, "What can I do today to make a worthy difference for this student or group of students?" Be prepared to take calculated risks on behalf of your students. Make your classroom a place of intellectual vitality.

All children have the right to an education that includes exploration of topics of interest and relevance, that results in personal fulfillment, and that leads to becoming an inquisitive and informed citizen, prepared to fully participate in our fragile democracy. We teachers have always been the keepers of the dream, the providers of hope and inspiration for our students. We must remain so.

Thank you for your dedication and all your valiant efforts.

With admiration and deep respect,

ENGAGEMENT

If students are not engaged in school, everything else that goes on in the name of education is pretty much beside the point. The costs of students turning off or dropping out are far higher that those of investing in schools that excite students to learn in the first place.

—*Ken Robinson*

How do we ensure that all students are engrossed each day in meaningful and challenging work, receive expert teaching, have equal opportunity to learn, and experience learning as joyful? I believe that is the key question for us as educators and also that such an outcome is only possible within a culture of empowerment. That is, in a physically, emotionally, and intellectually safe and rich environment, students and teachers feel encouraged and supported to let their voices be heard, explore their passions and interests, develop deep knowledge, and become their fullest and truest selves.

Picture this. You walk into a classroom—whether it's kindergarten or high school—and no one looks up. The students and teacher are so absorbed in meaningful work and productive conversations, pushing each other to higher levels of thinking, that they literally don't see you at first. They are deeply involved in learning that is social, personal, fulfilling, and intellectually challenging. They are in a state of "flow"; they are mindfully focused, involved, and motivated by the task or experience at hand, which is exactly the learning culture we want for all learners.[1] Such a desirable learning state begins with engagement. Yet, in my experience, classrooms where students are fully engaged and empowered are scarce. To change that dynamic, we need to understand and apply the factors that make engagement probable.

By *engagement* we mean the attention, commitment, and eagerness learners show in inquiring, creating, and responding to a question or a learning opportunity. Students—and teachers—who are engaged will risk failure, make their voices heard, work well with others, and seek to go on learning even when they face challenges. As referred to in this book, engagement is always connected to significant and authentic work that captivates the intellect and stirs the heart and mind. To be clear, engagement is not about compliance, complacency, following rules, or listening without an opportunity to participate.

Without engagement of both the heart and the mind, learning falters or remains superficial. Engagement of the heart, emotions, and intellect depends on multiple factors, such as a safe, risk-taking, organized environment; and a culture that promotes respect and kindness, celebrates strengths, welcomes errors and questions, appreciates effort, and teaches students to become self-directed learners. In this kind of environment, engaged learners willingly make a commitment to put forth their best efforts to do meaningful work. The byproduct is the joy, satisfaction, and love of learning that come from taking on a challenge and succeeding.

Active engagement is usually associated with deeper learning and activities that are worth our students' and our time and efforts. Expert teachers work to connect curriculum and standards with students' curiosity and real-world audiences and purposes, all of which make it more likely students will be engaged with learning. Disengaged students are far more likely to be bored, off-task, or display inappropriate behaviors. When students are asked to do recipe-like work, isolated exercises, or "cute" projects, some might be motivated to do the work and even enjoy it—for a reward, a grade, praise, or the ease of doing; but frivolous activities are time-wasters for enriching the mind and promoting deep thinking and do not constitute worthwhile engagement.

This first section of *Literacy Essentials* discusses the conditions, principles, and actions that are necessary for an optimal learning environment; that is, a school culture where all learners thrive. We'll explore the role of the physical, social and emotional, and intellectual environments that contribute to high engagement, which is essential to all meaningful learning. It took me many years to understand and appreciate that schools are cultural entities and that high achievement across a whole school depends first and foremost on a healthy, collaborative school culture that empowers all learners.

Developing Trusting Relationships

I f there's one crucial lesson I've learned in more than forty-five years of teaching, coaching, and mentoring, it's this: trusting relationships are a necessity for students and teachers to engage in serious learning and for all learners in a school to flourish. We simply cannot maintain the energy and focus on improving instruction and raising achievement without a whole school of trusting relationships. In fact, trust between and among teachers, principals, and parents is the greatest predictor of substantial improvement in student achievement.[1] *High achievement and good test scores are a byproduct of a healthy, thriving school culture.*[2]

However, in the high-stakes world of teaching, if school culture—and trust, in particular—is considered as a factor in school improvement, it's usually in a supporting role, not a leading one. Yet, a thriving, trusting culture helps any organization succeed and is a major factor in why people choose to stay. Without trust, we are all less likely to invest our energies in taking on new tasks and challenges. Everything meaningful that happens in a classroom, a school, and a district depends on a bedrock foundation of mutual respect, trust, collaboration, fairness, and physical and emotional safety.

Build Trusting Relationships

If the way people in a school relate to each other determines the success and achievement of the students, teachers, and principal, how do we establish those trusting and caring relationships? A principal recently asked me for advice on how to be successful in her first year in a new school. "It's all about relationships," I told her. "Celebrate teachers' and students' strengths every day, get to know your staff as people, earn their trust, respect confidentiality, and don't make major changes right away." For any of us who work in schools, or in any organization, we have greater opportunities for growth when we can freely and joyfully collaborate with colleagues. This is no easy task. It requires accepting that every person has a different perspective and way of thinking; that respecting and valuing colleagues' views, talents, and background are a necessity for developing trust; and that gossip is not conversation.

In a recent visit to a school where I did not yet know the staff, during our "working" lunch on the first day, the principal, curriculum director, and literacy coach each had a notebook in hand. I know they were surprised when I said, "Let's not work through lunch. Let's take a well-deserved break and just enjoy our time together." We wound up talking about our families, hobbies, cooking, and favorite things to do and eat. At the end of the lunch, I felt closer to each one of them. We had lots of laughs, learned about each other's lives, and knew each other better.

We simply cannot underestimate the power of positive relationships on the health, well-being, and achievement of all school community members. Without excellent relationships between students and teachers, teaching teams at and across grade levels, teachers and administrators, and students and their families, it's difficult to raise and sustain achievement and have a thriving school culture. In fact, *I have never seen a school increase and sustain literacy achievement without a schoolwide culture of trust and respect.*

Look for ways to identify and comment on something a colleague or staff member has done well. Honest compliments build trust, and high-trust organizations are more likely to be collaborative and high achieving. Thoughtful gestures matter. Recognizing our colleagues' strengths results in a more robust learning culture. When we feel personally and professionally valued, we are apt to be happier, more productive, and more likely to take risks as teachers and learners.

 ## Take Action

- Get to know students, teachers, and community members, and greet them by name. (See pages 284–285 on the power of honoring students' names.)

- Express appreciation specifically and often. Most of us do not hear often enough that our efforts are valued. For example, thank a colleague who has shared a successful lesson, opened up his or her classroom for colleagues to observe, offered support to a new teacher, or raised an important schoolwide issue in a positive way.

- **Remember colleagues' birthdays,** special occasions, and individual accomplishments with a personal congratulation, a short note, an e-mail, a text message, or a card.

- **Invite all staff members to attend professional development meetings.** Include specialists and teaching aides. Consider, as well, inviting a parent, a board member, or the superintendent. Our school community members can be our biggest boosters and advocates. Having some "open" PD meetings sends an inclusive message and makes our work transparent.

- **Publicly acknowledge a colleague's achievement in a staff meeting.** Or, before a scheduled professional development meeting, we can ask a peer to bring or share a student work sample, lesson plan, class-authored book, or anything outstanding we have noticed. Not only is a colleague's work publicly celebrated, but also we all benefit from learning about the excellent idea.

- **Provide families a welcoming school culture.** Ensure that a highly visible, welcoming message greets visitors as they enter the school building. It can be daunting for families whose children have mostly known failure to even enter our schools and classrooms. Resist judging families, even when they fail to "show up." We never know how many hardships a family may be facing or what fears or negative past experiences may be keeping them from attending a conference or returning a phone call. Continue to reach out in a positive manner.

- **Treat secretaries, office staff, volunteers, and custodians as valued players in a school's success.** Use Thanksgiving, Valentine's Day, and other holidays to write them class-authored gratitude letters. Invite them into the classroom to talk about their jobs. Proudly include them in any whole-school activity that celebrates the school's achievement. Organizations that flourish treat all employees and volunteers as team members.

- **Perform acts of kindness each day.** For example, listen without judgment to a colleague who has had a tough day; volunteer to pick up a colleague's class from a special activity; share a lunch with a teacher who has forgotten his or her own or had no time to bring one. For a colleague who is not a good speller, offer to read a newsletter before it goes home to families. Acts of kindness foster relationships, and kindness can be taught. Through our own kind gestures to our colleagues and students, we model and encourage thoughtful, kind deeds. (See more on kindness in "Teach Kindness," pages 17–19.)

10 Actions That Promote High Trust and Achievement

1. Celebrate strengths and successes.

2. Assume a collective sense of responsibility for all students and staff.

3. Hold high expectations for all learners (teachers, students, and principal).

4. Use common language and shared beliefs that align with research-based practices.

5. Engage in continuous professional learning centered on authentic and relevant work to increase student learning.

6. Implement a viable curriculum with accompanying first-rate resources and texts.

7. Embed meaningful and respectful conversations and feedback that move learning forward.

8. Employ coaching experiences that leave the learner feeling "I can do it!"

9. Promote ongoing assessment, mostly formative.

10. Ensure that data use, analysis, and application are sensible and practical.

Taken together and put into daily practice, these actions foster trusting relationships, which build capital when tough issues arise. These actions and principles are discussed and demonstrated throughout this book because a trusting culture is a necessity for all of us—students, teachers, coaches, leaders, learners at all levels—in order to put forth our full efforts, even under challenging circumstances.

Bond with Students and Colleagues

It's difficult to learn from someone we don't trust. Years ago, esteemed New Zealand educator Don Holdaway noted, "You don't have to love every student, but you do need to bond with each one of them if they're to learn anything at all." Bonding means forming meaningful and respectful connections with all students and their families—and making an effort to do the same with our colleagues. I'll never forget the story Don told about going in to see his daughter's kindergarten teacher when he and his family were living and working in Cambridge, Massachusetts. His daughter was not getting along well with her teacher and felt the teacher didn't like her. In his booming voice Don told the teacher it was her duty as his child's teacher to bond with her. From that day on, the trouble between teacher and child seemed to vanish, with the teacher taking Don's command seriously. Part of that bonding meant valuing the child and sending the message: *I see you, I know who you are, I understand you.* Too many of our students—and colleagues and families, too—remain invisible to us. Even if they are physically present, they are often mostly silent and unseen. Attempt to "see" through respectful eyes all members of the school community and to affirm each one of them.

 ## Take Action

- Let every parent or guardian know something positive about the student. A phone call, text message, or note early on—and often, throughout the school year—serves to build trust and saves time in the long run. A parent who believes his or her child and culture are valued will be more likely to listen without feeling threatened and to cooperate when there is a problem. Bonding with families makes it easier to bond with our students.

- Let every student know we value them. Through our daily gestures, body language, and words, let's affirm every student. It is important to let students know we are glad to see them, that their contributions to the class matter, and that we recognize their unique talents (even on days when it's hard to do so). Ask students, "What's one or more important things you would like me to know about you?" Tell students, "Here are a few important things I would like you to know about me." One thing I often tell students is: "I'm not interested in the 'right' answer. I'm interested in your thinking and how you got there."

- Let every learner know we want them to succeed. As one middle school student said, "You can always tell when a teacher wants to help all students succeed." That teacher demonstrates fairness, openness, effort, and flexibility. For example, if the whole class did badly on a test, the teacher willingly reteaches the lesson and gives a new test. As well, the teacher does quick check-ins with students to see how they are, if they understand the work, and what further support they might need.

◆ **Greet students warmly each day, which sets a personal, caring tone.** Check in with them every morning as they walk through the doors. Encourage students to wait their turn as others share quick greetings or stories as they file in. End each day in a similar manner. Even if it's just a smile, a handshake, a fist bump, or a high five, try to connect with each student at the start and end of the day or class period. Use that opportunity to show a sense of humor, make a kind comment, have a bit of fun, and make each student feel valued.

◆ **Get to know students, and help them get to know each other.** Find appropriate ways to learn about students' lives and interests. At the start of a class, take several minutes to ask a few volunteers to respond to such questions as "What did you do over the weekend?" and "Who learned or did something unexpected yesterday?" Ensure students are making friends and connections with other students, not just the teacher. Incorporate small groups for learning, and change them regularly, so students get to work with most of their peers.

◆ **Choose language and focus of remarks carefully.** The words we use have the power to encourage and motivate or to turn off students—and teachers and families—from even attempting a task or a requested action. Seek to first recognize and acknowledge the strengths of students, teachers, administrators, office staff, and community members. It's easy to pass judgment on someone who disappoints us or we don't know well. As much as possible, give students, colleagues, and families the benefit of the doubt and keep an open mind.

◆ **Model empathy.** Take time to talk with an upset student, validate all points of view, and show respect to every student through words, actions, and body language. An empathetic response to an emotional student helps to keep our learning culture positive for all students. When we embody a culture of empathy, we make our classrooms and schools safe havens for students and colleagues.

◆ **Share favorite books, websites, videos, podcasts.** Carefully select texts and resources to engage students, pique their curiosity and interests, and jump-start conversations where all can join in.

◆ **Create class traditions.** For example, create special class celebrations or a special song and tradition on birthdays or other celebratory days throughout the year. One teacher has her students make up their own version of the birthday song every year and often includes other languages in the song, depending on the students.[3]

◆ **Tell personal stories.** Ordinary stories from our lives supplemented with photos of family, friends, and our special interests connect us with students and staff and show our common humanity. I always share some personal stories as a way to bond with a new group of students.[4] Many such stories are a part of this book. (See more on storytelling, pages 77, 200, and 307; see "Stories Overview," page ix; and see the story "Bonding with My Granddaughters Through Storytelling," below.)

STORY ❖ Bonding with My Granddaughters Through Storytelling

When our granddaughters were 14 and 11, my husband, Frank, and I took them with us on a four-day vacation from Seattle, Washington, to the Oregon coast. We chose a town we frequented and loved and couldn't wait to share it with them. We stayed in our usual modest, cozy lodging where we did our own cooking and enjoyed the amenities of free bikes, movies, badminton, and picnic tables on the grounds. The location was ideal, a quiet beachside village close to a bustling town, a beautiful state park, and many seaside attractions.

It took a couple of days to realize we were not having any substantial conversations with the girls, especially with the older one, who was bonded and bound to her cell phone 24/7. No matter where we were or what we did, whether it was exploring sea life on the beach or seeing a gorgeous sunset, our 14-year-old granddaughter's most constant companion was the smartphone she held in her hand. Her primary vacation experiences were coming through the images she was viewing through the camera lens of her phone. It took a while to figure out what was happening, that she was uploading photos to Instagram and immediately sharing vacation moments with her friends. Although clearly the phone use was excessive, we were not her parents and felt we could not and should not intervene. But what to do? We felt we were losing the strong bonds we had forged with her over her growing-up years.

Late in the afternoon on the second day of the vacation, I announced we would be having cocktail hour before dinner. "Ladies," I said to them, "cocktail hour means wonderful drinks for everyone, special appetizers, telling stories, and no devices allowed. Papa and I will start first." With drinks in hand (fancy fruit drinks for the girls and wine for the grown-ups) and delectable treats on the table, we pulled out all the stops as we told the story of a "lady in a black dress" who had recently attended her first Seattle Symphony concert and had created quite a frenzy. A bit of background here: In a savvy effort to attract younger audiences, Seattle Symphony conductor and music director Ludovic Merlot decided to include a bit of popular music culture in selected programs. That evening, the opening number was performed by famous rap singer Sir Mix-a-Lot, who at the beginning of his performance of his classic "Baby Got Back" unexpectedly invited the women seated up front to join him onstage. As about twenty women danced and shimmied to the rhythmic beat of the rap music, one woman stood out. Wearing a stylish black dress and dancing exuberantly and "wildly," it was impossible to take your eyes off of her. The entire scene was captured on someone's cell phone—especially the particular woman who came to be known as "the lady in the black dress." The video went viral with more than three million views on YouTube. As it turns out, "the lady in the black dress" is a friend of ours, and our granddaughters, who had seen the video (being the tech-knowledgeable kids that they are) were astonished when we casually mentioned that fact. "You know her?" they asked in disbelief. We, the older generation, had instantly become "cool." Now they were eager to talk with us and had actual questions that only we could answer.

As we passed the storytelling baton to the girls, at first they said, "We don't have any stories to tell." Slowly, over days and with encouragement, they each began to tell stories of their own and to pull out all the stops as well. And from the stories came actual conversations, the four of us sitting around the table and enjoying each other's company. The following summer, we took the girls on vacation again to the same spot on the Oregon coast, which they had also come to love. "Can we please have cocktail hour?" they asked before we left Seattle. Cocktail hour is now part of our family culture and lore, even when we are not on vacation. Storytelling, as generations of people from all over the world have known for millennia, helps us bond with each other. Stories humanize us and connect us. Stories promote the value of our lives through talk, listening, and conversation—all of which are necessary for a full and happy life.

Teach Kindness

Establishing a school culture of kindness is essential. Giving and receiving kindness makes us feel happier, less stressed, and more connected to others. Acts of kindness are not just nice; they are a necessity for optimal well-being and positive life outcomes, such as academic success and professional advancement. We actually feel better and learn more when we perform kind deeds. The good news is that kindness can be taught and is learned best through experiencing it, not just talking about it. Even small acts of kindness contribute to increasing our self-worth, compassion for others, and optimism.[5]

When a group of diverse fifth graders embraced a yearlong, hands-on research and practice study on how to reduce bullying in their school and neighborhood, the whole atmosphere of the school improved. Students and teachers not only acted more kindly toward each other; the school community became a more caring place. Bus behaviors improved; students consciously took time to perform small acts of kindness to peers; fewer incidents of bullying were reported each day, which meant fewer students went to the principal's office for behavior issues. Perhaps best of all, students learned through their own advocacy efforts that they could be positive agents for change in their own lives. They became more confident, worked better with their peers, and trusted each other more.[6]

Repeatedly performing small acts of kindness can permanently change how we perceive someone. A personal story illustrates that point. Many years ago, a high-level administrator in a district where I was working made it difficult for me to work optimally with teachers and principals. For years, no matter what I did, she found fault and let me know it. As a result, I didn't trust her, tried to avoid her, and saw her as my enemy. Then, unexpectedly, for reasons I never understood, she began treating me kindly. At first I was suspicious and thought, "What does she want from me?" But she persisted, month after month, doing and saying kind things. She wore me down with her kindness, and my attitude toward her changed. It took a long time, but I began to trust her. The mutual trust that slowly developed allowed us to eventually become colleagues and to work well together, which made us both better at our jobs. I learned that kindness is far more powerful than I had realized. It's not just that the two of us could now work together; a huge burden had been lifted. I was able to enjoy my job more and experience less anxiety when a problem arose, and I felt more confident and effective in my work.

Take Action

- **Help to create a schoolwide culture of kindness.** Students watch us carefully; they notice how we behave and interact with others. If they see us acting kindly and compassionately toward others, they are more likely to emulate those behaviors. Establishing bully-free classrooms and schools is especially crucial for marginalized students and adults who face increased bullying in parts of our society. More than ever, schools must become kindness zones.

- **Read aloud and discuss books that focus on kindness and the harmful impact of bullying.** A few outstanding titles are *Wonder* and *Auggie and Me* by R. J. Palacio, *Each Kindness* by Jacqueline Woodson, and all books by Trudy Ludwig. Check with a librarian for more recommendations and resources.[7]

- **Share research findings on kindness.** Here are some key findings to share with students: experiencing kindness makes us happier and more compassionate, improves self-esteem, increases our gratitude, and helps us learn better.[8] Ask, "What does this mean for us?" "What actions might we need to take to make our classroom and school a kinder place and a bully-free zone?"

- **Create class-authored charts and books on kindness.** Display these in prominent places. Students can also create poems or mottos of words to live by around the theme of kindness. Display or publish this work, or use a program like Haiku Deck or Keynote to create a presentation about kindness.

- **Have students practice and demonstrate small acts of kindness.** Demonstrate kind acts and gestures, and notice and celebrate students' acts of kindness—for example, talking respectfully to someone who has hurt us, speaking up when we see a peer being bullied, or offering to do a task for a friend in need. With guidance, have students try out their own language and actions of being kind.

  - Have students stop and think about a kind act they noticed during the day to share with a partner during a turn-and-talk time.
  - Create opportunities for leadership roles with older students mentoring younger students and showing kindness—for example, when they work together as writing buddies or reading buddies.
  - Consider schoolwide spirit days or weeks for celebrating and sharing examples of kindness toward each other.

- Use class or school Twitter, Instagram, or Facebook pages to take snapshots or record acts of kindness throughout the school.
- Create videos, raps, and songs about kindness, with and by students; share these at assemblies, with other classes, and with families at student-led conferences.

Make Parents Partners

Trusting relationships with our students' families greatly enhance a school's culture. Engaged parents, who understand, value, and support our efforts with their students, make our jobs easier and happier. When parents are truly viewed as partners and not obstacles, students are more likely to be successful regardless of where they go to school. Yet, based on their own former school experiences, a lack of outreach, or reasons we don't understand, some parents and families can find it very intimidating just to walk into a school building, especially if their children have mostly known failure. I still remember, when my son Peter was in first grade, how uncertain I felt entering the school for a conference I had requested—and I was a teacher in the same school system!

We need to do better in recognizing and appreciating the knowledge, skills, talents, and differences that families and their children bring to our school culture. As one parent leader eloquently put it, "I want a school where the parents and teachers are raising the same child."[9] Given how overloaded most of us are, it takes a deliberate, heartfelt effort to reach out and get to know students' families. The effort is worth it. If parents are fearful coming into our schools, we cannot effectively partner with or engage them. When families feel welcome, they show up in greater numbers for family nights, conferences, and school offerings.

As a whole school, consider welcoming signs, easy-to-read information regarding services the school offers, and, if possible, even a small room or space where parents can come to meet and converse with other parents, learn about school offerings and special programs, find out about opportunities for volunteering, sign out books on learning, learn how to best help with homework, and so on. Consider also working with the principal to offer an occasional "early morning coffee" for families, as a time to meet with the principal, available teachers, and other families to hear news of the school. Socializing with the people we work with and depend on goes a long way toward building trust within the school community. It's well known, in fact, that despite the media hype on the failure of our public schools, most parents give their local schools high grades. Parents and families are our strongest advocates, and we need to continually let them know we value them and their children and are here to serve them.

Take Action

◆ **Communicate clearly with families to inform and interact with them in a manner that engages them and that they can easily access.** Use e-mails, texts, phone calls, social media such as Facebook and Twitter, a school website, and informational videos to let families know what we are teaching and what students are learning, what our explicit expectations are for students and their families, and the best way and times to reach us. Keeping parents informed, including communicating their child's strengths before needs, goes a long way toward engaging them as partners. For nonnative English speakers and newcomers, use translations, technology, and welcoming adults and students who speak their language and understand their culture to be sure messages are received and understood.

⦿ *Invite parents to join us as partners.* We can ask parents to write or personally contact us to communicate information about their child—strengths, interests, worries, hopes for their child. First, send your own personal letter to parents of your students doing the same. Also, ask for parents' preferred way to be contacted—phone, e-mail, or text. (See also page 379.)

⦿ *Make contact early in the school year.* Call, e-mail, or text a quick and friendly message before any issues emerge with a student. Try to contact at least several parents every week—and not just those families whose students may be having difficulty. All parents—even those of top-performing students—appreciate kind, concerned, and positive feedback. Especially when we have taken the time early on to comment on something encouraging about their child—for example, a strength or an improvement in an academic or behavioral area— parents are more likely to listen and partner with us later on, when there is an issue that requires their support.

⦿ *Listen with an open mind.* Just having a call from their child's teacher can initially feel intimidating to some families. Let's be sure to listen more than we speak, which is not easy for most of us, myself included. Seek to find out what parents see as their child's strengths, interests, and passions before discussing needs. Ask questions that show our genuine interest and willingness to use the information they share with us in a positive manner.

⦿ *Share visual snapshots of life in the classroom* through Instagram and other social media. Adding an explanation underneath any photo or visual can be helpful for communicating with families for whom English is the second language. If sharing student information online is a concern, keep the social media account private, allowing only students, families, and those with permission to have access to the posted content.

- *Create personal, classroom, or school blogs* to communicate with families and students. Creating a blog with our students can boost parent engagement. Consider Kidblog, Edublog, and WordPress resources for creating different kinds of blogs. For composing a post on a classroom blog, use whole-class, shared writing or small groups who contribute to the blog on a weekly basis. Besides curriculum information and class news, consider including items like homework tips, rubrics (in kid-friendly language) for assignments, and videos on such topics as how to do an assignment, how to think about a hard math problem, or what was learned in a recent curriculum study. Tips, rubrics, and short videos can be created by students with our guidance. Students can also create personal blogs for journaling, keeping records and reviews of books read, and sharing books with a wider audience—much as I do in my occasional reading blogs on my website.

- *Provide easy access to information.* Whenever possible, have alternative ways for families to learn what's going on in the school and classroom as well as your expectations for their children and them. Find out early in the school year, through a survey or conversation, if families have access to the technology required to get news and information that is available through a class website, a blog, social media, or other means being used to connect with families. If such technology is not available to families, make accommodations to ensure they are fully informed.

- *Incorporate weekly newsletters,* with a message that more information can be found on the blog or website, as another option. Occasionally, newsletters can be written with students as a whole-class shared writing, with partners, and individually. Generate newsletter topics with the class as an evaluation of what students deem the most significant learning that week. Consider a web-based newsletter, using a tool such as Smore (www.smore.com), which allows users to send out content, access a variety of multimedia, and track how many people read the shared content and for how long.

- *Give families reminders for important dates and deadlines.* All of us lead busy lives, and reminders are appreciated. Provide a monthly or daily agenda that reminds families to check out the class blog, attend an event, and so on. Remind, a free communication tool that is easy for parents to sign up for, sends reminders to their phones. Those messages can include daily recorded messages about upcoming events, as well as information about what is happening in the classroom. (See Appendix D: Technology Tools That Help Support Schoolwide Literacy Learning.)

- ◆ **Welcome parents into the school.** Consider an "open learning time" for families every few months, when they are welcome to come into classrooms for a specified time to observe and even participate in what's going on. Plan and carry out this time with students, and use it as an opportunity to showcase learning in the classroom, with students explaining to parents what they will see and what to especially notice. For example, if a shared-writing lesson is planned, families could be asked to notice how all students' thinking is honored and how we collaborate with students to shape their thinking.

  - ◉ *Ensure that the first messages families see as they enter the school are welcoming and worthwhile.* Walk into the school building with the eyes of a parent. What's the first thing you see? Is it a blank wall, pamphlets with lots of small print, a message that might be daunting for some? Make sure what's posted is positive in tone, attractive, easy to access, and worth reading and viewing. First impressions matter.

  - ◉ *Encourage parent feedback.* Ensure that communication with families is not one-sided. Put in place an easy process for parents to give feedback to teachers and the school, whether it's through social media, e-mail, a place to leave a handwritten note, a designated time teachers and others can be reached, a special place on the classroom or school website, or a monthly coffee time with the principal. Let parents know their feedback is welcome, not just to express their concerns but also appreciations. Make certain anonymous feedback is an option, when preferred.

  - ◉ *Promote student-led conferences starting in kindergarten.* With teacher guidance as needed, students take the lead to demonstrate and talk about their learning and goals. Having a child direct his or her own conference is a great way to showcase for parents what students have learned. It is also an opportunity for students and their families to participate as partners with the teacher. Together, they notice and celebrate the student's strengths and interests, acknowledge needs, and set goals.[10]

  - ◉ *Celebrate families.* Use the school website, social media, or a quick personal note or message to express gratitude for small, kind gestures and shows of support. Also, congratulate families and caregivers on special accomplishments, both little and large.

Endnote

Our students, colleagues, and families are watching us. They want to know if we can be trusted and if their children are safe in our classrooms and schools. I'll never forget a colleague speaking up at a faculty meeting for the first time and finally being open to making some needed changes. When I asked what took him so long (he had been silent and immovable for years), he said, "I needed to be sure I could trust you." Trust is paramount to collective success, and building that trust takes time, expertise, and delicacy. What had I done that allowed that colleague to feel emotionally safe enough to begin to trust me? I think it was truly seeing and appreciating his strengths before his insufficiencies.

It's the same with our students. Sitting side by side in a one-on-one reading conference with an older student, I began by highlighting the student's strengths—picking a book he thought might be interesting, getting the gist of the story despite limited word-solving skills, using what he knew about the series to make predictions. Only then did we begin to discuss how and what he might work on to become a better reader.

Instead of thinking, "What's wrong with the learner?" let's ask, "What might I offer or do differently to ensure the student is successful?" Sometimes it just takes some compassion, honest but kind feedback, and easy-to-implement ideas to get students moving. Kids are always eager to learn. Our job is to find a way in, and that way in depends on students, teachers, and families knowing they can trust us. We must do everything we can to ensure that trusting relationships are the foundational, caring heart of our teaching and learning. Without high trust, nothing of consequence regarding engagement, excellence, or equity will be possible. With that trust, the possibilities for what we can accomplish are endless.

Celebrating Learners

Celebration is the heart and soul of my best teaching. I say that because every time we congratulate the learner on something done well, we affirm the behavior, skill, strategy, or effort and, therefore, make it more likely the learner will do it again. This is as true for us as educators as it is for our students. Celebration is not just the actions we take or the words we use; it's a mind-set and demeanor that propel us to primarily see, observe, and value strengths. By celebration, I mean noticing and commenting on everything the learner does well. To be clear, celebration is not about giving casual compliments, such as, "I like your reading corner" or "That suit looks really good on you." Celebration recognizes and identifies a learner's actions and efforts, as in "The lead in your essay is much clearer now that you've stated your purpose up front" or "You figured out how to spell that tricky word by checking the word wall."

One of the most dramatic and meaningful changes I've made in my teaching and coaching is to notice and celebrate everything the learner has done well. Again, when we celebrate the learner, we make honest statements that explicitly acknowledge and name the learner's accomplishments. Teachers are more likely to celebrate their students' strengths if principals celebrate their teachers. For example, in an "instructional walk" where the teacher takes observational but nonjudgmental notes,[1] a principal who is knowledgeable about literacy might say something like this:

In your public writing conference with Juan, when you said _____ [restating actual language the teacher used], you validated his risk taking and word crafting by naming exactly what he did and why it was effective for the reader. Then when you said, "Kids, when you go to revise your writing today, you might want to try some of the techniques Juan used," you made it clear that all students are expected to try and apply their learning from a peer's public writing conference.

Significantly, it's been my experience that teachers who are regularly celebrated by their principals are more likely to choose to remain in a school. Savvy principals make teacher celebration integral to the school's culture.

Perhaps what I love best about celebration is its power to change and elevate a student's life, in and out of school. Especially in writing, I have literally seen students who envision themselves as struggling change before my eyes after they have been well celebrated. They sit up taller, look you in the eye, and dare to smile. Not only that, but their standing among their peers improves, and the culture of the classroom is enriched and improved. Peers who previously thought "He can't do that very well" or "He's not very smart" are now beginning to shift to "I didn't know he could do that. He knows more than I thought." With that shift comes a more positive stance toward the student and a stronger, more trusting community of learners.

Highlight Learners' Strengths

Seeing all learners through a positive mind-set is a necessity for learners to thrive. My training as a Reading Recovery teacher decades ago helped me make a permanent mind shift from focusing first on a student's needs to noticing and acknowledging strengths.[2] If the child in Reading Recovery knew only the first letter of his first name, his evaluation noted that fact first, and that's where the teaching began—building on that child's strength. It was a revelation to me that you didn't write down what the child couldn't do!

Discarding a deficit mentality is difficult. Many years ago, when visiting schools in New Zealand, I bought a bag of potato chips. "Please dispose of this thoughtfully" was written on the back. I was taken aback by that positive language and looked for just the right place to discard the bag! What a difference affirmative language makes in the actions we take. In the United States, the typical message would be "Don't litter." Celebration does indeed have the power to change not just actions but also students' and teachers' lives.

Celebrations are an opportunity to take intentional notice of what the learner is attempting to do and to comment on it in explicit language that validates the learner's efforts. In a reading conference, we comment on the learner's specific strengths—for example, the strategies and actions used when choosing a "just right" book, figuring out vocabulary, getting the gist of the story—before we might zero in on one or two teaching needs. In a conference on writing content, we comment specifically on the language the learner has used to engage and sustain the reader's interest—for example, by reading aloud the actual beginning lead and commenting on the language craft. A cause for celebration in writing might be as small as dating the paper (for a student who has previously ignored the importance of dating a piece of writing) or as big as a student taking the initiative to reread a draft and then rewrite a stronger conclusion. If it's a public conference, we let observing students know that "one of the reasons we're having a public conference is so that you can learn from all the terrific things another student has done and apply them to your own writing." In fact, our explicit celebrations of one student become teaching points for all students.

Being able to highlight the "terrific things" a student does in a manner that moves learning forward depends not just on our positive mind-set but also on our beliefs and how knowledgeable we are as educators. For instance, in working with a typical intermediate-grade student, if we see decoding as the most important strength to emphasize in reading or view correct punctuation and spelling as the most important thing to highlight in writing, our student will not advance very far. Noticing and aptly commenting on deep comprehension strategies, author's purpose, craft of language, and so on, require that ongoing, high-level, professional learning be integrated into our teaching lives.

Take Action

- **Focus first on everything the learner is doing well and attempting to do**—for example, when conferring or coaching in reading or writing. Name those strengths, write them down, and read or speak them back. Eventually, with practice and guidance, have the learner list and name his or her strengths and then state only what has been left out. Noticing a learner's strengths before moving to suggestions is as necessary for teachers as it is for students.

- **Give at least several honest, positive comments before making a suggestion.** Research has shown, and it's common sense as well, that most of us need to hear some positive comments before being open to constructive criticism and suggestions.

- **Name the exact, unique language a learner has used** in writing, coaching, speaking, or evaluating. Doing so provides a model for other learners and allows us to say something like, "Notice how Anna phrased that question. You might want to try it that way too, in your writing or speaking."

- **See all adults in the school community as learners**—teachers, principals, coaches, superintendents, district administrators, support staff, parents, and so on.

Develop a Positive Mind-set

It's difficult to highlight a student's strengths if our view of the student's capabilities is a limited or negative one, so it's essential that we recognize the magnitude of a positive mind-set. Holding a positive mind-set as educators—that is, mentally and emotionally seeing learners' strengths before their needs—is a prerequisite for supporting all students so they can excel and reach their full potential. To be clear, I believe holding a positive mind-set is not exactly the same as holding a growth mind-set. In a growth mind-set, we believe a learner's abilities can improve with effort, but I would contend that as long as we adults still hold low expectations for the student, that belief offsets chances for optimal student growth. Carol Dweck, who pioneered the work on growth mind-set, has revised her thinking to include a fixed mind-set, which takes into consideration the complexity and duality of mind-sets we all hold and acknowledges how slowly most of us change our mind-sets.[3]

Significantly, most teachers will say they already have a positive mind-set and hold high expectations for their students. However, in fact, many of us only become aware that our expectations and mind-set lean toward pessimism when we "see" our students achieving something we did not think was possible. That "seeing" factor has been one of the greatest benefits of our residency work in shifting teachers' mind-sets.[4] Because my colleagues and I work in classrooms with students whom teachers know well, the "yes-buts" often disappear. We don't know the students and what they "can't do," which is an advantage. With high expectations, interesting and meaningful work, sufficient frontloading (see pages 129–131), and respect for students, they "can do." Their teachers then gradually adopt a more positive mind-set. The unfortunate reality is that often our students first have to prove to us they are mentally worthy and capable.

In many decades of work in underperforming schools, I have observed that the culture of low expectations by adults in the school contributes more to low achievement than any other factor. Those diminished expectations often lead to a watered-down curriculum, low-level language use, skills taught in isolation, and scripted programs that isolate students from potentially rich and authentic literacy and language experiences. If we believe a student can only do such-and-such, that student is not likely to do more under our tutelage. It won't matter much if we have all the latest technology and resources or a great curriculum. Students will still fail to excel in our classrooms and schools. When teachers and leaders continue to hold a negative mind-set with accompanying low expectations for students, a school's culture is never celebratory or thriving.

Finally, a positive mind-set includes the importance of passion. "It is a particular form of passion—a passion based on having a positive impact on all of the students in the class."[5] I don't believe that kind of passion can exist without us holding a positive mind-set. Only then are we able not just to see and celebrate students' strengths but also to promote the joy of wrestling with complex ideas in a safe, nurturing, and intellectually invigorating environment.

 ## Take Action

- **Seek to do better.** With higher expectations and excellent, targeted teaching, we can raise achievement and change lives.[6] Get together with colleagues and take a brutal and honest look at the issue of whether or not the staff holds a positive mind-set for all students.
- **Find out what students are passionate about** and support those interests. (See the story "What Is He Good At?" on pages 30–31.) Seek also to create opportunities for students to find their passions. (See examples, pages 67 and 285.)
- **Self-evaluate the language of daily feedback.** Are our words and actions focused on improvement before noticing and celebrating strengths? Are we choosing our language carefully to boost students' efforts, confidence, and competence? Have a trusted peer listen to and write down our language during a conference with a student. Evaluate together to determine if the language reflects a positive mind-set. If not, what steps are needed to change that view?
- **Consider the gifts, not just the needs, of students.** Find a way to capitalize on each student's "gift." All students have unique talents. It's up to us to find them.

STORY ❖ "What Is He Good At?"

A mind-set that focuses first on a student's strengths and not on his weaknesses can dramatically alter a child's life. A close friend and colleague, who is a former elementary school principal, tells the story of how her grandson's life was transformed by a savvy and wise principal.

Robert was a kindergartner who had difficulty conforming to daily routines and expected behaviors, especially sitting quietly without moving his arms around and creating a disturbance. When Robert's grandmother received a phone call from her distraught daughter in late fall saying that Robert's teacher had called to set up a conference and that the principal would also be there, my friend responded, "Oh, honey, that's not a good sign that the principal will be there. Would you like me to be there to support you?"

The day of the conference arrived, and both mother and grandmother were taken aback when Robert's principal began the conference with these words: "What is he good at?" Without missing a beat, Robert's mother responded, "He's good at doing jobs." The principal immediately responded, "I will create a very special job for him."

The next day the principal took Robert aside and explained that she had a very important job for him to do. He was to stop by her office every day after lunch and to deliver a box of books to the library. (The designated time was deliberate; Robert's inappropriate behaviors seemed to be at their peak following lunch/recess.) So began the daily ritual of Robert bringing a box of books from the principal's office to the librarian. He would show up on time in the principal's office and she would say, "Are you here for your box? Thank you, Robert." A proud Robert would arrive at the library saying, "These are big books with little print, and only a principal can read it. And I'm the only one allowed to bring them to you." The librarian would warmly greet him each day, thank him, and say, "What a special job you have, Robert, and you do it so well." Robert kept his unique job for the rest of the school year. He never did seem to figure out that the box he was transporting each day was filled with, more or less, the same books. He only knew that the principal and the librarian were counting on him, and he was doing a good job—just as his mother had said he would.

Although Robert's teacher initially viewed him as a child who was creating a problem for her, Robert's principal saw a child who needed an opportunity to show off his strengths, and that positive mind-set made all the difference. The daily interactions with both principal and librarian made Robert feel important and cherished, and that opened up more possibilities for him in the classroom. Once his teacher saw how beautifully Robert responded to the celebration of his efforts, she eventually shifted her mind-set and attitude. As Robert began to feel more valued, his confidence grew, and he began to experience more success in the classroom.

"What is he good at?" is a grand question and one we need to be asking ourselves about each student, colleague, and leader. Then, we need to discard deficit thinking, focus on each individual's strengths, and do what we can to ensure that each member of our classroom and school community feels appreciated and successful. Only then can we support learners to reap maximum benefit from their unique talents and to move forward in a productive manner.

Express Gratitude and Appreciation

We all need to become gifted at showing gratitude and make visible for others and ourselves the little and big things we appreciate. Gratitude and focusing on the positive are not just feel-good, self-indulgent exercises. A planned or unexpected expression of gratitude has the potential to positively affect the giver and the recipient. Certainly that has been true for me. I feel more hopeful, less stressed, and more energetic when I show empathy and gratitude toward others. Research has shown that "practicing gratitude actually makes us happier . . . coaxes one's brain into processing positive emotions," and "brings out the best in those around us."[7]

When I give a professional presentation, I almost always publicly acknowledge my thanks to the audio-visual technician, state his name, and ask the audience to give him a round of applause. My thanks are sincere; I am dependent on the technology working well for an effective, seamless presentation. (I present wirelessly off my iPad, including video.) It gives me pleasure to publicly thank and celebrate someone who deserves special mention. As we might predict, the AV technician then goes out of his way to ensure all goes well during the presentation, which allows me to focus on the message to my audience. Afterward, the AV tech person almost always privately confides it's the first time he's ever been publicly acknowledged for his assistance and skill. It's been a win-win situation for us both.

A great example of how one school practices gratitude every day is its tradition of "Appreciations." At the conclusion of all events and performances, even a story read aloud, students note the features that made them happy or caused them to think more deeply.[8] The whole school becomes a happier place. When we let people know we value them and their specific actions, they are more apt to be open to trusting us and to listening with an open mind, which is critically important when we have to relay a difficult message or a request. (See pages 33 and 344 for more on appreciations.)

 ## Take Action

- **Begin with "interior gratitude,"** giving thanks privately.[9] Start with a mental assessment of someone whose actions you are grateful for. Then express gratitude in private to that person.

- **Look for ways to practice publicly expressing gratitude.** Start with someone with whom you have a trusting relationship. In the staff lounge or at a PD meeting, say aloud something you appreciate about a colleague, something that is taken for granted and not usually expressed. It could be as simple as "I'd like to thank Colleen for taking the time to rearrange the chairs in the library for our meeting today."

- **Write a handwritten note.** I'll take a short handwritten note over an e-mail any day. I save most handwritten notes I receive; not so with e-mails. As part of teaching writing, consider having students write expressions of gratitude to give as a gift to people they appreciate—for example, for an upcoming holiday such as Thanksgiving, Valentine's Day, Mother's Day, or Father's Day. Unless students have great difficulty using a pen or pencil, have them handwrite it. A handwritten note has personality and style, not to mention the opportunity to teach and value handwriting. (For more on handwriting, see pages 248–250.) Not to be minimized, handwritten notes can wield important influence. Former president Barack Obama depended on reading the carefully selected 10LADs (ten letters a day) as a way to gauge the mood of the country and pay more attention to the voices and needs of ordinary citizens.[10]

- **Recognize people's successes.** Whether it's a parent of a student who has gotten a job promotion or a colleague who took a risk and tried something new, be generous with noticing and affirming others' accomplishments.

♦ **Express gratitude to someone you wouldn't normally approach.** A contentious relationship can begin to heal when we let the person who has offended us know something about him or her that we appreciate. Our expression of gratitude might be enough to make a neutral conversation possible.

♦ **Show appreciation to unsung heroes.** When someone "steps up" to make a worthy difference for us, whether it's a grounder or a home run, let that person know. Have students write letters or communications of gratitude to a family member, former teacher, friend, or significant person in their lives describing a special moment, an act, or an action that has affected them. Model first with your own letter, perhaps, to a colleague who has done something very supportive and unexpected. Next, write one together, and construct a simple rubric with students (see page 326) before sending them off to write their letters.

♦ **Research and write about local and national heroes** or people who have contributed to the community or country, such as war veterans, Nobel Peace Prize winners, and people who have made notable contributions to the medical community, the sciences, or the arts, or invented something that makes a difference in people's lives. (In Canada, examples are Frederick Banting, a physician and surgeon, and Charles Best, a medical student at the time, who co-discovered insulin in 1921.) Make a book or create a blog about these heroes that becomes essential reading for the school and classroom libraries.

♦ **Celebrate daily acts of kindness by school community members**—crossing guards, bus drivers, volunteers, secretaries, curriculum directors, families, students, teachers, administrators, parents, and more. Through oral and written communications and heartfelt "thank yous," acknowledge the thoughtful acts.

♦ **Begin a tradition of classroom "appreciations."** Start demonstrating verbal expressions of gratitude for acts of service, kindness, and generosity. Expand to include actions that are specific to student work. Resist connecting gratitude with routine behaviors we expect—such as courtesies, following rules, working with others—or to any kind of reward system. Appreciations might take the form of a class-authored shared writing, a letter, a short video, a blog for the school's website, or an oral presentation, to name a few possibilities.

♦ **End the school year with "appreciations."** Have departing students from a grade level, content area, or their elementary, middle, or high school leave an expression of gratitude to another student, teacher, librarian, peer helper, guidance counselor, custodian, volunteer, crossing guard, or other school member. Or better yet, have them write to the principal or a key person at the school about what they appreciate most about their learning and time spent at that school. As well, consider compiling these into a school keepsake for departing students, new incoming families, and teachers. Use exemplars as models for future students' written appreciations.

Enjoy Teaching

Celebrating learners is all about joyful teaching and learning. Yet we often say we don't have time for joy and celebration. In too many schools, the pressure to raise achievement is relentless. The required high-stakes testing, teacher evaluation, program mandates, implementation of the latest standards, and curriculum demands sap our energy and pleasure. Yet without joy in our daily teaching we cannot be highly effective. Plain and simple, it's difficult to be great at something we don't like doing. Sadly, I have never been invited to do a reading or writing residency in a school because the kids hate and fear writing or dislike reading, although that is often the case. In almost every instance where I have been invited to a school, it is "to raise the test scores." Our national obsession with testing is like a disease gone viral. It is out of control, damaging, and hard to cure.

It is the joy of teaching and learning—the sheer pleasure and energy that come from teaching authentically and purposefully—that drives us to do better and to enjoy teaching more. A teacher at one of our residencies commented, "When you talked about the joy factor at the beginning of the residency, many of us rolled our eyes. We were thinking, 'We don't have time for that joy thing.' We had curriculum to cover, lessons to plan, and district mandates to worry about. But by the end of the week we saw that that joy thing was everything."[11]

 ## Take Action

- **Do your part to promote a positive and joyful culture.** Keep in mind that joy and fear cannot coexist and that a culture of fear is an unhappy and unproductive place. Make Steven Wolk's "Joy in School" mandatory reading for his excellent suggestions on how to make joyful learning flourish in our schools.[12]

- **Model joyful learning and teaching.** Do our students see us teachers as enthusiastic readers, writers, and learners? Do we embark on a learning journey *with* them as we read a new book or tackle a skill or learn about a new topic? Do they see us as teachers who are passionate and excited about learning? Students need to know that their teachers are curious and love learning related to all kinds of subjects—including math, science, and social studies. I defer here to my learning collaborator Trish Richardson:

When I began the frontloading for the polar bear–endangered species study with my class last year, I knew little about polar bears as we began reading, viewing videos, and listening to guest speakers. I recorded what I thought I knew and corrected many of my own misconceptions in front of the students. I recorded questions I had alongside them. I couldn't wait to open the stack of books that we had collected about polar bears. I was excited to learn alongside them, and they in turn were inspired and excited to learn alongside me. This study was memorable for many reasons, but one of the main ones was because of the joy learning brought to all of us as students.[13]

♦ **Take more time to celebrate small victories** and to notice and comment on what students and staff are doing well. Seeing a student's or a teacher's face light up with an "I can do it" spirit inspires us and our students to work harder and set challenging goals.

♦ **Plan occasions for the staff to socialize.** Potluck lunches, special treats before a PD meeting, and planned events outside of school can all contribute to the staff getting to know each other better, which makes work time more enjoyable.

♦ **Reevaluate how planning and instructional time is spent**—for example:

  ◉ Do we really need to have long writing projects, which place high demands on us for conferring, revising, and editing; or can we teach what students need to know with shorter assignments?

  ◉ Are the projects and management we are creating for students worth the time and effort they take? Can we simplify those and still maintain high quality? Is students' dependence on us sapping our energy and joy?

  ◉ Do we really need to have guided-reading groups with all students every day, or might we be more effective and enjoy teaching more if we allowed more time for closely monitored independent reading and daily conferring?

♦ **Leave school at a reasonable hour,** and try not to take much work home, so there's time for those activities that bring pleasure, enrichment, and peace of mind. (See more in "Live an interesting life," pages 60–61.)

♦ **Recognize that change takes time.** Try not to be too hard on yourself when lessons fail, you err in judgment, or you experience a misstep. Becoming a more effective teacher, leader, and learner is a lifelong process. Take credit and pleasure in recognizing and analyzing your errors and then finding ways to do better.

Endnote

It's hard to overstate just how crucial celebration is and how foreign it is to most cultures, not just education. A personal story brings home the point. A few years ago when my hometown Seattle Seahawks lost the Super Bowl, I was reminded of our national obsession with winning at all costs. The fact that our football team played a great game and had a wonderful season mattered little in the end. In sports, as in education, the prize goes to the top scorer, the highest number, and all the steady good work that occurred before the high-stakes game or test counts for little. Something is very wrong with that scenario.

What if Seattle had a celebration anyway for our deflated team? What if people gathered and cheered and said, "Thank you. We're proud of you even though you lost." Wouldn't that have been something? It would have said to the coach and team members, "You played your heart out. You did your best. We admire and respect your talents." Instead, our city's message was, "You disappointed us. You don't deserve a celebration. Better luck next time." That's exactly the message we give to schools when their test scores don't measure up. No matter that excellent teaching may be going on under the most difficult of circumstances or that students are putting forth best efforts. Too often, only the top number matters.

We could all take a lesson from the dignity and decency of Coach Pete Carroll. He accepted full responsibility for the Seahawks' loss and did not berate the team in any way. He stayed true to character, appreciating their spirited team effort and vowing to learn from his "mistake" and do better next time. He created a team with heart and soul, with players who care about each other, play with and for each other, and do so with relentless effort every time. That's why they will all heal and triumph. Amid the crisis, the team's leader was transparent, was available to answer questions, and faced the media and his team with honesty, hope, and resilience. Like all great leaders, he will continue to motivate and inspire his team and earn their trust.

And there's this: What if Pete Carroll's final call wasn't a wrong call? Surely, if the Seahawks had scored that final touchdown, the coach's call would have been seen as perfect. The fact is that we—coaches, educators, most of us—make the best decisions we can given all the information, expertise, and experience we hold. Sometimes even a "right" decision can yield an unsatisfactory result. Luck, randomness, and unforeseen circumstances can sometimes influence an outcome that otherwise would have been predictably successful. It's as true for us in education as it is for football.

Let's disrupt the status quo and not just measure and value the final number. Let's appreciate and celebrate the ongoing effort, perseverance, skill, and grit of our hard-working students and teachers. True champions are more than the highest scorers. Look closely. True champions are all around us—our colleagues, school families, community members, and more—and they deserve to be recognized and celebrated.

Creating a Thriving Learning Environment

For most of us, having a pleasing, workable, and flexible environment where we feel respected, safe, and valued is a necessity for our best thinking, learning, and communicating. It's the same for our students. Optimal achievement and engagement depend on settings that facilitate learning. Yet we tend to underestimate the crucial importance of our classroom and school environments—the physical, social and emotional, and intellectual elements that determine a school's culture—for fostering engagement. How we think about and develop those mental, social, and physical spaces and the decisions that we make depend largely on what we value and believe. Those values and beliefs, whether visible or invisible, translate to the decisions, actions, and practices that determine our school's culture, achievement, and well-being.

Our schools are cultural entities defined by our shared beliefs (see pages 113–118) and values, which in turn determine our practices, structures, and traditions as well as the stories that come to characterize us. Typically, culture has not been seen as crucial to schoolwide achievement, but research suggests that "change designers have failed to appreciate the dynamics of culture and cultural change."[1] In fact, "In order for there to be a durable change in teacher practice, there must be a change of the culture in which the teacher works."[2] Much of this book is devoted to showing how teacher practice, school culture, and school change are interconnected.

After a lifetime of working in diverse schools, I firmly believe that the culture of a school determines its success. The physical, social-emotional, and intellectual environments—which encompass engagement, excellence, and equity—make it possible, or not, to establish and sustain a trusting culture that invites and inspires openness, joyful learning, high achievement, and empowerment. For clarification, I view environment and school climate as integral parts of the culture, not as separate entities.

Take an honest look at your school's culture with your staff (see Appendix A: Culture Matters, and Appendix B: A Healthy and Thriving School Culture). Celebrate the areas where you are doing well, have hard conversations where needed, and commit to making changes to better your school's culture. Although *culture* does not have the urgent cachet of *standards*, *testing*, or *data*—terms that drive teaching these days—culture is everything. Without a safe and vibrant culture, no substantial achievement will occur or be sustained. "A positive, caring, respectful climate in the classroom is a prior condition to learning."[3]

Physical Environment

The way we use our spaces where we work and live can determine how well we interact with others, how comfortable we feel, how flexibly we behave, and, ultimately, how effectively we work. Aesthetics matter. Being in a beautiful, organized, and peaceful space can free us to imagine, create, and complete ordinary tasks with ease and take on challenging work with gusto. For me, having fresh flowers and farm-market vegetables lovingly arranged on my kitchen worktable makes cooking and baking more enjoyable. The room takes on a vibrant, colorful look and feel that relaxes me and beckons me to create something tantalizing. I am in a space that is more than a kitchen; it is a personalized setting that encourages me to spend more time there, to slow down, to enjoy my life. Very few of us talk of creating beautiful and peaceful spaces in our schools, but such spaces add a sense of order, comfort, and calm that can make engagement, productivity, and enjoyment more likely.

Create a beautiful and meaningful environment

Some of the most beautiful schools I've worked in are very old ones. These are schools where the custodian, principal, students, and families take great pride in their building. You can feel the love and care. A beautiful and useful space not only lifts our spirits; it also is an excellent public relations vehicle for showing off our literacy and learning community. So it's important to work with our students, colleagues, and community to make our spaces as attractive, organized, tranquil, and efficient as possible. We spend most of our days as teachers and leaders in a classroom, an office, or a school building. Those spaces serve as our home away from home; therefore, we need to be deliberate about how they look, feel, and work for us.

When spaces in my home and home office become too cluttered and disorganized, I feel anxious and less productive. I have to pause to take the time to rethink and reorganize, even when I have pressing deadlines. I prioritize current needs, remove nonessential "stuff," and reset my space for maximum use, relaxation, and—not to be minimized—beauty. Only then am I fully productive. At this moment, I am writing in a room in my home that serves as my office and writing space. By design, I am surrounded by photos of family and friends, bookshelves packed with favorite fiction and nonfiction works, a bouquet of dried hydrangeas from my summer garden, framed paintings and drawings that have special meaning to me, and lighting that creates a sense of serenity.

Take Action

+ **Analyze your classroom environment for inclusiveness.** Imagine that you are an outsider entering your classroom for the first time. What are your first impressions regarding what you see? Would you feel welcome and at ease in your own classroom? Is the feeling one of "my classroom" or "our classroom"? Seek to create an "our classroom" environment.

  - Are spaces peaceful, comfortable, well organized, and beautiful?
  - Does the classroom reflect the personalities and interests of all of the learners?
  - Does what you see reflect a personalized and thriving literacy and learning culture? If not, what changes might you advocate for making?
  - How might you include your students, for example, in your classroom's room design—including the design for seating and a peaceful reading area—as well as what goes on the walls? How are charts, rubrics, and student work created and featured? (See page 46 for an example of student input in a fifth-grade classroom.)
  - Ask a trusted colleague to look carefully at your classroom environment and give honest feedback. Be specific about what kind of feedback you want.

+ **Let students personalize their space.** While all of us like having a special place that reflects our personal identity, a personalized space is especially important to students who move often, are homeless, are refugees, are marginalized, or are struggling in some area of their life. Here are just a few possibilities to consider for students:

- Encourage students to put family photos and photos that showcase their interests on the cover of their writing notebooks.
- Let students decorate their lockers or book boxes with pictures of favorite things, people, special interests, or books.
- Allow students to have a small, memorable keepsake on their desk or table. (On my writing desk, I have a few small shells and rocks from a favorite beach as well as a couple of buckeyes from a beautiful nearby tree. I look at and hold those items often, and they bring back peaceful memories.)
- Have students use math patterns, original artistic designs, covers of favorite books, photos of class happenings, class raps, and so forth to make distinctive and personal borders for bulletin boards.
- Invite a student to handwrite a class chart that everyone will use as a resource.
- Save a special place in the classroom and school library for student-authored books, and showcase that space so it's highly visible, attractive, and accessible.
- Use school photos of students on borders, word walls, and doors—to teach patterns and word work, and to honor every student by name and face.

 Student-authored books, prominently featured for sign-out in the school library

♦ **Beautify the spaces you have.** When possible, use hallways and other areas in the school to create inviting spaces with couches and chairs to sit and read, and places where small groups can work. In the classroom, create different corners and areas where students can curl up with a good book or piece of writing or work in small groups using alternative seating. Rugs, beanbag chairs, and stools are great for alternative seating and can be spread throughout the room. Sometimes, when teachers ask, parents will donate an item, such as a couch or a rug that they are no longer using but that's in decent condition. Consider adding lamps and comfortable seating, such as pillows, to the reading or book corner.

♦ **Arrange furniture—desks, tables, chairs—to foster easy collaboration.** Group desks in clusters so students can collaborate at least some of the time. Groups of three to four work well for small-group work and conversation. (See pages 143 and 157 for why heterogeneous grouping is important.) Make it easy for students to find the resources and basic materials they need to successfully complete the work—paper, pencils, electronic tools, and so on. When possible, for student comfort and variation, provide multiple seating options.

STORY ❖ Presentation Matters

My husband, Frank, and I have a favorite luncheon spot in Seattle. Chinook's at Salmon Bay is a large, popular, family-style seafood restaurant with a great panorama of the water and working fishing boats. We've been frequenting the place for many years and have never been disappointed. We know some of the servers who have worked there for a long time, and we enjoy conversing with them. We usually sit on stools at the salad bar counter, where we have a close-up view of the preparation of all salads and desserts for the restaurant. A recent visit in midsummer got me thinking about how important a thoughtful and beautiful presentation is for enhancing enjoyment, satisfaction, and worth in whatever we do and for whomever we do it—even in a large organization.

Every salad at Chinooks is individually crafted. That is, even if there are multiple orders for the same salad, the chef on duty carefully makes and mixes them one at a time. All ingredients and resources are first rate. Every lettuce leaf and avocado slice is perfect—in freshness and appearance. The amount of dressing applied is just right—never too little or too much. And you can have your salad any way you want it. There's lots of choice within structure here. Without hassle or fuss, you can add or subtract any item that's usually included—or not—and make any changes that suit your whim. And, always, service comes with a smile.

As for the desserts, we always indulge, because they are gorgeous and taste out-of-this-world. Every dessert is made on the premises using the freshest seasonal berries and fruits from local farms. Nothing canned here. Only real whipped cream and fruits in season are allowed. If it's May, rhubarb desserts are featured. In June, it's strawberries, and in July and August it's all kinds of berries—raspberries, blueberries, marionberries, blackberries. Raspberries were featured the day we were there, and we personalized the kitchen's key lime pie with luscious raspberry sauce, topped with assorted fresh berries added to the usual preparation of pie with whipped cream. We watched as the cook carefully cut a slice of pie and made it look beautiful with all the toppings, a sprig of mint, and a curled zest of lime on the side, and then appraised the creation and wiped any excess from the plate's rim. We've eaten at a lot of restaurants over the years, and I'm a tough critic when it comes to fruit pies, tarts, and shortcakes. Chinook's is part of a large restaurant chain, and yet their desserts are the best we've had anywhere.

As I watched the cooks carefully preparing and crafting the salads and desserts, I thought a lot about how individualized presentation affects how we perceive quality and satisfaction. I thought about our schools and classrooms and how important it is to present ourselves and our classrooms to students and their families in a welcoming and flexible manner. Even though the schools and districts we work in may be large organizations, like the restaurant, we can design our offerings in an intimate, personal way—one school, one classroom, and one student at a time. For example, we can have attractive and well-organized welcoming messages and brochures to greet visitors to our schools and classrooms. We can structure our schools and classrooms physically and emotionally in a way that makes students, families, and teachers feel cared for and valued. We can set up the initial framework but allow and encourage choices and participation within that structure—with seating, bulletin boards, classroom libraries, routines, and how the classroom and school function on a daily basis. Most important, within our realm, we can personalize learning so students willingly return year after year, knowing they will be served up the best we have to offer—every day, to each and every one of them.

Rethink our prime real estate

It seems we never have enough space for everything we want and need, so we need to prioritize what is most useful for enhancing engagement and learning in our classrooms and schools. Our walls talk and tell visitors and us much about our school's culture, how we teach, what we believe, and what we value. Walls and hallways covered with commercially made charts with standardized graphics impart an impersonal look and feel. Not only that: students tend to ignore those mass-produced charts. Many are written in academic vocabulary suitable for adults instead of in kid-friendly language students can understand and access.

After one flexible, astute fifth-grade teacher and her students concluded there were too many charts in the classroom and at least half were commercial and group charts they rarely used, students wrote reflections with recommendations (see next page) to improve the situation. Those individual reflections and classroom discussions led to a much less cluttered and more beautiful room, a more peaceful environment, and the posting of information that students now accessed daily for reference, reading, and writing. Perhaps most noteworthy for the students and the teacher, the classroom now belonged to all the inhabitants, not just the teacher, and everyone was pleased with the change in dynamics.

Julia

Classroom Organization

1. I some of the reading posters are kind of the same then you will only need 1 so there arn't so many posters. Get rid of the rest.

2. I think you could take down the (Stop! Ask 3 Before Me!) poster because I don't know what it is and we barley look at it

3. You might want to return some library books so they don't get overdue, and to make more room for books.

4. You should move the book nook chart in the library, above the trampoline chair. You will make more room on that wall.

A fifth grader's recommendation for improving the organization of the classroom, especially as pertains to the use of several wall charts

Take Action

- Take an environmental walk around the school. What are your first impressions regarding what you see? Would you feel welcome in your own school? Are the spaces peaceful and beautiful? Are the posted messages and work affirming and celebratory and worth the space they are consuming? Does what you see reflect a personalized and thriving literacy and learning culture? If not, what changes might you advocate for making?[4] (See also pages 240–241.)

- Make wonderful libraries in the classroom and the school a high priority. Research has repeatedly shown that students who read more are better readers. Access to books matters. Although libraries will be discussed in depth in this book, they are mentioned here to underscore their importance. When arranging the classroom, think libraries first. (See next section, pages 48–51, and Equity, pages 262–263, for much more on libraries.)

- Make sure displayed work, word walls, and charts are legible, accessible, relevant, and current throughout the school—posted at students' eye level; written in language students understand; useful as student resources; clear in purpose; and accurate in facts, format, spelling, and grammar. Make sure that posted student writing is current and that your charts and work reflect research-based beliefs about teaching and learning.

- Aim for having the majority of posted work in classrooms and hallways created by students with teacher guidance. Think about having students handwrite, hand illustrate, or word-process class-generated charts and basic information students need for referral. Also, as noted earlier, consider having students make borders for bulletin boards. An example is shown on the next page—a photo of uppercase and lowercase alphabet letters created by a first-grade student who was struggling to learn his letters. Creating an original alphabet border that all students referred to boosted this first grader's self-esteem, created a lot of interest for visitors who entered the classroom, and—best of all—enabled a struggling student to learn all his letters.

- Consider use of QR codes on bulletin board displays to allow videos and other tech-based projects to be easily viewed by visitors, students, or parents. Use a QR code scanner such as i-nigma, one of the most widely used barcode readers, on a smartphone, tablet, or iPad. There are many free QR code generators, such as QRstuff.com.

An alphabet border created by a first-grade student who has been struggling with—and is now succeeding in—learning his letters and sounds

- ◆ Make certain that posted work throughout the school is focused on learning across the curriculum and celebrating students' accomplishments, rather than on decorations or management behaviors and rules. Choose work to post that demonstrates student thinking, choice, and appropriate challenge. Avoid cookie-cutter, recipe-like work in which all student contributions look the same except for a few details. Continually ask, "Are the posted messages and displayed student work affirming, celebratory, and worth the space they are consuming? Do they accurately reflect our school's beliefs and culture?"

Establish a rich and relevant classroom library

A well-organized and well-stocked classroom library is a precursor for a classroom grounded in reading, writing, and inquiry. You can't be a writer without being a reader, and you can't become a reader without easy access to interesting texts and sustained time to read them. The first thing I look for when I enter any classroom is the library—its location, appearance, organization, quality and diversity of texts, student access—and whether or not it's "our library" (the students') or "my library" (the teacher's). Sometimes there are few books or there is no library. That has sometimes been the case even when a large number of computers or tablets have been purchased, with the notion that most reading materials will be accessed on a screen via a device. While e-books have their own appeal and advantages, there is no substitute for excellent classroom libraries.

Classroom libraries can be a game changer for students' reading achievement. For one of my first teaching residencies, I was invited to a school to raise reading achievement and test scores. It was a typical school, just outside a large urban area, where the teachers believed they were doing everything they could as teachers of reading, and yet achievement—based on test scores—was stagnant. It took only one day to figure out the problem. Not only were students not reading much or enjoying reading, there were no viable classroom libraries or teaching for deep comprehension, and there was an overreliance on a core reading program. Our focus for the entire first year was on creating beautiful and accessible classroom libraries with student input; teaching students how to self-select "just right" books in various genres; setting up a daily, carefully monitored independent reading program; and relying on further reading of the text-in-process as our primary follow-up work to guided-reading groups. For the second year, with the libraries as the mainstay of daily reading in every classroom, we moved our focus to guided reading, but it was guided reading as a means to facilitate students being able to read, comprehend, and self-monitor on their own, not as an end in itself.

 ## Take Action

- **Make the classroom library the centerpiece of the classroom.** Look closely to make sure the library corner is prominent, attractive, and well organized, with book covers facing out, as much as possible, for easy browsing and accessibility. Rain gutters are one inexpensive, quickly installed way to showcase many books. Consider the use of plate stands on a shelf to display books. Also, where possible, include an adjacent floor area or designated space where students can read comfortably.

- **Involve students in organizing, setting up, and maintaining the classroom library** and give them choices in the types of texts, genres, series, and authors they prefer. Have book titles, including student-authored work, facing outward for easy access and browsing.[5] Develop common agreements on how books are shelved, cared for, and handled. Work out a checkout system with students that they can easily manage.

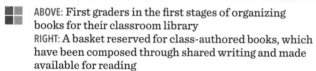

ABOVE: First graders in the first stages of organizing books for their classroom library
RIGHT: A basket reserved for class-authored books, which have been composed through shared writing and made available for reading

Start the collection, if need be, by borrowing a large number of books from the school and public library and, if possible, securing loans from students' home collections too. Include a variety of series, predictable and patterned books, informational books, poetry, texts by favorite authors (including student authors), graphic novels, and whatever kinds of texts interest your students. Balance the collection by having at least 50 percent of it consist of nonfiction works. If books are in bins, have students handwrite the category labels for the bins to create a personalized look. Be sure the library is organized with students so there is joint ownership, which increases usage and enjoyment.

Create a shelf or an area that displays books that are students' favorite picks. Have book recommendations attached to the book or a QR code in the book that can be scanned for a video of a book review done by a student or group of students.

- **Celebrate the classroom library with a grand opening.** After students have organized and labeled library sections at the beginning of the year, hold a grand opening and ribbon-cutting ceremony. Students can write letters to invite the principal and other school staff and also write and deliver speeches about the importance of their library, how they organized it, and how they choose great books.

- **Be cautious about leveling books.** Just as we would not expect to be directed to a particular level of books in the public library, think about grouping books by categories rather than levels, and explicitly teaching students how to select books they can read and understand. Leveled texts can be useful for guided reading and for students still struggling to choose books they can read, but for most of us, having a wide range of choices works best. (See pages 207–208 for teaching students how to self-select books and pages 121 and 220 for research and information on leveling texts.)

◆ **Connect reading conferences to independent reading.** Because almost all reading is done silently and independently, provide daily, sustained reading practice time on self-selected books. Then confer one-on-one with students to celebrate their strengths, ensure they comprehend deeply, and determine teaching needs (see pages 221–225 for specifics). For emerging readers, some of that time might be spent reading the same book with a partner.

◆ **Advocate for books for classroom and school libraries,** which are typically underfunded. Prioritize and budget for purchasing books ahead of the latest technology. Although e-readers and e-books have their place and many students benefit from e-reading, most students—and adults—still prefer holding the physical book in their hands. Also very important: a high-quality, diverse collection of books expands our planning and curriculum options as well as students' learning experiences and choices.

Social and Emotional Environment

Social and emotional well-being in the classroom and school are a necessity for students' optimal achievement. In fact, recent research indicates a stable social and emotional school setting is a determining factor in student achievement.[6] Although it's inevitable that some of our students may come from unstable environments, it is our job while they are in our schools to attend to their social and emotional well-being, not just their academic achievement. School may be the only opportunity for some students to effectively learn and experience how to be part of a community or group, be empathetic to another's needs, be safe physically and psychologically, solve problems with others in mind, and consider others' perspectives. Positive relationships among students, teachers, and peers, in which students learn to work well with others and self-manage their behaviors, can go a long way to improving students' social and emotional awareness in multiple settings.

Social and emotional well-being is also a necessity for us as educators. All of us need to feel psychologically safe before we willingly take risks and speak out, give suggestions, or voice concerns in a group. Without that comfort and buffer zone, we are much less likely to work effectively with our colleagues.

See the classroom through students' eyes

What would it be like to spend a whole day in our classroom if we were the students? It's easy to organize our classrooms to fit our own needs and personal styles and to forget what it was like to be a child, a preteen, an adolescent, or even an adult learner. If we truly want students to excel, we need to be sure the setting, tone, and classroom culture encourage and enhance risk taking, deep conversations, and meaningful learning. We educators set the temperature and controls for learning. The language we use, the choices we make possible, the learning structures and supports we set up, and the way we foster peer relationships and collaboration are vital to learners' emotional and mental well-being, regardless of the age of the learner.

 # Take Action

- ◆ **Evaluate access.** Ensure that selected resources—such as charts, word walls, dictionaries, libraries, technology devices, and websites—are top-notch, student friendly, well organized, and easy to use and understand without too much teacher direction and guidance.

- ◆ **Look at opportunities for interaction and collaboration.** It's difficult to sit quietly in one place for most of the day. Check that we are providing adequate time and space for movement, conversing with peers, working with a partner, being part of a small group for problem solving and discussion, and hearing all the voices.

    Middle school students admire and appreciate teachers who ensure students learn to work well together. One student noted that she appreciates when teachers switch seating around each month so all students get to know each other: "This is a community where we all work together, rather than against each other in a competition."[7] Such mixed grouping is vital for helping English learners—and all learners—feel valued for their culture and language.[8]

- ◆ **Consider whose classroom it is.** Make sure we are not giving the message that we own the classroom and that our students are our tenants for the year. Although the final decision may be ours, do involve students in deciding how the classroom is organized—the library, jobs, rules, bulletin boards, room arrangement, and design—so students feel some ownership and comfort in a space they reside in for part or most of their day. Also, consider eliminating the teacher's desk to allow more room for flexible use of space. (See also "Balance the Power in the Calssroom," pages 337–340, and "Establishing Routines and Rituals Together," pages 340–344.)

◆ **Establish criteria for learning requirements with students.** Again, although the final decision may be ours, without some consideration for giving students meaningful choices and input for doing "the work," we will always fail to engage some of our students. Even with required curriculum and standards, do provide some input and choice on books to read, writing topics, required assignments, questions to research, format and form of final product or presentation, criteria for rubrics, and so on.

◆ **Demonstrate empathy.** Imagine how it would feel not to understand the language, vocabulary, and concepts or to be a student who is new, hungry, unstable, overtired, or homeless. Would we feel at ease in our own classrooms? How well would we fare? What can we do to ensure we and our students create a welcoming and thriving learning environment for all? Empathy, like kindness, is necessary for all students to succeed.

◆ **Self-evaluate.** At various intervals, give students a questionnaire or an open-ended evaluation that does not require their signatures (see one example on page 167). Ask for advice and feedback on how being in the classroom has worked for them. Ask students what they think about topics such as choice, respect, fairness, problem solving, teacher effectiveness, group work, and whatever else seems important. Include space for an unlisted topic or topics of their choice. Invite students to first state what is working well before they offer suggestions. Let them know that, like them, we are always seeking to do better and will take their comments and suggestions seriously. Consider, also, providing parents a similar opportunity to offer suggestions on how being in our classroom and school is working for their child. Always assure students and families—and follow up with actions—that there will be no reprisals for their honest feedback.

Make sure students are engaged, not just on-task

A middle-grades teacher who invited me into her classroom told me her students were participating in sustained reading of self-selected texts every day, but many of them were not engaged. What should she do? A show of hands confirmed that at least half the class admitted to not enjoying the book they were reading. To an outside observer, the impression was "these students are engaged," but silence, making eye contact, and compliant behavior can be deceiving. In some classrooms, silence indicates students have had few opportunities for conversations, they don't know what their questions are or how to make informed choices, or they don't feel safe enough to risk expressing their opinions and making their voices heard. Engaged learners are "hooked"—they are working in their learning zone. They know what they are doing and why, and they possess the skills and learning habits to be successful. They are motivated, value the task at hand, and can discuss its purpose. They can solve problems when meaning breaks down.

Take Action

- **Make instruction and learning relevant.** Take the required curriculum and personalize it for students. Make it relevant, content rich, and memorable (see a lesson plan on environmental stewardship and climate change, Appendix C and on this book's website, as an example). Ensure that the questions we are asking to drive curriculum study are significant ones that have the potential to expand student thinking and learning in meaningful ways. Provide more opportunities for productive group work (see pages 143 and 156–157) and conversations in which students take the lead.

- **Offer more choice within structure.** Even if all students have to meet the same requirements, whenever possible build in some choice. We all engage more when we have some say in what we are being asked to do. (See pages 90–93 and 232–233 for more information.)

- **Move at a steady pace.** Moving at a steady pace, with work that is relevant and appealing, is probably my best strategy for keeping all kids engaged.

- **Talk for only about ten minutes.** Then give students a short break through "turn and talk," small-group conversation, or movement so they have time to process and respond to what they've heard.

- **Assess as we go.** Check that students are "getting" what we are teaching. Use questioning, turn and talk, shared writing, and short written responses. Also, when students move to the guided-practice stage, when they are trying to apply what we've been teaching, encourage them to jot down any questions or confusions—for example, concepts, vocabulary, or visuals they don't understand. (Don't require complete sentences and perfect spelling, especially for very young students. We're assessing here just for understanding.) Have students then share and solve any problems with a partner before possible sharing with small groups or the whole class. Then, note areas of confusion and reteach and regroup as needed. It's hard to stay engaged if we don't understand what's going on.

Teach with a sense of urgency

Teaching with a sense of urgency means focusing relentlessly on what's most important throughout every single day, moving at an efficient and effective steady pace, seizing problems and failure as opportunities for growth, and changing course as needed. It does not mean speeding up lessons to teach faster; in fact, it may mean slowing down to teach more deeply so students are more successful when they attempt a task—which saves time in the long run.

Teaching with a sense of urgency means making every minute count. That may mean abandoning a lesson or an action, even though it's written in our plan book, if it's not working. In a recent residency, with many observers looking on, teachers and visitors were flabbergasted when I stopped a shared writing lesson in process and said something like, "Kids, this isn't working very well, so we're going to change course." At the time, I didn't know why the kids were not engaging with the activity the teacher and I had jointly planned, but the lack of interest as demonstrated by the fidgeting and the meager verbal responses from students made it clear it would be a waste of valuable time to continue. In the evaluations by teachers at the end of the residency, it was the act of giving myself permission to change plans midstream that had the greatest impact.

Perhaps most important, teaching with a sense of urgency means knowing our priorities and not getting sidetracked. Stay focused on the main event! The essential ingredient in teaching reading is reading; in teaching writing, it's writing. That is, we must devote most of our literacy time to sustained reading and writing of complete, relevant texts that engage our students and not on activities and exercises *about* reading and writing.

 ## Take Action

- ◆ **Keep the flow of teaching going** through purposeful, engaging, and relevant lessons that connect to students' interests and needs as well as to required curriculum and standards. Notice when a lesson is not meeting students' needs and interests, and be ready and willing to take a different path.

- ◆ **Be efficient** in the directions and the language we use. Be concise, clear, and explicit. Ensure that we don't take so much time giving directions that we drain students' energy and interest in doing "the work." Make every minute count.

- ◆ **Stop while energy is still high** and the students and you can come back to the lesson with energy and excitement.

- **Try not to stop teaching because of off-task behaviors;** when possible, move a student right up next to you with a statement like "Chris, come right up to the front. I need someone to help me with _____."

- **Evaluate** as you go along. Ask yourself, "Is this lesson or activity working as planned? Are students clear about the purpose? Are students engaged? If not, why not? What else might I try?"

- **Be prepared.** Have an alternative plan ready to go in case things don't work out. For example, when facilitating a guided-reading lesson, I always have several sets of books next to me when introducing a new book. The designated level on the book is not always accurate, sufficient, or "just right" for a particular group. Students' interests, culture, and vocabulary knowledge play a role in whether or not they will be able to read the book. Sometimes we just have to try out a book or plan to see if it's workable.

- **Do away with unnecessary routines, procedures, and activities** that take lots of time but don't move learning forward—for example, creating and posting classroom charts in academic language that students cannot understand, or setting up elaborate learning stations that keep students occupied but often with activities that are never evaluated. Rethink to ensure that what students and we do in the name of learning is worth the time and effort involved.

- **Do more frontloading.** (See pages 129–131.)

Eliminate distractions and increase efficiency

If we are to teach with a sense of urgency and maximize learning, we must do all we can to minimize whole-school and classroom disruptions that impede instruction and learning. Deep reading, writing, and thinking require distraction-free concentration—rare in today's schools where new requirements and interruptions are the norm.

Nothing is as frustrating as being in the flow of an effective lesson only to have bells or buzzers go off or an inconsequential announcement come over the public address system. We lose not only our pace, thoughts, and momentum, but also precious time. Just ten minutes a day of unproductive time adds up to about three-and-a-half hours a month! Equally important, constant distractions—especially those out of our control—make it difficult for us to keep up an instructional flow and for our students and us to maintain focus.

Sometimes we teachers are unwittingly the cause of the disruption. For example, when we stop to discipline one or more students in the middle of a lesson and "wait" for everyone's attention, other students sometimes take that wait time as an opportunity to go off-task. Assuming our lessons are engaging, relevant, and appropriately challenging, moving on and ignoring minor behavior distractions almost always works for keeping all students' attention.

Also very important, when we are efficient in all we do and say, students feel calmer, can concentrate more, and are less likely to get distracted. When we are disorganized, talk too much, or give complicated directions, we lose our students' attention and engagement. Expert teachers are effective, in large part, because they are so efficient. Among other factors, that efficiency includes planning, management, giving directions, use of resources, discerning students' needs and emotions, solving problems, shifting gears as needed, and using time wisely.

Being efficient and not wasting a minute allows for more deliberate and sustained practice time, which is essential for mastering anything worthwhile as well as for ensuring maximum instructional time. Highly effective educators avoid busywork, worksheets and assignments that aren't worth the effort they take, complicated directions, and long transitions between activities, to name a few timewasters. Perhaps most important, we can't be efficient if we're not really good at what we do, which includes not just literacy and content knowledge but also management and organization. (See more on management, pages 221 and 291.)

 ## Take Action

- ◆ **Advocate for reducing teaching interruptions:**
  - ◉ *Discuss how to lessen nonessential, schoolwide, daily interruptions.* Take time at a staff meeting to talk about those nonessential staff meetings that drain teachers' energy and interrupt serious learning. Consider volunteering to be on a committee headed by the principal to deal with issues that don't require the entire staff getting together. Most important, devote whole-school meetings to professional learning.
  - ◉ *Eliminate or greatly shorten announcements* over the public address system as much as possible. For example, instead of an announcement stating a student needs to come to the office, try to work out a system in which a messenger delivers the request, orally or in writing, at least some of the time.
  - ◉ *Re-evaluate whole-school gatherings.* Ensure that such release times are connected to literacy and learning in ways that enrich and expand the

curriculum, such as drama and musical performances or expert speakers from various domains. Question whole-school pep rallies to boost test scores, which are cheerleading events that have little impact on increasing achievement and take valuable time away from purposeful learning.

♦ **Carefully self-monitor how precious time is used.** I'm a clock watcher when I teach. *Demonstrations*: I aim for ten or fifteen minutes. *Directions*: I self-monitor my language to ensure it is concise, clear, and relevant to the task. *Pacing*: I try to stop an activity while interest is still high, which makes it easier to return to it the following day if we need to. Being highly efficient helps keep students focused on the task at hand.

♦ **Have students take more responsibility for solving classroom-based issues,** which helps the classroom run efficiently. Use shared writing to brainstorm solutions for typical social and learning problems that occur. The shift from teacher-in-charge to student-in-charge of problem solving first requires guided discussion. Originally, most students in a grade two–three classroom (described on pages 82–83) placed "Tell the teacher" at the top of their list as the first and only solution for an ongoing problem of "Students annoying you when you are trying to do your work." Their "Solutions" on the first draft of the class-authored, shared writing quickly expanded, with "Tell the teacher" moving to the last resort:

  ⦿ Ignore them (do not talk back).
  ⦿ Tell them to stop.
  ⦿ Work it out with the person who is bothering you. Say, "Can you please stop bothering me?"
  ⦿ Walk away.
  ⦿ Move your sheet away. ("Sheet" refers to the stand-up folder some students use on their desks to have more privacy as they work.)
  ⦿ Tell the teacher.

♦ **Make expectations clear and prominent.** The aforementioned student solutions—along with solutions to other pressing problems—remained posted for the school year. Because students identified workable solutions, compliance was high. In those few instances when there was a lapse, the teacher only needed to refer briefly to the chart to keep students' undivided attention on their work, which meant she could instruct small groups or work one-on-one with students, uninterrupted. In another classroom where the teacher and students discussed appropriate behaviors toward one another, students worked together to create character education posters.

- *Have students role-play* how to deal with disruptive situations that may arise. Choose one or more students who are most likely to need a lot of guidance in this area. Use a lot of positive feedback as students act out their roles.
- *Make the students leaders!* When sending students off to work independently, invite two to four of them to model how this will look and sound while the rest of the class looks on. Commend them for their specific actions as they find their supplies efficiently, find a quiet spot where they are able to work, get started right away, use a whisper voice to ask a peer a question, and so on, in front of the entire class. Talk them through the procedures and behaviors upon which the class has come to agreement. Ask others to follow their lead. Such feedback sometimes takes a few extra moments, but it is well worth the time and gets students off on the right footing so there are fewer distractions once they begin the work at hand.

Efficiency Tips

- Don't go on too long.
- Give clear, concise directions.
- Aim for excellent pacing.
- Avoid distractions that take you off-task.
- Plan relevant lessons.
- Assess before teaching.
- Use peer tutors and cross-grade tutors.
- Be flexible; shift gears as needed.
- Release more responsibility to students.
- Have more student-directed groups.
- Do an excellent job frontloading.
- Plan with the end in mind.
- Stick with what's most important at this time.
- Keep your eyes on the goal(s).

All of these tips are embedded in other lessons throughout this text, because being efficient is essential for being fully effective as an instructional teacher, a leader, and a coach. A point not to be minimized is that being efficient eliminates most behavior issues. That is, when we are well organized, move at a steady pace, give students opportunities for input, and the work is relevant, interesting, and appropriately challenging, behavior issues become rare. As my esteemed and wise colleague Sandra Figueroa says, "Get rid of tools and practices that no longer meet the 3 Es—effective, efficient, and empowering."[9]

Intellectual Environment

Creating and sustaining a school culture in which conversations, professional learning, and student learning concentrate on scholarly pursuits is rare but necessary for full engagement, high achievement, and equity for all learners. Giving time, focus, and choice to investigating questions and issues that fascinate us is what scientists, mathematicians, historians, writers, and readers do. Even with all the restrictions and requirements we face as educators—mandates, standards, curriculum documents, time limits, and much more—if we and our students are to thrive, then we must find a way to devote time to critically inquiring, thinking, and acting like real-world learners while we are living our interesting lives. We need to begin with ourselves: What are we most passionate about? What are our burning questions? Schools around the world where students thrive create "a serious intellectual culture . . . one that kids can sense is real and true."[10] An intellectual culture also provides the resources and tools that support ongoing inquiry and learning—first-rate literature and libraries, technology that enhances and promotes deep and personalized learning, access to the arts and humanities, and opportunities for collaboration.

Live an interesting life

Years ago I was in danger of becoming a very boring person. Most of my time outside of work was spent reading and studying educational issues. I was not a fascinating conversationalist at parties. I could not talk confidently about history, world issues, or great literature. My husband, who is an artist, encouraged me to expand my horizons. How we live our lives outside of school matters. When we have interesting stories to tell and new ideas and burning questions to share, we enter our classrooms with a sense of rejuvenation and wonder. If we spend most of our evenings and weekends on crafting time-consuming lesson plans, devising elaborate projects, and grading papers, we come into school without the energy and spark to energize our students and peers. To foster a healthy social, emotional, and intellectual environment in our schools, we need to model that culture through our own actions.

Make time for reading for pleasure and information, exercising with a friend, gardening, dancing, cooking a special meal, walking, visiting with loved ones, learning about a topic outside of education, or whatever brings you pleasure and satisfaction. Remember, there is no research that shows that those of us who spend the most hours planning lessons and marking papers have the highest student achievement. An evening spent attending a marvelous theater performance, creating a splendid meal, dining with friends, listening to classical music or jazz, or reading terrific nonfiction or fiction gives me energy to teach.

Make time for your own passions. My ongoing intellectual passion is seeking to improve the literacy and learning lives of underserved students. My newest passion for sheer enjoyment is tennis. I have just resumed playing after more than twenty years and find I feel energized and renewed; plus I'm still a pretty decent player—to my surprise. While I like getting regular exercise doing something I love, what keeps me playing is how much fun it is. (See the story "10 Lessons Learned About Teaching and Living from Taking Up Tennis," pages 63–66.)

 ## Take Action

- **Prioritize.** Time is always in short supply. To find the time to do the things we love, we often have to let something go. For example, I do take time each weekend with my husband, Frank, to go to one of our year-round farmers' markets, which inspires me to cook creatively. On the weekend we also relax with coffee and pastry at a local café and take an urban walk in an interesting part of Seattle. I also make time to read every day—newspapers, books, professional journals, magazines, blogs, tweets. As well, just about every day I write something that feels important to me. And yet. I still have unpacked boxes from a move to Seattle fourteen years ago, my closets are disorganized, the oven needs cleaning, and my house will never be a dust-free zone. I will get to those chores as best I can, but they are rarely my top priorities.

- **Keep a reading log.** For many years I've been keeping a monthly reading log where I record the title, author, and genre of the books I read in a simple spiral notebook. I add a star next to a title if the book is exceptional. Keeping the log encourages me to read at least two books a month, and looking back on what I've read helps me balance my upcoming reading choices. I share my reading history with my colleagues and students, and many have been encouraged to keep a similar record of their own reading. Because reading—especially great fiction and nonfiction—is so integral to my life, I love having my reading history documented. Just do it! It's never too late to begin. Teachers who begin to keep a reading history report finishing more books more frequently. Reading books is good for our health. A recent study found that people who read more books, especially fiction, lived longer.[11] As an alternative to chronicling your reading choices on paper, you may want to consider becoming part of an online community of booklovers, such as the social media site Goodreads, and create your own online virtual bookshelf. My reading history over many years, with related commentary, is available on my website on my "What I'm Reading" blog.

◆ **Nurture your intellect and spirit.** On an evening or weekend, take time to see an exhibit, read a nonfiction book on an important topic, hear an author speak, attend a play or drama, or hear a concert. Growing up near New York City, seeing a Broadway show was a regular and favorite part of my childhood and teenage years. Musical theater and live drama are still passions. So is hearing an author speak.

After I heard Colum McCann's inspired talk at the Seattle Public Library, I bought and read—and reread—his magnificently crafted book of fiction *Thirteen Ways of Looking*.[12] And, again, I recently took the opportunity at our local bookstore, Elliott Bay Book Company, to hear Jacqueline Woodson talk about her latest book, *Another Brooklyn*.[13] I took notes during her talk and was conscious of listening like a writer. I came away inspired, renewed, and informed. Several meaningful quotes: "You learn to write by reading." "All you need is a pencil and paper and a story." "I always have to write because I have questions, not answers." "It's so important to write yourself into the bigger picture of the world."[14]

STORY ❖ 10 Lessons Learned About Teaching and Living from Taking Up Tennis

When I was a teenager, I spent much of my free time and weekends playing tennis with my best friend. When weather permitted, we would bike to neighborhood courts and play tennis for hours. It was free, it was fun, and all that practice turned us into darn good players. I continued to play for the next few decades and then stopped. Who knows why? I got busy raising a family, working, writing, and following other pursuits.

I took tennis up again recently with a specific purpose in mind: I wanted to meaningfully interact with my 16-year-old, tennis-playing, very busy granddaughter. If you spend any time with teenagers today, then you know face-to-face, in-person time is not their favorite contact sport. My granddaughter, like so many of her peers, prefers text messages, Instagram, Snapchat, and the like; Facebook, e-mail, and talking on the phone are relics from her past. Her dad had told me, "She'll play tennis with anyone," so I didn't flatter myself when she accepted all my invitations. But I had my pride; I wanted her to see me as a competent player. So I joined the same public tennis club where my granddaughter and family played. I treated myself to private lessons every other week and took up tennis again in earnest.

The ruse worked in ways I hadn't expected. I did get closer to my granddaughter, and that has been rewarding for us both; but the main benefits have been more far-reaching and surprising. What I learned has made me think more deeply about teaching, learning, and living.

1. It's never too late to improve.

Even though I hadn't been on a tennis court for over twenty-five years, my tennis playing got a lot better, even after just a few months of occasional lessons and practice. My desire to be a decent player propelled me to invest full mental and physical energy into the effort. I pushed myself, and though I was badly out of shape, I didn't get discouraged. Small improvements that were named and noticed by my teacher spurred me on.

2. Having fun makes you feel good.

I had forgotten how much I enjoyed tennis. I felt exhilarated when I played. And here's the surprising part: although part of my motivation was to get exercise I badly needed, having fun eventually overtook every other reason for playing. Playing tennis made me happy. If we are investing a lot of effort and time into teaching and learning, shouldn't joy be a by-product for both us and our students?

3. Doing something for yourself is a luxury and a necessity.

Like you, I don't take much time to treat myself to things that are just for me. Life's demands and guilt routinely intervene. So I was amazed how marvelous it felt to indulge myself in a pleasurable pursuit that was purely personal. I loved taking those tennis lessons and having one-on-one time with a teacher dedicated to helping me improve. Even being stuck in rush-hour traffic on my way home did nothing to dampen my spirits. Following a pleasurable, self-chosen pursuit continues to lift my spirits and give me energy to deal with the "hard stuff" life offers. Investing time in what brings us joy—whether it's reading, biking, painting, baking, creating, and so on—gives our lives richness and balance. Sharing such stories with our students can help them bond with us and engage more fully in what we are teaching them.

4. Having an excellent coach makes all the difference.

When I signed up for lessons, I got the luck of the draw and wound up with a superb teacher. As a skillful coach, she strikes the right balance between praising, nudging, demonstrating, practicing, supporting, and letting go. We start off each lesson with easy practice, rallying the ball back and forth, warming up with familiar volleys before adding any challenges. When I hit the balls well, she lets me know with a simple "good." As needed, she stops, shows, or explains what modification or specific moves would help me play more effectively. Her tone and demeanor are always kind and encouraging, which makes it easy for me to try again and want to do better. She is exactly the kind of teacher I try to be and want for all children.

5. How you follow through determines the end result.

One of my weaknesses in tennis is following through all the way when I hit the ball. I often start the swing in good form but then fail to move my arms and racquet in a manner that ensures accuracy and power, hampering the outcome. I hit the ball into the net and have little control over where the ball goes. The end result is I come up short. I've learned that starting well is insufficient; what happens all the way through the act of doing determines whether or not we succeed.

6. Informing your practice doesn't require a rank or rating.

It's common practice at our pubic tennis club and at most similar clubs that players are put into categories that define them by skill levels. As a practical matter, this makes sense for group lessons so players are matched with those with similar abilities. For adults, but especially for kids, competitive rankings can be problematic. For some, having a lower rating translates to "less capable" rather than to "moving forward appropriately." Even students placed at advanced levels stress out over the extreme competition and the pressure to maintain their status. The joy then goes out of the game. We need to be questioning and decrying the overemphasis on ratings and levels and the negative impact those kinds of evaluations have on teachers' and students' self-esteem, as well as their ability and will to do better.

7. Avoid overreaching.

Several months ago I took a serious fall while playing tennis with my son. The entire weight of the fall landed on my dominant right hand. Although X-rays revealed no break, I had severe ligament damage in several fingers and a near-dislocated joint. The healing process has been slow and humbling; the fall could have been avoided. Normally sensible about my physical limits, why did I run for that ball that was clearly out of reach? Was it because I was playing with my son for only the second time in over twenty-five years and I wanted to impress him? Did I trip over ill-fitting shoes? Did I think because I had not fallen before, falling wasn't possible? Probably all of the above. How often do we add a new initiative or accept a new challenge to our already too-full plates—in schools, in classrooms, in our lives? Things are going along reasonably well, and then we inadvertently tip the balance. Recovery can be painfully slow. Sometimes it may be wisest to put our efforts and energies into sustaining what's going well and not take that next leap. We need to advocate for staying the course for several years when working to improve, for example, writing achievement before adding another major professional development emphasis, such as math. Otherwise we are likely to lose many of the gains we made.

8. Invest in excellent resources.

When I took up tennis again, I hadn't given much thought to the equipment I'd need to play well. I already had a racquet purchased secondhand and a pair of old athletic shoes, so I made do with those. I learned that you actually need shoes that are made for playing tennis (the soles are specially constructed for the sport), and not having those shoes may be part of why I tripped and fell. You also need a good racquet that fits your size, strength, and needs. Not knowing how to purchase those on my own, I consulted with the head coach of the tennis club, and he personally helped me select what best suited me. In our schools, why do we settle for second-rate literature and resources that shortchange us and our students and may even do damage?

9. Relax your grip.

"Relax your grip" may be the best advice my tennis coach gave me. Especially after the fall, I felt like I was holding on for dear life when I picked up the racquet again. My fingers were wrapped in protective tape and I had about 65 percent mobility in my hand. "Relax your grip" forced me to slow down, take deep breaths, and loosen up—all of which resulted in being more relaxed and playing better. Isn't that true in all aspects of our lives? Holding on too tight—to people we love, to our students, to our families—doesn't work out so well for us or for them.

10. What you've truly learned stays with you.

I was astonished. After resuming tennis slightly handicapped and not playing for almost four months, I was playing as well as before the fall. My coach commented and I agreed: "You haven't lost a beat. You're playing very well." I left that lesson pain free and exhilarated. How was it possible that I had no loss in skill? I think that when we are taught well and deeply on topics we are passionate about, learning sticks. Choice and deliberate practice also matter a lot, but perhaps most important of all, joy matters. It was the remembered joy of playing that gave me the impetus and will to play again, even knowing new missteps were bound to occur.

Instill a love of learning

I would like to see as a requirement that the content we teach—and how and why we teach and assess it—promotes a love of learning; that our instruction and the experiences we provide students inspire them to inquire, seek more knowledge, ask deeper questions, and go on learning. That statement is as true for us as educators as it is for our students. Professional development that is overly focused on data analysis and raising test scores crushes our love of learning. What we spend time on must not only be worth learning, it must also lead to a desire to learn more. Some of us have been fortunate enough to have the experience of being smitten by a subject in which we initially had little interest. Because our instructor shared his or her passion, made it fascinating, and presented the information in a manner we could understand and participate in, we came to love the subject too. We must provide similar experiences for our students.

Provide opportunities for students to "find" their passion. Share the inspirational life story of Ryan Speedo Green with middle and high school students.[15] Speedo (his preferred name) is now an international, supremely gifted opera singer. Growing up, he had no passions other than responding with extreme violence to his life of poverty and other severe challenges. And then one deeply caring teacher took his class of students with severe behavior and learning issues to the Metropolitan Opera in New York City, and Speedo saw and heard opera for the first time. He was mesmerized by the magnificent voice and stage presence of a black opera singer, a superstar who looked like him. He was so moved, he thought, "That's what I'm going to do with my life." And against all odds and probabilities—and with the continuing support of that one teacher and other caring mentors—he achieved his dream.

In an interview with Tavis Smiley on National Public Radio, Ryan Speedo Green stated, "I had the love for music *before* I had the voice."[16] Sometimes our students' lives are so fraught with anxiety over just trying to exist, there is no room for thinking about a passion or love of learning. That's where we come in. It was a teacher's action that changed the course of Ryan Speedo Green's life. Through one action—taking him to the opera—his teacher took him away from his desolate, dispiriting world and showed him another world—one that grabbed his heart and mind and never let go. By his own account, that passion for opera gave him a reason to live, and today his life is joyful.

Make learning memorable. I recently asked a group of high school students what learning experience affected and inspired them most in their elementary school years. Although a few cited a teacher they loved, no one cited a lesson or unit of study or specific classroom learning. What had an impact on these students were occasions with their friends, field trips, school plays, musical events, lived activities that involved hands-on doing and interaction. Sadly, for many students, school is still not a very relevant or interesting place for learning.

One high school student described his required geography class to me this way: the teacher lectures; they read out of a textbook as a whole class; daily homework takes about two hours as students are required to write out definitions of many geographic terms and then use each in a sentence; there is no connection made to real-world places and current events. Predictably, the student dislikes geography, finds it boring, and resents the hours of irrelevant homework.

Imagine a different scenario. Integrating required curriculum and standards, the teacher plans the course around places in the world where geography has been or is a determining factor in shaping the lives of everyday citizens: India, Pakistan, Israel, Palestine, Syria, Iraq, Nepal, and China, to name several. The fascinating story of how geography and climate change are interrelated can also be included—for example, by studying the places where rising sea levels are compelling people who live on islands or near a coastline to consider moving to higher ground. The teacher embeds current events, news articles, primary sources that include first-person narratives, podcasts, videos, and social media into the content. With the teacher's encouragement, students ask questions about why and how geography matters. Students are given some choice in the required homework and projects. They are encouraged to present their findings through writing, speaking, and multimedia projects. Or perhaps the teacher focuses on a local environmental event such as a damaging landslide, a past volcano eruption, the overcutting of trees, and so on, that permanently altered the geography and living habits of a place students know.

I predict the same student might leave that class enthused and smitten with geography for life and much more likely to pay attention to worldwide current events where geography plays a role in people's lives. The student might even become a lifelong concerned and active citizen who is personally invested in how geography and related climate change will continue to have an impact on people's lives, including his own. What a different outcome than the outcome resulting from just covering a required curriculum and moving students through the same boring activities each year!

"Do no harm," the credo and foundational precept for physicians, must also apply to us educators. When we fail to excite and incite the intellect and instead squander curiosity—that most precious of natural resources that all human beings possess— we endanger a love of learning that should be, I believe, a birthright for all people. Our credo must become "Inspire a love of learning." Then, inspiring our students, teachers, and leaders must become our highest priority.

Take Action

- **Share your passions** with colleagues and students. When I work in schools and speak at conferences, I talk about my ongoing passion for wanting *all* students to succeed. Almost all my work is in high-poverty, high-needs schools because so little changes for our underserved students, and that inequity literally keeps me up nights. I am committed to doing whatever I can—one district, one school, one teacher, one student at a time—to make a difference.

- **Provide more choice**, which can be a game changer for students who are not engaged or making a full effort. Also, for independent thinkers, choice allows students the freedom to be more creative and think more ingeniously. (See also pages 54 and 90–93.)

- **Find a way to make required curriculum relevant.** As much as possible, find and create real-world connections that capture students' hearts and minds. See our online lesson plan at sten.pub/literacyessentials, which took the required social studies curriculum, science curriculum, and standards and integrated them to teach writing and reading in depth while also focusing on local environmental issues.

- **Assign students to read one or more news articles** and bring in articles that interest them to share with the class. Students can use these articles as jumping-off points for their own inquiry projects. High school teacher Kelly Gallagher's "Article of the Week" web page deftly uses the reading and discussing of news articles to help build students' prior knowledge, something that is especially important for the many who lack the foundational background knowledge necessary to understand current news and world events.[17] (For more on current events, see pages 211 and 267–268.)

- **Invite specialists from the community into the classroom** to talk about how they use, for example, geography, math, history, science, or geology, and so on, in their jobs to give students a sense of purpose and understanding of the subject matter being taught.

Create a need to know

After meeting with the aforementioned high school students who could not recall any academic experiences from elementary school that had made a lifelong impact on them and silently acknowledging the same was true for me, I changed my usual course in planning with teachers for an upcoming writing residency. Along with keeping curriculum and standards at the forefront, as previously noted, I almost always have begun thinking and planning with the question "How can we engage students' hearts and minds?" This time our first question to ourselves was "How can we create a learning experience so significant and memorable that it might have a lifelong impact on students' lives?" (The "big" questions we asked to frame the study are on page 87. The lesson is described in detail online. See also Appendix C: Lesson Plan Framework/Overview and "Ask More Vital Questions," pages 161–167.)

The questions we and our students ask determine the direction and outcomes of our learning. Inspiring "a need to know" is an essential first step. Director James Cameron begins his movie *Titanic* with video footage of the ship's sinking. In 2012, he revisited the facts that informed his 1995 conclusions and asked: "What could have happened?" "What actually happened?" "Why did it happen?" Cameron still had so many unanswered questions on a topic he was passionate about that, with a team of experts, he investigated, once again, the possible causes and explanations for the extensive damage to and quick sinking of the ship. The "need to know" drove him to explore and scrutinize further, reanalyze all the facts, and reach new conclusions. That intense curiosity is exactly what we want to foster in our students—and ourselves.

When I ask a group of students "What do we mean by revision?" there is no response and not much interest in knowing. The teacher has been assigning most of the writing in the classroom and directing any changes to be made, so, not surprisingly, most students don't value writing or see a connection between in-school writing and real-world writing. Without a need to know—in this case, knowing what revision is and why it matters—students will not improve much as writers and thinkers. Teaching by telling, with teachers giving the explanations and solutions to students, has been shown to be far less effective than responsive teaching, which, through teachers' thoughtful questioning, probing, and interaction with students, creates a need for inquiry. Although we may be restrained by required curriculum and standards, we must present content in a way that entices a hunger to know more, which, in turn, creates the motivation, engagement, and persistence that lead to new and lasting learning.

Take Action

◆ **Find out what students are passionate about and "need to know."** Encourage investigation of a topic of interest. Provide excellent resources. Do a lot of frontloading. (See pages 129–146.)

◆ **Demonstrate the research process** and how one comes to an informed opinion. Follow the Optimal Learning Model. (See pages 136–146 and online lesson plan.)

◆ **Value uncertainty.** By the types of questions we pose (see "Ask More Vital Questions," page 161), we challenge students' thinking. Not relying on one perfect answer promotes curiosity and a continuous desire to learn. Begin, as James Cameron did, with these essential questions: First, "What do we know now?" Then, after some investigation, "What have we learned?" Next, "What else do we want to find out?" and "How can we find that information?" Finally, "What are our conclusions, based on all the evidence and analysis?"

◆ **Challenge students' thinking.** Rather than giving students the answer, ask, "What do you think?" or "How could we find that out?" Explicitly demonstrate and show how curious people find information to answer their questions so that, with our encouragement and guidance, students can search, browse, read, research, and collaborate to find answers to their important questions. It is this process that can lead students to see themselves as smart, sometimes for the first time. (See my story "Feeling Smart" below.)

◆ **Pose your own "need to know" questions.** For example, investigate such possible issues as why so many students are being labeled for special education, why the writing at two adjacent grade levels looks about the same, why so few students reach the proficiency level in reading, or other specific burning questions related to your or your school's ability to maximize achievement, engagement, and more. Model wondering and asking questions during read-alouds. Go to the website Wonderopolis.org for the Wonder of the Day and many more wonders.

STORY ❖ Feeling Smart

All the years I was a student in public elementary, middle, and high school, I was never really sure if I was smart. I liked school, and my teachers liked me. I was an A student and a compliant one. My work was done to specification and completed on time. I figured out what people expected of me and, mostly, I worked for teachers' and my parents' approval. I don't remember any passion for learning or memorable study that made me feel challenged in a way that pushed my thinking. School was about getting good grades, being with my few close friends, and following the rules.

Conversations around our dinner table every night with my parents and two younger sisters revolved around my dad's work, general questions about school, and polite, superficial talk. I don't recall feeling intellectually stimulated, although both my parents were readers and thinkers. My dad read several newspapers cover to cover each day, and my mother always took refuge and pleasure in reading popular fiction. Still, what they were reading and thinking about they did not share with us.

Something shifted for me when I went to college. I wasn't consciously aware of it until my first visit home my freshman year when my dad declared at the dinner table that I was different, "intellectually curious" he called it. I was flattered and surprised. I remember I was taking an art history class, which I loved. I knew so little about art and found what I was learning and viewing to be riveting and wonderful. I also savored a class on American literature taught by a dynamic professor. We read, discussed, and wrote about books by such authors as John Dos Passos, Ernest Hemingway, William Faulkner, and similar literary giants. As I had not become an avid reader until my late teens, these authors and books were eye-opening. A whole new world opened up to me; I became a lover of literature and a voracious reader.

But it was a philosophy of education class in my junior year that made me think that perhaps I might be smart. On the final exam, each of us had to complete three essay questions, one of which we were expected to create during the exam without consulting notes or peers. Our own question and response to it were expected to be thoughtful, to demonstrate deep knowledge of the chosen topic, and also to encompass what we believed was most significant to our learning and education in that class. I loved creating and answering that unique question, showing off my knowledge, and having the sustained time to do it. I remember still, all these many years later, the exhilaration of formulating my own important question. I felt smart and valued as a "big" thinker for the first time in my life.

I went on to become an elementary school teacher, believing that to be my destiny. My parents' mantra was "Teaching is a good profession for a woman," and I never believed I had any choice in the matter. The unspoken message was I was going to college to find a husband—not all that uncommon for my generation—and that my real career would be as a wife and mother.

I loved being wife and mother—and still do—but something was missing. I needed to use my mind and intellect. I wanted to make a difference that mattered beyond my family. I went back to school, got my master's degree as both a teacher of reading and a teacher of students with learning disabilities. I taught part-time in a high-poverty school, where the population was over 90 percent African American and most students were failing to successfully learn to read. I became passionate about changing that tragic outcome, read every professional book I could find on the subject, and wrote a grant to flood a first-grade classroom with real books and daily journal writing instead of the usual basal manuals and worksheets. That journey and success is documented in my first book, Transitions: From Literature to Literacy.18

All that time, during weekly phone calls with my dad (my mom had died by that time and I was teaching full-time), my dad never asked any questions related to my teaching career. He asked questions related to what I was cooking, how my husband's career as an architect was going, and matters related to child rearing. Like the "good girl" I had always been, I never took the lead to shift those conversations to also include my work. All that changed on my fortieth birthday, when I exploded on the phone and raged at my father for never showing any interest in my teaching career. It was the first argument I ever recall having with him. To my surprise and to his credit, he listened well, apologized, and almost immediately changed his behaviors and actions. Always a loving and caring father, he became my biggest champion and even insisted on attending some of my professional talks at conferences. At the follow-up book signings, he would stand by my side and offer, as "proud father of the author," to also sign my books. Those were very tender moments.

It is only recently that I realized I began to write books to prove to myself that I was smart. I believe my reasoning went something like this: Smart people write books, so if I can write a book that gets published and that people read, that must mean I'm smart. I have now written about a dozen books for educators, and I do feel competent in my area of expertise; but I always see myself as a learner-teacher and not the other way around. More important, I take seriously that ensuring each of our students feels smart is a vital part of our role as educators.

I was not a very good teacher when I began teaching, although I know I was a caring and conscientious one. I taught my students as I had been taught—with textbooks for science and social studies, whole-class reading aloud of these texts, lots of worksheets on isolated skills, phonics-based reading, formula writing, and an emphasis on grades. I don't remember promoting hands-on learning, science experiments, literature conversations, authentic writing, or encouraging students' inquiries.

Over the years, as I gradually became a reflective reader, thinker, collaborator, questioner, and champion for all students, my thinking and my methods improved. Today, in my ongoing literacy teaching, coaching, and leading in diverse schools, always uppermost in my mind is posing relevant "big" questions that will challenge and captivate students' and teachers' thinking and engage their hearts and minds. I still treasure a handwritten note from a former student who wrote, "You are an expert at smartness." I want each of our students and teachers to feel they are experts at smartness as well. This requires that we create and sustain an intellectual culture in our classrooms and schools.

Work toward a culture of "collaborative expertise"

When I began teaching, most of my time was spent behind closed doors with my students. I have few memories of co-teaching, coaching, or working with colleagues. It was pretty much a "lone wolf" culture, and part of me preferred it that way. I could "hide out." My mistakes or failed lessons would not become public knowledge, and I didn't have to take many risks. If I'm an effective teacher today, it's largely because of what I've learned with and from others—through professional reading, professional conversations, observing experts, seeking feedback, and, especially, through ongoing collaboration with colleagues. In fact, in all high-achieving schools, professional collaboration and trust permeate the culture and day-to-day relationships of the school. Meaningful collaboration, the ability to work well with others, and effective communication are attributes of workers in highly successful organizations of all types.

John Hattie, in his remarkable text *Visible Learning for Teachers: Maximizing Impact on Learning*, uses the term "collaborative expertise" to connote the collective knowledge and wisdom of the whole group, which is a necessity not just for schoolwide learning but for developing an intellectual culture.[19] Applying collaborative expertise depends on a trusting culture. It is insufficient for a school to have a few brilliant teachers; whole-school achievement, well-being, and equity depend on our collective expertise in action. That is, we are focusing on the cognitive development of not only our students but also us educators.

In fact, engaged learning for all of us depends on intellectual environments that promote not just collaboration and cooperation but also ongoing interaction rooted in expertness. Much of that expertise develops through working with others in a professional learning culture. That is, when working together with a partner or group, teachers and students know why and how to discuss and exchange ideas, raise pertinent and intelligent questions, give actionable and useful feedback, deal with disagreements, and collaborate in a way that respects everyone's thinking. All of these actions first need to be demonstrated, practiced with guidance, and continuously supported to work well.

Collaborative expertise also includes knowing how, when, and why to use technology to augment instruction. Technology-enhanced instruction means our technology use provides students equitable and sufficient access to devices, along with appropriate and relevant content, purpose, and audience for the work.[20]

Not to be minimized, establishing an intellectual culture depends on all learners—students and teachers—believing and trusting that their school's physical, social, and emotional environments (see pages 40–60) make them feel safe enough to make their true voices heard, raise hard questions, and risk failure.

 ## Take Action

- ◆ **Evaluate your school's intellectual culture.** Aim for a knowledge-centered school, not a test-centered one. As a leadership team or as part of a professional development meeting, discuss the following:
  - ◉ *Are the topics of study and discussion meaningful and worthy of the time and effort they take*—that is, between and among teachers and the principal, are we mostly centered on applying principled literacy practices and supporting all students and teachers to inquire and learn more, or are conversations primarily focused on data, behavior issues, and testing?
  - ◉ *Are the questions we are asking our students and ourselves vital ones* that cause deep thinking and reflection on core literacy and real-world issues, or are they mostly about procedures, problems, and management?

- *Are teachers and leaders routinely reading professionally* and questioning and augmenting current practices, or are they putting all their faith into dutifully following a prescribed program or curriculum?
- *Is the necessary infrastructure and environment in place to support an intellectual culture?* If not, what's the first priority that needs to be addressed?

◆ **Work toward highest-quality professional learning.** Much of what is called professional development in schools today is actually what one principal labeled "random acts of professional development." That is, the PD is often top-down, superficial, and scattered, and nothing of importance changes for teacher and student learning.

- *Use multiple sources of classroom and school data to determine the area of greatest need for the whole school.* Start there (for example, improving the teaching of writing), and stay with that focus for at least one to three years so that positive changes are deep and sustainable.
- *Seek to establish ongoing and high-level professional learning* at your school, even if you have to start the process yourself with just a few colleagues (see pages 105–110).
- *Admit what you don't know* and seek out, observe, and have a dialogue with more-knowledgeable peers. Ask a trusted peer to review a lesson plan, give feedback on a lesson, or co-teach.
- *Ensure collaboration with colleagues occurs in vertical teams as well as horizontal ones*, and that enough time is given to think deeply about an issue or lesson.
- *Work to get a highly capable Literacy and Leadership Team in place* to guide the ongoing, schoolwide professional learning. (See pages 124–125.)
- *Try out and apply learning from PD meetings in your classroom*, with support and feedback from a mentor teacher, colleague, coach, or principal.
- *Work with the principal, coaches, and specialists to schedule times for mentoring* another teacher or being mentored, common planning for grade-level or content area teachers, peer observations, and peer coaching.
- *Do all you can to promote a school culture of co-teaching and coaching*, both of which depend on trust, respect, shared beliefs, and shared knowledge.

Ensure that the heart and mind go together

Finally—but also first and foremost—we must do whatever we can to first capture students' and teachers' hearts before worrying about how much we are instructing them. Have you noticed that no one ever says "mind and heart"? That's because if we win a person's heart, the engagement, effort, and intellect of the mind are more likely to follow. To reach the heart, we appeal to people's interests, needs, and curiosity; respect their culture and background; value them as individuals; and care about their well-being.

We can start with stories—our own, the students', family stories, the books we love—regardless of the age of our learners. A well-told, interesting story can connect us with others, increase our understanding of life issues, and engage us in a way nothing else can. The power of stories deepens literacy learning, humanizes us, and gives enhanced meaning to our lives.[21] "Stories" are sprinkled throughout this book for that reason, primarily to touch our hearts, inspire our thinking and actions, and expand our horizons. Make personal stories and storytelling central to your classroom and school's speaking, listening, and writing culture and community. For rationale, ideas, and great guidelines—especially for middle and high school students—see The Moth: The Art and Craft of Storytelling (https://the moth.org/) as well as the *SmartBrief* piece "Stories Stick with Students."[22]

As well, rely on writing—stories and content across the curriculum—to connect the heart and mind and make us smarter. I know that if I can engage students' hearts in an authentic topic and audience that matters to them, I can stimulate their intellect and also teach them everything they need to know about writing—organization, craft, elaboration, grammar, revision, editing, and so on—and they will willingly do the hard work of writing and wind up with very good results. However, without that heart–mind connection, writing efforts—and other academic efforts—will often be lackluster and minimal.

 ## Take Action

- Get to know students and colleagues—their backgrounds, interests, and families—by welcoming, encouraging, and honoring their culture, stories, customs, hobbies, and unique characteristics. Sharing our stories with students and staff members increases the connections, empathy, and trust we share with one another, which makes it more likely we can engage hearts and minds. (See the story "Being Known," on pages 287–289, for the importance of others knowing our life story.)

◆ **Read aloud great picture books to colleagues as well as students of all ages.** We educators also need the heart-mind connection for full engagement. I often begin a professional development meeting by reading aloud a great picture book. It's five to ten minutes beautifully spent as we slow down after a busy day, reflect, and allow ourselves to be moved by the power of story. A few personal favorites are *Breathe* by Scott Magoon; *On a Beam of Light: A Story of Albert Einstein* by Jennifer Berne; *Each Kindness* by Jacqueline Woodson; and *A Child of Books* by Oliver Jeffers and Sam Winston.

◆ **Let the people we spend time with every day know we value them**—through caring actions, verbal comments, facial expressions, short notes, kind gestures, and thoughtfulness in all we do. Through the collaborative classroom and school culture we establish, promote curiosity and risk taking by encouraging multiple points of view, welcoming conversation and student talk, and nonjudgmental listening. Establishing a storytelling culture goes a long way toward making all learners feel valued.

◆ **As much as possible, make students' interests central to the curriculum** through project-based learning, reading materials in classroom and school libraries, choices of writing and speaking topics, and respect shown for students' talents, differences, backgrounds, and needs. The more relevant, interesting, and enjoyable the work is, the more highly engaged our students become.

Endnote

As I was completing the writing of this book, a literacy specialist wrote to me wanting to know about the research supporting "joy." Although she was pleased that her district's school board had just included "joyful literacy learning" as a key literacy strategy outcome, some principals were not yet convinced and were requesting to see "research" and "measurement" information regarding joy from scholars and researchers. Although, based on her own classroom experiences, the literacy specialist was convinced that joy is essential, she needed some backup. In addition to recommending some resources,[23] I also wrote her the following:

> *"Measuring" joy seems silly (don't quote me!); it's like measuring happiness. We know it when we experience it. Common sense applies here too. All of us who are human have found that when an experience is enjoyable we are more likely to invest in it, take risks, and make a full*

commitment. Joy is not the same as fun. Joy comes from the celebration we do of teachers' and students' strengths and efforts.

Finally, I told her that joy is the main event. In my work in schools, the main reason the teachers and principals "buy in" is not because test scores go up—and they do—and not because kids become better readers and writers—which they do. It's because the work and the learning are so joyful for students, teachers, and principals.

It seems fitting and important to end this chapter on "Creating a Thriving Learning Environment" with a reminder to keep joy uppermost in our teaching and learning. Everything else is commentary. A joyful school culture determines whether or not teachers collaborate, stay at a school for a long time, come to work happy to be there, and all members of the school community prosper.

Teaching with Purpose and Authenticity

It's not easy to refashion required curriculum, standards, and programs to connect with real-world purposes, but it's essential. Instead of thinking, "How can we 'cover' all the requirements?" think, "How can we engage students, spark curiosity, and promote inquiry in a manner that propels a burning desire to read, write, question, and learn more?" Without a passion for learning, students don't remember much of value or consider the time spent on a topic, an assignment, or a study worthwhile. And neither do we. Think about the audience for writing and reading across the curriculum. For the most part, our audience needs to be a real-world one, and our and our students' efforts need to reflect that. Otherwise we waste that precious human capacity—the will and commitment to put full mental and emotional energy into the task at hand.

There's no need to make authenticity harder than it has to be. The real-world purpose for making independent reading of free-choice books a number-one priority is that readers read whole, meaningful texts, mostly of their own choosing. They don't spend most their time in guided-reading groups and on skills and strategy work. The latter are important, of course, but only as a temporary scaffold and means to an end—that of becoming comprehending, self-directed, and joyful readers. And the same is true with writing. Writers write for readers, not for bulletin boards or just the teacher. Writing for a real-world audience can be as easy as writing for students in the classroom and school—for example, having students write and publish engaging nonfiction and fiction pieces for the purpose of providing interesting texts for the classroom and school libraries. The authentic purpose is to provide appealing, relevant texts for real readers. As such, the published or displayed writing pieces and books need to follow real-world conventions and be easy to read and follow—that is, the writing is well organized, well crafted, and accurate.

Given how complex and uncertain life can be for so many students and their families, it's important we raise not just readers and writers, but also informed, thoughtful citizens who can contribute to a more equitable, sustainable, and caring world. That effort begins with ensuring that our teaching and assessing are relevant, purposeful, and engaging.

Infuse Purpose and Authenticity into All We Do

All of us want and need to be inspired by the work we do. That inspiration and passion is far more likely when the work matters to students and to us. When students understand and value the "what" of curriculum and standards, they are willing to invest in the "how." When they don't see the relevance of the lesson or activity, many make minimal efforts and even shut down. If we want students to invest full energy into their schoolwork, they must see the work as important to their lives in some way. One middle school student put it this way: "If there isn't an obvious, real-world connection, at least make the work interesting! Let us know this is something that will actually help our minds."

A growing body of research confirms that the more authentic and meaningful our instruction is, the greater gains students make. That is, when we embed real-world genres and purposes into teaching reading, writing, speaking, and listening, students are more engaged and more likely to understand at a deeper level.[1] Always we need to remain flexible in our instruction and be led by such questions as "What do students need to succeed in doing ____ in order to learn ____?" and "What's the most meaningful way to teach and guide them so they succeed?" Being flexible and teaching authentically include being willing and able to change course and modify our instruction based on the immediate needs of our students, which must always take priority over our lesson plan. In fact, changing plans midcourse may prove to be more valuable to student learning than the lesson we originally planned. An example follows.

In a recent residency focused on improving writing instruction, it became clear when planning with the teacher in whose classroom I would be demonstrating and coaching that although improving writing was our focus, student behavior issues were at the top of her—and her colleagues'—list of concerns. So I suggested we prioritize that concern by making it our writing topic. On the first day of the residency, after spending some time introducing myself to the students and sharing thoughts about my life as a reader and writer, I said something like the following to them: "I understand that inappropriate behaviors are a big problem in your classroom—so much so that they interfere with your teacher doing her job and prevent many of you from learning. So take a few minutes and turn and talk to the person next to you about the problems this class is having that interfere with learning." Those problems and the solutions we came up with together totally engaged the students. It turned out that the students were as distraught about the continuing behavior issues as the teacher was!

By focusing on students' interests and needs first, we were able to teach students—and observing teachers—almost everything about effective writing that we had set out as important end goals for the week, such as having the writing form match the purpose, rereading and revising to craft a clear and coherent message, editing for spelling and conventions to provide a seamless text for the reader, enjoying writing, and self-evaluating writing effectiveness. It was a thinking shift—from "How do we get kids to revise and edit?" to "How do we engage students' hearts and minds in a highly relevant, meaningful way?"—that made it possible to maximize our effort to teach writing well, all of which culminated in excellent results. The outcome was not just quality writing but also a classroom where students took increasing responsibility for managing their own behaviors. (See page 58 for results of that authentic writing.)

A couple of years later at the same school, students' foundational writing abilities were solid. In working to build a thriving environment, the school had developed a culture of trust, collaboration, celebration, and professional learning. Classroom management, which is really about students' self-regulating their own behaviors, was no longer a major issue. Teachers were now poised to use reading and writing for larger purposes. Thinking about purpose and authenticity had expanded from a singular literacy lesson to deep study and critical thinking about important topics that integrated literacy across the curriculum. Thinking about student engagement now included a wider question: *How can students use literacy to have agency in their lives and make their world a better place?* (Examples of that broader intellectual thinking are exemplified in the lesson plan featured in Appendix C, pages A5–A7, and online at sten.pub/literacyessentials.)

Take Action

- When planning, consider first the question "How can we engage students' hearts and minds?"—even when schoolwide pressure to raise test scores is driving instruction. When the work is relevant and stirs students' interests and curiosity, when we focus on significant ideas and high-level thinking, and when we provide great literature and frontloading, students and teachers surprise us with what they can do.

- Constantly ask, "Why does this instructional practice or activity matter for students?" For example, it may not be helpful to do a picture walk for every guided-reading lesson in the primary grades, use whisper reading for every guided-reading lesson in the intermediate grades, pre-teach most vocabulary, or follow a predetermined sequence for teaching skills. Expert teachers critically examine the objective of the lesson and rethink and rework their instruction to make it purposeful and relevant.

- State the purpose and goals of every lesson, task, activity, or change of plan. Be sure the language we use is student-friendly and comprehensible, and always make our thinking visible. Perhaps say something like this:

  - We're going to be researching _____. Here's why you need to know this.
  - We'll be working in small groups today to try out and practice _____ before you attempt it on your own.
  - We're going to change our plan for today because I noticed _____.

    Assess, through questioning, turn and talk, or a quick-write, to be sure students understand the learning goal. Many teachers post the purpose of the lesson and constantly refer to it to keep students and themselves on track.

- Have students wrestle with real-world issues, with guidance, by reading, researching, discussing, and writing about relevant and complex topics and ideas in social studies, science, politics, health, and the arts, and incorporating more primary-source texts and resources. Make every effort to provide firsthand experiences and to personalize required curriculum study to students' lives, cultures, and backgrounds. Think big, think broadly, and think deeply about important topics that affect students' lives now and in the future. Some examples that could work for K–12 include, but are not limited to, the rights of the child, human rights, social and economic justice, environmental stewardship, global warming, endangered species, cultural diversity, immigration, why elections matter, and how historical events can help us to understand the present.

◆ **Make meaningful connections between subject areas.** The only way to "fit" everything in is to integrate other subjects—for example, science and social studies—into the language arts and to view reading and writing as every teacher's responsibility. At times, math can also be included—for example, using measurement to shed light on a science problem.

◆ **Write and publish for authentic audiences and purposes.** My experience and teacher research confirm that this is the single most important factor for having students invest their full energies into composing, revising, and editing.[2] (See "Teaching Writers," pages 234–235, for many ideas for writing short pieces.)

◆ **Question the use of inauthentic resources,** such as worksheets on isolated skills, senseless activities in adopted programs, and the overuse of and overreliance on test preparation materials. Also, critically examine the use of workstations and centers as well as homework, and ensure they are promoting learning, not just keeping students busy.

◆ **Explain posted writing** so that the audience and purpose of writing featured in school hallways and classrooms is clear and the posted work will actually be read with understanding by students, teachers, and visitors. Compose a paragraph with students to explain the background, content, and goals of the posted writing. Once we've modeled and practiced how to do this with students, partners or small groups can volunteer to write an overview and explanation for readers. Without a big-picture explanation, many posted pieces become just artifacts and are not read or appreciated.

◆ **Get students involved in classroom, schoolwide, national, and global initiatives.** Once students, with our guidance, are routinely examining, inquiring, discussing, and reading and writing about important real-world topics, expanding the work to a purpose beyond themselves is a natural outcome.

   ◉ *Use an everyday concern to resolve a widespread challenge and behave as responsible citizens.* Knowledge really is power. When students have been researching, studying, raising questions, and talking about such topics as pollution, garbage disposal, world hunger, homelessness, the need for clean water, and so on, their awareness is heightened. As a primary grades teacher notes, even young students start to notice issues close to home and strive to do their part to make a difference beyond themselves:

Students in my class got very concerned over what was happening to all of our used-up markers at the beginning of the year when we discovered I couldn't throw them into the recycling bin easily without removing the ink cartridge. We tried to remove the ink cartridge and discovered it very challenging and messy! So we did some investigating. We actually stopped our whole lesson and Googled it. There was some great information out there, and we discovered other classes that had the same concerns. We found out we could collect the used markers and send any type of marker back to Crayola (colorcycle), or we could bring them into Staples. From here we began our own schoolwide marker-recycling program. We wrote letters, made announcements, and created informational posters around this project for our school.[3]

- *Consider fundraising for a local or global charity* connected to the current area of study. Students can learn about the people, their issues, and the area they are fundraising for. Students can be a part of choosing the charity, researching the charity and location, developing fundraising ideas, writing letters, composing blog posts, planning assemblies, and counting money raised through these fundraisers. Initiatives might include collecting food for local families in need, raising money for research on endangered animals, or building wells for clean water for communities around the world. (See examples online of the website lesson plan.)

Plan with the End in Mind

The hardest, most intensive, and time-consuming part of the residency work is the planning and deep thinking that take place weeks before we begin the actual demonstration teaching and coaching in classrooms. If we can get the planning "right," in general, the week successfully unfolds. The host classroom teachers and I plan with the end in mind for both students and staff; that is, our driving question is "What do we want students and teachers to experience, think about, know, and begin to apply (by the end of the week)?"

Planning with the End in Mind Requires That We Do the Following

- Examine the most pressing literacy issues through a careful look at data, standards, and required curriculum.

- Ask significant questions; that is, questions that stimulate curiosity and deep thinking.

- Know and apply proven research and best practices.

- Respect and use teachers' and students' backgrounds, strengths, needs, and interests.

- Invest in frontloading (see pages 129–131).

- Promote guided discovery and inquiry.

- Build in choice within structure.

- Remain flexible and open to a change of plans.

- Consider instructional alternatives.

In writing residencies in Winnipeg, Manitoba, in March 2015, host teachers Trish Richardson (for primary grades) and Daria Orloff (for intermediate grades) and I co-planned for our upcoming study of the endangered environment and the impact of climate change. The focus, for the primary grades, was on the endangered polar bear and, for the intermediate grades, endangered Lake Winnipeg and the right to clean water. Both of these real-world issues affected the students' lives and their communities beyond one school year.

We began our planning by generating four "big" questions to guide the work, which integrated the social studies and science curriculum with reading, writing, and the arts:

- What's happening to the environment to endanger it?
- What are the causes and "cures"?
- What can we do to help?
- Why does all this matter?

To then set the stage for the high-level thinking teachers and students were about to undertake, we asked ourselves some key planning questions. Note that these questions also served as our overarching learning goals.

- How can we make the work and audience for the writing so authentic and personal that students will invest their best efforts and will remember the experience, even as adults?
- How can our work give students agency and purpose in their lives?
- What kind of frontloading will be necessary so students know the content well enough to interpret it and apply it with minimal support?

By "frontloading," we mean the necessary support, structures, and scaffolding students require to be successful. In that regard, we asked these questions:

- What resources/texts/literature/technology can we find to support and enhance our work—including picture books, videos, online texts/blogs, experts, photographs, literature, firsthand accounts, news reports, opinion pieces?
- What structures—for example, fact gathering, shared writing, small-group work, resources, interviews, field trips, guided conversations—do we need for students to experience and practice before they can successfully work on their own?
- What genres, forms, and formats might the writing and communications take?

Ensuring we could accomplish our big goals in a week would depend on our extensive planning with the end in mind, which included the almost month-long frontloading by both teachers before the residency in each classroom took place. The first part of our frontloading was creating a detailed lesson plan, beginning with our goals and learning outcomes. (See Appendix C: Lesson Plan Framework/ Overview. See sten.pub/literacyessentials for the complete lesson plan. For more on frontloading, see pages 129–131.)

Fourth-grade teacher Daria Orloff reflects on how planning with the end in mind has made her more reflective and intentional:

> *My biggest take-away from all of this work is that I am now more thought-ful in planning writing projects for my students. I am more careful when I examine curriculum documents. I look at the general and specific learning outcomes, and then I choose a topic or a theme based on those outcomes that I feel would be the most valuable for my students—topics that will lend themselves to meaningful, purposeful, and authentic read-ing, writing, and learning experiences.[4]*

Take Action

- **Plan for less coverage and more depth.** Think in terms of important topics and big ideas worth teaching and learning about, rather than small units and isolated skills. Ask questions worth students' time and inquiry. Create a worthy lesson plan. As an example, see the first part of our plan "Overarching Goals and Outcomes" for grades two–three. Day-by-day and week-by-week specifics of that detailed plan, including Plan at a Glance, Teacher Talk, Tech Tips, Teacher Reflections, examples of frontloading charts, student work, student reflections, and much more are available online at sten.pub/literacyessentials.

- **Make meaningful connections beyond literacy.** For example, while researching and writing about the polar bear as an endangered species, Trish Richardson went beyond reading and writing to include math and art. In math, students compared the sizes of baby, female, and male polar bears. They examined the size of bears' feet. They learned about the distance polar bears could swim. They wondered whether a polar bear would fit through their classroom door when standing on its hind legs. In art, students used the research they'd done on the polar bear's habitat to make illustrations for the final published book. Students also used drawing apps on the iPad to layer in and draw different things they might see in the Arctic. The following year, as the study continued, a locally and internationally well-known artist was invited into the classroom to talk with students about how she uses paintings of polar bears to advocate for protecting them. (See page 373 for more.)

- **Keep end goals and purpose visible** so all students are clear on what they are working on and why. As noted, many teachers publicly post these and have students write the purpose and goals on their daily work. Always make sure learning intentions are clear and relevant. (See pages 344–346 for much more on learning goals.)

- **Let the audience and the purpose determine the format.** For example, in the lesson on polar bears and their endangered environment, deciding that the audience for our class-authored, nonfiction book—which comprised entries from each student plus whole-class entries—would be students in grades one, two, and three helped us define and determine the book's structure, categories, organization, size of font and amount of text on a page, illustrations, and more. (A complete copy of the gorgeous forty-six-page book, *Polar Bears Are the King of the North,* is available online at sten.pub/literacyessentials.)

In conclusion, the question "How can we engage students' hearts and minds?" remained central to our planning, instructing, and adjusting of our plans. Without student engagement, our study of polar bear endangerment in grades two–three and Lake Winnipeg in grade four could have become another isolated unit of study that students quickly forgot. Instead, students were fired up and exhilarated by the real-world content, the importance of the learning to their own lives, and the difference they could make in improving their local—and national—natural habitat.

Finding our audience and making the writing meaningful and authentic were key to our success. Trish Richardson reflects:

> *Throughout the entire process we kept the question "Why does this mat-ter?" at the forefront of our minds. At first there was some uncertainty, but there was no uncertainty about the fact that we wanted students to leave with a greater understanding of environmental stewardship. We wanted them to come away with the idea that they could make a difference and that their words and ideas mattered. This project was supposed to be meaningful. We wanted students to remember it. Could we write a letter? Write to whom? Why? Could we create a book to impart our knowledge to other Grade 1, 2, and 3 students? They loved this idea!*[5]

Provide More Choice Within Structure

Many of us feel that if we give up any control, chaos will result. I like as much order and control as the next person, but here's what I've learned: we get far greater results—not to mention better engagement, enjoyment, and higher quality of work—when students have some choice in what they do. We are still in charge and have the final say, but together we set up expectations and parameters that adhere to curriculum guidelines, standards, and mandates and, at the same time, consider students' background, interests, and needs. Providing students some choice, along with appropriately challenging and relevant curriculum, often forestalls any engagement issues.

As an example, see the sign-up chart for grade two–three students in the aforementioned project. Although we teachers directed the criteria for the writing, based on the literature students were hearing and reading, students had a wide choice of writing topic. That wide choice led to great enthusiasm to do "the work."

Choice within structure (controlled choice)—students sign up to write about one or more questions/issues on curriculum topic of study

Choice within structure also means that once we've taught students how to do something and they have demonstrated their competence, that activity can become a "free-choice" one. For example, students could choose to write poems, book reviews, or persuasive essays once they have completed required work satisfactorily or at designated times when free choice is an option. (See "Teaching Writers," pages 232 and 235, for many authentic writing ideas for short pieces that offer students choice.)

Free-choice reading of relevant, interesting, and appropriately challenging texts—and sustained time to read them—is a game changer for turning all students into readers. Promote reading choice across the curriculum. That is, within curriculum requirements, always allow for some student choice. (See also "Teaching Readers," page 209.)

 Take Action

- **Structure assignments within a required framework, but within that framework, give students choice.** Here are a few examples:
  - *Have students communicate their gratitude to someone* who has never been properly thanked for his or her actions. Every student would be expected to follow a writing rubric collaboratively created by teacher and students, but within those requirements students could decide to whom they would write, the personal content, and even the format, such as a letter, video, podcast, and so on.
  - *Within a required genre, allow students some choice*—for example, choosing to read three required books from a list of twenty or choosing resources they find on their own plus using one or several from a list of recommendations we supply. Or, as related to a particular study in a content area, we might require each student to read one or more texts in a specific genre or use information from various multimedia formats, such as websites and YouTube videos. Students could also have negotiated choice for how they present their learning—for example, a reflection, a poem, an original multimedia format, and so on.
  - *Allow students to create one or more questions to demonstrate their understanding of a concept* once they are well practiced in responding to and creating open-ended questions. (See page 72 in my story "Feeling Smart.")
- **Create a bulletin board of choice-within-structure activities.** Use your prime real estate to feature possible writing choices. For example, in a kindergarten classroom, we have a writing wall. Every time we teach a new writing form or genre, we name it and post it on the wall with one or more student exemplars.

Students consult the wall daily for ideas. Not only that, the postings serve as a reminder of what has been accomplished throughout the year, and students stop saying to us, "I finished my work. What should I do now?"

- ◆ **Give students some say in how activities will be carried out** once they know and apply classroom routines and expectations—for example, choosing places to sit during self-selected reading time, selecting a facilitator and scribe for small-group work, or suggesting a different format for an assignment.

- ◆ **Encourage more choices and formats that reflect real-world reading and writing** aimed at a wide audience, such as blogs, videos, tweets, podcasts, and e-publications. Use social networking tools such as Edmodo and Kidblog (see tech tools in Appendix D for others).

- ◆ **Have exemplars available for students to use as resources.** Save student work samples from the current year's class to share with future students. Then, with guidance, ask those students what they notice about the work—format, style, craft, organization, language, accuracy, and so on. Use such exemplars to showcase a wide range of possibilities and choices, not just expectations for the work.

Embrace Technology That Enhances Meaningful Learning

I confess: I've been slow to apply new technologies to my teaching. Unlike my granddaughters, who are growing up with these new literacies like a second language, I bumble along and need hand-holding every step of the way. Still, I am a convert. I know that the right technology tools can help us do our jobs better and make our teaching more interactive, authentic, motivating, and self-directing for our students and us. That said, as technology is increasingly influencing teaching and learning, we must ensure any use of technology supports and enhances worthy purposes.

My favorite and most successful use of technology to date involves using my iPad, connected wirelessly, to present information to large and small audiences. I upload albums using Photos on my MacBook, and these albums include videos, photos, text, and student work samples. My goal is not to use the latest technology. In fact, my iPad purchase and use has been for this one purpose only—to communicate more effectively with my audience. With fewer barriers between the audience and me and the ability to move and walk around, I feel I can be more personal and conversational, which is my desired presentation style. As well, I can be more authentic, flexible, and specific. Depending on the audience and their needs and interests, I can alter my original plan. I can quickly enter and exit various albums on different topics and also easily zoom in on children's writing to make it highly visible. In other words, the tech use and application function as a tool that supports and enhances my goals, content, message, and presentation.

Middle and high school teachers report that their use of Google Docs has changed their teaching for the better. In language arts and content area classes, students share with teachers what they are writing as they write, which enables quick and effective communication between teacher and student and ensures individuals and teams are all contributing and have up-to-date information. A big plus is the easy, automatic saving of drafts so nothing gets lost. Elementary teachers who transfer student writing into accurate books that become reading texts in the classroom library find Book Creator and similar technology tools a great support for effective and efficient publishing of student writing.

Still, I am not a confident technology user, and the technology stream feels like a torrent coming at me; the flow never stops, and I don't know how to shut it off or even if it's wise to do so. I know there are terrific technology tools for igniting passion in learning, equalizing the playing field for students and teachers who learn differently, and for inspiring creativity and inquiry, just to name a few possibilities. However, the big challenge and question for many of us is this: How do we sift through the myriad technology offerings, make informed judgments, and then buy, use, and apply only what's excellent and what serves our learning purposes?

Even when we have the "right" tech devices, we must ensure teachers, principals, and coaches have first been well instructed and practiced in its use, that students are involved in authentic learning and are not just moving through levels or programs, and that the feedback students receive is meaningful, that it moves their learning forward in thoughtful ways. When choosing an app, a tech project, or an integration of technology into the curriculum, consider the following:

Evaluating Technology Use

- Does the technology support and enhance our goals and shared beliefs for meaningful instruction, study, inquiry, observation, assessment, or application of learning?

- What is the purpose for "the work"? Who is the real-world audience for communicating our information and results, and how will we make our findings easily accessible and comprehensible?

- Is the technology use inclusive and adaptable? Will learners be able to participate in a way that gives them usable information, control, and choice, and that also advantages their style of learning?

- Is the technology simple and flexible enough that its use eases, rather than burdens, the teacher's or the students' daily efforts and time constraints?

Important to note: we can substitute the word *program* for *technology* in these questions for a new initiative our district, school, and we are thinking of adopting or adapting. In fact, as responsible educators, we must thoughtfully explore such questions before investing money and time into any new technology, program, or initiative.

One excellent and innovative use of technology that meets all of the above-stated criteria is the way principal Sue Marlatt gives feedback to teachers after conducting instructional walks in their classrooms.[6] Using an iPad and its camera, she seamlessly takes nonjudgmental notes and photos to explicitly celebrate teachers' strengths before making possible suggestions, all with the purpose of moving student learning forward. The combination of text plus photos quickly provides a vivid, organized, and detailed snapshot of the classroom, the teacher's work, and the students' work. Although my personal, highly recommended technology for recording information in these instructional walks is pencil and paper, I recognize that when technology use is meaningful, skillfully integrated, and nonthreatening, it has the potential to work well for documenting information.

Sometimes you just have to experiment with different technologies to see what works best for you. After trying out a number of apps and styluses for his instructional walks in classrooms, tech-savvy principal Matt Renwick moved to a paper-based, unformatted process when a survey of his staff revealed almost all preferred his taking and sharing notes on paper. He comments:

There is just something about having that immediate feedback, written out on paper, which made my visits more concrete and tangible. Because my instructional walks are strengths-based and not evaluative in nature, they could physically come back to these notes, reread what I noticed, and take pride in the quality of education they provide for their students.[7]

In my experience, too often technology becomes the go-to solution, especially in schools where students are failing. Chromebooks, iPads, apps, and the latest devices are purchased without a lot of thought and debate as to how student and teacher learning will actually be improved. Although the technology may be fun and interesting, if it does not lead to deep, meaningful learning, we must question its use. For example, in a high-poverty school where students were failing to learn to read successfully and where classroom libraries were scarce, iPads were purchased for all students for the primary purpose of moving K–5 students through leveled texts in an online "library of books." These were not "real" books but texts written for the online reading program. Not surprisingly, students did not become great readers. Had the district invested instead in developing effective teachers of reading through ongoing and expert professional learning along with providing excellent classroom libraries with accompanied sustained time to read books of choice, students as competent readers would have been a much more likely outcome.

Meaningful purpose must accompany technology use. The possibilities for making teaching and learning more dynamic, engaging, and efficient through technology are plentiful, including access to videos, YouTube for Schools, wise use of social media, smartboards and document cameras, interactive Internet formats, film, e-textbooks that can be continually updated, podcasts, webcasts, various art forms, blogs, wikis, student-made videos, school and district websites, and live chats with people across the globe. Our students have unlimited options for accessing information, uniquely expressing themselves, and communicating. Still, there is a caution. Computers, tablets, videos, computerized programs, e-readers, and other devices do not guarantee better teaching and learning. The goal is not more technology use but more effective, engaged, and purposeful teaching and learning. Technology, when it is used wisely, has the potential to fulfill that goal.

 ## Take Action

- **Use technology to communicate more effectively:**
  - *Create classroom, school, and district websites.* Publish book reviews and newsletters to parents, including subject-matter work and commentaries by students. Create a welcome packet for new students and their families. Principal Matt Renwick and his staff created an official school welcoming video for new students and their families. The video was embedded on their website, which also included maps of the school, informational videos, important and current information, upcoming events, and more.[8]

- *Using guidance and presentation software, have students make a class-authored presentation* for the school server to teach other students, parents, or community members a concept or content.
- *Establish online blogs* and other formats that provide information and perspectives on science experiments and observations, community studies, key political and social issues, and more.
- *Create class or school Twitter accounts and hashtags.* Share classroom and school events and celebrations with families and the local community and beyond. Include curriculum study and questions raised, book reviews and author chats, school policies such as grading, and much more.
- *Access outstanding websites*, such as www.edutopia.org and www.ReadWriteThink.org, for inspiration, innovation, information, and excellent resources to support curriculum and instruction.
- *Post student- and class-made videos* that explain content learning and thinking across the curriculum.
- *Create a tutorial in language that is clear and concise to help parents* understand the latest standards, report cards, homework guidelines, school rules, and so on.
- *Do demonstration writing using a document camera to project the work.* The document camera also works extremely well for public conferences after the student has read the writing at least once and the focus is on content, and for public editing conferences as well. (See page 176.)
- *Send persuasive letters and editorials* to local and national newspapers, school boards, and national organizations.

- **Embed technology that increases student engagement and motivation.** Consider novel uses for Twitter and other social media; have students, for example, compose book recommendations or summaries limited to 140 characters. Explore the possible use of e-publishing, digital books, and websites such as Edutopia, which can provide interactive diagrams, audio and video tools, and technological flourishes that illuminate and enhance content and concepts. Observe teachers who are using technology well.

- **Ensure that the technology used is worth the time and effort.** It's easy to turn responsibility over to a computerized program or an electronic device and assume, perhaps falsely, that students are progressing and learning more. Be sure you can *reliably* assess everything you ask students to do. For example, the online tests students take on computerized reading programs are almost always at the literal level only. If we want a true assessment of students' full comprehension, we need to confer with them or create an assessment that embodies deep comprehension. (See Appendix D for recommended technology tools.)

Finally, keep in mind that all new technologies take time to be meaningfully integrated into our lives, and that some old technologies survive and thrive. In the fascinating book *Hamlet's BlackBerry*, by William Powers, the author makes an important point: "Older technologies often survive the introduction of newer ones, when they perform useful tasks in ways that the new devices can't match."[9] Some examples are the continuing use of (for some of us) paper and pencil for writing, physical books and newspapers for reading, and paper notebooks for jotting and recording by hand.

These old technologies endure because they are aesthetically appealing, useful, and meet our needs. I like the calmness, peace, and higher state of consciousness I feel when I read a paper newspaper, write a poem by hand, and pen a letter to a friend. Make sure that whatever technology is employed, it brings some sense of happiness, human connection, and worthwhile benefit. Being techno-driven, continuously huddled around a screen, does not nurture our hearts and minds. Our challenge is to use technology so it adds richness and meaning to our lives, not just additional digital pursuits. "Digital busyness is the enemy of depth."[10]

Most important, we must never lose sight of the fact that although we may have machines and apps to aid our thinking and intelligence, no technology can build deep relationships of trust, love, and compassion. Those things have to be "uploaded the old-fashioned way, one human to another."[11]

Endnote

Do all you can to ensure the culture of your school is increasingly collaborative, trusting, and intellectual, with inquiries and actions that extend beyond required curriculum and standards. Grades two–three teacher Trish Richardson reflects on how teaching with purpose and authenticity has permanently had an impact on the culture of her diverse school:

> *The benefits of our teachers and school collaborating and guiding students in rich, meaningful ways have had significant effects on the success of our students beyond the classroom. Students have learned to think critically and have become global citizens. Our staff is committed to critically*

examining our beliefs and planning the instruction of literacy to ensure that is it rich, deep, and inclusive. Teachers are embedding deep learning throughout the school community from an early age, which is vital. Whether our focus is on a classroom, schoolwide, or world issue, teachers at our school continue to inspire and make strong connections to audience and purpose for our students when writing. Our audience can range from fellow peers, to families, or editorials in newspapers. Our ultimate goal through the use of literacy is to guide and inspire our students to be life-long learners and leaders in their world.[12]

The end result of focusing on engagement through developing trusting relationships, celebrating learners, creating a thriving learning environment, and teaching with purpose and authenticity is that all students come to love inquiring, researching, writing, and reading. Once students become impassioned about a topic, and we support them with expert teaching—the focus of Excellence, the next section of this book—even those students who did not see themselves as readers and writers flourish.

EXCELLENCE

The greatest influence on student progression in learning is having highly expert, inspired, and passionate teachers and school leaders working together to maximize the effect of their teaching on all students in their care.

—*John Hattie*

Excellent teaching and teacher effectiveness are inseparable. Of all the factors that have an impact on student learning, teacher effectiveness is the number-one determinant. However, what teachers are effective at matters, and collective effectiveness greatly matters if we want high achievement across a whole school. If we view excellence through a lens of high test scores, moving through book levels, or implementation of a program with fidelity, we will never achieve the high-level thinking that is the hallmark of intellectual, thriving school cultures. Teacher effectiveness that empowers and challenges all learners to achieve their full potential depends on a school culture of high trust, high expectations, and high-quality work; solid principal and teacher leadership; collaborative expertise; authenticity and responsibility in instruction, assessment, and learning; and ongoing, adept professional learning.

Excellent teachers possess key qualities (listed in the text box below and on page 103) that contribute to making them highly effective teachers and learners. Notice that most of these attributes cannot be effectively measured or scored against a rubric. Yet these combined qualities—which are just as important for us to develop in our students—can tell us more about excellence than any test score. Without these qualities, we cannot foster intellectually rich classrooms. These qualities are not isolated entities; excellent teachers apply and adjust them interactively, responsively, and seamlessly as they instruct, assess, and push students' thinking and actions.

Ten Key Factors for Excellence

1. *Adaptive expertise*—Take our deep knowledge of research and practice and expertly and flexibly apply it across the curriculum to students, standards, programs, and technology.

2. *Intellectual curiosity, focus, and open-mindedness*—Explore our passions, ask deep questions, and wrestle with complex thinking.

3. *Intentionality*—Know the what, why, and how of what we do and embrace real-world purpose and authenticity along with a whole-part-whole approach to teaching.

4. *Expert interpersonal skills*—Get along well with and communicate adeptly with students, teachers, administrators, and families.

5. *Common sense*—Follow our knowledgeable instincts and act in a sensible manner based on reason, research, experience, data, and the students we are serving.

6. *Creativity*—Have the ability to see things differently and to use and refashion information and ideas in unique ways.

7. *Joyfulness*—Fully engage with students in a manner that demonstrates and ignites passion and inspiration for learning.

8. *Ability to self-critique and self-assess*—Use self-knowledge and reflection to continuously adjust, improve, and set new goals.

9. *Relentless pursuit of excellence*—Constantly strive to make a worthy difference.

10. *Willingness to mentor and collaborate with others*—Generously and nonjudgmentally coach and co-teach and share ideas and techniques.

Expert teaching cannot be downloaded. No teacher ever became excellent without deep and ongoing study and reflection, without useful and actionable feedback on his or her instruction and assessment, without clear and timely communication with students and their families, and without helping to facilitate student goal setting. I would also add that expert teaching requires humility and kindness. Expert teachers share what they know, seek to learn more, and treat all members of the school community with respect, dignity, and care. Excellent teachers are also role models for how we conduct ourselves and behave toward others. That is, excellence extends beyond instruction to include admirable personal qualities such as inclusiveness, fairness, empathy, and generosity.

Excellence also means that students retain and apply key concepts they have learned, that they think critically and creatively, are resourceful, solve problems, communicate effectively as writers and speakers, set ambitious but achievable learning goals, and seek to make the world a better place. All of the aforementioned depend on moving beyond basic skills and "coverage" to instruction that includes ongoing opportunities for meaningful talk, questioning, and analysis; sustained reading and writing for information and pleasure; collaboration with peers; and more investment in tasks and projects that mirror learning and include participating in the world outside the classroom—which includes giving time and space to students' learning passions. Also, of utmost importance, we will continue to leave some students behind unless we ensure that excellence is accompanied by engagement and equity for all learners.

Embedding Professional Learning

Our journey to excellence in teaching begins with a commitment to professional learning. There are no shortcuts or detours or one best route that works for everyone. The journey takes time and starts with the desire to learn more and do better—for our students, our school communities, and ourselves as educators. I deliberately favor the term *professional learning* over *professional development* because in too many schools professional development has come to mean top-down learning, outside experts on multiple topics, a focus on implementation of the newest programs, or sporadic staff meetings centered on data or the latest district initiative. Unsurprisingly, resulting improvement is limited at best; teacher effectiveness and student learning are not much affected in the long run.

As a profession and as a nation, we greatly overrely on core programs, outside experts, commercial resources, curriculum mandates, or upgraded standards to improve and sustain achievement. So we continue to tread water and march in place, and not much of significance changes for far too many students, especially our underserved ones. We must do better! We need to seek teacher education, not teacher training.[1] Too much professional development overemphasizes data, program implementation, and short-term needs that do not necessarily translate to helping us educators become smarter, better teachers for the long term.

In more than four decades spent working in diverse schools in the United States and Canada, I have never seen a school improve and sustain literacy achievement without ongoing, high-level, schoolwide professional learning within a trusting, collaborative, intellectual culture. And yes, the "intellectual" part is a necessity; learning how to read is insufficient. We must be able to read and think deeply about topics that matter. The reason such professional learning is still so uncommon is that we persist in seeking that "right" program or expert—often from out of town—to "fix" things, when, instead, we need to be looking to ourselves as experts who have the wide knowledge needed to meet students' needs and interests and to selectively use programs as resources. As well, unrelenting pressure to raise test scores and rate teachers has led to prescriptive, mandated workshops that negatively affect teacher morale and ultimately do not lead to increased student learning.

Make Professional Learning a Priority

What we prioritize says everything about what we value. Testing, data gathering, programs, interventions, curriculum, standards, new initiatives—that's where we put our time and money. Professional learning? Not so much. Yet without that essential component, schoolwide achievement stalls every time. Be bold! Take the lead in ensuring that high-quality professional learning is at the center of your school and district culture. *I have never seen a whole school of teachers develop a professional learning, achieving culture without deep and ongoing study, collective reflection, and application of learning to their classrooms.* And such study takes time.

According to research, to be effective and sustainable, professional development must be ongoing, composed of at least thirty to one hundred hours of time over the school year, connected to classroom practice, and geared to fostering collegial collaboration.[2] Although some recent research has called into question the value of professional development,[3] the specific "professional development" research in question is often based on "training" in isolated skills such as phonics and focused on improving test scores, neither of which has been proven to lead to growth in reading comprehension or more proficient teaching.[4]

When we focus professional development, coaching, and intervention on low-level skills—without an accompanying emphasis on reading and writing for meaning—we shouldn't be surprised that understanding and content knowledge don't improve much. Professional learning is about effectively educating for thinking, analyzing, reviewing, reflecting, inquiring, collaborating, questioning, and communicating—and applying our learning so we and our students think deeply and learn more.

Professional learning communities, commonly called PLCs, have proliferated for many years. However, those PLCs that focus mostly on structure and data do not routinely lead to greater student learning. I have renamed PLCs Professional *Literacy* Communities to prioritize that our focus is always on raising student *literacy* achievement across the curriculum.[5] Although examining data is an important part of this work, data results are only as useful as our ability to improve literacy practices and student learning. Interpreting data to make it actionable for increasing student learning requires highly knowledgeable teachers and leaders.

One of my most important insights as an educator has been that we teachers need to observe what effective literacy practices look like in diverse schools and classrooms, hear the language of that responsive teaching, and discuss and analyze that teaching *before* we can apply those practices in our own classrooms with our own students. That knowledge was the driving force for developing my multiyear, video-based, literacy PD series for schools, principals, teachers, and literacy coaches—with an emphasis on professional reading, lesson analysis, and shared learning.[6] While standards guide us with the "what" of teaching, the "how" and the "why" are our responsibility, and that responsibility requires expert, ongoing professional learning and study.

Primary-grades teacher Melissa Kirkland notes:

> *The teachers in our building that I admire the most are the ones who are constantly reading, continually researching, constantly reflecting, and changing their practice, even though they have been teaching for many years. That needs to continue, to have book clubs or article clubs where we share and discuss, inspire and lead each other.*[7]

Even if we are in a school or a district with inadequate professional development, there is still much we can do as educators to improve our instructional knowledge of research and practice and to become more effective and informed.

 ## Take Action

♦ **Seek to make professional conversations integral to school life.** High-achieving schools are sustained through ongoing literate conversations—throughout the school day—with highly informed teachers, coaches, specialists, principals, and other leaders. It is those probing, thoughtful, reflective conversations that drive a "need to know" and that propel us forward. The entire school works to become an active and ongoing professional learning community committed to getting smarter about teaching, assessing, and learning each and every day.

◆ **Stay focused on the literacy emphasis.** It's common to move from one initiative to another from year to year. Use data analysis, formal and informal, to establish what the school's literacy focus will be—and stick with it. Our successful work in improving writing in many diverse, high-needs schools in Winnipeg was in no small part due to a multiyear initiative prioritizing expert teaching of writing.[8] By contrast, when a new literacy or numeracy implementation is added to a current initiative too soon, gains in the newest initiative are apt to be limited.[9] All our professional learning time and efforts must focus on a very limited number of "powerful and proven practices" with lots of opportunities for application and feedback.[10] The deep learning required for worthwhile and sustainable change takes time, and patience for improved results is rare in most school, district, and provincial settings.

◆ **Establish teams that work well together.** For professional learning to work well, establishing group norms—which includes treating all members respectfully—is a necessity. So is a culture in which members feel emotionally safe to voice their ideas. "The right norms, in other words, could raise a group's collective intelligence, whereas the wrong norms could hobble a team, even if, individually, all the members were exceptionally bright." The "right" norms promote "conversational turn-taking and empathy."[11] Ensure also that professional conversations are both vertical (across grade levels and content areas) and horizontal (within the grade level or content area) for forging connections, open communication, and clear goals across the whole school. (See the National School Reform website for useful guidelines on developing norms and much more: http://www.nsrfharmony.org/free-resources/protocols/. Also see "Developing Trusting Relationships," pages 9–12.)

◆ **Take responsibility for your own professional learning.** Become a member of a professional organization such as the National Council of Teachers of English (NCTE), the International Literacy Association (ILA), the National Council for the Social Studies (NCSS), or the Association for Supervision and Curriculum Development (ASCD), to name several. Advocate for a school membership, so all staff members have access to the organization's professional journal and other offerings. Besides educational journals, seek out books and websites from publishers such as Stenhouse, ASCD, Heinemann, Scholastic, Corwin, and Teachers College Press. Lead a book study on a professional book that seems to fit your school's needs. Join Twitter and follow educators you respect and websites such as Edutopia, Education Week, and MiddleWeb, to name just a few. Also, at your school or in your district, seek out a knowledgeable colleague you respect, observe a lesson, ask questions, and notice the language and actions your colleague employs.

Attend professional conferences. Choose wisely and seek to hear key leaders in the field of education. Go with at least one colleague or, better yet, a school team headed by the principal. Compare notes, and share and discuss what you learned that can be applied to your school and classrooms. As well, take the lead in ensuring PD meetings are geared to high-level thinking and learning. If your school does not have a leadership team, encourage and support the principal to create one to plan and carry out schoolwide professional learning. (See also "Read Professionally," pages 121–123.)

◆ **Collaborate with colleagues.** Ask a knowledgeable colleague you respect and admire to give feedback on an observed lesson. Let the colleague know, in advance, the kind of feedback you desire. It's not necessary for the colleague to be in the same grade level or content area. For example, if you want feedback on pacing, engagement, relevancy of your lesson, shared writing, how well you listen to students, and so on, choose the colleague who is an expert in that area regardless of the age of her students or the subject matter she teaches. Advocate for common planning times with grade-level or content area colleagues and for time to co-teach. Coach each other. Collaborative conversations about what we see and hear professionally push and solidify our thinking. Savvy principals occasionally take over classrooms for an hour and serve as a substitute teacher to promote collaboration among and between teachers.

◆ **Participate in coaching experiences.** When we have developed a trusting school culture, coaching experiences with colleagues have the potential to greatly improve teaching, especially when we have a schoolwide coaching model that includes collaborating, planning, and/or co-teaching.

◆ **Evaluate the role and influence of any adopted program.** Here's what I've found to be true every time: if teachers and administrators are overrelying on a program—even a good one—beyond year one, it's a sign expert professional learning is not regularly occurring. Figure out how to adapt, modify, or work around the program so it meets students' needs. As teachers and leaders become more knowledgeable, programs serve as resources and frameworks, not total curriculums. Do an honest staff assessment: *Are we implementing a program with fidelity or with flexibility and integrity? Are we prioritizing implementing a program or putting students' needs and interests first?* We must advocate and teach each day with what's best for students uppermost in our minds.

◆ **Keep a reflection notebook.** So much happens during a teaching day, it's impossible to recall our insights, aha moments, further questions, and so on. I keep a spiral notebook handy and jot down the date and my thinking as close to the actual teaching as I can. Some teachers prefer digital reflection, through a free tool such as Evernote, which allows for note taking, organizing, sharing, and archiving our thinking. Notability and Pages are other tools for taking digital notes.

STORY ❖ My Professional Learning Journey

My own professional learning began in earnest well after I had graduated from college and taught for several years in various contexts. With the exception of a philosophy of education course that expanded my thinking, I can't recall any education classes that prepared me to teach well. I learned how to thread a film projector to show content area filmstrips (one of the technologies of choice before videos and the World Wide Web existed), but I knew nothing about how to teach science or social studies concepts. I learned how to teach handwriting but nothing about how to teach students to write. In reading, I knew how to teach phonics in detail and how to use a basal reader, a commercial reading program, but I knew little about the importance of access to all kinds of literature and free-choice reading. The only thing I recall from my fourth-grade student-teaching experience is the homemade-pizza recipe my mentor teacher gave me, which I still make to this day.

My first teaching job was in a fourth-grade classroom in a low-income community. What I remember most is the full-weekend preparation before the teaching week and the many hours required to go through the teachers' manuals I was expected to use. I know I was dedicated to my students and did as credible a job as is possible when relying almost exclusively on textbooks and worksheets. I was relieved when a former student recently contacted me on Facebook to say she thought I was a good teacher, even though it was my first year. I went on to teach various elementary grades in different states as we moved around due to my husband's job opportunities. I found teaching methods and materials were pretty much the same everywhere.

I don't remember questioning the way I taught or what students were learning until I became a reading teacher at a high-poverty school where the population was over 90 percent African American. Most students were failing to learn to read using basal reading texts; writing was relegated to completing worksheets; and there was no joy in learning. I knew the kids were being shortchanged, and I shortchanged them further, although I wasn't immediately aware of that at the time. As the school's reading specialist, I met with small groups of students for thirty minutes each day in a little corner room stocked with all kinds of resources dedicated to teaching skills in isolation. I was good at my job, but it wasn't any fun for my students or me, and I don't think they learned much beyond decoding. As a mother, I knew the value and joy of reading aloud children's books, and I began to question what and how I was teaching my students. That questioning led to my first big question and serious inquiry: What was the best way to teach children to learn to read?

Luckily for me, at about the same time and without my requesting it, my district sent me to my first educational conference, all expenses paid. My only obligation was to come back and share what I'd learned. It was the annual conference of the International Reading Association (now the International Literacy Association), and it was a revelation. I heard speakers, some of whom later became mentors and colleagues—Frank Smith, Don Holdaway, Marie Clay, Brian Cambourne, and Ken Goodman, to name several—and my beliefs and practices about teaching reading and writing began to shift. I saw possibilities I hadn't considered. I read everything I could about literacy, and many of those books came from New Zealand and Australia. I was on fire with a passion for learning, and, through a detailed written proposal, I convinced my school superintendent to allow me to co-teach in a first-grade classroom in the same school where I'd been working as a reading specialist. From my professional study on teaching reading and writing to young children, as well as my experiences as a parent, I adapted and applied all that I had learned. The result was that the overwhelming majority of our first-grade children learned to read well and to love to read. I documented our literacy success story, which included the students' high test scores, and wrote about how my co-teacher and I used first-rate children's literature and children's own stories to teach reading and writing.

The success of that book, Transitions: From Literature to Literacy,[12] *and the power of the written word astounded me and gave me confidence to trust my own thinking. I began to speak out, to advocate for saner and better teaching practices, and to write more books. I continued to teach full-time while constantly reflecting upon my teaching, collaborating with colleagues, studying the research, and rethinking my beliefs and practices. I eventually created a new job for myself, doing demonstration teaching and coaching in literacy residencies in diverse classrooms and schools where underserved students were typically two years below grade level in reading and writing. As is still true today in similar schools and districts, discussion and attention centered on raising test scores, teaching the current standards, and overrelying on commercial programs for curriculum. Schools' limited and fragmented knowledge transferred to inexpert practices even if "professional development" was occurring. It was only as teachers and principals saw what students in their own classrooms were capable of that they began to raise their low expectations, rethink their beliefs and practices, and commit to schoolwide professional learning. That ongoing commitment included professional reading, study, reflection, viewing and analysis of best literacy practices with application to the classroom, and developing collaborative expertise.*

My searing frustration and heartbreak today is that, despite massive efforts, nothing much has changed for our students of poverty and color. Many teachers still do not learn how to teach writing as part of their teacher preparation and educational study, and often writing is the first subject to go when time is short. Basal texts are now called "core texts," and, as in decades past, they dominate how reading is taught. "How-to" commercial programs are still our go-to resources for teaching most subjects. Teachers are often expected to implement such programs "with fidelity," and, not surprisingly, too many students are still failing to thrive. Implementation "with flexibility and integrity" needs to be our mantra, but it is not. I've heard publishers and even some authors say, demeaningly, "Teachers need a script" with exactly what to say and do and in a prescribed sequence.

What we teachers need is expert professional learning. Yet our commitment to expert professional learning is still a rarity, even as it is our greatest hope for changing the dismal literacy trajectory for too many of our students. It was, and continues to be, deep and ongoing professional learning that is my lifeline for being an effective teacher, which, in turn, makes it possible for the students

I teach to engage and excel as learners. Once I became truly competent and not just compliant, I could take district requirements, standards, and programs and selectively use them as frameworks and resources to best meet students' strengths, interests, and needs.

We can positively increase student learning for all! However, first we need a deep foundation of knowledge that transfers to effective instructional and assessment practices in the classroom. I do "get it." I still teach, coach, and lead in diverse schools in the United States and Canada. I know that money is tight, time is short, pressure is high, new mandates appear, testing rules, and test scores matter. And yet! If we fail to take expert professional learning seriously and prioritize it in our schools each and every day, decades ahead we will still be talking about the achievement gap, rewriting standards, and seeking a new miracle "cure." You, dear reader, as a knowledgeable and inquiring educator, are the best hope for all of our students. Do everything you can to take responsibility for ensuring that expert professional learning is central to your life and your school's culture. Then, rewrite the script. Make it inclusive and captivating, and be sure to tell your story.

Develop Shared Beliefs

Make conversations about literacy beliefs the first priority in setting up professional learning for the school and the district. *Perhaps more than any other dynamic, positive and lasting change in a school accelerates and takes hold only when the principal and staff come together on commonly held beliefs that align with research-based practices.* Our everyday practices in our classrooms and schools mirror our beliefs even when we don't articulate those beliefs. Importantly, our stated beliefs must align with our practices and "show up" in our teaching; otherwise even the most commendable beliefs are just wishes. For example, many teachers say they believe that students need sustained time every day to read self-selected books. Yet their daily practices do not reflect that stated belief and priority. Only ongoing, expert professional learning makes it possible for teachers to implement in their classrooms even the most powerfully stated beliefs.

Coherence and consistency of beliefs between and across grade levels, content areas, and school divisions are essential for raising achievement across a whole school, and this is no easy matter. We all hold long-established beliefs based on our educational and life experiences, and these do not shift just because we adopt a new program or new standards. Resistance to change is the norm, and that resistance often stems from our core beliefs. When knowledge is low, we rely on "stuff," miracle cures, and past behaviors to provide us with our beliefs.

The importance of prioritizing the development of shared beliefs cannot be overstated. A distraught teacher recently wrote me that as a result of dramatic differences in beliefs and philosophies across her school and district, there is no clear message as to what her district values, which has led to mistrust, misunderstandings, and poor communication between and among staff, other schools in the district, and district leadership. Here is where a culture of high trust is essential; in fact, it is a prerequisite for having the hard but respectful conversations around beliefs.

When staff members first come together to examine and discuss their beliefs about reading or writing, it is not unusual to wind up with only one or two beliefs everyone holds in common. Especially in schools where there is dissension, where competing new programs are introduced every year or so, and where commercial materials, district mandates, and outside experts dominate curriculum and instructional decisions, teachers often don't know what they believe.

For example, in one middle school, about 50 percent of the staff believed that grammar should be taught in isolation, that spelling didn't matter much in a first draft, and that it was okay to post students' work with some errors if they'd done their "best" work. The lack of agreement schoolwide on those beliefs caused dissension and confusion, not to mention some ineffective teaching. As those middle school students moved from grade to grade and teacher to teacher in various content areas, they encountered different literacy expectations and requirements, which constrained full engagement and effort. Although the beliefs we hold are not right or wrong, when as a school and district we hold few beliefs in common or when there is wide disagreement, we must be responsible enough to read the research, have some hard but respectful conversations, and be willing to make adjustments. (See also Equity, "Advocating for Students," page 384.)

In the scenario described above, once the teachers read and discussed the research on grammar instruction, some began to think about and try out teaching grammar differently—in context, using students' actual writing, and often demonstrating how to do so in a public conference. (For more on teaching grammar, see pages 121, 175–176, 241, and 274–275.) Such changes do not happen quickly or easily. When we have an entrenched belief, it's natural to want to hold on to it. As one principal wrote to me:

When something is presented that is contrary to teachers' beliefs, they tend to find the exception to the rule to affirm their current thinking. "Well, one of my students could take off with . . . ." The disagreement that sometimes comes out of our conversations is really a good thing.[13]

Our beliefs drive our practices in every aspect of our lives, so it's crucial that we can articulate our beliefs, align them with sensible and research-based practices, and act upon them in a way that increases achievement, engagement, and enjoyment for our students and ourselves. Having a core of six to ten commonly held beliefs for teaching reading, for teaching writing, for optimizing the reading-writing connection, as well as for math and other subject areas, is essential for actualizing a school's vision statement and journey to higher achievement.

Be patient with colleagues. Developing shared beliefs can be difficult and time consuming as we and our fellow staff members remain at varying levels of understanding and readiness, based on the way we were taught and our cumulative experiences. However, without such agreement, schoolwide change efforts will stall. Not to be minimized: an achieving culture begins with developing schoolwide trust along with shared beliefs. Principal Stacey Wester speaks to the necessity of having shared beliefs:

Holding shared literacy beliefs has been invaluable for guiding us in short- and long-term planning, instruction, and literacy programming as well as for guiding us when some staff members wanted to go back to their old ways. I always refer to our beliefs as to why we are doing what we are doing. I don't know what we would do if we didn't have them! We will start the year off in January with a reminder of our beliefs and personal reflections about if classroom practices match our beliefs. My goal for next year is for staff to write instructional beliefs.[14]

 ## Take Action

- ◆ **Come to agreement on literacy beliefs.** In vertical teams (represented by various grade levels and specialties), get together as a staff a few times a year and have respectful and productive discussions around beliefs about teaching and learning.[15]

- ◆ **Evaluate what's posted on walls and in hallways.** We can often determine a school's collective beliefs by taking a brief walk through the school. Go with a small team and take notes. Share positives and concerns with staff.

- *Prominently post your school's beliefs* (see below) in the front hallway, teachers' lounge, and principal's office. Even if your school can only come to agreement on two beliefs, celebrate those and make them public. With ongoing professional learning, collective beliefs will evolve.

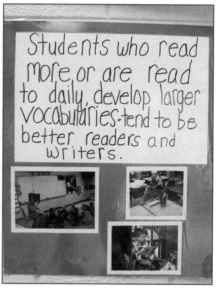

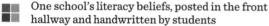
One school's literacy beliefs, posted in the front hallway and handwritten by students

- *Make sure messages and texts that are posted are relevant*, readable, accurate, and geared to real readers and writers. If postings are serving primarily as artifacts that decorate or cover blank walls, use that observation as an opportunity to discuss beliefs about what gets publicly posted, why it's posted, and whom it's for.

- *Note the language and format of class charts and resources* throughout the school. Look for charts that use student-friendly language and that have been created with students based on curriculum study, class needs, and interests. If most charts are commercially made, discuss what this says about the school's beliefs. For example, do teachers believe that charts written in academic, adult language will be accessible and useful to students?

◆ **Develop and use a common language** and understanding for widespread buzzwords and literacy terms, such as *close reading, balanced literacy, guided reading, rubrics, anchor charts, formative assessment, flipped classroom, differentiated instruction, personalized learning, best practice,* and so on. These terms mean different things to different people—based on what they've read, researched, and experienced. Without common agreement, confusion reigns.

For example, to me, *personalized learning* is connected to excellence and means meaningful and inspiring teaching that gives students choice and opportunity to pursue their interests and passions and to increasingly self-direct their learning. For others, it means students collaborating with teachers as learning partners in meaningful inquiry, which is interdisciplinary and grounded in real-world issues.[16] In the world of K–12 educational technology, personalized learning generally means using software and other digital technologies to tailor instruction to each student's strengths and weaknesses, interests and preferences, and optimal pace of learning. For some, it means a learning network.

To develop our beliefs and improve our practices across a school and district, we need to be employing the same specific, useful language and what it means, along with what to look for and how to teach in each literacy context. Even then, make no assumptions that the use of common terms extends to agreement on how those terms translate into instructional practices. As an example, when a principal looking to improve the teaching of reading surveyed her staff midyear, small-group conversations in vertical teams revealed an impasse due to confusion about how the word *text* was being defined. It was only after the staff came to a common definition that they were able to begin to agree on a few beliefs and then discuss how those beliefs could affect practices. (See quote on page 216 for a comprehensive definition of *text*.)

◆ **Make schoolwide beliefs known to families and students.** Use assemblies, literacy nights, school and classroom blogs, communications, and social media to highlight and discuss literacy beliefs and how they connect with learning goals and instructional practices.

◆ **Work to ensure that shared beliefs drive the selection of resources** and not the other way around. Often a school's resources and programs are purchased without rigorous discussion and group input about whether the resource aligns with credible research and the school's beliefs about literacy, instruction, and learning. Too often, desperation for better results leads to settling for a mediocre program backed by questionable research. When a program is driving the learning, it's likely that the program or resource is determining teacher practices and beliefs. Be on high alert! *We must first establish our beliefs, align them with "best" practices and relevant research, and then seek out the resources and programs that support those beliefs.* Make that process happen in your school and district!

◆ **Revisit and re-evaluate beliefs.** Devote a professional learning meeting near the start of the school year to developing shared beliefs. At least once during the school year, revisit those beliefs and use the results to help plan professional learning related to needs. Post and share widely so all members of the school community are clear on those literacy beliefs and expectations. Ensure that the beliefs are visible in practice.

  ◉ *Self-evaluate as a teacher and staff member*: If we believe such and so, then these are the instructional practices, actions, and behaviors we would see in our classrooms, school, and district. If alignment and visibility are not there, question why and bring that discussion to professional learning meetings.

  ◉ *Partner with a colleague for a tour of the classroom for constructive feedback.* Even just talking about the environment of the room and how, why, and where we have things placed or posted may open us up to some changes. Consider, with teachers' permission, providing sneak-peeks of the classroom environment—through photos in an online link or a QR code—into classrooms where shared beliefs and practices are in expert alignment.

  ◉ *Educate support staff on school beliefs,* including educational assistants and parent volunteers, especially if they are working with students in writing and reading.

◆ **Reflect continuously upon beliefs, practices, instruction, and learning.** Becoming an expert teacher is a continuing journey. It's easy to stay stuck in doing things the way we were taught or have always done them. Keep an open mind. We must view ourselves as learner-teachers, open to considering alternative approaches, new research, and revising our thinking.

Know Important Literacy Research

Beliefs that align with research-based practices depend on us! It is not enough for a school to come to agreement on a set of beliefs. As previously noted, those beliefs must align with expert practices that are supported by research and informed experiences. Highly effective teachers and leaders know important literacy research and how and when to question it. We have a strong foundation of knowledge for interpreting research and applying what fits and makes sense for our own teaching, learning, and assessing contexts. We use excellent research to inform our instruction without directing it—that is, we consider the research in light of what we know about literacy, subject matter, instructional approaches, and our individual students.

We also use our knowledge not just to teach better but also to communicate more effectively with our students and their families. When an instructional practice we apply is being questioned, being able to support our actions with credible research can go a long way to gaining parent and community support.

Expert educators use credible and reliable research to deepen understanding and improve literacy education.[17] Here is where professional reading is paramount for building a strong research base to help make sound decisions. As responsible educators, we must be fully informed on current issues and research related to teaching vocabulary, grammar, spelling, second-language learners, and so on. (For more on credible and reliable research, see pages 312–313 and 376.)

Dear reader, I know what you're thinking: "I don't have time to read research. I'm already overwhelmed and overextended." True as that may be, it's also true that knowledge is power and sets us free. The only way to avoid burnout, exhaustion, and frustration with all the demands we face is to focus on what's most important, to do less but do it well, and to teach for depth and substance. To do that, and to be able to advocate for sane and effective practices, knowing important research and knowing how and when to apply it—or not—to enhance, improve, and streamline our practices is essential. That said: be skeptical. If research results seem too good to be true, they probably are! We should initially trust but verify with our own students and contexts to see if the research results are applicable and reliable and hold true for our population. Just about all research results can work some of the time for some people.

See the following Take Action bullet points for key research that we can use to support exemplary literacy practices and question dubious ones. Knowing current and relevant research is an absolute necessity for advocacy for change. At the same time, knowing the best research won't matter much unless teachers and leaders can apply it in a way that increases student learning for the long run. As your school becomes more knowledgeable about research, including your own action research, create your own Take Action list of research that everyone on staff needs to know about.

 ## Take Action

Use the research cited here to apply and advocate for putting into place highly effective literacy practices. Use the list to jump-start professional learning discussions and to reflect individually and as a staff.

- Schools that are more collegial and collaborative have higher literacy achievement.[18]

- Highly effective teachers have their students read and write meaningful, continuous texts throughout the day, assign purposeful and challenging tasks, and support students with explicit demonstrations and grouping practices.[19]

- Reliance on "telling teaching" (a teacher-directed stance relying on imparting information) is not beneficial to students' reading achievement and comprehension.[20] "Responsive teaching," a student-supported approach with guided questioning, coaching, and ongoing formative assessment, leads to deeper and longer-lasting achievement.[21]

- Core reading programs are limited in their scope for effectively teaching reading comprehension.[22] (See also page 221 in Excellence, "Teaching Readers.") We teachers must take the lead in teaching reading for understanding.

- Expertly educated and trained kindergarten teachers can greatly increase the reading abilities of at-risk kindergartners.[23]

- Teaching reading and writing as reciprocal processes improves and accelerates both reading and writing.[24]

- Learners read and write more complex texts when the reading and writing activities are authentic—that is, when the activity has a real-world purpose and audience.[25]

- Students need to be able to read texts with a high level of accuracy and comprehension in order to learn content in those texts.[26]

- Writing enhances and deepens thinking and learning.[27]

- Reading and writing more nonfiction texts lead to higher literacy achievement.[28]

- The less knowledge teachers have about writing, the more test prep becomes the writing focus.[29]

- Excellent formative assessments must be integrated into our daily teaching for optimal instruction and learning.[30]

- Average and low-performing students do worse on written tests using computers versus writing by hand; high-performing students do better.[31]

- Collaborative expertise is a necessity for expert teaching, feedback, and assessment to significantly affect student learning and achievement across a whole school.[32]

- English language learners are more likely to thrive in language and literacy when instruction is in "high-quality two-language programs."[33]

- Relying on leveled texts is insufficient and inaccurate for fully determining students' reading ability and comprehension.[34]

- The formal teaching of grammar does not typically improve writing quality.[35]

- School libraries staffed by a full-time librarian increase both the amount of reading students do and their reading comprehension.[36]

Take the lead in sharing important, relevant research with colleagues. Consult the highly respected What Works Clearinghouse (WWC) at http://ies.ed.gov/ncee/wwc/ for reviews of research on programs, practices, and important educational issues and policies. (See more on page 376.) Check out the extensive and useful collection of WWC Practice Guides, which recommend specific classroom practices based on evidence-based findings. For more foundational research on effective literacy practices, see also http://regieroutman.com/inresidence/research.aspx.

Do access *Essential Instructional Practices in Early Literacy: Grades K to 3*, an excellent, comprehensive document by the Early Literacy Task Force (which included researchers Nell Duke and Tanya Wright) of the General Education Leadership Network of the Michigan Association of Intermediate School Administrators.[37] As well, consider following the International Literacy Association link to past blogs on literacy research at https://www.literacyworldwide.org/blog/literacy-research/.

Finally, we must value teacher research, including our own. We educators often don't know why a particular study was selected for research. University researchers tend to explore topics of particular interest to them, so some topics of interest to us as teachers may not be "hot" research topics. For example, I have not seen empirical research on the positive impact of group shared writing on students' reading and writing abilities or on the value of public writing conferences for improving all students' writing. Yet my teacher research of forty-five years and strong student results confirm the benefit of both practices for increasing literacy competencies. Just because credible, evidence-based research on a particular literacy practice doesn't yet exist doesn't mean the practice isn't valid.

Read Professionally

Noted but important enough to be emphatically restated: *Professional reading is a necessity!* Even if we are new to the profession, making professional reading a priority is essential. It is often difficult for inexperienced or even veteran teachers to believe that statement because we so often feel overloaded and exhausted. Ultimately, our deeper knowledge saves us time and energy, as we no longer follow programs in lockstep; we now know enough to figure out how programs can be used as helpful resources rather than as a curriculum. Also, in order to make the wisest decisions for our students and staff, we must be knowledgeable and up-to-date on current and reliable research, educational issues, and best practices. Otherwise we are unable to intelligently question publishers' resources and district mandates, teach at the highest levels, and effectively advocate for our students and ourselves. Reading professionally is a hallmark of an excellent educator. We may know a lot, but we still seek to question what we know, learn more, and do better.

 ## Take Action

- See if someone in your school or district will serve as a "knowledge sifter"; that is, a highly informed educator who reads and views avidly and is willing to sift through the "best" and most relevant research and practices from educational journals, publications, websites, videos, social media, and other online resources and to share those with colleagues. Print and online journals and news media such as *The Reading Teacher, Language Arts, Voices from the Middle, English Journal, Educational Leadership,* and *Education Week,* to name a few, are highly recommended publications for selecting relevant articles. Now, via e-mail and Twitter, I rely primarily on such reputable sites as Edutopia, MiddleWeb, Education Week (EdWeek), MindShift, TeachThought, and the Teaching Channel, along with SmartBriefs from ASCD and NCLE for well-written blogs, news, trends, and important research of the profession. Also via e-mail and Twitter, I rely on news of the profession from such reputable publishers as Stenhouse, Heinemann, ASCD, and Scholastic.

- Subscribe to a professional journal, or share one subscription with one or more colleagues. Whereas reading a professional book can be time consuming, reading an article or two a month is doable.

- Build a professional library at your school where teachers can sign out classic and current books on education, teaching, and learning as well as read professional articles and journals. Use Twitter to share excellent blogs and research and to encourage professional discussion. Lobby administrators to allocate money for outstanding professional books. Just as many bookstores do, invite teachers who have read and enjoyed a book to write a short handwritten recommendation, placed with the book.

Fifth-grade teacher Sherri Steuart selects and collects noteworthy articles and makes them available to teachers through iTunes U or a staff wiki. She created one iTunes U course that paired the staff's literacy beliefs with research-based articles. These articles guide discussion and reflection, ensuring beliefs and classroom practices are in sync.

◆ **Embrace social media.** Twitter has become my go-to source for staying current on research and best practices. Although it's frustrating that tweets with links to blogs and research come in at random all day long, what makes the process of wading through them worthwhile is the opportunity to find and read short, timely, relevant informational and opinion pieces that I would be unlikely to find anywhere else. Then I share the most significant of these through Facebook and Twitter postings via @regieroutman. Best of all, I continue to apply much of the research and practices I read about to rethink, confirm, and alter some of my teaching, assessing, leading, and learning practices.

◆ **Engage in schoolwide, professional conversations** around professional articles, blogs, research, or a book study. A well-informed staff can then intelligently ask "What does this mean for our literacy practices?" "What might we think about trying or changing?" "What else do we need to know?" and "What are our next steps?"

Once a month, as part of whole-school professional learning time, aim to read and discuss a selected article from a peer-reviewed educational journal, or read about relevant research and practices posted on a reliable social media site or website. Alternatively or additionally, consider a professional book study spread out over months, with the amount of reading for each meeting predetermined by the participants. See the items in the References and Resources section in this book, most of which have URLs (web links, easily accessible in online References), for notable articles, blogs, and research that may pique your interest. For recommended books—professional books and literature—see my reading blogs on my website, regieroutman.org.

◆ **Self-evaluate if and how professional learning is growing.** If we are excessively relying on a commercial program, it's more than likely that ongoing professional reading, reflection, and deep learning are not yet an integral part of the school's culture. If student achievement is flat or low, only ongoing, expert schoolwide professional learning has the potential to make a sustained difference. Take notice and advocate for change.

Become a Teacher-Leader

One of my greatest learning lessons in the whole-school change process has been this one: *principals have to know literacy, and teachers need to be leaders.*[38] I used to think that if principals were strong leaders and teachers were excellent at instruction, high student achievement would result. Certainly that has been true for some teachers and some students. But for sustainable change across a school, we need a whole school of highly knowledgeable, highly achieving teachers and students. That requires all teachers to assume a leadership role and for principals to assume a major literacy role as instructional experts. I define a leader as someone who recognizes what needs to be done for the good of the organization, initiates ideas, welcomes and seeks others' input and suggestions, and then takes appropriate action to help guide the organization to move forward in a respectful and collaborative manner.

A teacher-leader, in addition to the daily teaching of students, takes on a leadership role to improve instructional and assessment practices across a whole school, whether it is an elementary, a middle, or a high school. Because collective leadership has been shown by research to have a stronger impact on student achievement than individual leadership, shared leadership between teachers and administrators is a necessity.[39] Specifically, the teacher-leadership role across a school involves working to build trusting relationships (see pages 9–23), taking on the qualities of effective leaders, and planning and facilitating the professional learning—all with the end goal of improving student learning. Teacher leadership has traditionally been undervalued or ignored. Without it, schools and school cultures cannot thrive. Principal leadership is essential, of course, but because of the unrelenting demands of their job, principals need effective partnerships with teacher-leaders to be optimally effective.

A major role of the teacher-leader is as a member of the school's leadership team (see page 76). The leadership team, which typically has six to eight members headed by the principal, typically meets weekly (often over lunch) to take the pulse of the school community and to plan the ongoing professional learning. I have never seen a school sustain achievement gains without a strong leadership team or some similar structure firmly in place.

 ## Take Action

- **Take on the qualities of effective leaders.** The same qualities that make any leader effective apply to teacher-leaders.

- *Become highly knowledgeable*—whether it is in the area of literacy, special education, or a particular content or specialist area.
- *Hold high expectations* for colleagues and students.
- *Know and apply the latest and most relevant research*, and generously share and clearly communicate research, information, ideas, and resources with others.
- *Courageously speak up to ask the hard questions* on unresolved issues, suggest possible solutions, and encourage diverse opinions to be considered.
- *Actively listen* without judgment; strive to pay attention to others' thoughts on a topic before jumping in to speak.
- *Act as a humble and kind expert* who willingly mentors, coaches, and co-teaches with colleagues.
- *See yourself as a learner* who is open to change and who constantly seeks to get better at your craft.

- **Facilitate professional learning.** Ensuring high-level, on-site, ongoing professional learning is probably the most significant role for the teacher-leader. With the principal, teacher-leaders plan and carry out the professional learning in a school. To be an expert facilitator requires, in addition to being an excellent teacher, deep knowledge and pedagogy around teaching, learning, and leading, as well as skill with working collaboratively with groups, including administrators.[40]

  - *Share promising ideas* with your principal and colleagues. Distribute copies of excellent professional articles, important news of the profession, and timely research.
  - *Become a team leader*. Ensure that each grade level meets regularly to plan together, exchange ideas, and support one another. If no such team exists, start one and offer to facilitate the meetings. Request that another member take notes of the meetings and copy those for the team and the principal.
  - *Take the lead on schoolwide professional learning*. Even if you start with a small group of volunteers, begin to meet regularly to focus on improved instruction and learning. Go beyond looking at and analyzing data to observing, discussing, and applying—with collegial support—best practices to the classroom.
  - *Form a school leadership team* with the principal and representation by grade levels in order to plan, organize, and carry out ongoing professional development based on staff and student needs, data analysis, and agreed-upon literacy goals.[41] Consider forming a districtwide leadership team for ensuring common beliefs and common language between elementary, middle, and high schools. Without that cohesion, as students go through the grades they

encounter differing philosophies and beliefs and can become confused by conflicting approaches.

- *Seek to develop collaborative expertise* across your school and district. (See pages 74-76.)

Take Time to Reflect

Reflection time is rare; yet it is essential. When we quickly move from one event, lesson, or task to another, we lose the possibility for fully appreciating what we have done, considering alternatives, or improving upon our actions in some way. Be intentional in making time to reflect and seeing that time as a necessity for optimal functioning in all areas of life.

When I gave a blank journal as a gift to a principal and to a curriculum director, they laughed when they read the large gold type on the bright red cover, "Keep calm and carry on," a quote from Winston Churchill during the Second World War. Our lives move so quickly in and out of school that it's hard to remember what we did and said just a half-hour ago, and it's impossible to make sense of it all on the run.

Keep a notebook handy and record thoughts and ideas on anything related to teaching, learning, coaching, leading, or anything that strikes you as important to remember. I use one spiral notebook for all my reflections on daily teaching, professional development, conferences I attend, and things I'm thinking about. I date my entries, reread them, make notes in the margins, and return to them to clarify my thinking and next steps. Keeping everything together in one notebook, which can last me for a couple of years, means I can always find my notes! Although it may be old-fashioned, I still prefer paper over electronic devices for note taking and easy referral to past notes.

 ## Take Action

- Take a few moments between lessons or classes to record insights, questions that have arisen, new thinking, confirmations, ideas for future teaching, and so on. If we don't write our thoughts down, we lose them. Let students know why we do this reflective writing. They may want to try out something similar for themselves with their own notebooks.

- Record exact language used for instruction when observing a colleague or teacher, and give those words to the teacher. Doing so is nonjudgmental. Teachers can read their own instructional language later on and reflect upon it. In our moment-by-moment teaching, we rarely remember the words we have used, and words matter.

◆ **Carry a notebook** when leaving the classroom, attending a meeting, and heading home. That allows for "catching" thoughts as they arise and for rereading for focused reflection at a later time. Sticky notes and pads of paper in strategic places also work well. Especially when I am in the process of writing a book or an article, I keep pencil and paper on the table next to our bed. That makes it easy for me, even in the dark of night, to record the thoughts I don't want to lose that have disrupted my sleep. Not only that: knowing I have captured those thoughts allows me to relax and also creates space for new thoughts.

◆ **Purchase a smaller notebook,** such as a Moleskine, available in various sizes at bookstores and other shops, and carry it in a pocket or purse. I love mine and always have it with me. Kids love these too!

◆ **Take advantage of technical devices,** such as smartphones, iPads, or e-readers, to record thoughts, reflections, and memorable language. Use apps that are created for easy recording and retrieval, such as Evernote, Notability, Pages, and Office 365. (See Appendix D: Technology Tools That Help Support Schoolwide Literacy Learning, for descriptions.)

◆ **Consider using your notes to write an editorial, a professional article, or even a book for educators.** Although we may think all the important stories have already been told, it's not true. Our story in our own words is unique and needs to be heard. Truly, one of the major differences between a writer and a nonwriter is that a writer writes! I try to heed the wisdom of Donald Murray, Pulitzer Prize–winning journalist, teacher, and author, who said, "No writing is ever wasted" and "Never a day without a line."

◆ **Make reflection central to learning for teachers and students.**

◉ *Include a brief evaluation at the end of most professional learning meetings,* and have the school's leadership team use evaluation results for future planning. Ask such questions as "What worked well today?" "What did you learn that you can apply to your teaching and student learning?" "What support do you need?" "What suggestions do you have for ____?"

◉ *Occasionally ask students to evaluate lessons* with questions such as "What did you learn?" "What questions do you still have?" "What suggestions do you have for how this lesson might have been more engaging, relevant, or easier to understand?"

- *Use student self-reflections as quick free-writes* at the beginning of some content area classes. Most of the time, do not collect or read these. Occasionally ask students to review their quick-write reflections and to share one privately with you or publicly with their peers, if they are comfortable doing so. Use students' thoughts to further reflect and improve upon your own teaching. (See also pages 332–333 for examples of student reflections following a residency.)

Endnote

Prioritize first-rate professional learning as the best approach for achieving excellence in teaching and learning. Recently, a K–12 director of learning lamented, "We don't work on anything until it's broken." Our hurry-up, results-now culture works against building a sturdy foundation for long-term learning. The hard truth is that professional learning that leads to greater, sustainable achievement takes considerable time, commitment, patience, and skill. Although no one wants to hear it, my long-term experience working in high-challenge schools confirms it takes five to seven years to build a sustainable culture of excellence. And that means keeping a competent principal in a successful school for at least that long. Our teaching, leading, and learning foundation has to be rock solid to weather the inevitable changes that characterize school life.

When my husband, Frank, designed a tree house for our two granddaughters, putting in a strong foundation proved to be the most problematic issue. Getting up to the hilly, wooded area required going up a narrow, winding path, which made it impossible to bring in heavy equipment. The foundation had to be cleared and dug entirely by hand. So it is with teaching. A quick fix—the latest program or tech gizmo—over a weak foundation, hastily installed, just delays the necessary digging in and clearing away of debris. We must each do the hard, foundational work—slow and plodding as it is—to gain a solid underpinning of informed beliefs and practices that ground expert teaching and assessing. Only then will we know the important questions to ask, the "best" practices to apply, the resources that will best support us, and how to deftly deal with the inevitable challenges that come our way.

The educational pendulum will always swing, but we must not! Once we become highly knowledgeable, we may shift a bit to the right or left, based on relevant research, experiences, and the beliefs we hold, but if our foundation is rock solid, the shift will be an intentional, well-informed movement and not a full tilt. Any curricular framework or structure we employ is only as strong as the foundation that supports it. Not to be minimized: our students are dependent on our strong foundation of learning for their own optimal achievement. We can't let them down.

Expert Teaching Through Frontloading

One of the biggest changes I've made as a teacher is to slow down to hurry up. By that I mean taking the necessary time for thinking, planning, demonstrating, and practicing to ensure students have adequate background, information, resources, competence, and support to do "the work." When we expertly frontload—that is, sufficiently prepare students *before* we release them to try and apply what we are teaching—almost all students are likely to succeed. Excellent teachers at every grade level and in all content areas use frontloading to optimize learning success for all students. Although uncommon in practice, adequate frontloading is as necessary for high school students as it is for our youngest students. The same holds true for us teachers and leaders. When students and we are prepared, competent, and confident about the work we are about to undertake, we can maximize our time, efforts, and learning. As important, much less re-teaching is needed, which saves time and avoids frustration and loss of interest for our students and us.

Frontloading begins by consciously building a strong foundation of knowledge, processes, and strategies that will enable the learner to do the inquiry, problem solving, task, writing, reading, and so on, with minimal guidance and support. Continually assessing through teaching—before, during, and after—to determine what more needs to be asked, explained, modeled, adjusted, rethought, or revised is an essential part of the frontloading process. Such assessing is part of the ongoing responsive teaching that is a hallmark of highly effective teachers.

Frontloading may include, but is not limited to, providing some or all of the following information and actions *to* and *with* our learners so that they are ready to effectively work *by* themselves with minimal guidance:

Frontloading Possibilities

- Immersion in a real-world issue or genre (including noticing and naming features/qualities) through access to and interaction with excellent texts, multimedia, and relevant resources.

- Sufficient background knowledge.

- Pre-teaching vocabulary and concepts (e.g., when students wouldn't be able figure it out by reading text).

- Demonstrations and thinking aloud by expert(s).

- Multiple shared experiences.

- Hearing and discussing stories and texts read aloud.

- Exploring related websites.

- Viewing videos on the topic; listening to related podcasts.

- Partner and small-group work.

- Checking for understanding throughout process.

- Raising important questions.

- Lots of opportunities for talk and guided discussion.

- Purposeful and thoughtful guided practice.

Primary-grades teacher Trish Richardson reflects on how frontloading for a month preceding an in-depth study of an endangered species (polar bears) enriched her teaching and her students' learning and writing outcomes:

While I have recognized for a long time the importance and value of frontloading, I have not frontloaded to the extent that I did with my class in this study, and the positive results were evident. Students were engaged in the topic because the topic was deep and rich, which enabled us to spend a great length of time on it. Also, by the time students were ready to write, they all had a great deal of knowledge at their fingertips. When I sent students off to write, they were confident in themselves and their knowledge so that each and every student found their own voice. Students knew the information and it was so accessible to them that they were able to write in their own words with great success. Students became researchers, scientists, advocates for polar bears and, of course, non-fiction writers.[1]

To be clear—and important enough to be revisited—when we are talking about frontloading, we are focusing on meaningful and relevant work (see "Teaching with Purpose and Authenticity," pages 81–88) and dialogue that pushes our students' thinking, not preparing them for frivolous activities. We are asking significant "big" questions that open up the conversations and provoke high-level thinking (see pages 161–167 for questioning ideas and techniques). We are reading and writing for real-world audiences and purposes. We are also very transparent and intentional about our goals and expected outcomes and check to ensure our students know and value these as well. Perhaps most important, we are using our curriculum as thought, "to teach critical thinking, design, and problem solving—fluid intelligence. . . ."[2]

Trish Richardson's reflections illustrate a comprehensive study of an important topic that was connected to standards, curriculum, and real-world concerns. Trish's evaluation also noted how study of one worthwhile topic over time versus her past use of multiple writing projects made the quality of learning greater: "The less-is-more foundation allowed us to deepen our learning." (See more on the lesson in Appendix C and the full lesson plan online, including frontloading charts, photos, and student work examples.) Not only that: the students invested their full energy because they fell in love with the topic and wanted to make a difference that went beyond themselves.

It takes courage and a shift in beliefs to slow down, to take the necessary time for frontloading, and to teach for depth. One teacher told me that initially she didn't believe that teaching less, but teaching more thoroughly, would pay off. It took until the middle of the school year for her to see that her students were actually much further along as readers and writers. Not only that: the number of students needing intervention had significantly decreased.

Be More Intentional

Without highly intentional planning and frontloading—even when our teaching is effective—results will be limited in terms of student success, achievement, and independence. By *intentional*, I mean that both teachers and students are very clear about desired learning outcomes and that those outcomes propel students forward as readers, writers, and thinkers in meaningful ways. Although it is essential to clearly state and make visible our content and language goals and objectives—and check that our students know and understand them—those goals and objectives must be worthwhile ones and lead to empowering students as literacy learners beyond the lesson. Just because we post our learning targets each day and students can say what these are doesn't mean the work is worth doing. Being intentional also means being deliberately mindful in the act of teaching and changing course as needed.

Here's an example of what I'm talking about from a school where literacy beliefs were in transition. An observation of a strong kindergarten teacher showed that her lesson focus was on writing a book that recalled a recent class field trip to a farm. After the demonstration and frontloading, each of the students would be expected to write their own similar book. With the students seated in front of her on the floor, she told them, "Our goal is planning our book about our trip to the farm. What will we need in our book?" She then drew four pictures in four quadrants on a large sheet of chart paper to recall four key happenings. She did an excellent job asking questions and soliciting responses for the pictures and for words to go along with the pictures to make a complete story. But as my esteemed colleague Sandra Figueroa wisely says, "Our focus needs to be on learning, not just doing." Although the activity engaged the children and was worthwhile, by not being fully intentional about how the activity could potentially increase their skills and competencies as readers and writers, the learning was limited.

Being more intentional about literacy learning, the teacher could also do the following:

◆ *Create an authentic audience and purpose* for the writing. (Move the audience beyond the teacher.)

◆ *Make the print large enough for all students to see.* (The small print indicated that it was not meant to be read/seen by all students, even if the teacher intended it to be read.)

◆ *Reread and point to each word while reading.* (By not pointing to each word and not sliding her finger under each word as she read, she lost a shared-reading opportunity that can be highly supportive to emerging readers.)

♦ *Promote oral language* and hearing all the voices through "turn and talk." (The teacher did almost all the talking and deciding—that is, she was "telling teaching," which does not lead to optimal achievement. See research, page 120.)

♦ *Focus on reading-writing connections.* (There was no attempt to connect writing with reading. However, by saying something like "Writers write for readers, so our pictures and words have to match" and "Reread your story so it makes sense for your reader," even our youngest students can grasp this essential connection.)

It would not take much to move this teacher from strong to expert. In fact, after celebrating the terrific teaching she had done and asking her if she'd like any suggestions (she said she would), making her aware of these bulleted factors was enough to make her rethink her lesson and realize that an audience for the writing beyond herself would drive students to do their best writing; pointing to words that all students could see as she read aloud and invited students to read with her would increase their reading abilities and confidence; time to talk with peers could add richer language and more voices to the writing; and connecting reading and writing would benefit both processes—for example, using the text at a later date for word work.

To the teacher's credit and to the credit of the school's commitment to professional learning, it was not long before she and other teachers became much more intentional, which included raising curricular and literacy expectations for students and making the environment more student friendly. For example, she and other staff members began to reconsider the relevancy and placement of classroom charts containing academic language and dense print. Like all elements of expert and intentional teaching, setting goals that are more thoughtful depends on holding high expectations for students and a deep foundational knowledge of literacy, curriculum, and standards—all of which are best realized through ongoing, high-level, professional learning.

 ## Take Action

♦ **Focus on the learning** and ensure the process increases knowledge and understanding as well as mindfulness of what is not yet known. Ask the following:

  ◉ What is it that we want students to learn?
  ◉ What are the important learning outcomes that will result from this lesson or study?

- Will what we are expecting students to do maximize opportunities for worthwhile reading, writing, conversing, and critical thinking?
- How will this activity or study make students more capable, joyful, and independent as literacy learners and thinkers?
- How will we know what students have learned? How will students demonstrate their learning?
- What are our next steps for clarifying, sustaining, or increasing student understanding?
- Have we thoughtfully considered how we are best using the time we have?

♦ **Assess first what students know and need to know.** "Too often we fail to teach with intentionality because we do not have a sense of what our students know. As well, we wind up participating in professional learning opportunities that simply waste our time because we do not know what we need to learn to move our students forward."[3]

♦ **Make curricular outcomes accessible.** Ensure that lesson plans and goals are student friendly, attainable, and measurable, which is especially critical for students who struggle. Use multiple modalities—*see it, say it, do it*—to ensure all students have comprehensible input and understand what they are to learn and why they are learning it.

♦ **Seek out colleagues who get great results.** A school culture of mentors—that is, expert teachers who are intentional and highly effective—is a necessity for schoolwide achievement. Savvy principals find ways to provide support—such as occasionally hiring a roving sub or taking a teacher's classroom for an hour—so that mentors and mentees can observe and collaborate in either of their classrooms.

♦ **Be more intentional about data.** Do everything possible to ensure data collection and analysis is meaningful, balanced, fair, useful, and manageable. Often data use can be overwhelming for staff, leading to more testing, intervention, too much focus on data walls, and obsession with numbers. The first priority for data use must be improving student learning through improved and responsive instructional practices. (For more on data, see pages 322–325.)

Make No Assumptions

I have often taken for granted that students have enough background knowledge and experience to know the basic vocabulary needed to understand a read-aloud book, a guided-reading book, or a self-selected book. Then a student will raise his hand and ask, "What does [that word] mean?" Often it is a fundamental word, such as *disappointment* or *energy*. Time and time again, we assume that students—and teachers—have general knowledge and experiences about the world or instruction when they do not. For example, almost every time I begin a residency in a new school, the principal and teachers will say something like, "We've had lots of professional development, and we're very 'far along.'" In the past, I assumed the staff was knowledgeable, but I have learned that much professional development is fragmented and superficial, and that we cannot assume anything about what educators do and do not know.

"Make no assumptions" also applies to any set of standards we adopt. Even the "best" set of standards or curriculum requires that we educators know how to apply them—no easy matter. We cannot assume that schools and districts will be able to figure out how to implement standards so students learn more. In fact, successful implementation has proved to be a stumbling block for many.

Finally, "make no assumptions" applies to us as educators and colleagues. We cannot take for granted that our demonstrations are sufficient, that the terms we are using are commonly understood, that the support we are providing is helpful, or that the learning environment is a comfortable and positive one for all who inhabit it. Always we need to be responsively assessing all that we do and be willing to respectfully adjust our language, goals, methods, instruction, and assessment to maximize success for all.

 ## Take Action

- **Make it smart to ask questions.** Say something like, "If you don't understand something, a word or an idea, raise your hand and ask. Curious people ask questions. That's how we learn." Then, give students—and teachers, too—specific feedback when they follow through. Say something like, "Patrick, I'm glad you said, 'I don't know what revision is' and didn't sit there pretending to understand." Or "Gloria, a lot of teachers are confused about shared writing. I'm glad you asked about that." Or "Let's add that question to our list of things we want to find out more about."

- **Find opportunities to demonstrate and apply how to use keywords, concepts, and strategies** until their use is familiar and understood. For example, show, explain, and practice together the "how," "what," and "why" of revision and shared writing. Insert into daily speaking important words we expect learners to know and apply.

- **Check to be sure basic vocabulary and ideas are understood.** We often assume—often wrongly—that because learners are well behaved and looking right at us that they comprehend what we are teaching. Orally assess before, during, and after instruction. For example, ask and chart, "What do we know about _____?" Use that assessment to guide instruction. Then, as new words, concepts, content, and strategies are learned, add them to the chart. Date each set of entries, using a different color marker each day, to show growing knowledge as well as clarification of confusions and questions. Such charts are a good assessment for teachers as well as students. (See lesson plan online at sten.pub/literacyessentials for examples of some charts. For more on vocabulary, see pages 275–278.)

- **Include discussion of important current events related to issues in the community and in the world,** regardless of the age of our students. We cannot assume, for example, that students know the basics of how our government works or why free elections matter. (See more on current events and basic civic knowledge, pages 69, 85, 267–268, and 387–390.)

- **Provide additional frontloading** as needed. Even when we have done our best, it's typical to have a small group of students who need more frontloading—for example, our students who struggle, our English language learners, and those low in confidence. Pull them aside while the rest of the class gets to work. Then, when conferring on-the-run, check in with these students first to ensure they're off to a good start, which can prevent the need for reteaching, boost students' confidence, and give them energy to continue working.

- **Build in ongoing reflection for all instruction and assessment.** It can be as simple as asking "How many need me to explain that again?" "Turn and talk with your partner about _____." "Write down any questions you still have." Or "When reading the article today, jot down any words or concepts you couldn't figure out." Embedding ongoing reflection is as important for gauging understanding and next steps for us as professionals as it is for moving our students forward.

  Consider using apps such as Padlet or TodaysMeet so students and staff can add questions during and after a lesson or professional learning time. As appropriate, share with the group and adjust the lesson or professional learning.

Apply an Optimal Learning Model

I rely on what I call an Optimal Learning Model (OLM) for all my planning, teaching, and assessing.[4] The OLM is responsive teaching in action, or what some might call differentiated instruction. It is the expert frontloading and deliberate practice that learners need to be successful. The Optimal Learning Model evolved over many years, from a gradual release of responsibility (GRR) model developed by many scholars—beginning with Pearson and Gallagher[5]—to an Optimal Learning Model focused on learning; that is, "What do learners need to know, do, and understand in order to achieve optimal success?"

Although a gradual handover of responsibility is part of the OLM, the most important part is knowing what types of—and how much—demonstration, support, and practice are necessary *before* expecting the learner to productively apply what we are teaching. Researcher and scholar MaryEllen Vogt points out that one of the main differences between the OLM and the GRR is the OLM focus on what the student or students are doing versus the GRR focus on what the teacher is doing.[6]

The OLM is basically an interactive coaching model, which is applicable to students, teachers, and leaders at all levels. In applying the OLM, emphasis is on the learner who—as an active participant supported by an expert—assumes increasing responsibility for scaffolding and self-directing his or her learning while gradually becoming more competent and confident. Our responsibility as teachers is to do everything possible to sufficiently prepare students to take charge of their learning as early as possible in the process.

> *The Optimal Learning Model . . . puts the focus during a lesson on where it belongs: on student behaviors, such as negotiating understandings, collaborating, approximating, interacting, applying, problem-solving, clarifying, self-monitoring, initiating, independently reading and writing, and so forth. The point at which teacher-regulated learning becomes student-regulated is in the earliest stages of the process, not only at the end . . . ."*[7]

See the OLM chart (page 138) to notice who's in control of the learning and when that control shifts. See also the OLM cycle (page 139) and note that the learning process is fluid and recursive, not linear or rigid. I often call the model the "I do it–We do it–We do it–You do it" model because learners frequently need far more shared experiences than we typically provide them.

Optimal Learning Model

Who's in charge?	Instructional Support

Moving from dependence to independence

Teacher/Student	Demonstration
Teacher/Student	Shared Demonstration

Gradual handover of responsibility

Student/Teacher	Guided Practice
Student/Teacher	Independent Practice

Ongoing cycle of continuous assessment
Celebration of learning
Reteaching, as needed

© 2012 Regie Routman

Note. Adapted from *Teaching Essentials: Expecting the Most and Getting the Best from Every Learner, K-8* (p. 89), by R. Routman, 2008, Portsmouth, NH: Heinemann. Copyright 2008 by Regie Routman

Note two distinctive stages of "We do it" experiences: gradual shift from Shared Demonstration with teacher in charge to Guided Practice with student in charge

It's important to notice on the OLM chart that the "We do it" or shared-experiences phase has two stages. In the first stage, the teacher is still in charge; in the second stage, the handover has occurred and the student leads the way and does most of "the work." That deliberate-practice phase is essential for optimal learning; that is, once we have provided sufficient demonstrations/explanations and shared experiences,

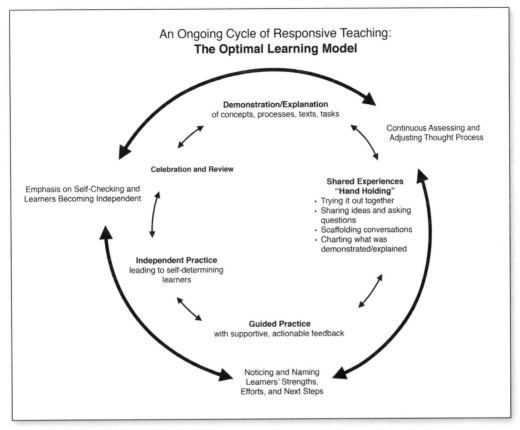

OLM as a flexible and fluid model for providing responsive teaching, differentiated instruction, and appropriate instructional support with the goal of learner taking on increasing responsibility and competence for doing "the work"

the student tries out, with our guidance, what we have been teaching and practicing together. The video of a scaffolded conversation, referenced on page 306, is one example of moving from stage one of "We do it," with teacher in charge, to stage two of "We do it," with student in charge.

Think about an "80 percent to 20 percent" rule here, with the majority of reading and writing time devoted to guided practice and independent practice—with the student leading and self-regulating most of the work and thinking—and much less time spent with the teacher directing the learning process. For example, if we are providing "just right" texts for reading and writing and have done sufficient frontloading, our support is minimal as the student attempts, mostly successfully, to direct and self-monitor his learning.

However, what actually happens in many classrooms is that many teachers overdo support to students; that is, we do too much for too long, which results in some students continuing to struggle or progress slowly. One common example in the elementary grades is guided reading; teachers frequently wind up doing most of the work or keeping students in the group too long. In this guided-practice phase, students are the ones who need to be in charge. We are mostly checking and doing the necessary affirming, guiding, and teaching so students have the mind-set and skills to read on their own as competent readers who consciously self-monitor, self-evaluate, and self-correct.

On the other hand, we sometimes move too fast from "I do it" to "You do it," which is especially common for students in middle school and high school, where curriculum demands can be great. Then both the students and we can become frustrated because we do not get the results we want and expect. Re-teaching is necessary, we feel exhausted, and we lose the joy that results from "I can do it!" and "We can do it!" experiences. It's all a delicate dance that requires close observation, ongoing assessment, and thoughtful improvisation as we teach. We always want to be asking ourselves, "What does the learner need most, at this time, to become more competent and independent?" Very important, none of the preceding OLM information matters much unless what we ask students to do is meaningful, usually involves some choice, and is worth their—and our—time and effort.

 ## Take Action

- **Get familiar with the OLM or a similar learning model.** For detailed, easy-to-understand explanations, see the blog "A Good Learning Model for New Teachers" (http://www.middleweb.com/23534/the-best-way-to-teach-learn-to-bake-tarts/).

- **Apply the OLM to big questions and deep learning.** See the blog "How to Fill Your Class with Joyful Learning" to learn how the OLM was the foundation for success for our lesson on environmental stewardship (Appendix C and online) and to understand the model more deeply (http://www.middleweb.com/24923/how-to-fill-your-class-with-joyful-learning/).

- **Self-evaluate your planning and instruction.** Ensure you have done excellent and sufficient demonstrations and shared experiences while allotting most instructional time to deliberate practice.

Do more demonstrations

Demonstrate everything you want students to be able to do well, from rereading when meaning breaks down to changing classes in an orderly fashion. Keep in mind that one demonstration is rarely sufficient. In fact, in a first demonstration, especially if it's something complex, we tend to pay attention to the procedural parts—steps to follow, details to include. We may not yet know what our questions are. Multiple demonstrations allow us as learners to get a gist of how the parts fit within a meaningful whole. For example, every time I push myself to learn a new technology, at the start I am only able to go step by step, in a prescribed sequence, without any real understanding of how these steps fit together. It's only when I've seen multiple demonstrations—including shared experiences with lots of handholding and the opportunity to try out with constant support how to "do it"—that I can begin to ask intelligent questions and gain confidence that competence will eventually come. For tips on effective demonstrations, see the article at http://regieroutman.org/files/4213/7842/4351/Tips_for_effective_demonstrations.pdf.

 ## Take Action

- ◆ **Explain exactly what will be demonstrated and why.** Check to be sure students understand the purpose. The demonstration might be done by us teachers or it could be done by another expert—even a student, an author through his or her book, a video, or an examination of exemplars of student work or other documents in which we point out important characteristics and qualities that make the work effective.

- ◆ **Think aloud as you read, write, create, and problem-solve** so students "see" your in-the-head thinking. Say something like, "I will be thinking out loud, so I can show you exactly what goes on in the mind of a good reader, writer, thinker. Then I want you to do the same kind of thinking when you read _____, so you can become an expert reader."

- ◆ **Be explicit.** Model exactly what it is you expect students to do. Chart, through a shared writing, what students noticed and saw you do in the demonstration. Use that chart as both an assessment and a rubric.

- ◆ **Take charge and be efficient.** Demonstrate for only about ten to fifteen minutes so students have time and energy left to "try and apply" the work. Demonstrations can be continued the next day. Remember, this is the time to model and explain, so do not get distracted by students who want to offer suggestions. Let them know they will soon have an opportunity to have a turn.

◆ **Be authentic.** If students will be expected to write on the spot, think about doing a demonstration writing in front of them (instead of showing them a perfect copy done at home) so they observe your struggles and see writing as a recursive process that requires revision, rereading, and rethinking along the way.

◆ **Check to be sure students understood and learned from the demonstrations** before moving on and expecting students to do "the work." Ask and, perhaps, chart responses: "What did you notice me do?" Depending on students' responses, you may need to repeat the demonstration—or parts of it—and ask again (adding on to the chart) what they noticed. You might also have students explain the task they are about to undertake through turn and talk with a partner or discussion in a small group. Then call on anyone in the group to explain the task. Repeat as needed.

Rely on shared writing

Regardless of the grade or content area we are teaching, using shared writing is one of the most effective and efficient ways to ensure literacy success for all students. In shared writing, the teacher "holds the pen" and does the actual transcription while leading, guiding, accepting, and shaping students' language and thinking. Shared writing makes it possible to raise expectations, show what's possible, and provide opportunities for all students to contribute their thoughts and ideas, without fear of failure. Often done in a whole-class setting or with a group, shared writing—when conducted in an atmosphere of trust and respect—makes all students feel validated and successful. Some examples of shared experiences connected to writing are co-constructing an editorial, essay, or rap together; examining writing exemplars from former students and noticing and naming what makes the writing excellent; establishing criteria for an upcoming writing project; and providing time for small groups to work before releasing students to work on their own.

For complete, detailed information on shared writing, see *Writing Essentials* (Routman, 2005b).[8] For tips on how to be successful with shared writing, see http://regieroutman.org/files/6713/7842/4352/Tps_for_shared_writing.pdf.

Take Action

- **Accept all students' ideas.** Even if a student is off track, try to validate some part of the student's thinking. The purpose is to affirm students for taking risks and to honor their thinking. Say something like "Say more about that," or "How about if we say it like this . . . ?" or "Let me come back to you again in a few minutes; listen to a few more ideas, and I'll help you put one of those in your own words."

- **Encourage all students' voices to be heard:**
  - *Call on a student who normally does not speak* and say something like, "Valerie, your thinking is important, too. Which idea do you like best so far? Can you read that one [on the chart] out loud? Do you want to add anything?"
  - *Put students into small, heterogeneous groups* to revise a class-authored, shared-writing draft. Give a word-processed copy to each group, appoint a scribe, and use the revised draft—signed by all group members—as an assessment of students' thinking and collaborative work. Bring the whole class back together, and have each group contribute its ideas to a final shared-writing draft that you help them shape.[9]

- **Turn shared-writing texts into shared-reading texts.** Because the texts are in students' own words, these are easy and engaging for students to read. Not only that, but all the word work students need—especially in the early grades—can come from these authentic contexts, which makes word study more enjoyable and far more efficient. Also, for second-language learners, creating shared-writing texts as bilingual books offers much support to them as emerging readers. Students can also illustrate different parts of the shared-writing text using a variety of art media, including paint, pencil, crayon, plasticine, or collage to help build comprehension.

  Consider using Book Creator to publish these shared texts, which can be printed or made into an iBook on an iPad. Texts can be air played and displayed on a smartboard. Use the Comic Life app to create a comic by adding photographs or students' individual drawings or other artwork for different parts of the writing. When introducing technology, apply the Optimal Learning Model.

- **Use shared-writing texts to teach older students who struggle.** Write texts for reading—for, with, and by students—and word-process the revised copies to be used for shared, partner, guided, or independent reading. Especially for students who have experienced years of failure and are turned off by school, meeting with a small group of reluctant readers and writing a text together on a topic they care passionately about, such as sports or video games, can be a turning point for becoming successful readers.

◆ **Create resources.** Use shared writing to create assessment charts, rubrics, research guidelines, procedures to follow, and explanations—all in student-friendly language that makes the classroom charts accessible and useful. In addition, having a class book devoted to student-authored shared writing, with new entries added continually, provides lots of familiar reading material. Rereading those entries builds fluency and competence.

Do more shared reading

Shared reading is ideal for building fluency, automaticity, stamina, reading skills and strategies, and enjoyment for learners of all ages. In shared reading, we teachers (or another expert) provide an engaging text to every reader—either through individual copies, an enlarged copy such as a "big book," or a projected copy that all can clearly see—and invite everyone to read along. (To see where shared reading fits in the Optimal Learning Model, see page 138.) Our reading demonstrations and support, as we read the text aloud together, give students the competence and confidence to eventually read and understand the text on their own. Sometimes the text is a familiar one, created through shared writing. Other times, it's an unfamiliar one that we have determined most of the students will be able to read and understand, with our support.

Shared reading is a terrific technique for improving reading competency, especially for beginning readers, elementary-age students who struggle, and English language learners. Once these students can read with accuracy and fluency, readers can focus on comprehension. Also very important, the support the shared-reading experience provides allows the use of more challenging content for all students, a crucial equity-access issue. (See also pages 145 and 211–212.)

 Take Action

◆ **Be sure students know the purpose.** Before shared reading, say something like "The reason we're reading this text together is so you can become a better reader, so make sure your eyes are on the text, even if you can't read every word." Or "We're going to read this text together and then notice and learn together how the author helps us figure out difficult words in the passage. Then, when you're reading on your own, you'll know how to do that." Or "We're going to read this aloud together to notice, enjoy, and appreciate the rhythm and language craft the author has created. When you finish your draft on such and so, quietly read it aloud to yourself and see if it sounds and works the way you want it to. If not, make some revisions."

◆ **Read and enjoy the text as a whole.** Word-process shared written work and project it on a whiteboard or screen so it's legible and visible to all. Read the whole text for enjoyment and information before stopping to do word work and other analysis (see "Apply Whole-Part-Whole Teaching," pages 271–275).

◆ **Help students track the print.** Use one or two five-by-seven-inch blank index cards (or opaque paper) to gradually expose the text line by line as you read aloud. Using one hand, place one index card underneath the sentence, go line by line through the text, and invite students to read along with you. For emerging readers or readers who struggle to track the print, also use a second card placed slightly above the first one to gradually uncover the text in each line as you are reading it aloud. Move along fluidly as you expose a sentence, phrase, or word at a time, depending on what your students need to successfully read along with you—either orally or silently. I also always have on hand and highly recommend using a sliding mask to expose part of a word, to frame a word or word part, or to highlight high-frequency words or academic vocabulary. These techniques work well in guided reading too.[10]

◆ **Assess as you go.** Have another student come to the front of the classroom, perhaps using a pointer, to lead a second or third shared reading on a whiteboard or chart so you can observe all students and intervene with students who are not on task. Stop and ask questions to check for understanding.

◆ **Use shared reading with older and younger readers.** Keep in mind that shared reading makes it possible for learners to hear, read along, and understand a text they may not yet be ready to read on their own. Use narrative and informational picture books as well as a chapter or portion from a fiction or nonfiction text, including news articles and content area texts. Add drama: when relevant, have students act out part of a shared reading.

◆ **Employ shared reading aloud**—that is, combine reading aloud with shared reading and interactive reading, which is a great vehicle for making nonfiction and fiction accessible and comprehensible to all students.[11] Keep the focus on enjoying and understanding the whole text before moving to instructional strategies. Then, for example, after demonstrating such strategies as summarizing, predicting, inferring, and figuring out vocabulary in a text you have been reading aloud and discussing, choose and project a paragraph or page that almost all students can read and have them read and analyze it with you. Then, have students "try out," first in a small group or with a partner, reading a portion and applying the targeted strategy or strategies. Revisit the text with students and have them confirm or disconfirm their responses. For example, we might say to a student, "Show me the line(s) in the text where it says _____," or "Let's read together the part where the author shows us _____."

Consider also creating a tableau. A tableau in drama is created when all the actors get into a position in the scene and freeze. This technique is great for management and adds movement and drama for a variety of learners. It can work well when reading a chapter book and some students need a movement break during the read-aloud.

- ◆ **Encourage rereading.** Multiple readings of a familiar, engaging text—especially one co-written with students—is a great confidence and competency booster for becoming a better reader. Once students can read a text with at least 95 percent accuracy, they can fully focus on meaning. Use partner reading, guided reading, and independent reading to have students practice the shared-reading text for fluency and strategies that have been demonstrated. Perhaps record the shared reading using the GarageBand app (See Appendix D: Technology Tools That Help Support Schoolwide Literacy Learning), and add the finished piece to a collection in a listening center.

Endnote

Essentially, expert teaching through frontloading means we possess the foundation, skills, strategies, and knowledge to be adept at teaching all students to learn and find joy in learning. Our deep knowledge of pedagogy, literacy, and content as well as our educational and life experiences make seamless teaching possible. That is, sufficient preparation, practice, tinkering, and reflection have brought us to the state where we are able to assess, adapt, and responsibly innovate during any lesson or collaboration with any group of learners. A related personal story, "Making Fruit Tarts," connects what I do when making a luscious fruit tart to highly effective teaching.

STORY ❖ Making Fruit Tarts

I've been making fruit tarts for about two decades, and it's taken me that long to become masterful—that is, able to turn out an excellent fruit tart just about every time. I don't say that to brag. I've had lots of failures over the years— tarts that had too much sugar, fruit that got mushy, crusts that weren't fully done, berries that weren't tasty—even when I was following a trusted recipe. Those failures taught me that thoughtfulness and analysis were also essential ingredients. I still mess up occasionally, but what I have learned is that although a recipe is a basic and necessary starting place, it is insufficient. Fruit varies, depending on the climate, time of year, growing-season conditions, quality of care, stage of ripening, transport to market, and any number of unforeseen and unknown factors. For example, all fruit has pectin in it, but we can't see it. The amount of pectin determines how ripe the fruit is, which determines how much sugar and thickener we need to add and how long the fruit needs to cook. So a successful maker of fruit tarts needs to consider many factors.

In many ways, learning to bake a superb fruit tart is similar to becoming a highly effective teacher. It takes many years of trial and error, deepening knowledge, professionally informed judgment, first-rate resources, practice and experience to master the craft, and ongoing self-questioning and self-monitoring. In making a fruit tart, self-questioning and tinkering are essential to the process because every batch of fruit varies and requires unique attention. How much sugar will this batch require? Will fresh lemon juice or orange juice be better? How much cornstarch should I add as a thickener? How long will this tart need to bake? *So, too, do highly effective teachers recognize that every student and group of students varies and has different needs based on former "growing conditions," many of which are unknown to us.* How much demonstration is enough? Will a small group or a one-on-one conference be most beneficial? How long does the group time need to last?

When we're new to the profession, we may need to follow and master a "recipe" or framework before we can responsibly and responsively adapt and innovate our teaching. Learning foundational steps and procedures, in order, over and over again, initially helps us cement basic routines and procedures so we don't have to think about them much; they become second nature. And, like my recipe for a fruit tart, it's a necessary first step, but just a beginning one. That solid internal framework, along with a growing store of knowledge, frees up mental space. That space gives us the energy and will to make the evolving judgment calls of effective, in-the-moment teaching and to do the inner self-questioning that expert teachers constantly embrace: Why isn't this lesson working as intended? What do I need to add, change, delete, or redo to get the results I want? What resources can best support teaching and learning? How can I engage this group of students? *I no longer use a recipe when I make a tart. I know from years of experience how to "measure" what's needed for optimal results.*

Finally, the quality of the resources we use is paramount. You can't make a first-rate tart with second-rate fruit. And you can't tell the quality of the fruit just by looking at it. On the surface, berries can look excellent, but until you taste them, there's no way to know. So it is with instructional and assessment resources, standards, and new curriculum. They can look like the "new best thing," but they have to be "tasted," studied, carefully examined, and tried out in the context of relevant research, experiences, and resources that have already proven their worth. Resources have to be top-notch, or they should not be used. Just as I serve my cherished family and friends only a beautifully made, tasty tart, we must not compromise what we "serve" to our students if we want "delicious" results.

Listening, Speaking, and Questioning

That Elevate Teaching and Learning

One of the most powerful actions we can take as teachers, leaders, and parents is to impose less and listen more. Scholar and educator Jonathan Kozol speaks of "the teacher who mattered most to me and has a continuing influence on me to this day." Kozol notes it was from Fred Rogers of *Mr. Rogers' Neighborhood* that he learned "to listen to children and to draw wisdom out of their voices."[1]

Listening fully is an act of respect, admiration, and even love. Genuine listening is not just hearing another's words and waiting our turn to speak. It is turning our full attention and energy to the speaker so that we might discern that person's thoughts, questions, concerns, and viewpoints without judgment. It's very difficult to listen well, but it is essential. How we listen determines what and how we understand, value, question, speak, and relate to others. As teachers, leaders, and colleagues, hearing everyone's voice is essential for well-being, optimal achievement, and a respectful school culture. It means making every effort to truly "see" the person speaking.

I still recall being in a principal's office to seek her advice about a student. I admired her vision and commitment to raising achievement. Yet while she was talking to me, she never looked up to make eye contact. Decades later I can still visualize the scene and feel my discomfort anew. Shuffling through paperwork on her desk and in her desk drawers, she said, "I am listening, but I need to get this work done." I remember feeling I had not been heard, that my request was not important enough to warrant her full attention. After several similar incidents, I sought out her advice less often, and my admiration for her moderated. Listening well and with an open heart and mind requires respect, effort, and resolve—in short, a mind-set that values listening as something of primary importance.

Especially today, when multitasking is the norm, listening well is more important than ever. Adept listening has the potential to raise the quality of our questions and conversations. With social media and instant response the currency of communication for our middle and high schoolers (and often their parents and us), active listening can be uncommon. "E-mails and phone calls are so yesterday," a high school sophomore told me. Face-to-face conversations, in which we as listeners can observe facial expressions, hear voice tone, see body posture, and make adjustments when responding to the person in front of us, have become even less common.

Oral communication and the ability to work well in a team are the top two qualities employers seek, as well as the top two predictors of success.[2] Therefore, we need to be explicitly and skillfully teaching and practicing effective oral communication to all students. Skillful listening and speaking—and especially questioning for depth and substance—are also necessary for optimal instruction and learning, and not just in reading and writing. Productive talk, listening, and questioning are key areas in math, science, history, and other content areas. In fact, success in the twenty-first century requires that all of us be able to think critically, collaborate, listen well, and know how and when to speak up, raise important questions, and effectively and courageously communicate our ideas.

Become an Active Listener

Most of us who teach talk a lot. It's been well documented that, for the most part, we talk much more than our students. On average, teacher talk accounts for 70 to 80 percent of classroom instruction time, and the higher the grade level, the more talking teachers do. Also, most of teacher talk is "telling" students. "Barely 5% of this instructional time was designed to create students' anticipation of needing to respond."[3] All that talking means we're not actively listening to our students much of the time.

My professional belief and life experience indicate that adept speaking and questioning depend on being able to astutely listen. That is, we listen with nothing more in mind than "What is this person trying to say?" "What does this person want me to know or understand?" "How can I facilitate useful and respectful communication?" "How does what this person says and how he says it inform my actions?" That open mind-set and single-minded concentration are crucial for our successful and appropriate verbal and written responses, for conferring in writing, for understanding our peers' points of view, for making every member of the school community feel valued, and for hearing all the voices (see "Promote Significant Conversations," pages 153–158).

Becoming an active listener means valuing our audience. When feasible, before any presentation or workshop, I try to learn as much as possible about my audience. For example, before a keynote talk I arrive early, walk around, and try to meet and talk briefly with as many people as possible. The reasons are twofold: I want to welcome and connect to individuals close up, find out who they are—job designation, grade level, content area—and listen to what's on their minds. I ask, "What's going well in your district?" "What's an issue you're struggling with in your school/district?" "What do you hope to learn today?" As a speaker, I try to encompass some of what I have just heard into my talk or workshop to make it more relevant and personal—even in these last minutes. I use active listening to inform, adjust, and revise my thinking and behaviors in an attempt to be as relevant as possible for my audience, in the same way expert teachers respond to the students in their care.

Becoming an active listener is also about how we learn to process and remember what's most important in a speaker's message or a teacher's lesson. Encouraging students to take notes by hand is one significant way to encourage active listening. Taking notes by hand forces us to think hard about what's most important to record because we can't write fast enough to get down every word. By comparison, when students take notes by computer, they tend to act primarily as stenographers attempting to transcribe every word.[4] Finally, active listening is crucial for students' optimal progress. If students are not good listeners, even useful feedback won't benefit them much. The same is true for us educators.

 ## Take Action

- ◆ **Increase the amount of time and opportunity given to students to participate in focused discussions.** Provide more turn-and-talk time with a partner, as well as more small-group collaboration, both guided and self-directed. Value active listening as much as speaking.

- ◆ **Remove barriers to active listening.** Be physically and emotionally present: make eye contact, lean in, nod to show affirmation, and make sure your arms are not crossed. Kneel or pull up a chair or stool beside desks or tables when listening to young children. For small-group conversations in classrooms, seek to remove or set aside distractions that impede listening, such as tablets and other devices, and arrange seating so students can easily converse with each other.

The same guidelines also apply to us educators. During professional learning meetings for administrators, whenever possible we have them sit in groups on chairs in a circle. With no tables and no place to hide devices or secretly check ever-present cell phones, participants are fully focused on group members and the topic at hand. Nobody picks up a cell phone. Such transparency in the physical setup leads to focused listening, which leads to richer conversations.

- **Value pregnant pauses.** Sometimes students' most innovative thinking happens because we take the time to actively listen before we respond. This is equally true for us as educators talking with one another. Try to allow at least ten seconds of wait time.

- **Do not repeat what a student says.** When we do so, we give the message that other students need not listen to anyone except us teachers. We not only stifle students' voices, but also we inadvertently encourage students to ignore what their peers are saying.

  - Say something like "I'm not going to repeat what Mario says, so, Mario, you need to speak loudly so your classmates can hear you. And, students, you need to pay close attention to what Mario says."
  - Have students turn and talk with a partner. Ask, "What did Mario just say?" Call on anyone. If a student cannot respond, ask his partner to tell him what Mario said, and then have the first student either put those thoughts in his own words or repeat what his partner just said.
  - Have Mario repeat what he said if both students in the pair cannot respond. Then repeat the entire exercise until students can respond.

- **Let students know we will give easy-to-follow directions only once.** If students know from our past behaviors that we will restate everything they are to do, there's no reason for them to listen the first time. Of course, for directions and expectations that are complex and might well require clarification for understanding, going over directions more than once is warranted.

- **Establish and practice listening guidelines with students,** such as making eye contact with the speaker, not interrupting, adopting a mind-set of putting the listener first, and demonstrating respectful posture, such as sitting up tall. Chart and post agreed-upon listening norms with students.

◆ **Expect all students working together, with a partner or in a small group, to be able to state the groups' findings.** Say something like "It's important for you to listen to each other. At the end of group time, I should be able to call on your partner or any group member to say what you learned, decided, questioned, concluded, and so on."

◆ **Listen to the quality of discourse** between students as they talk with each other. Are the questions and comments of quality and significance? We need to remember to model effective discourse and questioning techniques throughout the day.

◆ **Follow students' leads, discerning their spoken and body language.** Change course when students are not engaged and a lesson is not working. Sometimes that means abandoning a lesson and starting again.

◆ **Teach note taking.** Apply the Optimal Learning Model (see pages 136–139) to demonstrate and practice with students how to listen to a speaker's message and take meaningful notes on the most salient points. Demonstrate taking notes on paper as well as digitally. Some apps allow for typing, photos, and handwriting. Investing in a stylus makes it easy to draw and write on an iPad.

◆ **Do more shared writing.** Shared writing (explained on pages 142–143) is a terrific way to promote more speaking and active listening. Because we teachers are shaping the writing, if we have created a culture that is safe for risk taking, students feel free to voice their opinions without fear of correctness, rebuke, or failure. It is our job to listen carefully and try to discern what the student means, and to record and respect the language he or she uses. That language can be modified later.

Promote Significant Conversations

Meaningful conversation is a necessity for success and fulfillment in all areas of our lives. Conversation can lead to "intellectual communion. . . . Conversation is a kind of intimacy. You don't just get more information. You get different information."[5] In that regard, I have instituted what I call "'coffee' and conversation" with each of my teenage granddaughters, an occasional after-school visit to a local bakery where we attempt to commune beyond the superficial "How was your day?" to important heart-and-mind matters. Students today, accustomed to communicating largely through social media, need demonstrations and practice on how and why meaningful conversation is an artful necessity for optimal living and learning.

Productive and collaborative talk increases engagement, helps clarify meaning, improves retention of information, shapes and improves thinking capacities, leads to deeper understanding, and results in more enduring learning. "Learning how to interact effectively with others may be the most important skill that students develop in school."[6] Our role is to stimulate, clarify, and moderate the conversations so students do most of the talking. I tell even our youngest students, "Scientists (researchers) have found out you learn more from talking with each other than from just listening to the teacher. So it's important you listen well to each other."

Although lots of talk goes on in our classrooms, we need to ensure that most of that talk results in worthwhile conversations with and by students about texts worth reading and writing and content worth learning. Such conversations promote debate, curiosity, and thoughtful questioning and can lead to considering and valuing multiple perspectives, even for our youngest learners. Renowned researcher John Hattie notes that such conversations are rare.

> Teachers love to talk—to clarify, summarize, reflect, share personal experiences, explain, correct, repeat, praise. About 5–10 percent of teacher talk triggers more conversation or dialogue engaging the students. Please note that this is not how teachers perceive what happens in their classrooms, but what is happening—as shown by video analysis, class observations, and event sampling.[7]

Unfortunately, it is still uncommon to walk into a classroom and hear rich, issue-related discussion that is primarily directed by engaged students, and this is especially true for high school students.[8] Yet such ongoing dialogue is a needed shift for us. Masterful oral communication is a necessity for optimal application of digital media and for success in all aspects of our lives, including the work we do with others. Because face-to-face conversations can be infrequent in our age of social media, we educators must ensure we promote and facilitate students' opportunity to talk and experience productive conversations in our classrooms and in their lives outside of school. *Of utmost importance: if we want students to invest in complex thinking and sharing of ideas, they must believe their voices matter.*

Let's strive to put into practice recent research on how the most highly effective teams speak to and with each other. Research commissioned by Google reported that the most successful teams feel psychologically safe to take risks, trust each other, and be themselves; that is, "conversational turn taking" and high "social sensitivity" are the norm.[9] Also, in high-functioning teams, as long as everyone got a chance to respectfully speak for about the same amount of time—"equality in distribution of conversational turn-taking"—the team did well. "But if only one person or a small group spoke all the time, the collective intelligence declined."[10] Learning through talking requires us to intentionally guide students in how to effectively participate in meaningful conversations.

 ## Take Action

◆ **Demonstrate what a literate conversation sounds like** through viewing and analyzing quality videos with two or more speakers; have students observe you discussing something with a colleague or student and naming and explaining what you say and why you say it; or set up and facilitate a "fish bowl" demonstration conversation (see also page 349), with an inner circle of heterogeneously grouped students in a teacher-led, guided discussion and an outer circle of observing students who are noting and recording characteristics of effective speakers and listeners. (Students' written observations also serve as an assessment.)

◆ **Create more opportunities for dynamic talk and discussion.** Hearing all the voices in a classroom is about celebrating what students have to say or are attempting to say. Encourage students to respond to each other, not just to us. Having a silent classroom is not a virtue and often says more about a culture of compliance rather than an environment that promotes inquiry, active listening, and lively discussion. When students know we value their thoughts and we are not just seeking "right" answers, they speak up.

Stop often during a lesson, after about ten to fifteen minutes, when you are doing most of the talking, and have students turn to a partner, or to two to three students, to discuss what has been presented, raise a question, make a prediction, justify their reasoning, and so on. Use those times to assess what students are learning and where you need to adjust your instruction.

Educator Angela Watson provides the following "8 ways teachers can talk less and get kids talking more":

1. Don't steal the struggle.
2. Move from the front of the classroom.
3. Teach students signals for your often-repeated phrases and for transitions.
4. Use non-verbal reinforcement for behavior whenever possible.
5. Turn your statements into questions and prompts.
6. Instead of asking, "Does that make sense?" say, "Can you put that in your own words?"

7. Stop repeating yourself.

8. Notice moments when you summarize/review for students, and instead get their input.[11]

♦ **Have more conversations** about books. Make literature conversations and ongoing book talk with peers, not just the teacher, part of the reading and content area curriculum at all grade levels. Self-directed literature conversations are excellent for promoting student-guided talk about all kinds of texts.[12]

♦ **Promote significant conversations across the curriculum.**

⦿ *Ensure your students and you have the tools to make productive discussions possible.* See "Talk Moves to Support Classroom Discussion," superb suggestions by Elham Kazemi and Allison Hintz, in Appendix E.[13] Although the authors are writing about leading math discussions, their apt suggestions apply to language arts and all content areas.

⦿ *Have students, with pre-established classroom guidelines, explain their thinking* on a project they've completed, a problem they've solved, or a topic they've learned about. Have students practice their presentations in small groups before speaking to the whole class. Demonstrate how to give authentic and useful feedback.

⦿ *Set up weekly book talks* that students can sign up for to convince others to read a favorite text. First demonstrate what an excellent book talk sounds like, using a read-aloud book all students are familiar with, and establish criteria and time limits.

⦿ *Give more time and value to small-group work,* which affords more opportunities for rich conversations. Letting students know their work will be assessed as a group, not just as individuals, raises expectations and encourages higher quality. (See pages 143 and 157 for more on small-group work.) David Carr, acclaimed writer and journalist, told his students:

We will be working in groups . . . the goal is that you will leave here with a single piece of work that reflects your capabilities as a maker of media. But remember, evaluations will be based not just on your efforts, but on your ability to bring excellence out of the people around you.[14]

⦿ *Follow students' ideas.* Demonstrate and encourage students to ask and respond to open-ended questions such as the following:

- ☐ Say more about that.
- ☐ What else might it be?
- ☐ Add on to _____'s [name student] thoughts.
- ☐ Can you give another example?
- ☐ What do you think about why _____?

◆ **Turn over responsibility for productive talk to students.** Once it is clear, through classroom formative assessments, that students understand the directions, text, or work to be done, put them in charge. Often even the most competent teachers retain responsibility too long, which deprives students who are ready for the opportunity, for example, to problem-solve, to work with a small group, or to begin work on their own.

- ● *Consider multiple, heterogeneous groups of three to four students* discussing a portion of a text, news article, or math problem that is projected or photocopied so all can see the print. Students can read silently or one student can read aloud for all because the purpose is high-level thinking for all, not reading ability. Then walk about to affirm, assess, support, guide, and instruct each group as needed. Because you may not get around to every group, and also as an evaluation of the thinking that took place in each group, designate a scribe to record group thinking with everyone's names included. First be sure to apply the Optimal Learning Model to demonstrate and practice how a self-directed group functions and what a record of the group's thinking might look like.

- ● *Refrain from jumping in with an answer.* Ensure students have enough schema and experiences so they can do most of the mental work, deal with uncertainty and even failure, and create their own meanings that they can back up with evidence and well-reasoned opinions.

- ● *Emphasize becoming a better speaker and communicator*, which requires much deliberative practice. Before we flip for the flipped classroom (in which delivery of instruction occurs at home through online sites and videos while classroom learning takes on "homework" and interactive learning), let's ensure our students are strong oral communicators. Adept oral communication often determines which voices we pay attention to when considering new ideas and actions—in and out of school.

◆ **Promote significant conversations with colleagues.** We need to be courageous enough to raise our voices and the level of conversations in our schools and districts. Model respectful discourse related to such topics as student learning and engagement, choice, reading for understanding, authentic assessment, and so on. Ensure that gossip, test scores, and deficit thinking do not dominate the discourse. (Apply research on successful teams, as discussed on pages 154–155, and see pages 157 and 304 for specifics on successful group talk.)

+ **Self-evaluate the dominance and quality of teacher talk.** Invite a trusted colleague to observe a lesson, videotape it, or script the actual dialogue. Note the time period and the proportion of teacher talk to student talk. Self-evaluate if your talk has led to productive, student-engaged conversations. Strive to do better where needed.

Teach Public Speaking

Presentation literacy is a necessary life skill that we must be teaching, learning, and applying to ourselves as well as our students. Most jobs of the future will require that ability—that we orally synthesize and clearly communicate ideas to others; yet most of us of have had little experience or education in that domain. I'll never forget how terrified I was when I began publicly speaking to educators decades ago. A big part of my fright was my total lack of experience. In all my years of schooling I was reticent to speak out and recall little encouragement or guidance to do so. Not surprisingly, my lack of experience greatly affected my initial confidence and competence. What finally made me take the risk to speak publicly was my sense of urgency to communicate what I believed to be important principles, findings, and approaches for improving literacy and learning.

Being a clear communicator is more important today than ever before. The earlier students start learning and practicing how to orally communicate ideas to a real-world audience, the easier it will be for them to master this art and the more comfortable they will feel doing so. Regardless of our line of work, many of us are likely to be called upon to make an effective presentation to a group. Teacher leadership, for example, is a growing and necessary role that goes beyond our own classrooms. I have written extensively on what that role entails,[15] and part of that role is being able to lead a staff in professional learning, which requires being an organized planner and a capable speaker and communicator.

Although presentation literacy involves many forms—such as videos, podcasts, and written formats, all of which are discussed in this text—this section will focus on public speaking, the most common and basic form. "Public speaking is the key to unlocking empathy, stirring excitement, sharing knowledge and insights, and promoting a shared dream."[16] And effective public speaking can be effectively taught.

To become an effective and engaging public speaker even to a small group, we need to be knowledgeable about our topic, pay close attention to the appropriateness and relevance of the content we present, anticipate the needs and interests of the audience, gauge the pacing of the talk, consider what's most important to say and how to say it in a limited time frame, and integrate technology support when it enhances our goals. Very important, we need to "read" the audience throughout the presentation and determine if they are engaged or if we might need to modify our course. That modification might be as simple as slowing down, leaving out information, and giving the audience a quiet thinking or talking opportunity to process what we've presented with another person and, possibly, give us feedback.

Perhaps most important, to inspire our audience to dream big and think differently, we need to passionately speak from the heart and let ourselves be known. "You'll never convince your audience of anything if they don't trust, admire, and genuinely like you."[17] This is certainly true for me. The speakers I've learned the most from are people I greatly admire.

Teach and practice the following public speaking tips, which can also be applied to successful writing, videos, podcasts, and other presentation formats:

- Remove barriers between you and your audience.

- Consider starting with a personal story to engage the audience and get them excited about the topic.

- Decide the most important message/big idea you want the audience to come away with and work backward from there.

- Support your important end message (big idea) with three supporting messages, and elaborate on each of those with subpoints that include compelling stories and examples.[18]

- Enhance the presentation with relevant visual images—graphics, photographs, and videos.

- Practice relentlessly; revise as needed.

- Finally, be yourself. Try to enjoy the delivery; you're prepared!

 ## Take Action

- **Demonstrate, analyze, practice, and apply what effective public speakers do.** Listen to and view excellent media forms such as highly effective video and audio talks—for example, TED Talks for students, which are limited to fewer than twenty minutes and are mostly done without notes. (See TED Talks websites: www.ted.com/talks, ed.ted.com/; and a program called TED-Ed Clubs that "allows any teacher to offer a group of kids a chance to give their own TED Talk."[19]) With your guidance, discuss and chart with students what you observe and might be able to try and apply. Sufficient time to practice is crucial to success.

See nationalspeakingweek.org for excellent classroom lessons, teacher and student resources, videos of model speakers, recommended digital tools and sites, and more.

- **Notice what else successful speakers often do:**
  - Demonstrate knowledge of the topic and stay on topic.
  - Say something compelling and back it up with stories, experiences, and facts.
  - Display enthusiasm and energy in talking about the topic, question, or issue.
  - Make the purpose of the talk clear and relevant.
  - Customize the talk for a specific audience.
  - Have a well-crafted delivery.
  - Make points succinctly and clearly and back them up with evidence.
  - Know what's most important to include and to leave out.
  - Have an inspiring closure that listeners can remember.

That said, like all skillfully written and spoken texts, a checklist or rubric is insufficient for appreciating the whole text. How a speech affects us is what resonates and stays with us. As one example, a universally praised speech by former US first lady Michelle Obama ". . . is worth studying for the poetry, the beauty, and elegance of her words."[20]

- **Know your audience,** the purpose of your talk, and what you want your audience to understand, see, hear, and take away from your talk/comments, as well as how much background you need to provide to ensure maximum understanding and enjoyment. One important example is having students present a portfolio of their learning as part of a school's or district's reporting to parents. The student portfolio could be a physical, digital, or video portfolio that showcases work over time. Regardless, to create a portfolio that is effective and can be understood by families, students must be expert explainers and communicators.[21]

- **Promote in-school public speaking occasions** through daily, whole-school announcements that students prepare (following the Optimal Learning Model); provide opportunities for groups of students to explain their learning on a nonfiction study to other classrooms through talks, podcasts, radio broadcasts, videos, and so on. Students can also promote and explain schoolwide events—for example, a fundraiser—and create videos to communicate their message both in school and on social media. Book reviews and recommendations, shared publicly on podcasts, are another way to articulate thoughts and to practice fluency in speaking.

◆ **Reflect on speaking.** With students, develop criteria to follow for public speaking. Record their speaking through a video or podcast. Have students self-evaluate their public speaking, discuss their strengths and needs with them, and, perhaps, offer one or two suggestions if the student seems ready for them.

Ask More Vital Questions

Significant conversations rely on asking and thinking about powerful questions that hook students and push their thinking. The questions we ask our students and ourselves reflect our knowledge, priorities, beliefs, and experiences, and those questions have the potential to limit or expand our instruction, knowledge, innovation, thinking, students' learning, and relationships with our students and colleagues. In fact, the quality of teacher and student work and talk is largely determined by the questions we ask as well as the questions students raise. Well-educated people are curious, in pursuit of questions, and they push their thinking and others' through thoughtful and provocative questioning.

Researchers estimate we spend at least half of our instructional time asking questions, so most of those questions need to be promoting deep learning and inquiry. Unfortunately, that tends not to be the case. Of the hundreds of questions teachers ask each day, the great majority are low-level, cognitive questions related to factual recall (60 percent) and procedures (20 percent); such questions "often serve as the glue to the flow of the lesson."[22] Low-level questions—for example, those limited to skills-teaching and test preparation—also tend to dominate our professional development and teacher talk in a school. So although we teachers ask a lot of questions, relatively few of them are questions that probe and check for critical thinking and deep understanding—especially during a lesson.

By continuously assessing, mostly through asking high-level questions while we are teaching, we can adjust and tailor our instruction to better meet students' needs, interests, and our required curriculum and standards. Do not immediately jump in when students "don't know." Let them come to know, through relevant questioning, additional teaching, shared experiences, and guided practice that you will support them to figure out their own "answers." Use informed judgment. Sometimes stepping in to help a student or group of students is necessary—for example, with a scaffolded conversation (see page 305) or demonstration that can avoid an unproductive failure.

All of the aforementioned is responsive teaching at its best, not "telling teaching" (page 120), which may hold back students' best thinking. In addition, students who develop a mind-set of self-monitoring, problem solving, self-questioning, and goal setting are more likely to do well on standardized tests, because they have internalized and can independently apply the habits of successful readers, writers, thinkers, and problem solvers. They are also more likely to become self-determining learners (see pages 335–337).

Several self-assessment questions for higher-level questioning can guide our professional learning, instruction, and thinking:

♦ Are most of our questions, ideas, and lessons aimed at promoting and generating high-level student thinking?

♦ Have we created an intellectual and trusting culture where students feel encouraged to think about and share complex ideas?

♦ Are we sufficiently preparing students to successfully do most of the talking, thinking, questioning, and "the work"?

♦ Will the feedback we give learners build on their strengths and give them the will, skill, and confidence to ask and seek answers to the questions that can help them move forward?

♦ Are we showing our students how we self-question our own thinking, intentions, and understanding in the process of teaching, assessing, and learning?

♦ Are we giving students enough time, space, demonstrations, and guided practice to pose their own sophisticated questions and engage in rich dialogue with their peers, not just the teacher?

♦ Are our questions ultimately leading our students to become critical thinkers who ask critical questions themselves?

Higher-order thinking happens when students apply what they know to an idea or a situation and transform it into something new.[23] Initially that thinking often begins with a vital question. It was our in-depth study of an endangered species in the primary grades—framed by the high-level questions we posed (see page 87) and accompanying frontloading (page 88)—that led Connor, a student who had not previously seen himself as a reader or writer, to write on his Evaluation of Learning: "I thought a groundbreaking thought!!!" He beamed with pride and joy and went on to do more reading, writing, and questioning than he had ever done before.

 ## Take Action

+ **Ask key questions that lead to deep and sustained learning across the curriculum.** "What if we changed the question from how to get kids college- and career-ready to how to engage hearts and minds and inspire love of learning?" That tweet generated one of my largest responses on Twitter. "How do we create schools where all learners—students, teachers, and leaders—are joyful, engaged in meaningful work, and self-directed?" This is the question I keep uppermost in mind when I start planning any study.

    By contrast, if our big question and focus is "How do we raise the test scores?" or "How do we cover all the material?" we are likely to get stuck in a spiral of continuously seeking the "perfect" program or expert to tell us what to do. If we focus on creating a safe, intellectual learning culture, as described in the Engagement section (pages 60–61) and the Equity section (pages 263–268), high achievement will follow.[24]

    Use curriculum documents, standards, and students' interests and needs to determine what's most important for students to learn, know, and be able to do, and then determine how to ensure they learn it and choose to go on learning.

+ **Ensure questions asked are worth the time and attention they take.** For example, reading for understanding requires concentration, engagement, and momentum. When we interrupt the flow with endless questions, we impede optimal understanding and enjoyment. Notice the essential questions Trish Richardson and I raised in our environmental study with students (see page 87). Check yourself, using the questions in the text box on the next page.

Self-Check on Our Questioning

- *Are most of our questions directed at student thinking,* or are most of the questions we ask focused on student behaviors?

- *Are students doing most of the talking and thinking,* or are we micromanaging the conversations?

- *Are we listening for and encouraging divergent thinking,* or are we waiting for the "right answer" we already hold in our heads?

- *Are students confident raising their own important questions,* or have we neglected to teach and encourage students how and why to raise vital questions?

- *Are we using students' questions to self-reflect, revise, and extend teaching and learning,* or do we sometimes find students' questions an intrusion on our planned lessons?

If the answer is "yes" to the second question in any of these bulleted items, rethink your learning culture; consider revising your actions to move closer to the more constructive actions embedded in the first questions (in italics).

- **Ask more open-ended questions that require students to think more deeply,** find evidence in a text to support their reasoning, and ponder possible solutions— questions such as these:

  - What do you notice?
  - What seems most important about _____?
  - Why do you think that _____?
  - What else could account for _____?
  - What's another way you could say that?
  - Have you thought about _____?
  - What is the author trying to convey about _____?
  - What evidence leads you to conclude _____?
  - On what assumptions is the evidence based?
  - What's another possibility?
  - Where could you find that information?

Notice these are appropriate questions for any grade level or content area. Give sufficient wait time; encourage multiple answers as acceptable possibilities; call on students who don't volunteer and let them know their voices are important to the conversation.

- **Request that a colleague observe a lesson and write down the questions you ask of your students.** Self-evaluate. Check that most of your questions and responses are not just about management and literal-level thinking and that you are asking and demonstrating important questions and thinking that lead to rich conversations and deeper understanding.

- **Teach and encourage students to ask more thoughtful questions.** Create a trusting classroom and schoolwide culture (page 9) where students feel safe to ask a challenging question, risk making a mistake, or ask for clarification in front of their peers. It can be difficult, even as adults, to ask a question that may indicate our lack of knowledge or understanding or that reveals our confusions. Celebrate the risk taking students do. Say something like "Carlos, I'm so glad you asked what that text passage means. Making sure we understand before moving on is what thoughtful learners do."

  Teach and demonstrate how to create more open-ended questions (responses that trend toward multiple possibilities and explanations, which can expand learning) versus closed questions (responses that trend toward a "right" answer, a yes-or-no answer, or a quick answer, which can limit and shut down learning). Build on students' questions and inquiries to promote project-based learning opportunities, spark curiosity, and support students' interests and passions.

  Two excellent books for learning how to ask better questions in our lives and in schools are *A More Beautiful Question: The Power of Inquiry to Spark Breakthrough Ideas* by Warren Berger and *Make Just One Change: Teach Students to Ask Their Own Questions* by Dan Rothstein and Luz Santana.

- **Aim for students to eventually self-question** and self-direct the inner questioning that is a hallmark of reflective, self-sustaining learners. Perhaps create a criteria chart with your students for expected self-checking, as in the list in the text box on the next page.

Self-Questioning Criteria: A Sampling

- Do I need to reread this passage to be sure it makes sense?

- Have I understood the essence of what the author or speaker is trying to communicate?

- Have I drawn reasonable conclusions from the evidence?

- Are the sources or news I read (or viewed or listened to) and cited credible? How can I be sure?

- Are there other possibilities I have not yet considered?

- Can I figure out the meaning of the unknown word or concept by reading the sentences that come before and after it, using the visuals, or attending to clues the author provides?

- Where might I look to find the resources or information I need?

- Will the lead in my writing engage and orient my reader, or should I rewrite it?

- Have I provided enough background information for someone unfamiliar with the topic to understand it?

- Is this assignment or text ready to hand in? Have I checked it thoroughly so it's accurate, clearly organized, legible, and has my best spelling and conventions?

With demonstrations, shared experiences, and guided practice, even primary-grades students can be taught to ask and answer their own significant questions—for example, in their guided-reading groups, literature conversations, small-group work, peer talk, independent work, and self-evaluations. See, also, questioning as part of demonstration (page 142) and priority questions as part of planning (pages 87–88).

- **Take a risk and have students write an anonymous evaluation,** such as the following open-ended example.

Student Evaluation of Teaching and Learning

In terms of engagement, challenge, support, feedback, enjoyment, personal connection, having your voice heard, or anything that seems important to you:

- What has worked best for you as a learner?

- What do you wish I would do differently?

- What are a few actions I could take that might make your experience as a learner more satisfying?

- What other advice or comments do you have?

Thank you for taking the time to give me honest feedback. The purpose of the evaluation is to improve my teaching so that you can learn more effectively. Your comments will not be used for any other purpose.

Use students' responses to celebrate, strengthen, and improve your teaching and relationships. Consider giving such an evaluation several months into the school year and again near the end, to evaluate your impact. Listen for the wisdom of learners' collective voices. Also, the evaluation can be modified for feedback at the end of the school year with next year's students in mind. Note: a similar evaluation might be given to a mentee from the mentor teacher, to teachers by their principal, or to principals by their superintendent.

Endnote

Finally, I have told this story before, but it's an important reminder—as noted in the first paragraph of this chapter—of the need to take wisdom from children's voices. When a disruptive first grader offered his suggestions for a class shared writing-in-process, I wrote his mixed-up words exactly as he offered them, without judgment, on a blank chart adjacent to our class-written chart. He quieted down a bit, followed along in the lesson for a few minutes, and then raised his hand: "Would you write my name next to my words?" Such a simple and profound request; it took my breath away. He wanted only what we all want—to be seen, heard, and valued. Having his name next to his words made him feel that, like his peers, his words mattered, and for the moment that seemed enough for him.

Embracing the Reading-Writing Connection

A teacher recently told me she was not allowed to attend a writing workshop because the district would only pay for professional development related to reading. Despite the fact that reading and writing are reciprocal processes that nourish each other, this most logical of literacy connections is often overlooked and undervalued. You can't be a writer without being a reader, and extensive reading enhances reading comprehension and writing.

Writers write for readers and are always thinking about their audience and purpose; discerning readers read like writers and apply what authors do to their own composing process. Although the latest standards do not directly connect reading and writing, they do specify an integrated model of literacy: "The processes of communication are closely connected, as reflected throughout this document."[1]

Although the benefits of the reading-writing connection still have not been fully explored, recent research "results suggest that an individual can learn to read by writing as well as by reading and can learn to write by reading as well as by writing, as reading and writing involve some of the same subprocesses."[2] Another finding in the same research study, involving middle school students who are second-language learners, is that "for writing, the reading–writing connection seems more evident for those second-language learners whose language proficiency exceeds a certain linguistic threshold." In other words, students need a rich language bank to write well, which is common sense. Vocabulary and facility with language matter.

Without exception, regardless of grade level or content area, I begin my work in schools with the reading–writing connection. It's how I begin to bond with students and teachers. Most often, I read aloud an outstanding picture book—even to older students—one that I've specially chosen for my audience and the content of our upcoming work. Together we savor the beautifully written and illustrated text, its special features, its riveting story. We notice what authors do and carry this into our writing. I also share my reading and writing life and explain how I could not be a writer if I were not a reader. I show students and observing teachers my reading log, where each month I record the books I've read by title, author, and genre. (See sample, page 196.) With middle and high school students, I talk as well about the impact specific books and authors have had on how I read, write, and think.[3]

In kindergarten, in particular, the reading-writing connection is crucial for efficient and effective literacy and language growth, engagement, and enjoyment. As students are sounding out words as they write, they are trying out and cementing their phonemic awareness and phonics knowledge. In fact, looking at kindergartners' writing is a valid and easy assessment for determining their phonological awareness and skills regarding beginning and ending consonants and blends and medial vowels. In working with kindergarten classes, I see that in every case in which these children excel as readers and writers, the reading-writing connection has been fundamental to that success.[4] In such classrooms, what the children write becomes a large part of what they read. Student- and class-authored stories become texts for reading, enjoying, and embedding word work.

Embedding the reading-writing connection in all literacy work pays big dividends for students becoming discerning readers and writers. Applying the reading-writing connection in high-poverty schools makes it possible for most kindergartners to read and write well by the end of the school year. That success, when shared across the school, leads to higher expectations for what's possible at every grade level, kindergarten through high school. A smart move is to invite high school principals into unexpectedly high-achieving kindergarten classrooms and talk about insights gleaned that can apply to high school students.

Share Inspiring Stories

If we want our students to be excited about reading and writing, we must read, tell, and write interesting stories and texts to engage and inspire them. That's why the first thing I do when I work in a new classroom is to share stories. My favorite books, whether they are fiction or nonfiction, weave an engaging tale. I also tell stories from my life as a way to bond with students and teachers, and I enthusiastically pull out all the stops when telling a personal story. All writers are storytellers. Nothing holds students' attention like a well-told story. (See also pages 15, 77, 173, and 199–200.)

I held a third-grade class mesmerized when I told them stories of taking care of Percy, our son's family's anxious, rambunctious, and endearing dog. And when I wrote those stories down with great detail and mailed print copies to the class at their request, the students voluntarily read and reread them and begged for more. It's important to note that this kind of close reading (see pages 215–216), a current reading emphasis, is not just for informational texts. Students do read closely when they enjoy a text and want to know more. "Close reading is about rereading with purpose, including what is important in the text, what is confusing about the text, the multiple meanings of words and passages, and reading like a writer."[5] Reading like a writer is at the heart of the reading-writing connection.

Well-told stories appeal to people of all ages. It's fascinating and comforting to know that in Grenoble, France, short stories can now be downloaded for free in various public places. With the push of a button on a dispensing machine in places such as train stations, tourist offices, and bus depots, people looking to fill "the dead time of a commute" can choose one minute, three minutes, or five minutes of fiction printed out on rolls of paper.[6] How wonderful is that! And it's encouraging to note that requests for replicating the French process have poured in from countries all over the globe—including the United States and Canada.

 ## Take Action

+ **Seek out the very best nonfiction and fiction literature** and bring those texts into the classroom—as read-alouds, inspiration for further reading and writing, part of the classroom library, models for demonstration writing, and models for showing and noticing what authors do. I gravitate to nonfiction books so students can hear a great story and also increase their world knowledge and vocabulary.

Here are some favorite inspiring nonfiction and biography picture books that are suitable for both younger and older readers (see also page 212 for additional titles):

My Name Is Blessing, written by Eric Walters, illustrated by Eugenie Fernandes

Ryan and Jimmy: And the Well in Africa That Brought Them Together, written by Herb Shoveller

Nubs: The True Story of a Mutt, a Marine, and a Miracle by Brian Dennis, Kirby Larson, and Mary Nethery

Unlikely Friendships: 47 Remarkable Stories from the Animal Kingdom by Jennifer S. Holland

When Marian Sang: The True Recital of Marian Anderson, written by Pam Muñoz Ryan, illustrated by Brian Selznick

I Dissent: Ruth Bader Ginsburg Makes Her Mark, written by Debbie Levy, illustrated by Elizabeth Baddeley

Radiant Child: The Story of Young Artist Jean-Michel Basquiat, written and illustrated by Javata Steptoe

Check with a librarian or bookstore for other extraordinary picture books.

♦ **Choose stories that inspire hope.** Students who are living in poverty, are homeless, or face severe hardships need to hear and read true stories of people, like themselves, who overcame overwhelming odds. See the "I Can Do It!" booklist under Text Resources on the *Teaching Essentials* companion website for many excellent nonfiction picture books that present role models of people who struggled mightily but went on to make significant contributions.[7]

♦ **Include hip-hop, song, rap, dance, film, and other art forms and media** as effective nonfiction and fiction vehicles for storytelling and for learning sophisticated language skills. Our students today, even our youngest ones, are growing up immersed in all kinds of music, film, and multimedia presentations. Many students come to school "deeply rooted in the cultural practices, traditions, and mindsets of hip-hop."[8] So we need to learn from our students and engage them using the familiar modes that resonate with them.

Consider reading, rereading, and analyzing the lyrics and storytelling of famous singers and icons such as Adele and Bob Dylan, who was named the Nobel laureate in literature in 2016. Study hip-hop and rapper artist Lin-Manuel Miranda for examining, appreciating, and teaching the power of language and storytelling, and the relevance of history (see page 189 for more on Miranda). Another hip-hop group to consider is the Black Eyed Peas. Their songs "Where Is the Love?" and "I Gotta Feeling" lend themselves well to immersing older students in popular culture while presenting a positive message of social justice and finding happiness. Also, don't miss the riveting and inspiring girl-power video-song, "What I Really Really Want," advocating for girls' rights throughout the world and appropriate for high school students.[9]

- **Make storytelling central to life in classrooms and schools,** whether it's historical stories, family stories, great fiction, or other genres. Consider an area in a prominent place in the school where free short stories and poems are available for the taking, similar to the story dispensers described earlier. Of course, to be published, these would need to be well written, legible, and accurate. For why stories matter and ideas for how to bring them to life in our classrooms, see *Story: Still the Heart of Literacy Learning*.[10] See also StoryCorpsU, a terrific program and website for guiding middle and high school students to tell their life stories through an interview process, "... designed to help students in high-need schools find their voices and develop a sense of empathy."[11]

- Incorporate elaboration and details from oral storytelling when demonstrating writing; do not just write a bare-bones story. Put meat on the bones! To accomplish that, we may need to choose to focus on just one moment or part of a story when we write or create a podcast and encourage students to do the same. (See the final bullet on page 231 to access the link for embedded video with oral storytelling.)

- **Make parents and caregivers aware of the power of the reading-writing connection** for young children's literacy development. Encourage reading aloud, talking about stories, and writing stories. Recommend having writing tools (paper, pencil, pens, paints, or whatever is available in the home) and showing children how to use writing to communicate—composing notes, to-do lists, get-well wishes, and birthday greetings, as well as blogs, e-mails, and tweets. Emphasize the importance of a home library; it's well known that children who do well academically in school grow up with lots of books in the home.

In fact, having lots of books in the home is more closely connected to higher reading achievement than parents' education level or standard of living.[12] And, of course, being a reader greatly affects becoming a writer. Do whatever you can to get books for students who can't afford them. Encourage parents and community members who can afford to do so to donate money so that when there's a book fair every student can afford to buy or order a book. Check out First Book Marketplace for high-quality books greatly discounted for low-income students.[13] At the very least, we must guide families that cannot afford to buy books to make optimal use of their local public library. Also, be sure to recommend limiting television time and time with devices for all students.

Read and Write More Texts

Quantity and effort matter. *If we are able to assess all the pages students read and write, they're not reading and writing enough.* Students need to be reading and writing authentic and continuous texts for uninterrupted and sustained periods of time every day at every grade level and in every content area. Deliberate practice matters, along with choice and access. Research has unequivocally shown that students in high-challenge schools can become unexpectedly high-achieving when everyone—teachers and their students—are reading and writing numerous relevant and engaging texts each day, applying authentic and engaging literacy practices, and doing a minimal number of activities *about* reading and writing.[14]

Award-winning author Kent Haruf told his creative writing students:

> *There is no lack of talent for writing. But there is a lack of talent for hard work. Read everything you can get your hands on. Read, read, read. Write and write and write. Every day. Get black on white. Write what you know. Don't let other people overly influence your own voice. Listen to instructors or teachers but then let it all go and be true to your own vision and voice.*[15]

Quality also matters—a lot. What we read, view, and listen to influences how and what we write and create. "In order to have a chance of making great work, you have to consume remarkable work."[16] Here is where the texts we read aloud, have available in our libraries, and use for teaching language arts and content curriculum influence student thought and creations.

Take Action

- **Make sustained reading and writing time a priority.** It's in this deliberate practice stage that students get familiar with authors and their unique styles, attempt to apply what these authors and we are teaching them, experiment with language, figure out new vocabulary, notice what authors do, reread for clarity, gain fluency, build stamina and discipline, self-monitor, and ideally become their own best teachers. With older students, skillful content area teachers demonstrate for their students how they are focused on reading to understand content, and they support students to recognize and apply significant concepts, vocabulary, text features, and formats. Expert middle and high school teachers recognize and put into action that we must *all* be teachers of reading.

- **Revamp schedules for longer blocks of language arts time.** For middle or high school students, that might mean three to five days in a row devoted to reading, followed by three to five days in a row devoted to writing. That way, teachers have time to go deep and students have time for deliberate, sustained practice. In elementary school, integrating reading and writing in science and social studies—at least part of the time—works well. For example, in the lesson plan on endangered environment (pages 87–89), almost all reading and writing for about six weeks was centered on that topic of study.

- **Count the number of texts we read to and with students each day.** For younger students, aim for at least six to ten texts a day. A text is defined as a read-aloud, a shared reading, a rereading of a class-authored text, reading of student-authored text, reading of a chart, and so on.

- **Emphasize reading and writing authentic texts,** and minimize isolated passages and excerpts that lack sufficient context for understanding. Integrate reading and writing into math, science, and social studies. Seek out short texts, such as well-written editorials, letters to the editor, and blogs to read, analyze, and use as exemplars for student writing. Create with students math and science books that explain processes and concepts and propose problems for other students to solve. (See also "Read Like a Writer," pages 183–186.)

- **Embed grammar instruction** in authentic reading and writing. Formal, isolated grammar instruction has not been shown to improve reading comprehension or writing ability.[17] Students internalize most grammar through immersion in wide reading. Explicit grammar instruction before middle school is not generally useful.

Even then, only the formal teaching of combining sentences has been proven to affect reading and writing.

- *Avoid grammar exercises disconnected to meaningful writing.* Such exercises do not yield better grammar use. For example, instead of identifying nouns, verbs, and adverbs in isolation, focus on the application and correct use of nouns, verbs, and adverbs in speaking and writing.
- *Use student writing of authentic work-in-process.* Project student writing on a screen or make photocopies, with the student's permission, and demonstrate how to edit for grammatical errors. Read one sentence at a time. Ask, "Does it sound right?" "Is this how we'd see it in a book where we expect standard English?" "What do we need to fix?" Then, following the OLM (see page 136), have small groups of students work together to edit for grammar before expecting them to do it on their own papers.

- **Publish more class-authored and student-authored work.** Publish these into individual books and collections in various forms and formats that students can reread throughout the day and school year. Use Book Creator and other recommended technology tools to create nonfiction books, comics, graphic novels, poetry collections, and much more. (See Appendix D for technology tools and useful apps.) House class-authored and student-authored publications in the classroom library, and place the best of these in the school library (see photo, page 42). Share, too, on class and student blogs. Students can also publish work in their own Evernote account, creating a digital writing portfolio to share anywhere.

  As well, try a "zine," an eight-page mini-magazine made by folding one piece of paper, and an easy and engaging way for students of all ages to self-publish and share their ideas.[18] I have used this format for many years as an easy, affordable way to give every student a consumable copy of a text, song, or story to read, enjoy, and reread. Kids love these mini-books.

  For all learners, but especially for our English language learners and students who struggle, stories and texts about their lives, interests, and culture—in their own words—are always the easiest for them to read and understand. Bilingual books also work well here and promote both reading and writing. (See also page 235 for many more ideas for purposeful writing.)

- **Integrate art and music whenever possible,** and write about finished pieces— the processes and purposes—as a class and individually. Music teacher Randal Bychuk integrates music, art, and literacy by having his elementary students listen to notable music such as Modest Mussorgsky's suite of ten pieces, *Pictures at an Exhibition,* and then—collaborating with the classroom teacher and an art specialist—has students analyze the experience through interpretative movement, art, and writing (see also "Incorporate Music and the Arts" in Equity section, pages 369–373). Using the movement "The Old Castle," students analyze the arrangement, discuss the emotions evoked after listening, and then create a visual-art piece interpreting what they might see outside the old castle. This exercise extends into descriptive writing, with the writer imagining a person staring out the old castle window, what that person might see and how he or she might be feeling. The art and writing directly correlate to the musical integrity of this classical-music gem.

- **Save a variety of exemplary, student-authored texts** each year. Have students keep their "first edition," and then make a "second edition" (with students' permission) to put in the classroom library for before-school reading and independent reading time. At the start of a new school year, the classroom library will have a lot of student- and class-authored works available as high-interest reading texts and writing models.

- **Lessen summer reading loss.** At the end of the school year, send home booklets for each student with most or all of the class-authored texts and shared-reading pieces and poems bound together. Include directions for families that encourage rereading of texts for fluency and enjoyment. Seek out ways to ensure students participate in some type of summer reading program—for example, open the school library several times throughout the summer for book checkout. Also, find unique ways to encourage summer book sign-outs. Ensure that there are some type of roving libraries, such as book buses or book mobiles, in neighborhoods where access is limited; allow large numbers of books chosen by students to go home, and don't fret too much if some are not returned; and have community volunteers establish "Little Free Libraries" for students in neighborhoods where book access is limited. (See also Equity, pages 362–363.)

- **Make the reading–writing connection seamless.** Beginning in the primary grades, support students' writing with excellent reading texts. For example, if students are writing about planets, sharks, or plants, bring in well-written texts they can read to provide evidence, facts, charts, images, and ideas to support and enrich their writing. If such texts are unavailable, write your own with the students.

Integrate Word Study

The only way to "fit everything in"—because there are never enough minutes in the day—is to be as efficient as possible. Learning is faster and more likely to be long lasting when our students and we can see the value of the work and immediately apply what is being taught. Explicit daily word study, in the context of the literacy or content lesson, is a big shift for some of us, but most teachers quickly see the benefit—more learning that's relevant and that sticks.

Midyear in a kindergarten classroom, when students were learning about nutrition and their community, each student wrote a restaurant review that got sent to the local restaurant. Using vocabulary and concepts students had learned from our reading aloud of relevant books, examining real-life brochures and menus, and discussing personal experiences, we first wrote a restaurant review together on chart paper. On the first and second reading, we read it through line by line, and on the subsequent reading, we used a sliding mask to highlight high-frequency words such as "red" in our review of a Red Robin restaurant. The second day, the whole class read a word-processed copy of our class-authored review. Then we zeroed in on a few high-frequency words and, word by word, talked about the "tricky part," visually highlighted and studied each word for a few moments ("take a picture in your brain"), and had each child write the designated word on a whiteboard. The restaurant review, which we covered up for each individual word-writing assessment, was then uncovered as we reminded students, "Check yourself. Do you have it right? If not, fix it up." Just about every student could write—with some self-correction—the words *red, love,* and *food.*

 Take Action

- Post word walls in science and social studies for key vocabulary that students will be expected to read and write in a particular study. Use those words daily in speaking and writing. For older students, consider content area word charts for classroom word walls or personal reference. "No excuse" spelling words can be part of students' writing notebooks.

- Use individual whiteboards to have all students quickly write and read featured words. Include challenge words. In the aforementioned kindergarten restaurant reviews, *pizza* was our challenge word, and almost every student— midyear in a high-needs, half-day kindergarten class—spelled it correctly! They could all read *pizza* too. Examples of challenge words connected to content study that I've used in similar kindergarten classes near year's end are *oxygen, butterfly,* and *dinosaur.*

♦ **Expect students to self-check spelling** by using room resources such as charts and word walls, checking with peers, and looking at familiar texts. Teach, practice, and expect self-correction.

♦ **Create with the students, from their ongoing reading and writing, charts that conform to the word study in process**—for example, a chart of "ee" words or an important vowel combination, or words with specific prefixes or suffixes or important roots. Students can use sticky notes to attach words to the chart and, if the words are correctly spelled, add them to the chart. The same applies for charting with older students for teaching prefixes, suffixes, root words, etymology of words, and so on.

♦ **Highlight features of words in familiar texts,** using a document camera or a whiteboard, or on charts. Use a sliding mask to feature a word and to blend word parts.

♦ **Evaluate everything being taught in word work.** One quick and reliable way is to take a familiar text, such as a class-authored one (for example, our restaurant review), and give each student a word-processed copy. Read through the text as a whole. Afterward, direct students to circle designated words, turn their papers over and write those words, and then self-check and correct for accuracy. Send home such papers weekly and have students read the text to their family and talk about the text and their word-work learning.

Write Book Recommendations

We ask students to do a lot of writing about their reading. Some of that writing is useful and encourages deeper reflection. Some of it is not especially helpful for pushing students' thinking; that time might be better spent giving students more time to read. As in all things we become expert at, choice and practice play a big role, and choice in reading depends on easy access to excellent books and texts in various genres and forms. Knowing how and what to choose is also essential.

When I enter my favorite local independent bookstores, the first thing I do is head over to the book displays and walls that feature best-selling fiction and nonfiction as well as bookstore employees' favorites. The lure for me is the short handwritten book recommendation, which fits snugly underneath each featured book, with its full book cover facing outward. Almost always, after reading some of these recommendations, I can't resist buying a book or two. I justify the spending as doing my part to keep independent bookstores viable. I take on this buying responsibility seriously and joyfully. I also take advantage of sale books and am always on the lookout for great familiar titles I've not read—and sometimes, unknown books that reel me in with their enticing cover and back cover copy.

I'm personally a big fan of book reviews—especially the *New York Times Book Review* each Sunday—but for getting students to write about books they love, I favor book recommendations. They're short, easy to write, often handwritten, and are great advertising for letting peers and others learn about favorite books. (See one student's book recommendation on pages 181–182.) Best of all, they can be written quickly, and, if not overdone, they don't dampen students' enthusiasm for reading. Students need only include the title and author, the genre, their opinion about the book, and who should read it. Of course, legible handwriting, correct spelling, and editing are a given. Students and all writers need to respect the fact that when we write for readers, we have an unsigned contract to get the conventions right so the reader can easily focus on the message.

Think about devoting a classroom wall or school hallway to book recommendations. These need not be just for students at a particular grade level. Older students can write recommendations for younger ones, which can be especially validating for those older students who struggle as readers and writers. Teachers can write short book recommendations for their colleagues. Although, thankfully, many teachers no longer assign book reports, which have no real-world meaning for students, too often students are still required to do extensive writing about a book. And although some writing can cause students to deepen their understanding of a book, too much writing can kill a student's enthusiasm for reading. Our job as educators and parents is to entice kids into reading by ensuring we provide choice, access, and variety and keep pleasure and enjoyment at the forefront.

To recap, the main purpose of book recommendations is to get kids reading and enjoying reading. Along with my book soul mate, Toby Gordon, who is my most reliable source for recommending books I come to treasure, I also rely on the Sunday *New York Times Book Review* and a couple of other book-lover friends whose reading preferences closely match mine. That way I wind up spending almost all my precious reading time on books I love.

Name: Eva

Date: Jan 11 2017

Do you love fairy tales but crave a little action in your reading life? Well then the Land of Stories would be the perfect book for you! This fantasy for ages 8+ is action packed with suspense, mystery and surprises. Follow Alex and Connor's adventure to get back to their world. They race against the clock to find the ingrediants to the wishing spell, their only ticket home - and find that they have another competeto Chris Colfer takes you into another

A book recommendation by a fifth grader

> The
> dimension in ˅Land Of Stories: The Wishing
> Spell, the first installment in the Land Of
> Stories series. Available where books are
> sold.

 A book recommendation by a fifth grader (continued)

Take Action

- Read book reviews and book-related websites, frequent bookstores, and get to know librarians and seek out their recommendations. Find out what genres students prefer and share the latest and "best" books and texts. To teach reading well, we teachers must also be readers. Since 2007, I have been writing a semiannual blog, "What I'm Reading," which includes lists of favorite books as well as descriptive recommendations of several fiction and nonfiction books detailing why I've found these particular books outstanding (see regieroutman.org).

- Rely on social media. Consider following respected publishers on Twitter, authors who post about upcoming titles, and librarians and educators who recommend new titles for students and adults. Goodreads is a reliable site for finding books for readers of all ages. Recommendations include helpful lists of books by genre and reading interests. School Library Journal Blog Network (http://www.slj.com/slj-blog-network/) reviews quality literature for children and teens and houses the outstanding Classroom Bookshelf by Katie Cunningham, who reviews new books and provides a wealth of teaching ideas.

- Make available and accessible outstanding texts in various genres. Include picture books for younger and older readers, and outstanding fiction and nonfiction. Give brief book talks in a variety of forms and media to introduce new books and authors to students.

♦ **Present more book recommendations,** blurbs, blogs, book reviews, and other real-world book promotions to students. Once we have written some book recommendations together and established criteria with students, we can have them write short recommendations, give brief oral remarks, or create a one-to-three-minute podcast or video for potential readers. Save exemplars of book recommendations, including podcasts, videos, and book trailers, as models and choices for current and future students. I like the weekly *New York Times* author interview feature, "Tell 5 Things About Your Book"; question 5 is "Persuade someone to read [title of book] in less than 50 words." Consider accessing former author responses to give students ideas for writing concise book recommendations.

Apply the Optimal Learning Model (pages 140–144) to teach, practice, and apply how to clearly and effectively create persuasive book recommendations. To make book recommendations part of the school and classroom culture, insert one-minute oral recommendations into daily routines. Use whole-school announcements, a designated weekly classroom time, and social media such as Twitter and Instagram to highlight great books and entice readers.

Read Like a Writer

Because I write for readers, I deliberately notice what other authors do in terms of tone, voice, word choice, language play, all aspects of craft, setting, character development, how I'm affected as a reader, and so much more. So it's been a surprise to me how little of that we share with our students. We read aloud; we may write in front of our students; we talk about books; but in my experience it's rare for us teachers to make the reading-writing connection visible. Our students do not automatically think, "I'm going to try out in my own writing what that author just did." We have to explicitly demonstrate that transfer for them and encourage them to take risks and try out new styles, craft, and language.

As important as facts, research, and content are to my writing for educators, I continue to focus most of my reading on excellent fiction and narrative nonfiction. That's where I am most inspired by craft and where I derive the most joy. For books I especially enjoy and admire, I often reread them—or parts of them—to savor the language again, to enjoy the bliss that a well-told, well-written book brings me, and to get ideas for my own writing. Let students in on that secret.

I love what author Roger Rosenblatt writes: "I'm reading the book again for pleasure, and also to get its language into my system and steal from it the way writers steal. No fingerprints."[19] I savor his two words "No fingerprints." That made me smile; all writers, of course, borrow language from other writers. I sometimes use the sentence "And yet." in my writing to slow it down or make an important point. I happily stole it from author Christopher Hitchens.[20] The trick is to adapt and adopt language in a manner that creates fresh fingerprints—your own—while still honoring the original author by crediting him or her for any ideas, even two-word ones, such as "growth mindset" (Carol Dweck) and "collaborative expertise" (John Hattie).

Students need to know that it's okay to try on an author's style; all authors do it. Take the time when you read aloud to your students to occasionally stop, notice, and talk about what an author has done well and make the connection to students' own writing. Advise them when they read independently to pay attention to what authors do to capture and maintain the reader's attention. Encourage them to read like a writer and apply what they notice to their own writing. In particular, the craft of writing, which we learn from noticing and trying out what authors do, is not something students typically do on their own at any age. We have to repeatedly show them how to read like a writer and pay close attention to an author's language, style, voice, technique, organization, and so much more. It's been humbling to find out how hard all of that is to teach and do, but it's the icing on the cake for writing, the sweetness that not just holds the readers' attention but changes the reader in some way.

In too many schools, we don't focus on craft except in artificial ways such as teaching metaphors and similes and using a thesaurus to add lots of "vivid verbs" and "spicy words" that can often make the writer's voice sound artificial. Perhaps most lethal to a piece of writing is the prescriptive "adding details" to increase length regardless of whether or not those details enhance the writing. We also get a lot of lifeless writing these days that is overly focused on correctness, rigid form, organization, and mechanics and assigned without regard to authentic audience and purpose. Craft becomes an afterthought. But true craft is where the writing juice and engagement lie for the reader, the "I can't put this book down" feeling.

We teachers are rather adept at teaching kids the mechanics of writing—such things as starting sentences with capital letters, using correct punctuation, and indenting for new paragraphs—which, relatively speaking, are easy. But what we pay far less attention to, in my experience, is reading like a writer and crafting our writing with a reader in mind. Think about it this way. We can have a piece of writing with a beginning, a middle, and an end, and with perfect grammar and conventions. Yet if the piece is boring and the reader is disengaged and unmoved, that writing is a big "so what?" It's what the writing does for the reader that matters. That's why it's often best to just listen to a student's writing (as it is read aloud) without looking at the paper and prejudging it. Just try to discern and support what the student is attempting to do and say; put the writer before the writing.

 ## Take Action

- **Prioritize teaching the craft of writing,** not by doing exercises about craft, but primarily through reading aloud to students and making wide reading a high priority for our students and ourselves. It's immersion in notable authors' language in literary fiction, nonfiction, and poetry that inspires us. Ask any great writer what has been the greatest influence on his or her writing, and invariably the response highlights being an avid reader who has been affected by other writers.

- **Use exemplary texts and authors to demonstrate and notice what authors do.** Include student-authored texts. With our guidance, we can have students notice literary language, logical organization, engaging leads, satisfying closings, descriptive settings, effective transitions, and so on. Three questions can guide us:
  - ◉ *What did you notice the writer did?*
  - ◉ *What was the writer's intention?* (Or "Why did the writer do that?" Or "How did that affect you as a reader?")
  - ◉ *What might you try and apply to your own writing?*

- **Teach students to read like writers.** Occasionally, direct them to read for a literary or an informational device, such as an unusual, riveting lead or the use of visuals and organizational structure that provide additional information and text access. Or, during independent reading, occasionally have students mark with a sticky note a place where something the author did inspired them. Have them share with a partner. Celebrate when students try out a writing technique or idea they got from another writer, including a student writer.

  Students can also take snapshots of examples of craft they notice from their reading, using a tablet or a smartphone to share after reading time. Using tablets, students can air-drop their examples into one central location for sharing and discussing in small groups or as a class.

- **Use daily writing to teach reading to learners who struggle.** Students' own language and stories often become their most successful and enjoyable reading experiences, which can jump-start the entire reading process. Explicit word work can often be taught in the context of these texts (see pages 178-179). Encourage students to write for younger readers and think about what that younger reader needs, such as an enjoyable story, words and language the reader will understand, layout of words and illustrations on each page, captions, legibility, and so on. Then, find ways to have the student share the text with other students in an earlier grade—for example, having the student read aloud his book to a class or a small group, which can be a self-esteem builder.

Begin with Poetry

So much of what we want students to know and apply when they write in any genre is teachable through reading and examining poetry: titles, word choice, rhythm, style, structure, voice, closure, economy of words, organization, impact of our message on a reader—beginning in kindergarten. Reading a lot of poems can help students internalize grammar, the power of words, use of conventions, and the dramatic effect that changing the rules can have on meaning. Poems are often shorter than other texts, which can make them easier and more enjoyable for students to read, reread, analyze, and write. Poems also afford great practice in oral reading and fluency, especially when they rhyme. And, poems are open to interpretation; there is no one right meaning that resides in the poem.

Unfortunately poetry is often neglected in the reading-writing curriculum, despite the fact that exposing our students to poetry has great benefits that go beyond reading, writing, speaking, and listening. Writing is an act of discovery, and we remove that opportunity for students when we require rigid formats. Poetry sets us free to explore and break the rules. Poetry can also be a healthy outlet for our emotions and can promote trust, empathy, and connections with others. Noted poet Georgia Heard says, "Poetry is important because it keeps my heart open."[21]

When I want my audience to know me as a person, not just as an educator or a presenter, I write a poem in front of them or share a previously written poem along with my thinking-composing process. I believe we need to model what we ask and expect others to do, especially when it's risky and difficult. The other reason I choose poetry is to show how powerful connecting the heart with the mind can be in teaching, learning, and relating to others. So, dear reader, while I don't typically share personal feelings with people I don't know, here is a recent poem I wrote that was inspired by *What My Mother Gave Me*. It's a short poem, but it took me months to write it, as my relationship with my mother was loving but also complicated and incomplete, like so many important relationships.

Gifts My Mother Gave Me

It took me a lifetime to appreciate
the gifts my mother gave me

She died young, before I had become
the person I wanted to be

no longer absorbed with pleasing others
or hiding my truest self

finally embracing my mother's finest gifts,
her gracious way of being

her daily loveliness, patience and calm
even in adversity

her elegance, style and flair
in living and doing

her beauty and goodness, always on display
while sometimes masking her truest self

We played it safe, both of us
unable to shift our roles and discourse

from dutiful daughter and doting mother
to honest women and open hearted friends

leaving me with an abiding loss
for the mother I never fully knew

but also, at long last, with acceptance
and admiration for all she was

June 2017. Inspired by *What My Mother Gave Me: Thirty-One Women on the Gifts That Mattered Most* by Elizabeth Benedict, ed., 2013.

Poetry is also a terrific genre for equalizing writing success. Students who have been viewed as limited in literacy achievement often astonish us with their poems. Being able to write fewer words without concern for correct form and fixed rules frees up many students. Publicly celebrating students' poems can be a game changer for students who struggle, both for how they perceive themselves and how their peers view them. I have written a lot of books for teachers, but my *Kids' Poems* series are my most popular, best-selling books.[22] I believe it's because poetry writing engages kids, is doable and enjoyable, and everyone succeeds—and the same holds true for us teachers. Perhaps most significant for our students and for all who write poems is this: "Poetry means taking control of the language of your life."[23]

Poetry gives us a way to freely express our deepest thoughts, longings, curiosity, memories, and so much more. And poetry lives on. My husband Frank's favorite gift is the book of poems I wrote over several months for a milestone birthday. It touches me deeply that many years later he still keeps that book close at hand and rereads it often.

 ## Take Action

- **Do more poetry reading and writing.** Immerse students in free-verse poetry, notice and chart what poets do, and write some poems together before students write their own. Also, because many poems are short, they are excellent texts to use as writing exemplars and for rereading for fluency, analysis, and enjoyment. Consider expanding poetry writing beyond language arts into the content areas as one way for students to demonstrate their learning.[24] See *Rhythm and Resistance: Teaching Poetry for Social Justice* for excellent ideas and examples for taking political action through poetry.[25]

- **Consider beginning each day or class with a poem.** Read aloud a short poem that either a student or you have selected. It's a relaxing, engaging way to start the day or period, and it only takes a few minutes. Read the poem again and, perhaps, discuss how the poem affects the listener or what it means, or just enjoy the poem's language. For developing readers, we can sometimes project the poem as well and encourage students to follow along as we expressively go line by line and point to the words as we read. Acclaimed writer Kwame Alexander urges us to inspire our middle and high school students to read and write poetry by starting class with a poem we love. "Read it, recite it, play it, show it, let your students perform it."[26] Also, don't shy away from having students choose a poem to memorize and recite. Learning a poem by heart—not for testing or assessment but for pleasure—can be enjoyable.

- **Rely on free-verse poetry.** Most of the poetry in the world is non-rhyming, free-verse poetry. Rhyming poems are actually much harder for our students to write because so much energy goes into searching for the "right" rhyming word, often resulting in contrived, stilted poems.

◆ **Avoid overanalyzing poems.** Poetry is personal. Our own reactions to and interpretation of a poem are valid. Poems, like paintings, are art forms. Be cautious about coming to group consensus on what a poem means. I prefer to keep the focus on personal expression; an author's craft, such as unique use of language and form; impact on the reader; and enjoyment.

◆ **Introduce and encourage raps, hip-hop, and songs.** Lin-Manuel Miranda, who wrote and starred in *Hamilton*, one of the most celebrated musical shows of all time, spent much of his teenage years listening to records of hit Broadway shows. His consuming interest and constant immersion led him to memorize rhyming couplets and songs. He developed an intuitive and sophisticated feel for language and form that he put to spectacular use, creating a new genre that has garnered unprecedented appeal and acclaim. Encourage students to take their love of music and rhythm and create their own poetic forms—whether it's rap, hip-hop, free verse, or their own original form. Perhaps try cyphers, with students standing in a circle and taking turns contributing to the lines of a poem or a rap, one at a time. Collaborate with students to create unique forms.

◆ **Write a poem in front of students.** Do not write the poem out ahead of time and then present it as a perfect process. Prepare ahead by thinking about what you might want to say, jot down a few notes, and then have at it. When we take this approach, students appreciate the honesty of our struggle, our public thinking aloud, and our willingness to be seen as imperfect—all of which makes them more willing to take writing risks.

◆ **Read aloud early drafts of poems.** Reading aloud writing we've done affords us the opportunity to hear how the language sounds and whether or not we want or need to change words and phrases to get the rhythm we want, the lyrical feel, the intended meaning, and so on. Rereading poems or any writing is an effective way to improve oral fluency, emphasis, and expression. Asking students "Does it sound right?" or "Does it sound and look the way you want it to?" encourages rereading, revising words, and altering white space and line breaks to match the intended cadence and flow.

◆ **Encourage poetry writing as a presentation mode.** Use poetry writing and other poetic forms as a vehicle for demonstrating what students have learned. Poetry can be themed around endangered species, human rights, or any topic we are studying. View the YouTube video "Freedom Road," an original lyric video with call-and-response presentation mode, by third and fourth graders advocating for clean water for all citizens in their community.[27] Encourage middle and high school students to write free-verse nonfiction on issues that matter to them. Use acclaimed books such as *Brown Girl Dreaming* by Jacqueline Woodson and *The Crossover* and *Booked* by Kwame Alexander as inspirational models. Have students write "heart poems" to show love, appreciation, or gratitude to a significant person in their lives—for birthdays, holidays, or special occasions.[28] Hold a poetry reading for families and other classrooms, thereby increasing the audience and sense of purpose for the poetry writing.

◆ **Create poetry anthologies.** Put together with students a classroom poetry anthology, and make a second copy as a model for future classes. Poems by published authors—well-known poets and peers—can inspire students to write their own. You might begin by having students choose a favorite poem they wrote (even though it may not be your first choice) and get it ready for publication for a student-authored anthology that becomes part of the classroom library. Also consider putting together anthologies of favorite poems students love to read and reread. Use shared writing of poems in the early grades to practice reading as well as writing. Use individual binders students can add to, and create poetry collections for reading before school and for independent reading. Use a variety of art media, including oil pastel, watercolor, paint, or collage, to illustrate class poems and anthologies. (See Appendix D: Technology Tools That Help Support Schoolwide Literacy Learning for specific apps, such as Patext and GarageBand, to enhance publication.)

Endnote

Recently a group of knowledgeable teachers asked me to recommend a professional book for teaching the craft of writing. We had been collaborating for several years on improving the teaching of writing; students were writing reasonably well, but now the teachers wanted their students to be able to captivate their readers through artfully crafted writing. There was no "right" answer to their important question except one; in order to produce discerning and distinguished writers, we first have to ensure we create discerning and discriminating readers. You can't scam kids with junk reading—worksheets, fake books, poorly written texts, and test-prep materials—and expect them to become writers. They need the real stuff, excellent literature.

No shortcuts here. A professional book on how to teach craft won't suffice. Writers read—and read and read and read; and not just fiction. All my preferred nonfiction books have a narrative style—that is, those qualities that apply to excellent fiction writing and poetry apply to nonfiction as well. Want to teach high school students how to write amazing descriptions of character and place? Read aloud an engaging, superbly written book and discuss what the author does to mesmerize the reader. Unique and effective craft, style, and technique have to be inhaled and digested by an engaged reader who is immersed in one unforgettable reading experience after another.

Exercises in a book on craft might help us teachers know what to look for, but only deep, pleasurable reading and noticing what writers do will provide the sustenance and specifics that lead students to read like a writer and expertly craft their writing.

Teaching Readers

When I think of reading I think of pleasure, favorite authors, beloved books, libraries, bookstores, stories, and relaxation. I think of finding solace, of being suspended within the unique world a talented author has created. I think of language beautifully crafted and books so mesmerizing that afterward I want to tell other readers, "You've got to read this book." I do not think of levels, programs, grouping, or tests. Those are school things that ultimately do not determine who becomes a reader.

So let me say straightaway that although this chapter will deal with multiple aspects of *teaching* reading, those elements are in service to the desired end goal of helping students *be readers*. By readers, we mean those of us who choose to read for pleasure and information and to expand our worldview. By readers, we also mean those of us who read with understanding and appreciation for an author's craft, style, and unique ideas while also using our own background, experiences, and knowledge to interpret what we take away from our reading. And let's be honest here. Being a reader means we read, value, and cherish books. Of course, we also read news, research, blogs, song and rap lyrics, recipes, and more—often via social media and online; and we read magazines and journals of all kinds; but the mother lode is books. Plain and simple, books are the currency of being a reader.

If that last statement sounds presumptuous, consider the facts. Students who have more books in their homes do better in school and are more likely to earn more income over their lifetimes.[1] Students who have access to libraries read more, and how much one reads connects to growth as a reader.[2] My unscientific survey of noticing what people are reading on planes when I travel is heartening; more people are reading actual books than reading on a device. More significantly, sales in brick-and-mortar bookstores are on the rise for the first time in a decade; independent bookstores are rebounding and thriving; on-demand printing and binding of books from digital files is now a growing reality.[3] Reading books, an old technology, has actually become cool in our digital age. Yes, teens still do cling to their devices for social networking, taking and sharing photos, playing games, light reading, and more. However, given the choice, the overwhelming majority of teens and all students age 6 to 17 prefer paper books to e-books.[4]

Maybe it's because we're so often in a hurry, and we find reading a book to be a leisurely, slowed-down experience, an experience we secretly crave. At least that's true for me. Reading on the Internet can cause me to feel a bit frantic and jittery. There's so much material out there, I'm often overwhelmed with what and how to choose. Still, I do read quite a lot online—mostly perusing, scanning, and skimming, what is often called "light reading"—in a daily attempt to stay informed and up to date in all areas of my life. For example, reading online—primarily via Twitter—has been crucial to me for keeping up on the latest research and thinking while in the process of writing this book.

Still, when I want to save and savor a social media post, an Internet post, or a new research post, I print it out and read it in full. I read more deeply with the printed paper in front of me. Along with many others, I prefer the intimate feel of paper, the permanence of it, and the ease of returning to reread a passage and mark it up should I choose to do so. Perhaps most important, I feel more mindful reading on paper, page by page, as compared to scrolling down a screen often littered with pop-up ads and other distractions. In fact, recent research comparing print and onscreen reading by university students from around the world confirms that reading printed text is more likely to lead students to concentrate better, think critically, and learn more[5]—all of which are significantly important for understanding and analyzing complex content.

Reading also provides respite. Writing this book, for example, has been the usual combination of challenging, exhausting, and fulfilling. At some point in the day, usually by late afternoon or after dinner, I pick up a book and disappear into the author's world. This call-to-read feels as strong as my hunger for food, friendship, and love. In fact, the many books I read sustain me and give me a life beyond work. Beautifully crafted stories—both fiction and nonfiction, as well as poetry—satisfy my need for total escape, peace, knowledge, and entry into a space where anything seems possible.

Regardless of the content we teach, we need to establish a reading culture in our classrooms that promotes reading and readers. See Appendix F: Removing Roadblocks to Reading, for ways to ensure we are prioritizing what works for developing avid readers.

Be a Reader

Letting our students know we are readers and sharing our reading lives and habits with them is essential for turning them on to reading widely for pleasure and information. For some students, we may be their only reading role models. We must all assume responsibility for ensuring students understand content through teaching vocabulary, concepts, summarizing, interpreting infographics, and much more—regardless of the age level or subject matter we teach. Yet we cannot become expert teachers of reading—across the curriculum—without being readers ourselves.

Even if you do not yet see yourself as a reader, it's never too late! Start with short books, picture books, graphic novels, poetry, or anything at all recommended by a reader you admire. Or get to your local library or bookstore, 'fess up, and ask for some hand-holding in choosing a few books to read. Not only will you be enriching your life, you'll become a better teacher of reading because you'll be an insider to the process. My hunch is you will not be recording the number of minutes you read, timing yourself for speed, stopping to look up vocabulary, or answering questions in writing. You will be too busy being lost in a book!

Not only that: consider the strong findings of a recent study, which concluded that reading books is good for our health; those who read more books live almost two years longer than nonreaders.[6] Consider also that thoughtful leaders are readers. Former president Barack Obama attests to how daily reading has been a lifeline for him. Reading books gave him perspective, context, escape, and empathy and also made him a more thoughtful writer.[7]

 ## Take Action

- ◆ **Set aside time each day for personal reading.** Best times for me are late afternoons, before bedtime, or on weekends, especially rainy ones. Carve out a daily time and make reading, even for short periods, a priority. Then, consider keeping a reading record (next page) to ensure reading at least one or more books a month, and negotiate with your students to keep a similar record.

October 2016

✱ Originals: How Non-Conformists Move the World by Adam Grant
nonfic, studies & stories

✱ Nutshell by Ian McEwan
fiction

✱ Sing For Your Life: A Story of Race, Music, and Family
by Daniel Bergner
biography, inspiration

Excellence Through Equity: Five Principles of Courageous Leadership to Guide Achievement for Every Student
by Alan Blankstein & Pedro Noguera
professional

A page from my monthly reading record

- **Consider reading young adult books.** Talk with teenagers and see what they're reading and what they recommend. Follow their lead. Edgy young adult books are often as well written, gripping, and inspiring as any adult fiction. A few personal standouts include *Eleanor and Park* by Rainbow Rowell, *The Fault in Our Stars* by John Green, and *The Absolutely True Diary of a Part-Time Indian* by Sherman Alexie.

- **Try poetry.** If you're put off by length and appreciate poetry, book-length prose poems can be wonderful. A few favorites that are suitable for upper-intermediate grades through high school and joyful for us adults as well are *Brown Girl Dreaming* by Jacqueline Woodson, *The Crossover* and *Booked* by Kwame Alexander, and *Out of the Dust* by Karen Hesse.

- **Share reading choices with colleagues, too.** Our students love it when we bring our reading lives into our classrooms and talk about our favorite books and authors. Invite principals, teachers, and students to do the same. Create a book-reading culture. Prioritize talking about books, celebrating books and authors, and being a reader. Say, "I'm currently reading such and so. What are you reading?" Reserve a school wall space for posting what adults are reading. For my book recommendations with commentary, see my semiannual blog posts at www. regieroutman.org. (See also "Read Professionally," pages 121–123.)

- **Share personal reading habits and actions with students.** We can share with our students how and why we select books, sometimes abandon them, learn about new authors and illustrators, strategize to understand content and characters, talk about books with friends and colleagues, make time to read, decide what to read next, and so on.

- **Consider audiobooks.** John Norton, editor of MiddleWeb, describes himself as "an Audible addict who reads while walking the dog, shopping at the local superstore, and driving hither and yon."[8] I know many teachers who listen to books as they drive to and from school and find the power of storytelling relaxing and informative.

- **Believe it's never too late to become a reader.** This mind-set is especially important for readers of all ages who struggle, whether it is with decoding, fluency, motivation, or comprehension. "A great deal of research confirms that readers can improve dramatically in reading at any age, including adulthood, if they have access to interesting and comprehensible reading material."[9]

STORY ❖ Becoming a Reader

My earliest memory of reading was seeing my mother quietly reading, day after day, in the pale light of late afternoon. I envied her that zone of peacefulness and privacy and knew not to disturb that sacred time. She tried to invite me into that world by insisting I read old-fashioned classics such as When Knighthood Was in Flower, *first published in 1898. She handpicked similar masterworks at our local public library, and I resisted every one of them. I have no childhood memories of learning to read in school, of being read to at home, or of enjoying reading. Other than romantic comic books, which I savored well into my teens, reading was an unpleasant chore, something that had to be done whether one liked it or not.*

I was 15 before I formed my first unforgettable reading memory. It stems from an overnight with my grandmother. She read aloud Gone with the Wind *by Margaret Mitchell with such emotion that I was spellbound. I finally got it! So this was what reading and hearing great literature could do for the mind and spirit—transport me to another era, enable me to enter the fascinating and complicated lives of different characters, prompt me to rethink my own hopes and desires and become so thoroughly lost in a riveting story that time stopped and nothing else mattered. I was drawn in to savor the sounds and rhythms of well-crafted language—and I was hooked for life.*

I became an avid and discriminating reader. Reading became as necessary to me as breathing. Today I read for many reasons, including relaxation, curiosity, and to learn about the world around me—I want to be a knowledgeable citizen. How do I find the books I most enjoy? I rely on the Sunday New York Times Book Review, *friends' and colleagues' raves, bookstore recommendations, book sale browsing, and books written by authors I love. Of all the possessions in my home, I am most proud of my walls of books, the books I buy because I have to have them—not just to read but to touch, rearrange, revisit, cherish, and lend. Those books define me—fiction, nonfiction, professional books—and say much about who I am, what I value, and what kind of reader I am.*

Reading continues to keep me grounded, relaxed, invigorated, and joyful. My mother would be proud. I spend many a late afternoon and evening lost in the pages of a book. I bring my reading interests and passions into the schools where I teach. I always introduce myself to students through great books. I choose the books for students as carefully as I choose for myself and base my choices on their interests and curiosity. "I'm so excited, kids. Have I got a book for you!"

I open the book and begin to read aloud. Soon the room goes silent, and I can see that students are engaged. A great book has once again worked its charm and captured listeners' hearts and minds. And afterward, as always, I hear a chorus: "Will you read it again? Can I read it?" The reading magic has begun, and it is contagious.

Read Aloud Every Day

I almost always accompany meeting a new group of students and teachers with a beloved book, and most often it's an inspiring, nonfiction picture book. Gathering the students in front of me, I let the children and teachers know why I brought "this book" just for them. As I begin to read aloud, the students and teacher are quickly captivated by the work of a brilliant author and artist, their eyes riveted on each page, heads leaning in to listen to every word and examine each illustration or photograph. It is through fascinating stories and great books read aloud that I bond with students, an indispensable first step in reaching them and teaching them. "Reading to someone is an act of love."[10] Stories bring people together and humanize us.

Every time I work in a school, I bring books as gifts for the school and classrooms. Most of these are picture books that I choose carefully, often with the help of a librarian or children's book specialist at one of my local independent bookstores. I read aloud not just to K–12 students but also to teachers, principals, and other school leaders—in schools and at workshops. Taking the time to read aloud is a necessary pleasure. It slows us down, relaxes us, and reminds us of the joy and inspiration of a well-crafted story.

Here's a well-kept secret. It's not just kids, including teenagers, who love to be read aloud to and benefit from it; we teachers love it too. No matter how tight on time I am when facilitating a professional learning meeting at a school, I try to begin or end—or both—by reading aloud. It gets people settled, relaxed, content, breathing more easily. It shows us why reading matters and the power of a masterful story. A great book inspires, informs, and delights. Being read to puts us in a frame of mind for learning and increases literacy achievement.

Children of any age who routinely hear books read aloud score higher on national and state literacy tests.[11] These students are not just more proficient readers who delight in stories; they are often excellent writers with wide vocabularies at their disposal. Literacy informs and inspires their daily living. Not only that: repeated reading aloud of storybooks accompanied by opportunities for discussion strengthens children's vocabulary, comprehension, critical thinking, and ability to retell a story.[12] As well, focusing on storytelling provides an oral language foundation and can improve academic vocabulary, especially important for second-language learners.

So I always begin by reading aloud. I read aloud to students not only to bond and forge relationships with them but also to ignite lively discussions, jump-start a study in a content area, establish and improve the climate of the classroom community, inspire their writing, introduce them to great authors, and spark intellectual development. I deliberately choose challenging books, keeping in mind that students can listen to and understand books well above their instructional reading level. In fact, teachers are often surprised at how long an engaging book will hold students' attention.

A wonderful picture book working its magic through reading it aloud

Yet, teachers tell me they have no time in their busy schedules to read aloud. District requirements such as daily "focus lessons" on word work, grammar, and vocabulary—mostly taught as exercises with worksheets—as well as pressure to teach to standards and do well on high-stakes tests have leached the joy out of teaching reading. So I demonstrate: Here's what it looks like, sounds like, and feels like to be enthralled by a marvelous story read aloud. Slow down. Be enchanted. Great readers and writers are inspired. They have heard and discussed great stories, including the vocabulary, word crafting, informational background, learning about the author, and so much more—especially critical for students who come to school without a strong literary heritage.

In a residency in a diverse school where I read *Nubs: The True Story of a Mutt, a Marine, and a Miracle*[13] aloud to first graders, observing teachers were flabbergasted that these students, most of whom struggled with reading, not only understood this complex story with some difficult vocabulary; they enthusiastically listened to it in its entirety in one sitting, and they loved it! They applauded loudly when it was done. Following our discussion of *Nubs*, we did a shared summary writing of the story with the purpose of posting it in the hallway to encourage others to read the book. The classroom teacher later worked with the whole class to turn that summary into a Readers Theatre, with groups of three to four students each repeatedly reading and practicing a couple of lines until all could read them fluently. The end result was a two-minute, whole-class video, beautifully and proudly performed by all the groups and then shared with the whole school. As well, one student who was not a confident or successful reader wrote his own excellent summary of *Nubs* at home and proudly brought it to school to share with us. His teacher noted it was the first time he had ever taken the initiative to produce text on his own.

It's not easy to be a teacher these days. The demands and pressures are unrelenting. Reading aloud is a salve on our open wounds; it heals, soothes, and comforts, and does so without overwhelming effort.

 ## Take Action

- **Prepare for reading aloud.** Become familiar with the book and rehearse well; practice the cadence of the language, pacing, tempo, facial expressions, tone of voice; plan stopping points and teaching points.[14]

- **Make reading aloud a daily ritual.** If possible, do it several times a day, even if you have just five minutes to spare. Consider reading aloud for a peaceful end to the day. For kindergarten and first grade, keep track of the number of texts read aloud, and aim for at least several texts a day. Some texts we read aloud can be very short—for example, a class-authored paragraph, a morning greeting, poems, news items, jokes, and more.

Create opportunities to also read aloud news articles, book reviews, blogs, and exemplary student work. Occasionally project and enlarge some read-alouds so students can read along or follow along with their eyes. For younger students, track the print with a pointer or line marker. Reread favorite stories and encourage dramatic play and re-enactment for favorite, well-known stories.

- **Maintain a reading-aloud flow.** Don't feel guilty reading a book all the way through without stopping to ask questions. Use common sense. Stop only when it makes sense to question and talk about the book. Reading—and listening—for understanding requires concentration, engagement, and momentum. When we interrupt the flow with endless questions, we impede optimal learning and enjoyment.

- **Apply the research on the benefits of reading aloud.** Children are never too young or too old to benefit from hearing books and texts read aloud. Listening to stories stimulates imaginative thinking and creativity and helps children develop visual images, learn more vocabulary, and gain exposure to unique and complex book language.[15] As previously noted, reading aloud also increases language development and reading achievement. Reading aloud storybooks has the potential to increase students' comprehension and critical thinking.[16] Share the research with parents and caregivers.

- **Seek out inspirational picture books.** Because picture books are short and often inspirational, they work well in the classroom and for beginning or ending staff meetings in a relaxing manner. Several personal favorites for reading aloud to both students and educators are *On a Beam of Light: The Story of Albert Einstein* by Jennifer Berne, *What Do You Do with an Idea?* by Kobi Yamada, *Courage* by Bernard Waber, and *Breathe* by Scott Magoon. Some books and authors provide additional information through updates, sequels, documentaries, lesson plans, other texts, websites, or videos. Google the book's title and author to see what's available. Also, check with a librarian for the best in informational picture books. These days, I almost always bring nonfiction books to read aloud, especially when we are combining the language arts with content area study.

- **Introduce authors, illustrators, books, and series.** Read aloud the first book of a series, which often inspires students to read other books in a series. Or sometimes read aloud a compelling book and stop when interest is high. Or stop at the end of the first chapter and read no further. Students always want to know what happens next in a good story. Try to have several copies of the book on hand to encourage students who want to borrow the book and read on, which can also inspire collaborative book talks and book clubs.

Do include appreciation for talented artists and illustrators, including graphic and comic book illustrators, to inspire student art. A few notable picture book examples include the work of Lois Ehlert, *The Dot* and *Ish* books by Peter Reynolds, Eric Carle's books, and *Flotsam* by David Weisner. Seek out books by winners of the Caldecott Medal, awarded annually for best American picture book for children.

♦ **Solicit students' suggestions for read-aloud choices** for picture books, novels, short stories, informational books, and more. Elementary through high school students appreciate it when some of their favorite books become whole-class read-aloud books. Consider keeping a dated written record of read-alouds. Students love looking back on our read-aloud history.

♦ **Consider a yearlong theme or common thread.** For example, if the school or classroom focus is on kindness, bullying, rights of the child, forgiveness, the changing environment, and so on, choose a variety of read-alouds around that topic. These related books provide familiarity with a set of texts to refer back to and help to create a common foundation upon which students can build. Consider also becoming part of the annual Global Read Aloud: One Book to Connect the World (https://theglobalreadaloud.com/) where, internationally, teachers choose to read aloud the same book and make global connections with other classes.

♦ **Make students aware of the way authors choose and use language.** Guide and encourage readers to notice what authors do, including student authors, and to try some of those things out in their own writing. (See also pages 183–185.)

  ◉ *Stop occasionally and reread something an author has done well.* Say something like, "I just have to read this part again. Listen to how the author's lead, or beginning, hooks the reader right away. I can't wait to read on. Take a look at the lead in your story and make sure you pull your readers in."

  ◉ *Direct students' attention to a particular focus.* For example, before independent reading time, we might say something like "Today, when you're reading on your own, pay special attention to a place where the author describes a setting (or a character or an event) so you can picture it. You may want to attempt something similar in your own writing." Once in a while, have them mark that place with a sticky note and then take time to have students read and savor some of those passages aloud—to the class, in a small group, or with a partner.

◆ **Promote reading aloud by families, regardless of students' ages.** Many parents tend to stop reading aloud once children can read on their own, but reading to older children creates a strong family bond and can introduce them to the wonder of language in all types of texts and genres. Occasionally encourage young children to draw or illustrate what they "see" as they are listening to a descriptive or favorite passage.

Make Independent Reading a First Priority

One of my most popular tweets ever was this one: "Make daily indep reading #1 priority & work backwards from there. Use think aloud, guided read, shared read to support that end."

Despite the fact that most of us do know that wide, self-selected reading is a necessity for becoming a reader, we don't routinely put that knowledge into daily practice in our schools. We understandably get sidetracked and overwhelmed by mandated programs, standards and assessments, curriculum requirements, guided-reading groups, test prep, skills work, and more. It's no wonder sustained time for reading is so often the first to go when we are pressed for time.

And yet. Our students will only become fluent, comprehending readers who develop deep engagement, stamina, competence, content knowledge, and self-monitoring abilities if and when we prioritize free-choice, independent reading every day. Also very significant, wide independent reading is the primary source for most vocabulary acquisition.[17]

One of our core reading beliefs must be that uninterrupted self-selected reading is a necessity for becoming a reader. Then we must put that belief into daily practice by allotting a minimum of twenty to forty minutes a day for it, depending on the age and increasing stamina of our students. I worry that reading enjoyment and getting lost in a book are not seen as worthy school goals. We must work to change that. Kids today spend so much time "reading" their phones via Facebook, Twitter, and countless apps that we need to make sustained, deep reading a regular part of daily school life.

Children who become great readers read voraciously. As teachers and parents, we need to be careful not to derail kids' curiosity and interests with early restrictions. With freedom of choice and our gentle guidance, our students eventually move toward higher ground in reading. I believe it's because I spent so many years reading "lesser fare" through my teenage years—comic books and lowbrow popular series—that today I gravitate toward very well-written fiction and nonfiction. My own experience has led me to encourage teachers and parents to let kids choose to read any genre or form that interests them, whether it's comic books, graphic novels, or online texts. At the same time, we want to continue to read aloud great literature regardless of the child's age and to make engaging texts readily available.

Easy access to interesting books and time to read them in schools are a necessity, especially for children from low-income families who may not own many books or have access to a neighborhood public library. Evidence suggests that most US high school graduates today lack the reading proficiency necessary to meet the challenges of higher education and the workplace.[18] Although increasing poverty of school-children is seen as one probable cause, I would humbly suggest that another might be that time for voluntary reading becomes increasingly scarce as students go through the grades. You can't get good at reading if you don't read.

A caution here: just setting aside time each day for students to read may be fine for some students, but almost all need and benefit from having us do some monitoring of their reading to ensure they comprehend, self-correct, self-direct, set reasonable goals, and enjoy the books they are choosing to read. Keep in mind that for 90 percent comprehension, students need to be able to read texts with 95 to 99 percent accuracy, a crucial marker as most of the skills that proficient readers acquire are through self-teaching during voluntary, independent reading.[19] Therefore, independent reading time must include—as needed—teaching and coaching on book selection, applying word-solving and comprehension strategies, and discussing and analyzing the text. Most of that monitoring and feedback occurs during reading conferences. (See "Rely on One-on-One Reading Conferences" later in this chapter, pages 222–225.)

Independent reading works well when students:

- Have easy access to a wide range of interesting and readable texts.

- Know how to choose engaging books they can read and understand.

- Have sustained time and opportunity each day to read and talk about books.

- Know how and when to apply self-correcting and self-monitoring strategies to make sense of text.

- Confer with the teacher to ensure that understanding and enjoyment are occurring.

- Receive useful, actionable feedback for how they are doing as readers.

Take Action

- **Learn from expert teachers who get students to love reading.** Educators such as Donalyn Miller, Teri Lesesne, Franki Sibberson, Nancie Atwell, Kelly Gallagher, Penny Kittle, Laura Robb, Cris Tovani, Pernille Ripp, and others have done groundbreaking work in getting kids to read by ensuring engaging books are easily available and accessible. See their websites for their publications and blogs; connect with them through Twitter and Facebook. Soak up and apply their good ideas, not just for reading but for writing too. For one excellent example of a blog with some of their ideas, see "6 Simple Ideas to Get Kids to Read."[20]

- **Make few requirements.** If we want students to read and love to read, let's not mandate number of minutes to read each night, recording number of pages read, or extensive written responses. Our responsible intentions can backfire by undermining the desire to read. Keep in mind that as kids go through the grades, recreational reading declines. Make reading logs voluntary. I have students keep a reading history, similar to what I do (see page 196), and together we negotiate what to include. Also promote self-assessment (see page 330).

- **Put into practice the research on libraries, becoming a reader, and free, voluntary reading.** The quality of the school library is positively connected to literacy development. "Research also suggests that access to a good school library can offset, to a large extent, the negative impact of poverty on reading achievement."[21] As well, my teacher research over many decades confirms that outstanding classroom libraries, established with students for easy access, choice, and student interest, increase the amount and variety of reading students do. (See pages 48–51, 262, and 363 for more on classroom libraries.)

  Be sure to also share with colleagues, administrators, and parents the research that concludes that "in-school, free reading" leads to better reading progress, more reading even years later, and more positive attitudes about reading for most students.[22] My teacher research also shows results are strongest with a school culture that prioritizes daily, independent reading as described in these pages. "It is time spent actually reading that often distinguishes proficient from less proficient readers."[23]

- **Assess classroom libraries.** Whether we teach elementary, middle, or high school, I believe books need to be prominently displayed in our classrooms with most book covers facing out and a comfortable, inviting environment that advertises "We love to read." *Self-check.*

- *Are the books in our libraries captivating* and culturally relevant? Do they include titles and genres that will appeal to all types of readers?
- *Are books organized with students,* with consideration for access, readability, and choice for all?
- *Does the collection respect and honor students*—their preferences, interests, language skills, and reading abilities? Do we have sufficient titles for second-language learners—for example, some bilingual books and books in Spanish?
- *Is the collection well balanced* between fiction and nonfiction genres, and does it also include poetry?
- *Is the sign-out process easily manageable by students?*

- **Teach students how to select "just right" books.** I strongly believe that classroom and school libraries need to be organized like our public libraries, where we don't level books or limit student choice. At the same time, we need to ensure students are choosing books they can read and understand and that these are plentiful. Too often, developing readers and readers who struggle cannot find books easy enough to read. In teaching students to choose books they can read, apply the Optimal Learning Model and show and think aloud how to select a book that meets this standard: the reader can read at least 95 percent of the words and can tell someone what the book is about. Ensure students grasp that reading is about understanding, not just decoding and fluency.

Demonstrating to first graders how to choose a "just right" book from their classroom library and reading a few pages to ensure understanding

Poor readers' progress is delayed when they read texts that are too difficult for them.[24] They are unable to benefit from the purposeful practice and self-teaching—qualities of proficient readers—that occur when students can decode almost all the words, figure out unknown vocabulary, and grasp the concepts, information, and overall message. All of that said, be flexible about what makes a book "just right" for a reader. For example, a book that is a bit challenging might work if the child's background knowledge and motivation are very strong.

• **Get to know students' preferences.** Early in the school year, informally survey students for their reading histories, interests, and preferences. For reluctant readers who often have difficulty choosing a book, we may need to put a book in their hands and say something like "I chose this just for you because I know you like _____." Also, to widely expand students' choices to current and out-of-print books, consider POD (print-on-demand), which allows quick printing of a single copy or small numbers of a book via digital printing technology.

• **Adopt a mind-set that values massive free reading.** This belief holds for students of all ages and is particularly important for students who have not been successful early in their school careers and for high school students who have had little opportunity to read for enjoyment. If we make interesting reading materials available and accessible and teach students how to read them, the child can "catch up" anytime[25]; this statement also holds true for second-language learners. "In other words, 'once a good reader, always a good reader.'"[26] That means for some students, we may need to find out what their passions are and then write original reading materials with them.

A caution here: students do have to know how to read independently before we have them self-selecting books and spending lots of time reading on their own. Otherwise students can waste precious time as "fake readers," holding the book in their hands and turning pages, but without any real understanding. Here's how elementary teacher Trish Richardson guides book selection: "I have a set time for different groups of students to switch and pick up books. I often sit in the library and watch and guide the initial book selections. I also check in regularly with the students and their book selections to make sure they have balance."[27]

• **Value and promote audio texts.** Some students find it easier, at least occasionally, to follow a professionally narrated story, digital audiobook, or podcast that they can just listen to without worrying about decoding or fluency—and some audio recordings can be adjusted for speed. Significantly, audiobooks can transform elementary through high school students who have struggled with reading into students who see themselves as readers, as they finally have access to understanding and discussing the same engaging and high-quality literature as their peers. For English language learners, combining audio and text makes reading easier and more interesting for them. Make iPods loaded with high-interest books and headphones available during reading time.[28] Try e-readers, such as Epic and Reading Rainbow, that will read to students.

- **Be flexible with student choice.** Let's not limit students' selections to only what we deem appropriate. Teenagers love edgy books, some of which might not meet with everyone's approval, such as *Looking for Alaska* by John Green and *The Kite Runner* by Khaled Hosseini. That said, we need to give students the tools to analyze controversial books. Also, allow students the pleasure and freedom of reading more than one book at a time, at least some of the time. Years ago I recall telling students they needed to finish one book before they could begin another. Yet that's not what I do as a reader. In the past month, while writing this book, I've had three books going simultaneously, and I've read each one for different purposes, at different times of the day, in different places. My available time, mood, purpose, and attentiveness as a reader determine which book—or other reading material—I pick up.

- **Limit rewards.** Reading incentives such as special prizes are common for getting students to read more books or move to a program's higher level. Although these can be motivating in the short term, research has shown that in the long run such rewards work against students' desire to read and their enjoyment of reading.[29] Make sure reading is its own reward. Showcase favorite books in the classroom; promote book talk that students lead; allow more library visits; add compelling books that pique students' interest and curiosity to school and classroom libraries; and encourage families and communities to donate books to classroom and school libraries to celebrate special occasions and accomplishments or to show gratitude for their child's education or local public school.

Choose and Use Excellent Nonfiction and Fiction

The most critical piece for teaching reading well—that is, having students understand, enjoy, and self-monitor their reading—is the "right" text, and today that text might be digital. So it's important we take care when selecting books, texts, and websites for content area study, guided reading, literature discussion, writing models, and reading aloud. Be cautious about overrelying on preset levels, core reading programs, or textbooks, which may have been written exclusively for a school audience rather than a real-world audience and can work against creating readers. We need to examine texts ourselves and with our colleagues to determine their readability, suitability for engagement, authenticity, connection to students' lives and cultures, accuracy, language use, and potential to lead to deep and meaningful thinking and discussions.

We can't teach a first-rate reading lesson with a second-rate text, just as we can't effectively teach craft in writing without outstanding literature. Neither can we teach well and deeply in the content areas without primary sources and reliable resources that are accurate, well written, and appropriately challenging. Although it can be daunting to keep up with the most current and relevant texts that best suit our goals and purposes, we can consult websites, librarians, news media, bookstores, colleagues, and social media for recommendations. Then we can use our read-aloud times, demonstration lessons, whole-class and small-group work, and reading and writing conferences to show how authors and texts work (see "Create Access to Complex Texts," pages 215–217).

Current reading emphasis has shifted to a greater use of informational texts and complex texts. The Common Core State Standards for college and career readiness recognize that to do well in our complicated world, we need to read and understand more nonfiction. In fact, for most of us adults, nonfiction reading accounts for the majority of the reading we do. For example, in addition to print nonfiction books and daily newspapers, I also read directions, recipes, research, reviews, professional journals, articles, and so on—in print or online formats. Recognizing the importance of nonfiction, I often begin our literacy work in a residency with informational texts—those we read to students, those we write together, and those they research and write through our demonstrations, shared experiences, and guided practice.

At the same time, I continue to be a devoted fiction reader and worry that fiction may be deemphasized in our zeal for more informational reading and writing. Let's not underestimate the power and potential of fiction for helping students make sense of their world and develop the critical thinking skills that a well-told story can provide. It is, in fact, the close reading of fiction and understanding of complex characters and life situations that have helped me become a discerning nonfiction reader and more compassionate person. History is about his story and her story, and the nonfiction that most resonates with me is a beautifully told story with one or more central characters that I get to know and understand. In fact, close reading and deep understanding of fiction help prepare students to read and grasp the complex texts they will increasingly encounter in nonfiction forms and formats. Also, not to be minimized, reading literary fiction encourages us to empathize more with others.[30]

Award-winning fiction writer Charles McGrath reminds us of what fiction can do for us:

> *Here was a book that performed that special trick of fiction, the one that never gets tired. It lifted me out of myself, my grumbling and my self-pity, and in language just like the language we use every day, only better, dropped me down in another place and among people far more interesting, who had more on their plate than just a stack of books.*
>
> *I remember thinking, this is what reading used to be like: fun. I sat there for hours, getting up only once or twice, and finished the book before supper—in time to start another before going to bed.*[31]

It will be up to us to ensure fiction maintains its rightful and critical place in our curriculum and teaching, right alongside nonfiction.

 ## Take Action

Note: Because, for many teachers, teaching students to read nonfiction texts rather than fiction is a newer emphasis—and many say they find nonfiction harder to teach—the suggestions that follow prioritize informational texts but are applicable to all texts.

◆ **Use content-rich informational texts to teach comprehension.** Be aware that students' reading achievement in the elementary grades does not automatically transfer to middle and high school, most likely because of the increasing demands for specialized content and academic vocabulary in the content areas.[32] My teacher research also suggests that, in general, elementary students have not received sufficient and expert teaching and practice in learning how to read and comprehend nonfiction content.

Go beyond books and textbooks. Check out useful sites such as Newsela, TweenTribune, Wonderopolis, Google News Archive, and DOGO News for finding engaging, unique, and meaningful texts.[33] These sites also provide teachers and students free access to some excellent articles that can be used for current events and argumentative writing models. Also, don't neglect outstanding informational picture books, even for high school students.

◆ **Choose relevant portions of text for teaching.** Use online texts in shared and interactive read-alouds to demonstrate and model our thinking and expectations for reading (see pages 144–146). That is, while reading aloud or teaching a concept in a content area, occasionally project or distribute copies of a text portion so it is clearly visible for all students. (Copyright law does allow copying of a small portion of text for educational use. An advantage of paper copies is that students can make notes, underline, circle, or use other notations to help their comprehension.) Then guide students to do similar work with a partner or small group before expecting them to independently do the task.

- *Teach strategies,* such as these:
  - ☐ Use surrounding context to figure out vocabulary and concepts.
  - ☐ Substitute a word or phrase that makes sense and read on.
  - ☐ Determine what a paragraph is mostly about.
  - ☐ Pay attention to evidence the author presents and check for accuracy.
  - ☐ Detect key details in print, images, and infographics and notice how they influence meaning.
  - ☐ Observe and utilize how transitions orient the reader to a new idea.
  - ☐ Notice and name how text structures such as cause and effect, compare and contrast, and well-placed visuals increase meaning.
  - ☐ Incorporate knowledge and experiences to increase text understanding.

- *Assess during the learning process*:
  - ☐ How did you figure that out?
  - ☐ Find the line, chart, visual that shows _____.
  - ☐ Where does it say/confirm that?
  - ☐ Reread thus and so to find out _____.
  - ☐ Tell your partner in one sentence what that paragraph is mostly about.
  - ☐ What is the author's purpose in writing this text?
  - ☐ What are the key points the author is making?
  - ☐ What evidence supports those assertions?

An outstanding resource for teaching students how to read nonfiction texts is *Diving Deep into Nonfiction, Grades 6–12: Transferable Tools for Reading ANY Nonfiction Text* by Jeffrey Wilhelm and Michael Smith.

- **Incorporate nonfiction picture books**—some of which are biographies—to increase oral language, background knowledge, and academic vocabulary, and to spark interest in science and history. Teens who read and hear real-life stories of scientists are more likely to become interested in science. *Snowflake Bentley* by Jacqueline B. Martin and Mary Azarian and *The Tree Lady* by Joseph Hopkins and Jill McElmurry are but two of many excellent picture book examples.[34] Another one I love is *Women in Science: 50 Fearless Pioneers Who Changed the World* by Rachel Ignotofsky, suitable for upper-elementary through high school. For two inspiring picture book biographies of female US Supreme Court justices, see *I Dissent: Ruth Bader Ginsburg Makes Her Mark* by Debbie Levy and Elizabeth Baddeley and the bilingual book *Sonia Sotomayor: A Judge Grows in the Bronx* by Jonah Winter and Edel Rodriguez.

◆ **Keep teaching for strategies in perspective.** Become a teacher-mediator; that is, do whatever is possible to help make the text and its meaning accessible to students. Remember, we must all be teachers of literacy, regardless of the subject we teach, and accepting the responsibility to develop a strong foundation in general literacy instruction is a mind shift for many. Make the content and subject of the text central to strategy teaching, and keep the focus on understanding. For the most part, there is no need to teach strategies in isolation. Notice what you do as a reader. As readers, we apply strategies interactively, not one at a time. For example, try reading just to make connections, and notice that at the same time, we infer, summarize, question, use prior experience, and so on. When meaning breaks down or before assigning a complex passage or text, apply the Optimal Learning Model; demonstrate and practice with students what strategy or strategies can be applied—and connect the teaching to the content.

◆ **Teach rereading and slowing down.** Rereading is probably my number-one strategy when a passage is unclear. Sometimes the only strategy that works is to slow down and start again from the beginning of the sentence, paragraph, page, chapter—and sometimes the book. Many learners who struggle will read on whether or not they understand the text. Rereading a well-known text, such as a class-authored shared writing or a favorite book, also makes it easier to practice and achieve fluency, stamina, and greater comprehension. Selective rereading— for example, in a content area—may be the only way to achieve complete understanding and the "deep reading" state in which we fully immerse ourselves in the language, perspectives, sensory details, and analysis of the text.

  ◉ *Demonstrate rereading* as a powerful strategy for slowing down and thinking more deeply about a text, when both reading and writing.

  ◉ *Encourage repeated readings* of texts by students for gaining greater understanding of words and passages. Let students know research supports that strategy.[35]

- ◉ *Use partner reading* of natural-language texts to lead to improved reading competency and stamina, which is helpful especially for students who struggle and second-language learners.
- ◉ *Use Readers Theatre* to create texts from familiar stories to perform for peers. Doing Readers Theatre well requires multiple re-readings.

◆ **Teach reading print and digital texts.** Teens do much of their reading in digital spaces, and it's our job to teach them how to read critically in print and online, especially as more textbooks are e-textbooks. Still, demand for paper textbooks is expected to remain high despite the growing use of digital content. Recent results suggest that print readers demonstrate higher reading comprehension than digital readers.[36] And, in fact, for academic reading, many students prefer reading paper textbooks, which allow them to easily go back and forth between pages, rather than reading and scrolling down a screen.[37] We can only be effective teachers of reading in all modes if we ourselves are discerning readers. We need to pay close attention to what we do as readers to comprehend, and demonstrate and share our process and thinking with students.

Teach students of all ages how to do the following with print and e-books:

- ◉ Figure out word meanings (e-books often have a pop-up dictionary that shows pronunciations and definitions).
- ◉ Determine accuracy of a book or digital source.
- ◉ Self-question and strategize when meaning is unclear.
- ◉ Interpret charts and other visuals.
- ◉ Highlight and take notes (reading on a Kindle or other e-reader makes it easy to highlight words.)
- ◉ Summarize and analyze information.
- ◉ Decide when and how to apply deep, close reading strategies to a text or portion of text.

◆ **Teach students how to fact-check news stories.** In our fragmented media world, legitimate journalism and accurate sources are more important than ever, so it's imperative that we teach students how to evaluate the sites they are accessing for legitimacy and accuracy. Fraudulent news accounts, especially in online news websites, proliferate and spread virally in our social media age. Inaccurate reporting makes it a necessity that we teach students to be vigilant about how and where they get their news and facts. Misinformation and propaganda are skillfully packaged, and social media sites are not typically edited for accuracy.

♦ **Expand the definition of texts and reading to include multimedia.** Incorporate video, audio texts, documentaries, infographics, and other visual and audio platforms to explicitly teach how to view, "read," listen to, and analyze messages that various media, visual, and audio forms provide. Also, with the help of a librarian, seek out excellent nonfiction texts that integrate art or music or both.

Create Access to Complex Texts

I have been teaching reading for more than four decades—as an elementary classroom teacher, a certified and experienced reading specialist, a Reading Recovery teacher, a teacher of students with learning disabilities, and a mentor teacher. One thing I know for certain: matching students with texts they can read and understand is crucial. Marie Clay's groundbreaking research taught us many years ago that steady diets of books that are too hard make readers regress, not progress.

So although the latest standards emphasize that all students read complex texts—a worthy and important goal—I'm concerned we may be expecting students to tackle complex texts before they are ready. As well, the recommendation that students do multiple readings of a complex text and figure things out for themselves with little guidance is off the mark if the text frustrates students.

The best preparation for reading increasingly complex texts is wide background knowledge gained through successful experiences listening to, choosing, reading, investigating, questioning, discussing, and understanding a range of fiction and nonfiction, other genres, and authors. We teachers provide some of those experiences for students (see the second bullet item in the Take Action segment on page 217 that follows) but, mostly, as students become increasingly adept as readers, we continue to guide and support them to read and comprehend more intricate texts. However, we educators must first be discerning readers of complex texts ourselves and be able to think aloud and explain how we problem-solve and grasp difficult concepts before we can effectively teach our students to do the same.

Take a close look at close reading. Another critical point: with a greater emphasis on informational texts, *close reading* has become the expected norm for reading complex texts. *Close reading* is a current term for a familiar concept, what many of us used to call analytical reading. Analytical reading meant raising deep questions about the text and the author, inferring different levels of meaning, recognizing the author's purpose, examining text structure, figuring out vocabulary, and noting evidence to support claims—all of which first needed to be modeled, practiced, and discussed with the teacher. Then, as now, careful rereading plays a major role in such analysis.

According to the Common Core State Standards for Language Arts, close reading involves determining what the text explicitly says, making logical inferences from that text, and backing up those thoughts with evidence from the text. The text rules; making claims and inferences that also take into account our experiences and prior knowledge is not considered relevant, which I personally believe defies common sense and what we know to be true about effective teaching and effective reading. As discerning readers with varying experiences, ". . . we are thrown into conversation with the text."[38] Relying solely on the text for interpretation is not what readers do.

Our purpose always determines how we read, whether that purpose is to enjoy a text on our own terms, to analyze it for a classroom discussion, or to comprehend it on a deeper level. Often when reading, it can be more appropriate to skim, scan, or read just once. Sometimes we combine leisure reading with close reading; that is, we are going along, fluently reading for pleasure, when something in the text causes us to want to slow down and reread, analyze, think more deeply about the text. So it's important to clarify what we mean by *text*. Educator Heather Dean writes:

> *Our definition of text needs to expand to include not only written text, but also maps, political cartoons, photographs, art work, book covers, magazine covers and even advertisements. Students struggle to interpret "these" texts and close reading is an avenue for discovering the layers of understanding within visual text as well written text.*[39]

Not all texts deserve or need a close reading. Close reading and complex texts are not the end goal. It's reading for pleasure and information, always with the intent of understanding and coming away from a text somehow enriched, more curious, learned, and satisfied. When we focus on teaching close reading—or even on close listening—let's be sure we keep the awareness on important ideas, what those ideas mean, and why they matter. We also need to give students ample time for consideration and discussion of those ideas.

 ## Take Action

♦ **Advocate for and receive professional learning** that explicitly demonstrates how to read, question, analyze, and deeply understand weighty texts. That expert modeling must follow the same Optimal Learning Model we use with students and include shared experiences, guidance, and lots of practice. One recommended way to begin is with a schoolwide "book study." Rich and lively discussions with colleagues have the potential to raise deep questions, intelligently consider complex issues and ideas, encourage self-reflection, and develop teacher confidence for leading similar analytical discussions with our students.

♦ **Provide access for all students to increasingly complex texts** through daily reading aloud, thinking aloud, filling in needed background knowledge and explanation of crucial vocabulary and concepts, and, especially, demonstrating and fostering the habits, behaviors, and strategies of competent readers to the whole class, small group, and individual. Much of this access happens in the necessary frontloading stage of teaching—for example, in shared reading and shared read-aloud, discussed in detail on page 212.

♦ **Ensure students get daily, sustained reading practice with content-rich, relevant, age-appropriate books and other texts** that have just enough challenge so students can successfully figure out words, concepts, infographics, and text meanings. Without sustained practice with meaningful texts that students can read with at least 95 percent accuracy and 90 percent comprehension, comprehension will remain superficial. Also ensure that for most complex texts, students have the opportunity to read on paper. As previously noted, multiple studies show that our reading comprehension is usually better on paper than on screen.[40]

♦ **Emphasize reading for meaning right from the start.** Reading the world begins at birth. Reading to learn begins the moment a child interacts with a text. Use shared reading experiences, guided reading, and, especially, one-on-one reading conferences to ensure students understand what they read and are not just pronouncing words.

♦ **Encourage close reading, when appropriate, through questions.** One way thoughtful teachers encourage close reading is by the depth of the questions they pose to students and the questions they teach students to ask themselves as they read. If those questions are trivial or overly focused on details and isolated facts, or if the text isn't well organized, well written, and worthwhile, close reading is not necessarily beneficial or the best use of students' time.

♦ **Rely on silent reading.** Although oral reading is necessary and appropriate for emerging readers, we often focus too much time on it once students become readers. When the purpose is comprehension, students need to read silently to give their full attention to making meaning.[41]

Put Guided Reading in Perspective

Guided reading is out of control in many educational settings; instead of being an effective and temporary means to developing independent readers, it has often become the end goal for teaching reading. Many teachers ask, "How can I fit in all my guided-reading groups today?" before considering "What are the most important actions I can take today to move these students forward as readers?" and "How can I provide students uninterrupted time to read?" Equally troublesome, too often teachers assume most of the responsibility for doing "the work" so students fail to acquire the strategies and competence they need to successfully read on their own. So it's important we're clear on the realities and goals of guided reading.

Guided reading is most often defined as meeting with a small group of students at a similar reading level and supporting them through a manageable text. Group makeup is said to be fluid and flexible, but the reality is often quite different. Many students remain in their same ability groups all school year.[42] As well, structures such as "walk to reading"—in which elementary students leave their home classroom and teacher each day to be taught reading in another classroom with students at similar levels— are still flourishing. The research on ability grouping is unequivocal: results for both low-performing groups and advanced students do not justify the practice, with the impact on minority students—who are more likely to be placed in low-ability groups and classes—being especially detrimental.[43] Even when guided reading is done well, we have to be diligent in not making it the main reading event. Always, we must put the reader before the teaching of reading; that is, have a mind-set that we are teaching readers, not just guided reading.

In guided reading, the student is in charge and doing most of the reading work. The handover of responsibility has already occurred (see OLM chart, page 138). The teacher is checking to ensure the student can read the guided-reading text with at least 95 to 98 percent accuracy and with fluency and understanding. The teacher's role is "guide on the side"—nudging, scaffolding, prompting, encouraging, and explicitly teaching as necessary—so that when the student is reading on his own, which is well over 90 percent of the time, he can self-teach. That is, he knows, for example, how and when to problem-solve, self-monitor, self-question and reread, figure out vocabulary, determine the most important ideas, access useful resources, and interactively apply those strategies to understand the text.

Using the definition just presented, guided reading expands to encompass, for example, a one-on-one reading conference, a small group of students tasked with collaboratively reading and responding to a news article, or a literature discussion.

What is key is that students are expected to do the majority of the thinking and strategizing in this guided practice, learning stage. Then, during independent reading time—when students are expected to successfully read and comprehend on their own—they are well prepared for sustained, deliberate practice, acting as self-directed readers who effectively problem-solve, apply, learn, and extend what we have been teaching.

 ## Take Action

- ◆ **Self-assess the incorporation of guided reading.**

  - ◉ Does our guided-reading time mostly involve actual reading of high-quality texts?

  - ◉ Do selected texts include sufficient emphasis on nonfiction?

  - ◉ Are we personally checking that a book's designated level is accurate and appropriate for this particular group?

  - ◉ Are students able to read at least 95 percent of the words on their own so they can focus on meaning?

  - ◉ Are the texts we are using well written, well organized, culturally relevant, and engaging for our students?

  - ◉ Are most of the vocabulary and information in the texts comprehensible for our students?

  - ◉ Once students can read (usually by the middle to end of first grade), is most of the reading silent?

  - ◉ Are we connecting skills and strategy teaching and application to the act of independent reading?

  - ◉ Are students doing most of the reading work during guided reading?

  - ◉ Does the guided-reading group last between ten and twenty minutes?

  - ◉ Do most follow-up activities involve more reading?

⊛ Does our management system for what the rest of the class is doing result in students becoming better readers? How do we know?

⊛ Are we prioritizing comprehension and self-monitoring during independent reading—that is, using guided reading as a supportive means to that end?

If you answered "no" to any of the above, reconsider how you teach guided reading. Think of guided reading as the guided-practice phase of the Optimal Learning Model (see page 138), and remember to focus on whole-part-whole teaching. If we are teaching discrete skills in isolation, we are probably making reading harder for students.

- **Be picky about the process for choosing books and other texts.** Among other factors, consider language usage, vocabulary, background needed for understanding, length, format, and layout—for example, picture book or nonfiction text with infographics. Consider also genre demands, text complexity, relevance, authenticity, and interest level. Try to have at least two selections available, so if one turns out not to work with a particular student or group of students we have an alternative ready to go. As already noted, do not overrely on designated levels (see pages 209–210). With emerging readers, English language learners, or students who struggle, we may need to write some of these texts with our students in order to fully engage them and ensure successful reading outcomes.

- **Be cautious about teaching skills in isolation,** which is inefficient and ineffective for raising readers. As an example, many students who are drilled at the word and sentence level never do become fluent readers. They often don't understand or care why fluency matters, and they don't apply the skills-in-isolation training to the whole process of reading. Seek to apply whole-part-whole teaching. (See pages 271–275 for rationale, research, and ideas.)

- **Don't get caught up in a book-leveling frenzy.** Leveling is not a proven scientific process; it is, in fact, a subjective, complex act that requires professional judgment. Keep in mind that "instructional levels are not the same as instructional needs."[44] Although assigning books levels can be useful for guided-reading instruction and students not yet able to independently select books they understand, do organize classroom libraries—with students—by authors, categories, and subjects. Just as they would in the public library, allow students to choose.

◆ **Do not overrely on core reading programs.** The most comprehensive analysis of the major core reading programs conclusively shows, among other findings, that such programs do not adequately teach comprehension, teach too many skills and strategies, move too quickly from one skill or strategy to the next without sufficient practice time, and disadvantage readers who struggle by expecting them to read texts that are too difficult.[45] Therefore, it becomes a necessity for us teachers to fill in the holes and know how to teach reading comprehension in depth.

◆ **Ensure that time for carefully monitored, sustained reading practice is a daily priority.** Guided-reading groups often go on too long, often lasting for about thirty minutes, which means there will be scant time left for actual reading. As well, sustained reading time is often the first activity to go in the language arts block when we run out of time. Consider scheduling that precious independent reading time first.

◆ **Increase the number of opportunities and amount of time students have to read, respond, and participate in productive conversations** about the texts they are reading. Encourage partner reading and small-group discussion.

◆ **Limit oral reading for older readers.** Although oral fluency is a good predictor of reading comprehension for young readers, it is not a valid predictor of comprehension for older readers. Research has shown that "reading texts at high levels of oral reading accuracy is more important for beginning readers than for older and more accomplished readers."[46]

◆ **Consider having students write brief responses to a comprehension question.** Ask vital questions, such as "How was the problem solved?" or "What's the most important thing we've learned so far about ____?" or "What evidence does the author cite to back up ____?" Using small notebooks for this purpose works well. Having students record brief responses as a comprehension check is also important when we assign further reading, because once we ask a comprehension question orally in a group and one student responds, we don't know if the others "got it."

◆ **Reexamine management practices during guided reading.** Be sure that the management of what the other students are doing while we're with groups is not the main emphasis, overtaking our planning and teaching time as well as our reading priorities. Managing the management must be easily workable and worthwhile for our students and us. Too often, especially for readers who struggle, workstations or seatwork waste students' precious learning/practicing time with unproductive activities.[47]

♦ **Assess the learning.** Whatever activity our students are doing while we're with a group, we must have a way to evaluate their learning. It is not enough that students are working on-task; we must know if and what they are learning and ensure they're engaged in worthwhile tasks and activities, not "busy work."

Rely on One-on-One Reading Conferences

<u>*Put the reader before the reading*</u>. I'll never forget Maria. I wasn't supposed to have a reading conference with her. In fact, I wasn't really supposed to "see" her at all. She was a fourth grader in a high-poverty school, an English language learner who was still struggling with decoding and was reading on a first-grade level. Responsibility for her instruction had been mostly handed over to a literacy specialist who took her out of the classroom during language arts time for thirty minutes each day. In my residency work in schools, I insist that all students be present, so, because of that requirement, Maria was there for the entire morning. When I asked the students in her classroom "How many of you are fake readers?" Maria's hand was the only one that went up. "Maria," I told her, "because you're the only one who is courageous enough to tell the truth, you're the first person I'm going to have a reading conference with."

During that one-on-one conference, I was flabbergasted to realize that she could barely read. She had been in that school for several years, and in spite of caring teachers and the fact that she had been sitting with books every day for sustained periods of time during independent reading, she couldn't read anything but the very simplest text. Here is a crucial point: *deliberate practice without effective teaching and coaching doesn't guarantee growth*. In fact, students can stay stuck for years without much improvement.

After just one reading conference, Maria began to make huge gains. The things that propelled those gains were being honest with her, noticing and naming her strengths first, pinpointing her most pressing needs, setting immediate short-term and long-range goals, treating her as a reader, and providing the explicit instruction she needed. In Maria's case, that instruction centered on decoding and word-solving skills with applied practice reading engaging books. Her listening comprehension in our whole-class read-aloud and discussion, along with her ability to infer meaning from the little she could read, indicated good comprehension. After that conference and with renewed support from her teachers and the school and continuing support from her mother, she began to make rapid progress. Her whole demeanor and outlook changed. She—and her teachers—finally saw her first as a developing reader rather than a student with learning and language issues.

Tell the truth. I never lie to students. Our students and their families have the right to know the achievement realities and possibilities. If we are caring, transparent, tactful, and supportive in our language and motives, honesty really is the best policy. And telling the truth is not just for students who struggle. I will never forget a reading conference with Robert, a confident sixth-grade student who was speeding through complex chapter books. It was only through a one-on-one reading conference, assessing for deep understanding, that I learned he was a shallow reader. He never stopped to reread or clarify meaning. He could talk about plot but had only superficial understanding of a book's major themes or why characters behaved as they did, all of which I told him. I also said, "Robert, you're a straight-A student and your test scores are high, so it's likely no one will ever know you can do better. But you will know." Several months later he sought me out to let me know he had taken to heart my advice to slow down and read for greater meaning. With a huge smile he told me, "I'm loving reading now, and I'm taking my time. And I'm learning and understanding a whole lot more."

Make reading conferences a priority! Use the time set aside for daily, monitored, independent reading. It is during this sustained practice time that students cement the strategies and techniques we've been demonstrating and guiding them to try out and apply to their daily reading. The best way to know if students are deeply comprehending is to sit side by side with them, observe them reading silently—as we read along in the same text—and probe the depth of their understanding with thoughtful questions. (See guidelines for reading conferences, page 225.) Then we can truly ascertain what students know and need to know and plan next steps and goals. Again, already stated but important enough to be restated, do not over-rely on levels to assess reading progress. Although reading levels and computerized tests can provide easy-to-get-data, we can easily be lulled into a false sense of complacency with numbers that move upward while students continue to spend time with books they minimally understand.

Make conferences manageable. In conferring one-on-one with students, consider roving conferences two days a week for quick check-ins with many students, but devote most of the time to several in-depth one-on-one conferences. In middle schools and high schools, where large numbers of students are a reality, try public reading conferences a couple of days a week. These work very much like public writing conferences (see pages 243–245). Be sensitive about choosing students who, with their permission, would feel comfortable conferring with peers looking on. For video examples of one-on-one reading conferences, see Note 48 in this section.

For optimal comprehension in any reading conference, have the student bring in a book-in-process or recently completed text. Because almost all the reading we do in the world is silent, except in the case of beginning readers, have the student read a page or two silently—while we read the same pages silently and also observe students' behaviors and actions. Plan to record in detail the content and results of the conference; do it on the spot. Share the information with students and their families and keep it as part of ongoing, formative assessment. Most of all, keep uppermost in mind that when the student leaves the reading conference, we want him to be motivated to go on reading, to enjoy reading, and to see himself as a reader. Without that outcome, any teaching or coaching we did in the conference won't matter very much.[48]

 ## Take Action

- **Undertake a comprehensive assessment.** Important factors to assess for deep understanding and self-monitoring include, but are not limited to, the following:
  - *Choosing and accessing appropriate and readable text*—reading level, content, layout, organization, genre, interest, strategies used in selection of text, knowledge of author and genre, going beyond the "five-finger test" (where the student holds up a finger for each word she can't read or understand on a page; four to five fingers up indicates book is probably "too hard.")
  - *Reading with fluency* and at a suitable rate, connected to type of text.
  - *Figuring out unknown words*—applying word study and word-solving skills.
  - *Summarizing.*
  - *Inferring meaning* that is backed up by text evidence and experiences.
  - *Handling of unknown vocabulary, concepts, and infographics.*
  - *Having a plan of action when meaning breaks down,* such as rereading or seeking and using appropriate strategies and resources.
  - *Understanding character development,* motivation, and change—in fiction and in biography and history texts.
  - *Determining, retrieving, and consolidating important information.*
  - *Backing up claims and opinions with evidence* from the text.
  - *Self-evaluating reading strengths and needs* and setting important next steps and goals.

Conduct a Reading Conference: Some Guidelines

During the conference:

- Ask student to silently read a passage (one to three pages) of a book-in-process, or just completed—ideally a self-selected text to ensure optimal comprehension.

- Take notes on appropriateness of text, reading habits, strengths, and needs.

- Read along silently with student, and write down what you observe and also what you might want to question.

- Note the time started and approximate reading speed (number of pages read in three to four minutes).

- Check for subvocalizing, finger pointing, and pacing.

- Watch body language.

- Note if student rereads to figure out vocabulary or passage meaning.

After the student reads:

- Focus first on naming student's strengths.

- Have student read orally only if comprehension is missing, to check book's appropriateness and readability and student's word-solving skills.

- Ask questions to check for understanding on varying levels.

- Set most important next steps and goals for and with student—for example, rereading before going on when meaning is unclear—and discuss these with student.

- Have student restate his or her strengths and reading goals before leaving the conference; eventually, with guidance and practice, student sets own appropriate goals.

Endnote

It's not an exaggeration to say that one reading conference has the potential to profoundly affect a child's life. I'll always remember my conference with Kathy, a reader who struggled mightily due to limited word-solving skills but who still managed to pick up the gist and big ideas from the text. Her strong comprehension was also confirmed by her participation in class discussion during our interactive read-aloud. We celebrated that strength and others before talking about any learning needs. By building on her strengths, raising expectations, and targeting daily instruction to her needs, Kathy's competency gradually grew and her goals for herself expanded.

I kept in touch with Kathy for many years, mostly through e-mail but through phone calls as well. When she was in high school, she decided she wanted to become a lawyer to help underserved children. She confirmed that our reading conference changed her life because it was the first time she saw a "glimmer of possibility" for what she might become.[49]

Becoming a reader can do that for students; it gives them hope, opens up new worlds, and makes future dreams possible. It may well be the best gift we can give them.

Teaching Writers

I am a writer. It took me decades to feel comfortable saying those four words. Years of traditional schooling left me feeling I wasn't good enough or smart enough. I can still hear the stinging words of a fellow teacher when I told her I was writing a book for teachers. "What do you know?" (Not enough, apparently.) "What have you ever written?" (Nothing really, except some personal poems.) That feeling of not being legitimate, of not being a "real writer," remains an indelible memory. It's why I always "see" and celebrate the writer first—what the writer is attempting to say and do—no matter how limited those efforts or marks on paper may appear.

It is also through writing, especially writing poetry, that I discovered and clarified new thoughts and ideas about myself as well as the world. Becoming a writer allowed me to see how writing is integral to thinking. Former president Barack Obama said writing allowed him to sort through "a lot of crosscurrents in my own life—race, class, family . . . and integrate all these pieces of myself into something relatively whole."[1] Once we teachers recognize writing as a great tool for working through our beliefs and deepest thoughts and making us more fully human, we prioritize writing in all subject areas.

We are so vulnerable and exposed as writers. That's why our response as teachers must ultimately be respectful and affirming to the writer. As readers, we at least have the support of a written text even as we grapple with it. As writers, we create a text from scratch, often with a looming blank page or screen in front of us. However, once we've actually created a text—even just a sentence—we can manipulate it, massage it, and make it more meaningful. It is in the act of composing that we figure out what we know and need to know. I know that as fact, from decades of writing and taking on challenges I initially thought were over my head.

Pulitzer Prize–winning journalist and author David McCullough says, "To write well is to think clearly. That's why it's so hard."[2] Writing *is* thinking, and for most of us it's very hard work. That's why it's crucial that our K–12 classrooms and school cultures support risk taking, validating strengths before needs, and writing across the curriculum—for sustained time, each and every day. As teachers, let's think not only about having students learn content but also how we can show, teach, and guide students to think and write like historians, scientists, environmentalists, mathematicians, informed citizens, and so on, in an engaging and accurate manner that informs, entertains, or persuades their readers. If we can't clearly communicate what we know, we can't affect and influence others.

Also, let's not abandon narrative writing and poetry because of current standards' emphasis on expository writing. My favorite and preferred nonfiction reading always follows a narrative written form. Narrative writing, though narrowly defined in schools, needs to be expanded to include informational writing as well. Noted educator, author, and scholar Tom Newkirk notes, "Locate any widely read writer on science or medicine or the environment and you will find someone skilled at narrative writing, one who keeps before our eyes the human consequences of policies and discoveries."[3] With our guidance, what we teach students about narrative writing, poetry, and memoir can transfer to all writing genres and forms.

Each writing genre and form conforms to unique characteristics and formats; we want students' writing—including their informational writing—to aim for the same overarching goals and objectives:

- Engage readers in worthwhile content.
- Write with an organized and coherent structure.
- Present the story or information in a clear, comprehensible, and persuasive manner.
- Support facts, claims, and opinions with evidence.
- Craft language that captivates the reader and showcases a unique style and voice.
- Write accurately, fluently, and, even, elegantly.

(See also Appendix G, 12 Writing Essentials for All Grade Levels.)

Finally and simply, take to heart the straightforward advice of William Zinsser, famed author of the classic *On Writing Well.* "Write clearly. Guard the message with your life. Avoid jargon and big words. Use active verbs. Make the reader think you enjoyed writing the piece."[4]

STORY ❖ The Writing Life

I'm midstream in the process of writing a new book for educators, so I've been thinking quite a lot about what it means to be a writer in our schools today, with the expectations and demands of the latest standards, high-stakes testing, and just finding the time to write in our overstuffed curriculum. Most of all, I believe we must value writing for its own sake because of all the marvelous rewards that come from being a writer.

If we write well, we have read avidly and have noticed and learned from what authors do and say. If we write well, we have learned patience and what it means to stick with something worthwhile even when there are no early rewards. If we write well, we have carved out daily time each day; and even when we didn't want to, we sat in that chair for a sustained quiet time and rarely missed a day. If we write well, we have received effective feedback—even if that feedback has come mostly from our own continual rereading and rethinking. If we write well, we feel smarter because wrestling with thoughts and ideas and putting them together in a way no one else has ever done before brings a unique sense of accomplishment. I believe all of the above statements to be true for writers of all ages, including our students.

Here's what I know for sure. Our present standards will eventually be replaced by newer ones; "better" tests will always be on the horizon; new demands will make it easy to crowd out writing for something "more important." However, if we teach writing well, the students will do fine on the tests and will meet the standards. More significantly, we will be giving our students a lifetime gift that will bind their hearts and minds and enhance their communication and collaboration with others, regardless of their career path. Whether all students receive this precious gift depends in large part on us.

We teachers must be discerning readers and writers who demonstrate the thinking, actions, and habits of practicing readers and writers if we are to effectively teach the craft and the nuts and bolts of writing. Reading all kinds of texts with the lens of a writer as well as a thoughtful reader, taking notes and researching, organizing our information and thinking into a meaningful whole, backing up our pronouncements with facts and our own experiences, being able to communicate ideas clearly and persuasively, writing and publishing with an authentic audience and purpose, and doing all of this in our own style and voice is a crucial responsibility all of us educators must assume, regardless of the grade level or subject matter we teach.

Here's what else I know for sure. Being a writer means accepting that the work is messy and frustrating. We can be stuck for hours with no coherent paragraphs forthcoming. We can be easily distracted and discouraged. We can be totally off message. And yet. The writing life is a worthwhile one if we stay with it. After multiple drafts and day after day of composing, thinking, rearranging, rethinking, and just plain uninterrupted writing, ideas begin to cohere and pages begin to form that seem readable. When the writing flows, even for just a page, it's magical. We have literally made visible by our own hand and mind something of potential value for a reader, even if that reader is ourself. All students deserve to experience that magic.

Focus on the Writer First

Focus on the writer first and the writing second. Of everything we do to help turn students into writers, focusing first on the writer and trying to discern what the writer is trying to say is the most crucial. It is one of the hardest things to accomplish as a teacher of writing because it depends on us adopting a mind-set of noticing and celebrating student strengths, first and foremost. Focusing on the writer first also requires us to be thinking, "When the student leaves the conference, I want him to have the confidence, energy, and will to go on writing." Therefore, the feedback we give each student must be carefully worded to celebrate and to build upon the learner's strengths. This can be difficult for us as teachers because we sincerely want improvement as quickly as possible.

Most of us tend to be skimpy with honest compliments. Keep this in mind: the language we use with a student in a writing conference has the power to change that student's life. Time and time again, I have seen a student who struggles sit up taller, finally make eye contact, smile, gain respect from his peers, begin to take risks, and blossom into a full-fledged writer—all because the student has been celebrated for his specific writing efforts and what he is trying to say. Conversely, we can demolish a student's writing spirit for the whole school year by focusing first on weaknesses and strategies for improvement.

Writing takes courage and perseverance. Do view the three-minute video by Ta-Nehisi Coates, winner of the National Book Award for *Between the World and Me*, with colleagues and with middle and high school students.[5] Coates's advice is excellent for all of us: repeated practice is crucial; failure is a normal part of writing success; breakthroughs come from putting pressure on ourselves. It's because writing is difficult to do well and requires risk taking that we need to take great care with how we advise and respond to writers. It's also why it's critical that we teachers become writing risk takers ourselves and that our students see us writing, thinking aloud, and wrestling with words and ideas right in front of them. Only then can we truly appreciate why we must focus on the writer before the writing.

Take Action

- **Focus on the student's strengths.** Think first: "What is this student trying to think through and accomplish? What has he done well or tried to do? How can I best recognize and support his efforts?"

- **Choose and use language that moves the writer forward.** Think: "What's the most important thing I can say or do right now that will give the writer the will and energy to go on writing?" Sometimes, especially for a writer who has a history of struggling, the best judgment call might be to recognize the best-effort writing as "good enough" and to direct the student's energy to editing rather than more revision.

- **Pay particular attention to the language the writer is using**—or attempting to use—and how that language has an impact on a reader before worrying about structure, conventions, grammar, and so forth. Adopt a mind-set of looking for original thought, not perfect grammar.

- **Notice the student's body language and affect.** Students let us know, without speaking, how they view themselves as writers. Be sensitive to the signals they send us, and do whatever possible to boost the writer's competence and confidence.

- **Remove roadblocks to writing.** See my entry on the *MiddleWeb* blog for "10 Surefire Ideas to Remove Writing Roadblocks."[6] Embedded in the link is also a demonstration of the storytelling/writing of a memoir snippet.

Write and Publish More Short Pieces

Encouraging short writing assignments makes writing easier for students and us. Not only that: effective short writing is important for success in today's workplace; memos, summaries, agendas, reports, and other short forms are integral to many jobs. In fact, we can teach students everything they need to know about writing—such as leads, organization, word choice, elaboration and detail, closure, revision, and editing—with a short writing piece. A nonfiction report or essay does not need to be many pages long; such lengthy pieces can drain students' energy as well as our own. Even for older students, think about demonstrating, practicing, and assigning shorter pieces and assigning only one or two big writing projects a year. Shorter writing pieces, for authentic audiences and purposes, can move writing from being burdensome to being everyone's favorite subject.

An easy way for students to write shorter pieces is to legitimize social media—it's where our students live. "Social media can be a tool where students are encouraged to use their creativity combined with personal expression to improve and strengthen their writing."[7] It was only after I started writing blog posts that I realized that blog writing—done well—took as much effort and revision as any other form of writing. Blog writing is a great way for our students to reach large and specialized audiences. Twitter, which combines tweets and hashtags in a message of up to 140 characters, is but one of many popular, authentic, and unique forms of communication. Develop guidelines for tweeting to families, community members, and other students. Consider tweeting out information as a whole school or class to publicize and celebrate events, accomplishments, news, and more. Include photos and images for increased engagement.

To be clear, by "short pieces" I don't mean story starters, worksheets, or daily exercises about writing. It may seem counterintuitive, but we make writing harder for kids when we break it into bits and pieces—which is especially egregious for our students who struggle. The brain is a pattern finder; the whole really is greater than the sum of its parts. Always, start with a whole text and encourage students to tell the story first. (See "Apply Whole-Part-Whole Teaching," pages 271–275, and "Do more scaffolded conversations," pages 234 and 305–306.)

 ## Take Action

- ◆ **Provide more choice.** Choice within some structure makes all the difference for motivating and inspiring writers to put forth their full efforts. Within required standards and curriculum, give students some choice on topic, form, communication, or presentation format. However, too much choice, especially if clear guidelines are not included, can result in frustration and low-quality work. (See page 90 for more on choice, and see chart on page 91.)

- **Include social media.** We do need to teach our students digital citizenship and what is appropriate to tweet and text and communicate. Blogging and tweeting can be used to communicate with families, comment on current events, and deal with real-world issues. Also, consider texting as a means of communication in the classroom—a radical idea for many of us. For example, some teachers have students text questions to them, even in the middle of a lesson. Especially when small, self-directed groups are working together and the teacher is moving around the classroom—giving guidance as needed—a group's texts and the teacher's follow-up responses are an effective and efficient way to confirm, question, and push students' thinking. Keep in mind that our students are "digital natives" and that "texting is the primary communication medium of 14- to 18-year-olds."[8]

  Even if we're still learning how to use social media, we need to appreciate how powerful and natural it is for our students, especially if they are in middle or high school. Give it a go. Although it may feel risky to publicly try out a new technology, our tech-savvy students are more than willing to show us what they know and to jump in with tech advice. Also, seeing us educators taking risks, seeking guidance, making mistakes, and even failing as we are learning is important modeling for our students for what it means to be a learner.

- **Demonstrate only the amount of writing that most students are capable of doing at this time.** Follow the Optimal Learning Model (page 139). Write and think aloud in front of students, use shared writing (see page 142), and show writing exemplars. Be conscious of not taking valuable time (as well as students' energy and sustained time needed for actual writing) by demonstrating too much—for example, by modeling two pages of writing when most students are typically writing one page.

- **Model writing as a recursive process, not a linear one.** When demonstrating for students, show the back-and-forth nature of composing. That is, in the act of writing, we reread as we go along to figure out what to say next, to see if what we've written makes sense, to clarify our thinking, to be picky about word choice, to improve organization, and so on. We want students to inculcate the writer's habit of rereading, rethinking, and revising writing-in-process. Remember also to think aloud and tell the whole story, persuasive argument, or experience before writing it; then choose a meaningful part to write aloud in front of students. Give the message that we don't just write what we know; we write to figure out what we don't know.

◆ **Do more scaffolded conversations.** For our English language learners and students who struggle, having a supportive conversation about what they might write before they go off to write is often the game changer for whether or not they're successful. Much of a scaffolded conversation involves putting the language in a student's ear or offering language suggestions from which the student chooses what to use. (See Equity, page 305, and the video of Liam, referenced on page 306.)

◆ **Save exemplars.** Save excellent examples of short writing forms, such as news articles, blogs, editorials, letters to the editor, and poems—those written by adult writers as well as by students, with students' permission. When I read something especially well written and inspiring, I file it for possible future use with students for the immersion/demonstration stage. Then, together, we notice and discuss: "What did the author do?" "What makes the writing so memorable for the reader?" "What might you try in your own writing?"

◆ **Bring a piece of writing to a final, published copy often,** at least once a month, starting in grade two. Students need lots of practice in revising and editing if they are to become fluent, proficient writers, and short assignments make that possible. What is key for students to put forth best efforts is to have them write for readers who matter to them, which must be more than just the teacher and the bulletin board.

Because composing in kindergarten and early on in first grade can take so much effort, for most students I recommend, when publishing a piece, that we take responsibility for word-processing or hand-writing the student's final work while sitting side by side; have the student decide how much text goes on a page while we publish the writing error-free. Also, once students are beyond the stage where they need to draw a picture first to aid their writing, encourage them to wait and do their illustrations in their published books, which saves time and yields best-effort work.

◆ **Consider some of the following short writing forms and genres.** These need not be traditional pen-and-paper pieces but can take the form of podcasts, brief videos with text and music or sound effects, blogs, Instagram captions, tweets, advertisements, speeches, e-mails, raps, hip-hop, song lyrics, and more. Consider also quick-writes (see page 343), and don't forget shared writing (pages 142–144).

Here are more possibilities for short writing:

- *Letters* (thank you, inquiry, gratitude, persuasive, request, editorial).
- *Reviews and recommendations* (book, restaurant, magazine, video, audio text, play, movie, game, app).
- *Notes* (birthday, congratulations, holiday greeting, friendship, invitation, appreciation).
- *Announcements* (morning, assembly, celebration, accomplishment).
- *Advice* (for friends, readers, writers, new students, teachers, parents).
- *Explanations* ("how to" writing, directions, manuals, steps to follow, summaries, solving a math problem).
- *All about the author* (student profile to be attached to published writing—could take various forms).
- *Reflections* (memories, most important learning, personal gratitude, content learning, journal entries, self-evaluations).
- *Poetry writing* (free verse or hip-hop with rhyming couplets).
- *Developing a character* (as a prelude to fiction writing).
- *Informational picture books* (for peers or younger readers).

See also Appendix D for technology tools, presentation apps, and other aids to assist short forms of writing. For a novel and engaging writing and publishing format, consider typewriters. Kids love using manual typewriters, and the advantages for using them are many.[9] See *Writing Essentials* for many more ideas and examples of short writing for authentic audiences and purposes.[10]

- **Use pop culture to teach writing.** Encourage hip-hop and rapping as a possible communication/writing/publishing form. To engage and inspire students, use examples of rhyming couplets by Lin-Manuel Miranda from the hit musical *Hamilton* as well as word crafting from well-known rappers and hip-hop artists. After months of study on the issue of a polluted local lake and the urgent need for clean drinking water, music teacher Randal Bychuk and fourth-grade teacher Daria Orloff collaborated with their students to create a captivating three-minute rap video.[11] The students were passionate about the topic, and many of the facts they had learned easily became lyrics. They chose to rap the verses, sing the repeated chorus, and include a call-and-response section, which rivets listeners and encourages their participation.

Rethink Revision

When I am composing, I concentrate my efforts on writing a clear, coherent message. At the same time, I keep my audience and purpose in mind because they affect my tone, style, format, length, and choice of evidence and examples. Although I don't know exactly what my content will be (I discover and uncover that as I write), I do know before I begin whether I want to persuade, entertain, explain, advise, inform, call to action—or some combination of these. I do reread and make changes as I go along, but mostly I put my energies into maintaining focus on what I am trying to convey to my reader.

Re-vision, carefully re-looking at and re-examining a piece of writing as both a whole and in its parts—for example, at the paragraph, sentence, and word levels—can be time consuming and labor intensive. Therefore, we must deliberately demonstrate, teach, and practice the revision process with students before we turn it over to them. When we ensure as well that the audience and the purpose are meaningful and relevant to students—and that they have some choice in the writing topic—students do willingly invest in revising their work. For example, when students write blogs on social media, they do take time to carefully express their thoughts to their intended audience and rewrite as necessary. They want their message to be understood by their readers, and that motivation drives the writing. For me, even writing a meaningful tweet takes time.

Finally, be sure to separate composing and revising from editing. When our students try to do both at the same time, quality suffers. For example, when we are doing a demonstration writing or a shared writing with our students, simply write. Just do it. Put full energy into what we are trying to say. Award-winning author Kent Haruf always wrote with his eyes closed so his imagination could run free. "When he typed his first draft of each chapter, he would pull a stocking cap down over his eyes and write 'blind' so he wouldn't be distracted by spelling, syntax or punctuation."[12]

 ## Take Action

- **Ensure students know the difference between revision and editing.** Even older students sometimes equate the two processes or believe revision means "making corrections." Some students think revision means copying over their papers so they look neater, which is a time waster. Assess students' knowledge by charting their responses on a class-authored chart, "What We Know About Revision." Date it, and as students learn more from our demonstrations, shared experiences, and their own revision work, add those insights and information to the chart in a different color with a later date. Use the chart to determine students' understandings and what to teach next, and to establish criteria with students (often with a rubric) for their expected revision process.

◆ **Demonstrate our revision process.** We can save drafts of our family newsletters and other writing that has required some substantial revision and share those with students. Better yet, let them see our messy revision process by projecting our writing and thinking aloud as we make changes and explain why we are making them. Show and explain how to carefully reread with readers and purpose in mind. Let students know that rereading and rethinking can help us write more effectively. Value revising on paper. Even tech-savvy experts find revising on paper to be highly effective: "I do a lot more printing off of writing drafts, even blog posts. I catch things in print I would not otherwise on digital."[13]

◆ **Provide shared revision experiences** before expecting students to just "do it." That is, project a class-authored shared writing for a real-world audience and lead the class through the revision process. Accept and record all responses that make some sense. Come back to the piece later in the day or on another day and revisit the suggested changes. Continue to revise until the writing meets our expectations. Once students are competent with this process, have small groups tackle revision work together. Notice this is the handover—or second stage—of "we do it" in the OLM; students are now in charge as the teacher is available for limited guidance. (See OLM chart, page 138.)

◆ **Be cautious with writing to a rubric.** Rubrics, especially when they are written with students, are useful for evaluating and improving writing overall once students have a working draft. However, when we use the rubric as the mainstay for writing, judging, and improving a student's writing, quality suffers. Students and we wind up focusing too much on the parts and lose the sense of a meaningful whole. Also, overly focusing on a rubric detracts from giving useful, personalized feedback to the writer. (For more on rubrics, see Equity, pages 325–329.)

◆ **Make revision work matter.** A common practice is to have students substitute "juicy words" for boring ones or to "add more details." Substituting a more sophisticated word for a simple one or merely adding details to a piece of writing can derail the writing and actually make it worse. Discourage the use of thesauruses by students. Read and analyze authors who write clearly and directly without "big" words.

◆ **Schedule separate time devoted to revision,** not for all pieces but for selected writing that will go to publication for a real-world audience. Allow a time lapse; writers of all ages do a better job on revision when there is a short interim between the writing and the revising. Schedule time over several days so students can read each version with fresh eyes. If students can word-process their drafts and print out successive, clean drafts, those efforts are a plus but not a necessity.

- **Create "I Can..." statements with students** to help with their own expectations, revisions, and self-direction as writers. For example, the following are a few, key manageable statements and expectations created with a grade two–three class:

  1. I can write a lead sentence that pulls in the reader.
  2. I can back up my ideas with proof or evidence.
  3. I can wrap up my writing with an inspiring ending.

  Also use "I can" statements to hold students accountable. Consider having students place respective numbers—corresponding to a few key "I can" statements—on their drafts to show evidence of application before conferring with them or before accepting students' papers for feedback. See the photo on page 245 for many "I can" statements written with students on the classroom whiteboard; notice the three highlighted statements (one is obscured) match the numbered statements above, which are writing requirements for the writing focus on clean water issues.

- **Teach students to read the writing out loud for rhythm and language flow.** Teach students the author's device of reading aloud the piece, whisper-reading it, or reading it aloud in their minds. So often that's how many of us notice a word or phrase that doesn't "sound" right, an unwieldy sentence, or a missing transition between ideas. I read aloud much of my work in the process of writing and after I write, and I draw attention to that rereading in my public demonstration writing and revising. Reading aloud is especially important for reading and writing poetry.

- **Focus on craft.** Use read-aloud time, think-alouds, and conferences to point out an author's expert use of language, literary devices, leads, style, format, word choice, voice, and so on. Combine well-written current-events news articles, interview questions, and more for studying and applying an author's craft.

- **Date and save all drafts,** handwritten and word-processed, as a record and history of the writer's thinking, process, and efforts. Let students know we credit and value their revision work, not just the end product. Often students and teachers only save the final copy, and they, we, and their families never see the messy thinking work of revision and a student's writing work and growth over time.

  At grade levels, content areas, and across the school, come to agreement on an organization system for housing and dating all writing. One way for students to demonstrate and assess their progress is to have them revise a piece written earlier in the school year and note their improvements.

◆ **Teach revision techniques and shortcuts** such as these:

- ◉ *Cross-outs* in one line (not erasures) so we can see the writer's thinking.
- ◉ *Skipping lines* (to leave room for adding in words and ideas).
- ◉ *Writing or printing on only one side* of the page (to make cutting and pasting possible).
- ◉ *Lassoing* sentences with an arrow (for moving text around).
- ◉ *Adding symbols*, such as a letter of the alphabet or a made-up symbol before a section or sentence and using the same symbol in a new location (to indicate new placement of text).
- ◉ Demonstrate your online revision process as well.

◆ **Write more short pieces for publication,** which makes it more likely that students will have the energy and will to revise.

◆ **Remember that most writing never gets revised** and apply that principle to the classroom. Other than a word change here and there, I don't much revise text messages, e-mails, handwritten notes, greeting card messages, and so on. Also, I don't generally revise reflections and musings that I write for myself.

Rethink Editing

Editing matters. Editing is the clean-up stage in which we get ready for a nearly flawless presentation. That means spelling, punctuation, and grammar must be correct. Editing also refers to our final efforts for accuracy and clarity, which often includes finessing word choice and form. Students may have created an outstanding piece, but if we can't easily read or view their final version, the content won't matter much.

When students are in the composing and creating process, I seek to be as kind, sensitive, and attentive as possible. I choose my feedback language carefully and pay careful attention to the writer's demeanor. My focus is on celebrating and encouraging that writer to write a meaningful and engaging message for an authentic audience and purpose. But once revisions are complete, the focus is on the writing, not the writer, and I am relentless. I tell students: "Editing is about the reader; it's not about you. Out of respect for your reader, your piece must be as perfect as you can get it."

Once we collaboratively decide our editing expectations, usually through a class shared writing, students are responsible for editing their work with all-out efforts. Too often what happens is that we teachers continue to do most of the work, which makes the editing process cumbersome and exhausting for us and sends students the message that editing is not really their job. Turning over most of the editing responsibility to students is a win-win situation—less work for us and more skill and pride for students as editors. Not to be minimized, students come to relish the challenge of becoming competent editors, as the following story illustrates.

A group of proud students gave me a copy of their monthly class newsletter for families. The content was excellent, full of interesting and well-written information about the goings-on of the class—what they had been learning, doing, and thinking about. Here's what I told them after I carefully read the newsletter: "Your newsletter is excellent. You have engaging leads, great descriptions, and you communicate information clearly. I can tell you are serious writers. However, I was distracted by the spelling and punctuation errors. As a reader, I count on correctness so I can focus on the message." They "got it." From that point on, many students took responsibility for rereading the newsletter. They challenged me to find errors, and I never did. Correct spelling, conventions, and grammar are about respect for the reader. Readers expect and deserve a seamless read so they can focus on meaning. I tell students, "You have a contract with your reader to get it right."

Raise editing expectations! Ensure that whatever goes public is as perfect as possible. Poor spelling and conventions reflect poorly on us as educators and send a message to the public that spelling doesn't matter much. From early on in grade two, almost all students are capable of "fixing up" basic spelling and conventions if we expect them to do it, teach explicitly, and give lots of guided practice through writing and publishing for authentic purposes and audiences. For younger students, in kindergarten and grade one, if work is posted with invented spellings—especially in school hallways—be sure to accompany that work with a notice that says something like "Our best independent spelling" or something to that effect, so readers and the public know we are doing our job. Invented spellings are appropriate for those words we do not yet expect students to be able to spell and for encouraging the use of unique vocabulary so that students do not feel limited to basic, easy-to-spell words.

Take an environmental walk around your school. Look at what's posted on the walls in hallways and classrooms. Is the writing that's posted readable—that is, is it at an eye level and a size that students, teachers, and visitors can access? Is the writing legible? Are spelling, conventions, and grammar accurate? It's such an easy and important public relations win. Parents, board members, visitors, and others judge us, rightly or wrongly, by the correctness of what's posted in a school. In particular, grammar and spelling errors are often judged harshly, partly because the public views such errors as evidence of lowered standards. Provide students the demonstrations, shared experiences, and guided practice they need to self-edit and peer-edit. Then, be relentless about expecting them to do the editing work. Just as it is in the world outside of school, what gets published, posted, and public must be as close to perfect as we can get it.

Also consider this: Is the posted student writing worth reading? That is, is the information presented showing off important learning and thinking? Much of what we ask students to do as writers is at the surface level and does not push their thinking.[14] Wow your audience! Make sure posted work goes beyond basic skills and correctness to highlight and celebrate high-level thinking and learning.

 ## Take Action

- **Emphasize that writers write for readers.** Just like the students in the aforementioned story, once students internalize that we write for a purpose and a valued audience—beyond the bulletin board or the teacher—they take spelling, correct conventions, and grammar seriously.

- **Emphasize rereading.** Students are usually stunned to learn that rereading their writing once or twice is insufficient proofreading for finding and fixing up errors. Accustomed to us teachers doing most of the editing work, students initially require multiple rereadings to "see" editing needs and to believe we are serious about holding them accountable. Don't tackle all editing issues at once. Start with spelling. For some students, reading the writing backward, word-by-word just for correct spelling, helps them "see" misspelled words.

- **Place responsibility for editing on the students.** Only confer with students about editing once they have done, on their own or with peer assistance, everything they know how to do regarding correct spelling, grammar, and conventions and have checked their work against the class-established editing expectations. Consider telling students—orally or by denoting on their papers—how many errors exist in a line or a paragraph, and challenge them to find and correct every one. Hold firm! We disable students, in the long run, when we do for them what they can do on their own or with peer assistance.[15]

- **Have the student hold the pen or pencil.** In an editing conference, whether public or one-on-one, have the student make the corrections. Even when I give a correct spelling "for free," I will often write it on a sticky note and expect the student to correct his misspelled word. Be willing to fix only what the student can't do, an approach that initially shocks students who are accustomed to us teachers doing the heavy lifting.

- **Expect high-frequency words to be spelled correctly.** Even in a draft, expect word-wall words and agreed-upon high-frequency words to be spelled correctly. When they are not, put a penciled mark or symbol above the word to indicate the student is expected to fix that word.

- **Teach spelling strategies.** There are two parts to fixing spelling: inspection and production. Even students who struggle with spelling can often "find" many of their misspelled words. Once in the editing stage, expect students to circle or underline misspelled words and then attempt to correct those. Once a student has made her best efforts at production, I fix remaining misspelled words "for free." Before having an editing conference focused on spelling, develop criteria and strategies for spelling expectations with students. Some of these might be to try writing the word another way, to ask a peer, or to consult an easy-to-use resource. Full-size dictionaries don't work well unless we already know the first three letters of the word we are seeking.

- **Teach paragraphing.** Although my classroom-based research over many decades confirms that most students don't create paragraphs automatically before the end of fifth grade, we still want to teach as early as kindergarten that like ideas go together. Until students have enough language and literacy experience to know how and when to create paragraphs, they can still be shown—through reading and noticing, with our guidance, what authors do—how to use titles, headings, transitions, word crafting, infographics, and more to orient the reader, even in kindergarten. For older students still learning about paragraphs, one easy solution is to let students know authors sometimes indent or create a paragraph to give the reader's eye a break when there is too much print on a page. It's certainly a technique I occasionally employ for my reader's comfort when the sheer length of a paragraph looks overwhelming.

- **Provide student-friendly resources,** such as word walls, personal "word walls" in students' writing folders or notebooks, small dictionaries with high-frequency words, criteria charts with examples, and easy-to-use apps such as Book Creator. Teach students about spell-check when using word-processing programs. Keep in mind students still need to learn to spell when using spell-check because they need to be able to pick out the correct word spelling; one common example is the use of homophones, e.g., *there* and *their*.

Embrace Public Writing Conferences

Conferring with students is the single best way I know to move them forward as writers. In a public conference, one student has a conference with the teacher, usually sitting side by side, in full view of the whole class or group. The other students are looking on, listening, and thinking about how to apply to their own writing what they are observing and learning. From kindergarten through high school, students greatly benefit from seeing and hearing the language of useful conferring.

Separate content conferences from editing conferences and begin with content conferences. It's difficult to focus on content and editing at the same time. What typically happens when we do that is most of our comments tend to deal with correctness, conventions, and grammar because those concrete areas are easier and more comfortable for most of us to talk about. Spending time with content, figuring out together what the writer is attempting to say, requires our full attention, skill, and energy. And again: a perfectly edited piece doesn't matter much if the writing is not worth reading. Also important to keep in mind, students cannot effectively confer with peers until we have demonstrated and they have tried out, with our guidance and support, the language of helpful, actionable feedback.

Trish Richardson speaks to the power of public conferences and how they have affected her teaching and her students as writers:

> *Positive public writing conferences and celebrations, along with giving choice within the structure of writing activities, have turned students who did not see themselves as writers and who would painfully pull out one or two sentences for me into avid, voracious writers who create many texts. I now see this time and time again. I used to always do an author's chair that students liked when they shared their writing. We complimented each writer, clapped our hands and celebrated. Students liked these experiences but students did not necessarily leave with any real feedback to work with in their next writing, and the students who were watching took away very little. Our time was not being used to its fullest.[16]*

Listening to Carol Dweck recently speak on developing a growth mind-set, I was struck by how much of what she recommended aligned with the way my colleagues and I conduct our public and one-on-one writing conferences. Dweck noted that mind-set only changes to a growth mind-set when teachers take specific actions:

- Teach for understanding.
- Give deep and extensive feedback.
- Give students a chance to revise their work and revise their understandings.[17]

Of course, none of the above is easy to do well with writers. Figuring out what to comment on and focus on first and, especially, getting our feedback language "right" can be a challenge and takes much coaching and practice. Although we start by noticing and naming what the writer has done well, we also give suggestions when warranted. What's key is that we give feedback that propels the writer forward and gives the writer sufficient time for revision, if needed. It's all a delicate dance of knowing when to follow the student's lead and when to lead, facilitate, or guide.[18] (See feedback, pages 246–248.)

 ## Take Action

Note that almost all the suggestions that follow for a public conference also apply to a one-on-one conference.

- **Be explicit in how and why the public conference can benefit all students.** Say something like "We are having this public conference for two reasons. First and most important, we're going to celebrate everything the writer has done well. Second, you'll need to be listening carefully to get ideas for your own writing. Also, we may give the writer some suggestions. Again, you want to pay close attention, as I will expect you to reread your paper and to think about making revisions based on what might apply."

- **Check that students are clear on the purposes of the public conference.** Have students turn and talk about the purposes of the public conference. Then call on volunteers to respond. Just about every time I have ever done this quick assessment, the first responses are always along the lines of "improving the writing." "Celebration of writing" rarely comes up, even after I restate the purposes of the conference. A school culture of "need to improve" is so pervasive in most places that even when the work may be "good enough" and teachers say they support the idea of focusing first on students' strengths, years of questioning students around what needs "fixing" serve to make students initially immune to believing a writing conference might value strengths over deficits.

■■
■■ Celebrating the writer in a public writing conference: Grade two–three teacher Trish Richardson reading aloud Izan's writing on the importance of clean water and noting his strengths—after he has first orally read the piece aloud. (Notice shared writing of agreed-upon "I can" statements on whiteboard. See page 238 for more on "I can" statements.)

◆ **Adapt public conferences for middle and high school students.** Although there's no way to have a meaningful one-on-one conference with every student, several in-depth public conferences that address typical strengths and concerns can be invaluable for raising expectations for all and for having students assume more responsibility for both content and editing. It is generally not a good use of our precious time to spend hours beyond the school day putting detailed comments on students' work. Most students tend to ignore our suggestions and remarks. Also, most teachers' comments typically focus on corrections and suggestions—with disproportionately few comments noting writing strengths, which can discourage students who already lack confidence as writers. Consider having middle and high school students who are observing the public conference write down what they noticed, what they learned or confirmed, or what they might apply to their own writing. Occasionally collect those sheets and use them as an informal evaluation of what they are learning and what we might need to be teaching.

- **Have the first public conference with a typical strong writer,** so we have a good role model for other students, the work to be done is manageable for the student and us, and we feel successful. Consciously adopt a mind-set of seeing and commenting on strengths before focusing on needs.

- **Encourage the student to first read the piece aloud,** which respects the fact that the writing belongs to the writer. On the first reading by the student, try not to look at the writing itself, which can lead us to focus on grammar, legibility, or poor spelling. Instead, actively listen for and attempt to discern what the writer is trying to say and do. If the piece is long, have the writer first orally say what the piece is about; then have him choose to read one part where he wants feedback. An additional important point here: occasionally a student is unwilling to read his writing aloud. When that happens, I offer to read the piece aloud. Whatever the reason for the writer's reluctance—and often it seems connected to a lack of confidence due to a history of conferring centered on improvement—once the writer experiences the conference as a celebration, that hesitancy disappears.

- **As teacher, read the paper aloud a second time**—and a third time, if needed. The purpose is to think on our feet and go line by line to figure out what students are trying to say. Name and read aloud the exact language, craft, structure, organization, and so on, that the writer has used to affect the reader and convey his message. Naming the technique a writer has used—for example, using similes, transitions, or voice—does not, by itself, help the writer or the listening students we are also hoping to affect through the public conference.

- **Choose feedback language carefully.** Begin by acknowledging what the writer has done well or attempted to do well. Focus on the actual words the student has used and what those words convey to the reader. Again, it is not helpful to the writer or to other students listening in to say "I like your beginning" or "You used good detail" because we don't know what that means and can't emulate it. It is helpful to say "Listen to Martin's first lines [read the exact language aloud] and notice the way his words and rhythm entice the reader into the story. Make sure you have done something similar with your own writing."

  Some other examples of language that focuses on craft, not just mechanics and generalities, might include feedback such as the following:

  - *When you said (such and so), I could empathize with the* (sadness, joy, frustration) you were feeling.
  - *Your ending sentences [read those aloud] leave the reader with a sense of* (peace, astonishment, satisfaction).

- *The way you crafted your words in your lead paragraph [read paragraph aloud] immediately engages the reader and lets her know* (what the whole piece is about, why the topic is important, and what action you hope the reader will take).

◆ **Decide on what's most important to say and do at this time to move the writer forward,** and make one or two teaching points, if appropriate—for example, cutting and pasting for better organization, writing a better lead, or both. Remember that sometimes the writing content is "good enough" as is and it's wisest not to recommend revisions. Especially for writers who struggle, it's vital that the writer leave the conference with the energy, confidence, and will to do any editing work, as well as other writing.

◆ **Make conferring manageable.** Do one or two in-depth public conferences. Do not worry if such a conference takes fifteen or twenty minutes. Remember that "less is more" when we want students to think, learn, and apply techniques at a deep and meaningful level.

◆ **Ensure the conference language can be understood.** Not only are we seeking to have students apply what we are celebrating and suggesting, but also we are modeling the language of response for worthwhile peer conferences.

◆ **Leave final decisions to the writer.** Once strengths have been noted, make any suggestions carefully and respectfully. Too many suggestions or "constructive criticisms" can give students the message that our purpose and agenda are more important than their own. Although honesty is necessary when a piece needs improvement, consider giving suggestions through questions or statements that move responsibility to the writer, such as:

  - *I was drawn in when you said* _____. I'd love to know more about that. What do you think about adding _____? It's up to you.
  - *What do you think about removing this line?* You've already said something similar here.
  - *What did you want the reader to think right here?* [Read sentence or section.] Here's what I was thinking, but I'm not sure if that was your intention. Perhaps you might want to explain _____.
  - *When you went from talking about such and so* and then moved to a new topic, I was confused. What could you add that would make that transition smooth? Would you like a suggestion on how you might do that?
  - *I was wondering how it might work if* we moved this section to _____.

⦿ *Let me read your last few lines again. See if that ending imparts the sense of closure you want for your reader.* Think about what you heard and learned today in our public conferences. You might want to try out a new ending—or not.

Value and Teach Handwriting

Handwriting still matters—a lot. There. I've said it. In school after school and classroom after classroom, the writing of far too many students is undecipherable, sloppy, and done without pride. Poor handwriting is an epidemic that is adversely affecting students' writing fluency, stamina, competence, and confidence. We disadvantage students when they cannot and do not form letters properly, hold the pencil or pen awkwardly, or both. Many students are now writing slower and composing shorter, hard-to-read pieces—primarily because they have not been taught handwriting. Sadly, once students have established incorrect habits for letter formation, it can be very difficult to reteach them, even in grade one!

The solution is an easy one. We need to teach handwriting, formally and informally, beginning early in kindergarten. Somewhere along the way, many of us got the message that we should leave students alone to form letters and hold the pencil as best they could and not interfere. We are now seeing the results of those misguided beliefs. Not only that: recent research confirms that handwriting, including cursive, activates portions of the brain that stimulate language and learning processes.[19]

Fluency and ease with handwriting are vital even in our Internet age. As noted, teaching handwriting has the potential to improve students' writing, reading, and comprehension. When I write by hand—for example, when listening to a speaker—I think differently and efficiently. While listening to the speaker, I put significant comments in quotes, write in my own words and underline what strikes me as important, and write side notes in the margins—all of which make it easy for me to find, review, and recall information later.

There is something about writing on paper—at least for me—that provides a physical and emotional experience that I don't get with digital experiences. I still enjoy writing with a beautiful pen on special stationery and taking and sending notes by hand. And I am not alone. Business for the Italian company that makes Moleskines, those lovely small notebooks many of us carry around, is booming.[20]

Finally, fair or not, many do judge writing quality by legibility. Teachers are more likely to score a paper higher, even if the quality is the same as another student's, when the writing is easier to read.[21]

Take Action

- **Take responsibility for teaching handwriting.** Even if handwriting is not mandated by the latest local, state, or national standards, we still need to be teaching it. Keep in mind that without fluency in handwriting, we disadvantage students as they approach everyday writing, taking notes, and completing tests. When students are unable to form letters and words quickly, easily, and legibly, or hold the pen correctly or comfortably, they simply do not develop the necessary stamina for sustained writing.

- **Come to agreement on a schoolwide handwriting policy.**

  - *Get together first by grade levels* and then across grade levels. Spell out expectations and guidelines for when, what, and how to teach letter formation in manuscript or cursive writing and for the appropriate writing paper to be used by each grade level, and consider whether a formal program needs to be incorporated.

  - *Don't go overboard!* Ten minutes a day of "formal" handwriting instruction is probably sufficient until students have solid skills in letter formation. Also, take the opportunity to teach on the spot when students incorrectly form letters in everyday writing and when conferring with them.

  - *Consider a variety of materials to help teach letter formation* to younger students and students who struggle with forming letters, such as printing in sand, using whiteboards, tracing, painting, and using printing apps that help teach directionality, such as Handwriting Without Tears, which uses a stylus.

- **Value handwritten pieces.** Special handwritten notes to friends, family, and colleagues, and get-well and condolence letters, benefit from the personal touch by the writer.

  - Ensure that at least some of students' published work that is shared, distributed, and posted is handwritten.

  - Make exceptions for those students physically unable to legibly write by hand. Make accommodations with a computer or other device.

  - Depending on audience and purpose, consider incorporating handwritten messages into apps such as Notability (see Appendix D), which allow for handwritten notes as well as photos and typed text.

  - Consider having students write notes, either as a class shared writing or individually, as a gift to next year's students for how to be successful in that grade level or class.

- Write short, encouraging, handwritten notes to students that show our appreciation for them—their unique qualities, efforts, accomplishments, etc. A couple of notes each day is manageable, and students treasure these.

♦ **Apply the research on taking notes by hand versus using a computer.** When students take notes by hand, they understand the subject matter better than when they take notes with a laptop. Researchers found that when students took notes on paper, they paraphrased, summarized, and put the information into their own words; those working on a keyboard tried to write everything down verbatim, which resulted in lower retention of the content and shallower learning.[22] Certainly this is true for me. I use one spiral notebook to write down all my notes on teaching, notes when listening to a speaker, and reflections. I write notes in the margin, underline and highlight parts, and reread often.

♦ **Consider asking administrators to take observation notes by hand,** which many teachers experience as a more informal, nonjudgmental, and collaborative approach. It also encourages description and moving away from dependence on a checklist. (See page 95 for more.)

To conclude this section on teaching writing, consider the following typical questions many students ask us. If these kinds of questions dominate writing, take stock. Students stop asking these questions when purposeful writing for real-world readers—with student choice and ownership built in—dominates the writing culture.

- How long does this piece have to be?
- How many details do I need to add?
- How do you spell _____?
- Do I need to copy this over?
- What should I do now?
- How many sources do I need to cite?

When we teach writing well and students see themselves as writers, it becomes the most satisfying part of the day for our students and us. Students then ask questions like these:

- When will it be writing time?
- I have an idea for writing. When can I start?
- Can I go to the library and research _____?

- Can I take this home to work on?
- Can I share my writing with the class?
- And even, Can I skip recess and stay in and write?

Not only that: writing becomes joyful. Allyson Matczuk, collaborator and researcher on our long-term initiative to improve writing in high-poverty schools in Winnipeg,[23] corroborates what happens when students become writers:

> *Teachers did not need a prescription to manage classroom time. Time was managed by the interest and engagement in the subject matter. It was the meaning and structure of the various writing pieces being created that engaged the heart and mind of the students.*[24]

Endnote

When we teach writing well, we prepare our students to communicate clearly and even elegantly. Regardless of their future career path or job, students-as-writers are well positioned to effectively communicate their ideas, reasoning, and thinking, which is necessary for living a full and influential life. To that end, it's crucial that as well-informed teachers we offer students authentic writing purposes and audiences, which determine how and what they write and how much effort they put into conveying their message. Consider also that sustained time for writing is the most important part of teaching writing—not the lessons, the grammar, or critiques by others. Writing is an act of thinking; and rethinking and revising for coherence, relevance, and efficacy take time.

All of that said, becoming an expert writing teacher is no easy matter. We need to know and be able to apply "principled practices"; that is, we need to plan our instruction as knowledgeable teachers who apply credible educational research and engage in ongoing, reflective practice with others.[25] Such "principled practice" requires ongoing professional learning and study as discussed on pages 105–110. It was studying and applying the work of writing giants Donald Murray, Donald Graves, Lucy Calkins, and Nancie Atwell that initially launched me as a teacher of writing. Those mentors and others—plus being an avid reader—made me believe I might become a writer and a teacher of writing.

Take to heart the advice from Stephen King on writing well: "You learn best by reading a lot and writing a lot, and the most valuable lessons of all are the ones you teach yourself."[26] This self-teaching only happens when we write fearlessly and often. Share the advice of poet Jane Kenyon with your students and follow it yourself: "Tell the whole truth. Don't be lazy, don't be afraid. Close the critic out when you are drafting something new. Take chances in the interest of clarity of emotion."[27] And I would add, "Your voice matters. Let it be heard."

EQUITY

Solutions are complex, imperfect and uncertain, but the biggest problem is not a lack of tools but a lack of will. A basic step to equalize opportunity would be to invest in education for disadvantaged children as the civil rights issue of the 21st century.

—*Nicholas Kristof*

Equality and equity are not the same. As Pedro Noguera says, "Giving everyone a shoe is equality; making sure the shoe fits is equity."[1] To use a commonly accepted definition from the National Equity Project: "Educational equity means that each child receives what he or she needs to develop to his or her full academic and social potential." Easier said than done. Knowing how to best serve all children is their right and our responsibility; yet for too many of our students, we fall short more often than we succeed. In general, we serve the wealthy and privileged well but do not do well for the less fortunate. We fail them academically, financially, socially, and emotionally, and most of the students we fail are students of color and students of poverty. Our collective tragedy and shame is that every time we fail to successfully educate a student, we are rolling the dice with that child's life. Every illiterate or underprepared student we turn out is more likely to fail to function in everyday life and to become a burden to society rather than a contributor.

Poverty, and the cruel hardships that accompany it, is generally seen as the major factor in why many students fail to thrive in and out of school. A large research base confirms that school-poverty concentration adversely affects student achievement[2]; in fact, it is rare for a high-poverty school district to achieve at the national average.[3] The poverty issue is huge; in the United States alone, almost half of the children live in low-income families—including 21 percent who live in families below the federal poverty level—and are at risk for learning, health, safety, and issues of overall well-being.[4]

But there is some good news. The huge academic gap between high- and low-income students is narrowing, as evidenced by kindergartners who now enter school "more equally prepared" then they were a couple of decades ago.[5] And yet. Although the school readiness gap has improved, the overall educational inequality gap remains formidable. The quality of education and resources rich and poor students receive remains markedly different. We have a long way to go and must do better. All children, regardless of where they live or life circumstances, are entrusted to us so we can do everything within our power to help them succeed—academically, socially, and emotionally.

Tightly connected to poverty is the harsh reality of segregated schools in the United States. Desegregation by both race and socioeconomics, which most agree is an educational necessity for all students to thrive, remains an unfulfilled promise.

How to address poverty, segregation, and underperforming and failing schools is, I believe, the number-one issue the United States faces as a democratic society. As I am writing this section, I am reading a heartbreaking front-page news story about failing schools in one of the "worst urban districts in the nation."[6] It's a devastated city where charter schools have been seen as the answer to failing public schools, but for the most part—as has been the case nationwide—charter schools have not delivered on their promise. (See also pages 358–359.) I am not, per se, anti-charter, except when charters take away vital resources from our public schools, as they did in New Orleans and continue to do in other cities. One of the biggest lessons from the educational overhaul after Hurricane Katrina is this: "It is wiser to invest in improving existing education systems than to start from scratch. Privatization may improve outcomes for some students, but it has hurt the most disadvantaged people."[7]

So what can we really do? In *Read, Write, Lead*, I made it clear that the book was about school change, not school reform.[8] I still believe that school reform is out of reach for most of us; but I now believe we have to at least try to break through the political logjam that threatens to stall efforts at real and lasting improvement. The reality is that if we truly want to give kids the lives they deserve, we must find ways around harmful assessments, too many mandated initiatives, rigid restrictions, and the entrenched infrastructure that too often works against what we know is right and best for our students. (See "Advocating for Students," pages 357-364.)

This section will give perspectives on realities, possibilities, and solutions for ensuring more equitable opportunities for learning for *all* students, including those in high-poverty schools where success stories are rare. We must shift our conversations from complaining and needing to do better to taking proven actions that will expand students' literacy and learning lives—despite the real constraints we face. We need to break the cycle of failure that leads to hopelessness. There is no educational equity without engagement and excellence for all. Hope for equitable change begins with us.

Making High Expectations an Instructional Reality

I've never heard anyone say they hold low expectations for students, but, in fact, that is the actuality in many schools, especially high-poverty, underperforming ones. In my forty-plus years of teaching, mentoring, and coaching, it is low expectations on the part of adults in schools that most impede optimal student learning. Students in high-poverty schools are typically two or more years below grade level, despite caring teachers who believe they are doing all they can. Our diminished expectations often lead to a watered-down curriculum, low-level language use, skills taught in isolation, and scripted programs that isolate students from potentially rich and authentic literacy and language experiences. Minority and low-performing students are more likely to be placed in ability groups and have the "least effective teachers."[1] They are also less likely to take and be prepared for AP classes and AP exams and to graduate prepared for higher education. Nothing changes until teachers, principals, and superintendents come to believe their students can do better, and they embrace the moral obligation to ensure that teaching and assessing lead to increased student learning—for *all*.

Several years ago, I spent a day in a school where 80 percent of the students qualified for free and reduced-cost meals, and almost all were English language learners. Achievement at the school had been dismal for years. The talented principal, who was bilingual and bicultural, had grown up in this community, was one of the few in her high school to attend and graduate from college, and had returned with a steadfast commitment to increase possibilities for her underserved Hispanic students. After proudly giving me a tour around the school, where teaching and learning were now vibrant in every classroom, she was eager for me to meet the superintendent and assistant superintendent. In our conversation with them, I asked, "How many of the students in your district go on to college?" Without missing a beat, they answered, "Our students don't go on to college." Neither administrator could cite any numbers because they collected no such data; they simply didn't believe or expect that their students could be college material. Although their words were shocking and heartbreaking, such low expectations are not uncommon.

In far too many schools, we accept stagnant or low achievement and play a blame game. We use poverty and other outside factors to shirk our responsibility and maintain our low expectations, and we fail to acknowledge that we can do better. Although it is true that we cannot compensate for the myriad of complex issues many of our students come to school with, we can and must give them our finest efforts for the hours they are with us each day. We need to raise our expectations for what's possible, see our students as capable and resilient, and assume responsibility for the achievement of *all* students.

Equity means we provide all students equal access to an excellent education—that is, we ensure they receive what they need and desire to reach their full potential. That includes fairness and decency toward all, as well as a challenging and relevant curriculum. With higher expectations and excellent, targeted teaching, we can raise achievement and change lives.

STORY ❖ Expecting More and Getting It

My dad died several years ago at the age of 93. I don't think one is ever prepared for the death of a parent, even when it's expected. While my dad had become increasingly frail, his death seemed a bit surreal to me. I was relieved his struggle was over, but I missed the dad I'd known most of my life.

My husband and I had devoted eight years to taking care of my dad and enriching his life as best we could. Following his brutal stroke, we moved him from New York to Seattle, where we live. Although my dad was severely physically disabled, for most of those years his mind was fully alert and he understood everything, although it would be a while before he would learn to speak again. To keep his mind active, I read aloud to him, books on politics and other nonfiction I thought he'd find interesting, as well as articles from his favorite news source, the New York Times. We also did some shared reading of articles, with him following along as I read. Now and then I would pause, show him a line, and have him fill in the next meaningful word or the rest of the sentence. To make sure he was understanding what we were reading, I would ask him what the article was about, and with very few but precise words, he demonstrated he got the essential meaning.

I learned a lot about teaching from seeing how my dad was treated in the nursing home and how little was expected of him. As nursing homes go, it was an excellent one. For the most part, my dad received expert and compassionate nursing and medical care. It was his mind, however, that I worried about. The philosophy seemed pretty much to be "Keep him breathing," with little attention to "Keep him thinking." There were few expectations for engaging him in conversation, beyond the superficial "How are you?" or "Who's here to visit you today?" even though he was perfectly capable of making and receiving an intelligent or humorous comment.

Seeing my dad mentally starved reminded me of some high-poverty schools where the credo seems the same: "Give the kids a scripted program and keep them breathing. Make sure they have a pulse, that they're well behaved, but don't worry much about getting them to think for themselves." Sadly, when I've shared this commonality between nursing homes and schools with educators, there's always instant recognition.

The head nurse and my dad's physician told me they were surprised by his progress, that they'd rarely seen anyone who had suffered such a severe stroke able to mentally function at my dad's level. I hear the same thing in high-poverty schools where I do demonstration teaching in classrooms. Often teachers say, "I didn't know he could do that," to which I respond, "I didn't know he couldn't."

I believe one of the gravest educational injustices is how little we expect from our underserved schools and students. As one teacher once told me, "We all say we have high expectations, but the truth is the kids have to prove to us first that they are capable." Let's turn that around and really believe "they can do it" and teach in a way that respects and maximizes each individual's intelligence and potential.

Seek and Value Diversity

An important first step in moving toward equity for all children is to seek and value diversity as an asset and a necessity for a flourishing learning culture in and out of school. When my husband, Frank, and I made the decision to live and work in Shaker Heights, Ohio, in the 1970s, a prime motivation was that the schools were racially and economically integrated. Our son, Peter, who went from kindergarten through grade twelve in the local public schools, still maintains "best friends" status with four classmates, three of whom are African American. Just about every year since they graduated from high school thirty years ago, the men come from all over the country to enjoy several days of "play" and friendship together. Like many others, Peter's early experience with diversity has continued to serve him well in all aspects of his life.

> *Ethnic diversity is like fresh air: It benefits everybody who experiences it. By disrupting conformity it produces a public good. To step back from the goal of diverse classrooms would deprive all students, regardless of their racial or ethnic background, the opportunity to benefit from the improved cognitive performance that diversity promotes.*[2]

Not to be minimized is research that shows "a racially integrated student body is necessary to obtain cross-racial understanding, which may lead to a reduction of harmful stereotypes and bias."[3] Another important, related point: desegregating by class, rather than race, is often seen as an easier political sell and first step toward more equality. A strong body of research supports the fact that all children, but especially poor children, benefit socially and academically when they are in classrooms with middle-class and affluent students.[4] However, although more schools are making efforts to ensure affluent and less-advantaged children go to school together, ". . . in U.S. schools 92 percent of students remain in racially and socioeconomically homogenous schools."[5]

In spite of the research that diversity—racial and socioeconomic—is viewed by most as a necessity for educational equity, it still remains rare in many of our schools. Recent federal data indicate that "the number of high–poverty schools serving primarily black and brown students more than doubled between 2001 and 2014" and that majority-black and Hispanic schools "were less likely to offer a full range of math and science courses than other schools . . . ," denying equal access to the more academically rigorous courses students have in other schools.[6]

In Seattle, where I live and where my granddaughters attend public schools, approximately one-third of the city's white students attend elite private schools while one-third of the city's students of color attend a high-poverty school. As well, almost half of all African American and Latino students in the city do not graduate in four years, if at all.[7] Very distressing, these dismal numbers have held constant for decades, according to several friends who have been longtime residents. Despite supposed "best" efforts, there has been little change for our students most in need. As the principal of Seattle's Garfield High School noted, "Dismantling a system built to sort students will take more than good intentions."[8] Seattle, as well as Detroit, Philadelphia, Chicago, Dallas, Newark, Boston, Los Angeles, New York, and other urban hubs, continues to struggle with resolve, results, resources, and responsibilities despite consensus that our schools need dramatic improvement. At our own local levels, we must do better—in spite of poverty and other factors we cannot control.

 ## Take Action

- **Value different life and language experiences.** Diversity is growing in our communities and in our schools. We need more role models like Justin Trudeau, Canada's prime minister, who has taken a leading international role in celebrating multiculturalism in schools and championing why we must all work toward a diverse, open, and inclusive education system.[9] See diversity as a plus. Embrace the backgrounds, languages, traditions, and cultures that students bring with them. Use a world map to pinpoint where our families originated. Consider making schoolwide announcements in different languages. Embrace music and art from around the world. Read aloud books that celebrate students' unique cultures. Our students will follow our lead in accepting and celebrating newcomers, all students, and their families.

- **Promote cross-racial friendships and dialogue.** Recent research shows that teacher behaviors "may shape how students select and maintain friends and affect the longevity of interracial friendships."[10] Most children still form most of their friendships in school, so we need to do all we can to create deliberate access for diverse friendships to form—through mixed grouping, conversations, invitations, language use, opportunities to work and play together, and ensuring that all children feel good about who they are. Students in diverse classrooms who experience cross-cultural dialogue demonstrate increased civic engagement, are more likely to be open to alternative points of view, are less likely to stereotype "others," and are better prepared for working in our increasingly diverse, global economy.[11]

- **Examine classroom and school libraries for diversity.** Excellent literature with accurate and dignified portrayals of people of color is still in short supply. With students, determine if the classroom collection is balanced by gender, students' cultures, interests, fiction and nonfiction, and more. Check for gender and racial stereotypes. See useful resources, such as "Resources for Teachers Seeking to Use More Diverse Texts," in an article by Lorna Collier; Weneeddiversebooks.org; Jessica Lifshitz, for excellent suggestions from a fifth-grade teacher; and Jonda McNair, for superb ideas on how to develop a diverse classroom library.[12]

- **Strive to adopt a mind-set that views all students as capable.** Research suggests teachers often view students from low-income families as less able than their peers from higher-income families even when cognitive assessments return equivalent scores.[13] When we perceive students as being less skilled and teach accordingly, we deny them the high-level, challenging instruction we offer students from higher-income families. We have to consciously work to change that harmful dynamic.

- **Group students who might not usually work together.** My middle school granddaughter considers being expected to work with different groups of students as one of the most valuable strategies her "best" teachers employ.

- **Come to agreement on shared beliefs on how to promote diversity.** Until individual and schoolwide beliefs shift to valuing diversity as a strength, many students will remain underserved. (See pages 113–118 for developing beliefs.)

- **Question policies that keep schools segregated,** and work to change them. The academic achievement gap for poor, black, and Latino children increases when they spend time in segregated schools.[14] Even when poor and middle-class students or students of color do attend schools with whites and affluent students, a two-tiered system often exists. There may be unspoken rules and settings that restrict participation and access to only whites or blacks at the school. Find out what's going on in your school and district, share findings, write an editorial, and use social media to advocate for more inclusive policies—for example, promoting integration by considering socioeconomic status when assigning students to schools.

- **Evaluate the representation of minority students in various school contexts.** We must face and adjust our biased behaviors, which limit equity. Seek out students who have potential but need an extra push to succeed. Ensure that being a bilingual student or a student of color is not used as an excuse for exclusion from a gifted program. "Black students are three times more likely to be referred for a gifted education program if they have a black teacher."[15] As well, examine the school's discipline policy and actions for fairness to all. High-poverty schools with large populations of blacks and Hispanics are "more likely to use expulsion and suspension as disciplinary tools . . . ."[16]

Implement a Challenging and Viable Curriculum

Students' understanding of any content and curriculum we teach depends in large part on our expectations of what we believe they can achieve. One of the biggest advantages of the residency model and my on-site work in classrooms over time is that teachers who are observing see what their students are capable of, which causes the "yes buts" to disappear.[17] With higher expectations and excellent, targeted teaching, we can raise achievement and change the trajectory of students' lives. However, we have to first believe in our hearts and minds—and then get students themselves to believe—that low expectations can be supplanted with high expectations that are accompanied by appropriately challenging learning experiences. Often it's the students themselves who are our catalyst for change; they achieve something that was not thought possible, and that can cause us to alter our thinking and view "curriculum" more broadly—as the sum of all we do, promote, say, and believe.

Our main job is not to teach skills or how to pass tests but to instruct, guide, support, and inspire students to become passionate learners who read, write, think, and compose their lives in and out of school in ways that bring meaning and satisfaction to them and to others. Curriculum is more than content. Curriculum includes all we do to create and sustain an intellectual classroom and school culture that fosters inquiry and invites all students on an intellectual adventure. Rethinking curriculum is a necessity. As innovative thinker Terry Heick notes, "If our job is to teach critical thinking, design, and problem-solving—fluid intelligence—then thinking is our collective circumstance, and **our curriculum becomes thought**" (boldface in original).[18] Curriculum as thinking about real-world issues must apply to all students, not just our high-performing ones. Our low-performing students benefit mightily. "Across the grades, when instruction was challenging, relevant, and academically demanding, then all students had higher engagement and teachers talked less—and the greatest beneficiaries were at-risk students."[19]

If we teach thought, then we are teaching students to inquire—for example, to examine real-world problems, analyze and synthesize what they read, consider and communicate multiple perspectives on issues, raise deep questions, and apply their learning to new contexts. To do this, our students need multifaceted skills and strategies—not taught in isolation but applied to the context of meaningful work. To teach thought means to nurture curiosity and to give students time and space to inquire on topics they care about, to collaborate with peers, and to take action on important issues beyond the classroom and themselves. All of this requires that we develop collaborative expertise to ensure our instructional practices are excellent. Here is where expert professional learning across a whole school is required. Heed the words of William Parrett and Kathleen Budge, highly respected educators who work to turn high-poverty schools into high-performing ones: *"Professional learning and student learning are two sides of the same coin—they cannot be separated"* (emphasis added).[20]

My experience has been that deep thought and having students do most of the intellectual work are rarely at the heart of our curriculum. We do value deep thinking and problem solving, but the bits and pieces of daily requirements and mandates often overrun us. It is only when we relentlessly prioritize and focus on a few important goals and outcomes and maintain that effort over a sustained period of time—even years—that we see deep learning results.

Implement an instructional framework and curriculum that are consistent with your beliefs, vision, research-based practices, and the needs and interests of your student body. Curriculum and standards ought to be a guide, not a straightjacket, and be meaningfully connected to students' lives. In my ongoing, collaborative work in Winnipeg, Canada, with my esteemed colleagues Nancy McLean and Sandra Figueroa, we worked with teachers and leaders to promote inquiry and capitalize on students' interests while teaching them to be discerning readers, complex thinkers, effective communicators, and citizens dedicated to improving their world. Deep learning occurred because the work was interesting, important, and purposeful to the students, and the teachers had become expert at their craft through ongoing professional learning. (See more on authentic teaching on pages 84–90.)

When a group of those fourth graders took on the work of highlighting the plight of their local endangered lake, the initial and ongoing frontloading (see page 88) gave students the information, vocabulary, techniques, and choices to inquire and write with passion and great skill. Under the expert guidance of their teacher, Daria Orloff, students wrote to their families and government officials to inform them about toxic algae and other substances endangering their freshwater lake and to urge them to take specific actions to save the lake. They wrote editorials that got published in the local newspaper, conducted interviews, created a persuasive rap video, conducted fundraisers to help clean up the lake, and more. Students became prodigious readers and writers; literacy—accompanied by advocacy—became for them not just something that happens in school but also something that informed citizens do to live a full and meaningful life. Daria notes,

> *The students were so engaged in their learning that our time together studying about the lake became our favorite part of the day. Needless to say, the writing pieces that came out of this were outstanding.*[21]

Jal Mehta, one of the researchers on a "deeper learning" study in thirty high schools and a few elementary schools seeking to offer rigorous, challenging, and engaging instruction, found that identity, mastery, and creativity have to coalesce for students to learn deeply—very much what happens when students become self-determining learners (see pages 335–337). In classrooms that achieve deeper learning, teachers ask appropriate questions, do not readily give the answers, and encourage and expect students to wrestle with uncertainly. Because students do most of the mental work, they "create knowledge, rather than receive knowledge."[22] As such, deep learners are able to transfer what they learn from one context to another.

 ## Take Action

+ **Give students the message that they can achieve at high levels.** Research has shown that when we let students know we hold high expectations for them—and that if they are willing to put in the effort, they will be able to meet our high standards—most students will redo an assignment and put greater effort into their work.[23] Remarkably, even a single display of respect from a teacher can have profound effects on student achievement. When African American seventh-grade social studies students received a handwritten message from their teacher (who was white) "encouraging them to meet a higher standard and implying that the teacher believed in them as they tried to do so," these students ". . . had fewer disciplinary incidents over the entire next year and were more likely to be enrolled in college six years later."[24]

+ **Seek to spark imagination, curiosity, and desire to learn** in all students, and see those qualities as a basic human right for every child, regardless of the child's background or present achievement level. Let's start with those qualities in mind and share with students our own passions for learning; talk about and show what we are most curious about and how that affects our lives.

Self-Check Our Curriculum Expectations—Ask questions like the following:

⦿ Will students be expected to do some deep thinking—meaningful problem solving and communication with and for a real-world audience and purpose?

⦿ Are we providing the foundational knowledge that makes it possible for students to grasp complex ideas?

⦿ Are we asking important questions and encouraging students to do the same—that is, do the questions raised lead to deeper understanding on topics worth knowing about? (See pages 70, 84, and 162 on questioning.)

⦿ Will the lesson, task, project, and goals engage students in a manner that will make them want to go on learning?

⦿ Is there enough choice within structure (see pages 90–93) so students will want to engage in the lesson or task?

⦿ Are there ample opportunities for productive dialogue and collaboration with others?

⦿ Are the literature and resources that our students and we employ first-class—that is, accurate, unbiased, written by reputable authors, and easily accessible and comprehensible?

⦿ Are we providing clear and worthwhile goals and success criteria along with sufficient frontloading (see pages 88 and 129–131), collaborative experiences, and deliberate practice so students have the necessary support, competence, and will to "do the work"?

◆ **Connect science and social studies and STEM with real-world issues,** high expectations, and authentic problem solving. Organize curriculum around important themes or issues, big questions, and investigations connected to students' lives. For example, engage and challenge students with local, national, and international issues such as human rights (for example, the right to clean water, the right to a living wage), environmental concerns and rights (such as polluted local lakes, endangered species, climate change), social justice (such as racism, criminal justice, segregated schools, housing discrimination), and immigration (such as undocumented workers and their families, the international refugee crisis). Some topics, such as climate change and the rights of the child, can become a yearlong school focus across all grades.

- *Connect reading, writing, and research with required standards* across the curriculum—as much as possible, which allows for large time blocks for deep learning. See lesson plan online at sten.pub/literacyessentials for one such example.
- *Consult excellent websites*—for example, those of the US Environmental Protection Agency, the American Society for Engineering Education, NASA, the Library of Congress, the Smithsonian Institution, iCivics, Edutopia, and Exploratorium, for lessons, ideas, and much more.
- *Teach specific, adaptable skills* along with wide-ranging understanding.
- *Present findings and learning.* Connected to curriculum and learning must be evidence that the process and results inform and benefit students and the wider community, which can be demonstrated by presenting important information or urging advocacy—through a book, a performance, research, a video, an op-ed piece, a podcast, a multimedia creation, and so on.

♦ **Integrate civic engagement into disciplinary literacy and school life.** Make voting rights, fairness, and treating all people with dignity core equity issues across the curriculum and across the school. Give the message that good government is everyone's responsibility. Model how responsible citizens behave and act in ways that go beyond their own self-interest. Start with our youngest students and provide experiences in student council, collaborative group work, role playing, helping peers, preventing bullying, and much more.

♦ **Bring current events into the classroom** and help students understand various points of view on significant, present-day topics, such as immigration, homelessness, climate change, social media, racism, criminal justice, and more; such understanding contributes to becoming an informed and responsible citizen. Sustaining our fragile democracy demands that citizens, starting in elementary school, become committed to knowing and understanding history in the making, our system of government, and the forces that shape it.

News-rich classrooms also expose kids to the diversity of the world and help cultivate their development as responsible, global citizens. Also of importance, "Current events discussions offer ample opportunity for skill building (e.g., vocabulary development, reading and writing informational and analytical text, oral expression, critical analysis—all part of the ELA Common Core Learning

Standards."[25] For reputable news sites to use with your students, check out sites such as TweenTribune at http://microsite.smithsonianmag.com/tweentribune/, Newsela at https://newsela.com/, and Listen Current at http://www.simplek12.com/podcast/listen-current-podcasting/. (For more on current events, see pages 69 and 387–390.)

- **Strive for coherence and clarity**—that is, consistency and alignment in beliefs, practices, and learning goals across the grades and across the curriculum. A series of case studies found that ". . . schools that failed to improve were not able to achieve instructional coherence, despite being in systems with strong external accountability."[26] Coherence and clarity do not happen without strong teacher and principal leadership and a highly functioning Professional *Literacy* Community (see page 107).

- **Examine curriculum documents for relevance and usability.** Ensure that such documents are readable, focus on the big ideas, and are not broken up into myriad isolated skills. Also work to ensure any written document for a curriculum area is no longer than twenty to thirty pages. Unwieldy documents eventually become shelf documents that gather dust.

- **Implement worthwhile common assessments.** Ensure that these actually help us learn more about our students and teach better. Often, common assessments exhaust us and do little to improve teaching and learning.

- **Raise expectations for writing.** Very few writing assignments push students to think at higher levels.[27] As a staff and a district, evaluate what students and teachers are asked to do, and how. What does having students write a well-crafted essay, book review, or report entail? It goes way beyond correct grammar, punctuation, and a beginning, middle, and end; it includes an enticing lead, important and well-stated content backed up by evidence, a logical and organized sequence of ideas, interesting vocabulary, and a persuasive conclusion—all of which need to be modeled by the teacher. (See Optimal Learning Model on page 139 and Appendix G, 12 Writing Essentials for All Grade Levels.)

- **Recognize that reading instruction and "reading programs" are often inadequate** for many students. For example, workbooks and worksheets demean the intelligence of low-performing students, yet they remain common fare. Ensure the reading materials connected to curriculum study are first-rate and connected to high-level thinking—for all students.

Employ Standards Thoughtfully

The Common Core State Standards (CCSS) set a necessary, higher bar for what students should know and be able to do, especially as related to analytical thinking, communication skills, and conceptual understandings in reading and writing texts and in content knowledge. Those standards were developed as a direct response to many states' common practice of lowering standards and expectations in order to artificially raise student achievement. As a result, falsely elevated test scores on high-stakes tests did a terrible disservice to many students and their families, who came to believe students were progressing satisfactorily when they were not. Compared with scores on the National Assessment of Educational Progress in many states, the differences in achievement between the state test and the national test were stark. The good news is almost all states have revised their standards and the levels for considering students proficient on state assessments.[28] The not-so-good news is many teachers and leaders don't know how to reach those higher standards, and support to do so is often insufficient.

Issues with standards

In my experience, most teachers feel ill-equipped and overwhelmed by all that is expected of them in implementing standards, whether it's being expected to write their own curriculum, use district-produced materials or commercial programs, or find time for all the competing demands. Also, as predicted, higher standards have raised expectations but often fragmented instruction. Just like what happens when focusing on an extensive checklist, it's easy to lose sight of the students in front of us when we're concerned about the myriad details on the standards. Some teachers work so hard on trying to teach all the standards that they fail to help students connect all the parts into a meaningful whole. Another troubling result is that excessive pressure to meet standards and raise test scores has caused many teachers to question and discard what we know works from research and experience.

A regrettable consequence of an overemphasis on having all students meet grade-level standards—as opposed to an emphasis on expert teaching that meets each student's needs and interests while using the latest standards as a guide and framework—is that students who most need individualized instruction tailored to their needs do not get much of it and, therefore, do not improve much.

Very troubling as well, a mind-set of "standards before students" has led to excessive test preparation, which does little to improve student learning in the long run and much to damage teacher and student attitudes about the meaning of school and learning. As publishers have explicitly connected standards to new and costly tests, we have further escalated our national frenzy of "test more, teach less," with the result that test prep dominates day-to-day teaching in many schools, especially those where students are not thriving. Such overzealous test prep and testing continue to create less opportunity to learn, which perpetuates the achievement gap. In fact, "What is called 'the achievement gap' is actually an 'opportunity gap.'"[29]

So although the CCSS were developed with the noble goal of promoting equity, in actuality that goal has not been realized in most states. Partly as a response to low test scores on tests that are more rigorous, some states are considering lowering standards to boost high school graduation rates. Doing so will only exacerbate our current problem of students who do make it to college but are unprepared, as evidenced by the fact that so many wind up in remedial reading and math classes.

Coping well with standards

There is only one implementation route that will enable us to truly raise and sustain literacy achievement for all students, and that is a whole-school commitment to intelligent and effective professional development—what I call Professional *Literacy* Communities (see page 107). Such a commitment requires a national, cultural shift that recognizes that understanding and interpreting standards requires highly knowledgeable teachers and leaders. Standards delineate the "what" of teaching and the performance expectations—to effectively determine the "how" of teaching and the instructional and assessment moves that lead to student competency.

Keep in mind that there is no research that shows that states that adopted high standards have fared any better than those with low standards.[30] We educators are the ones who need to be on the front lines in determining the high-quality curriculum that will respect our students' cultural and language identities and provide the significant and targeted scaffolding learners require. We simply cannot assume that adopting standards will cause students to learn more.

Knowing and applying "best" literacy practices that respect the long-standing research base on literacy acquisition and application and holding fast to making principled decisions that honor our students' backgrounds, interests, and needs are essential to implementing standards with instructional integrity. Such knowledge is especially crucial as school districts are collectively spending billions of dollars, most of it from their own budgets, to buy standards-aligned programs, curriculum, and assessments—much of it of questionable quality.

Take Action

What follows are a few broad and significant areas we can focus our teaching practices on that are cited in the CCSS as necessary for college and career readiness. Note that these key areas are trademarks of highly effective and knowledgeable teaching regardless of what set of standards or programs happens to be in place at the time.

- **Emphasize critical thinking.** Focus on in-depth learning—not just right answers—requiring more analysis and real-world problem solving. Critical thinking includes teaching independent thinking—that is, reasoning abstractly, constructing persuasive arguments, understanding point of view, and asking questions that cause deeper thinking, such as "What made you think that?" "What's another possibility?" "How else might this information be interpreted?" (See "Ask More Vital Questions," pages 161–167.) A caution here is to not teach critical thinking—or any standard—as a separate entity, but to envision critical thinking infused throughout the day and across the curriculum.

- **Teach close and deep reading of texts,** including more nonfiction. Demonstrate for students and guide them in reading more closely and analytically—both informational and literary texts—by going back to a text to cite evidence, a necessary skill for proficient readers. That type of reading, recommended by CCSS, need not be exclusive; that is, we can do close reading of texts and still employ our experiences and prior knowledge, which are long-established, research-based hallmarks of strong readers. (See also "Apply common sense" on page 384 and "Create Access to Complex Texts," pages 215–217.)

- **Promote extensive writing across the curriculum.** Emphasize the teaching of clear and coherent writing in all subject areas and in multiple genres for various audiences and purposes, supported first by effective demonstrations of our own effective thinking and writing. Include persuasive arguments, research, narratives, reflections, explanations, and much more.

Apply Whole-Part-Whole Teaching

When I first started going into schools to do demonstration teaching and coaching of reading and writing practices in classrooms, teachers would typically ask, "Can you give me a list of all the skills I need to teach, preferably in the order I should teach them?" At the end of the weeklong residency, we would make a list of all the skills we'd taught, and teachers were amazed at how many more skills we had "covered" when we focused first on meaningful teaching and embedded the skills that were needed into the instructional context. Literally, our skills list was pages long!

You would think that it's easier and more manageable for students, especially the ones who struggle, if we break texts and activities up into little parts or discrete subskills. Actually, a fragmented approach makes it much harder for students to successfully learn. A colleague put it this way: "It's like putting all the pieces of a big puzzle in front of someone but never showing him or her the lid of the box." It's actually easier to learn when we can first get a sense of how all the pieces fit together— as in learning how to ride a bike. It's easier for the brain to make sense of something when we start with "seeing" the whole of a meaningful activity, text, context, story, or poem, and doing so makes success more likely, even for our youngest learners, as the following story illustrates.

I was working in a high-needs kindergarten classroom during the month of March, with students who had been reading and writing for authentic audiences and purposes since the beginning of the school year. The teacher and I were having the students write "how to" directions that would be posted in the classroom and around the school. We wrote "How to Line Up" together, as a shared writing; brainstormed many "how to" topics they could choose from; and had several public, scaffolded conversations with students before sending them off to write. We directed them to write only the first line, their lead, for two reasons: (1) we wanted to ensure they understood how to begin so they, and we, wouldn't have to redo, and (2) we didn't want to overwhelm them. To our surprise and chagrin, all students got down a meaningful first sentence, and more than half of them wrote the entire "how to" text in one sitting! What a big learning experience that was. It was actually easier for most of them to write three to five sentences and keep the flow of writing going than to stop after one beginning thought. Our meager expectations limited their capacity, but, luckily, most of them ignored us.

We are also limiting the capacity of teachers—not to mention squandering their precious time and energy—by district mandates that make it a requirement to deconstruct and teach the standards one by one, which reflects part-to-whole teaching that leads to narrow goal setting and shallow teaching. Many students, especially those who struggle, never do figure out how all the parts fit together. Connected to that unnecessary parsing of the standards are the inadequate resources that exist to help teachers implement and apply standards thoughtfully. That resource gap has often led to expecting many teachers to write their own curriculum, which is unrealistic for many reasons, not least of which are insufficient knowledge, support, and time—time that otherwise might be spent on more worthwhile pursuits.

And there's this: innovative thinkers, "start-up" people, creative problem solvers all think outside the box. They raise open-ended questions, consider alternative routes, and seek inventive solutions. When we lose the ability and desire to see "the big picture" and "a different picture," we remain limited to the small boxes we have put ourselves in, and that does a huge disservice to our students and us.

 # Take Action

- **With implementation of standards, focus first on the big picture of literacy.** Related to the CCSS, I rely on a one-page, double-sided laminated sheet that I keep on hand to remind me to stay focused on what's most important to teach. One side lists the four key areas, followed by explanations, of the College and Career Readiness Anchor Standards for Reading; the reverse side similarly lists the College and Career Readiness Anchor Standards for Writing. These apply to grades K–12. (See Appendix H: College and Career Readiness Anchor Standards: Reading and Writing.) Notice how the reading standards also apply to writing and reinforce the reading-writing connection. I have read through all the ELA standards, an exhausting process. With a deep and growing foundation of knowledge via ongoing professional learning, I am able to stay focused on what's most significant and not get lost in myriad details of the standards.

  Be sure to apply this big picture of literacy to any adopted program or resource as well. Often core reading programs and intervention programs, for example, rely heavily on canned lessons and skills in isolation, believing they are "teaching to the standards." This is not good teaching. Effective teaching prioritizes teaching for meaning and applying skills to purposefully communicate, understand, and reason—in and outside of school.

- **Apply an Optimal Learning Model** (see pages 136–146). The OLM is always about whole-part-whole, meaningful instruction. The Optimal Learning Model is differentiated instruction and responsive teaching in action, which is how we learn best. Based on the needs and interests of our students, we begin with a meaningful whole—a topic of study, a concept, an article, a book, a song—and then teach students to understand how skills, strategies, vocabulary, visuals, and so on, fit into the whole meaningful context. A part-to-whole instructional approach— with its accompanying belief that separately teaching the parts in isolation will eventually (and magically) add up to a meaningful whole—lowers expectations. As well, a part-to-whole approach often demeans students by diminishing their engagement, potential, and ability to excel and apply learning to other contexts.

- **Teach it first; label it later.** Of course, we can and must teach all the necessary skills, but when our students and we first have an understanding of the "big picture," teaching and student learning are easier and more effective. For example, we can teach and label transitions as early as kindergarten and make a chart of possible transition words and phrases starting with transitions from students' writing. First, however, we spend sustained time noticing and discussing—in the context of daily read-alouds, reading texts, and writing texts—how transitions make it easier for the reader to follow along. Here is some suggested language to try out:

  - "When the writer wrote such and such, he was letting the reader know he was changing subjects."
  - "We call those call-outs to the reader 'transitions.' They make it easy and logical to follow where the author is going."
  - "You might want to include transitions in your writing when you change topics so the reader can easily follow your [story, thinking, logic]."

- **Tell the whole story first.** Even if you only intend to write a small portion of a "story" or an editorial or essay, first give students a sense of the whole, and then how the parts fit within the whole. This advice applies to us and our students. Telling the whole story first encourages the use of elaboration and detail and helps us flesh out what's most important. Starting with oral storytelling, with guided support, also makes it easier for most learners to tell and write a complete story.

- **Provide some context.** When assessing comprehension through one-on-one reading conferences, have students bring a book-in-process or a completed book. Sometimes the reader needs to have read at least several pages or more before full meaning kicks in. Having some idea of the content and how the text works before an assessment makes deeper comprehension more likely.

- **Rethink exercises in isolation.** There is no research that shows that isolated skills work helps kids learn more or faster. Embed explicit skills teaching and practice within the context of the meaningful content we are teaching. Keep in mind that every well-written text contains multiple opportunities for teaching vocabulary, grammar, word work, writing craft, reading comprehension, and much more.

  For example, when teaching grammar, zoom in and out as needed between a meaningful whole, such as a paragraph or an essay, to the smallest chunk of meaning, such as a sentence, and guide students to see visual and meaningful patterns such as subject-verb agreement.[31] Also, with students' permission, project a whole piece of writing and go line by line demonstrating editing for grammar, spelling, and so on. Students invest in such an exercise when it's their own writing done for an authentic audience and purpose. Of course, we have first conferred about the content of the writing before emphasizing the editing.

- **Reconsider daily schedules.** Too often, schedules are configured to fit parts into a whole—for example, mandating that a language arts block be broken into pieces, such as starting the day with word work in isolation. In fairness, some districts mandate such work because they believe teachers are not teaching word work. Only schoolwide professional learning will bring things into balance. Then, savvy teachers figure out a way to make a mandated and fragmented schedule whole. As one example, primary teachers use shared writing and shared reading as a vehicle for required, explicit word work.

Integrate Word Study and Vocabulary Development

A principal recently told me that his whole-school focus for the year was on "vocabulary." I gently suggested he might want to think about changing that focus to wide reading. We simply can't directly teach enough vocabulary and word work to significantly increase students' achievement. It's widely known that students who own a rich storehouse of words tend to be higher achievers, and most of these students are avid readers. As an equity issue, we must ensure students become comprehending readers early on in their school years.

For our English language learners and students who struggle, understanding and applying key vocabulary words are vital. It is often a lack of academic vocabulary that severely limits students' understanding of content and concepts. Research has clearly shown that vocabulary knowledge is a constant predictor in comprehending informational text.[32] Research has also shown that once students can read independently, voluntary reading is the most effective way to increase vocabulary development in students of all ages, regardless of their socioeconomic status.[33]

Not only is a rich vocabulary a necessity for understanding and creating meaningful texts, but also it's fun to talk about and use words in various ways. Kids are naturally curious about words and word play, what words mean, and how words work, generally and specifically. It is never too early to start playing around with words and learning challenging vocabulary, and the two can easily go together. Learning to love words is something we can easily and deliberately incorporate into our teaching in all disciplines, for all students. Taking a bit of time each day to focus on and discuss fascinating words can pay big dividends.

Use the Optimal Learning Model to show students how to learn new words, enjoy figuring out meanings, and aptly apply word knowledge to enrich their speaking, writing, reading, and listening. Teach and practice how the most frequent prefixes and suffixes, as well as roots of words, can help unlock many unknown words. Demonstrate how surrounding text can also assist in deciphering word, phrase, and/or sentence meaning. However, context clues are only reliable if the surrounding text is meaningful and the learner has sufficient background knowledge to infer a reasonable interpretation.

Since our time for teaching vocabulary in an already too-full curriculum is limited, most vocabulary teaching—of necessity—must be self-teaching. Again, since most self-teaching of vocabulary occurs through wide reading, we need to be providing sufficient time for sustained, mostly free-choice reading. Not to be minimized, as part of a rich and deep curriculum, we must also be explicitly teaching those significant concepts and definitions that are essential to students' reading comprehension. Avoid requiring students to "learn" lists of vocabulary words and use them in sentences, an unproven activity for vocabulary retention and application. As well, turning vocabulary work into an unpleasant chore can turn some students off to reading, an especially egregious result for students who don't yet see themselves as readers. Implement a combined instructional approach: explicit teaching of crucial words and concepts, effective use of context, and extensive reading.

 ## Take Action

♦ **Develop a word-conscious classroom.**

  ◉ *Notice and talk about interesting words wherever they turn up,* demonstrate their use and meanings, and find opportunities to use key words over and over again—in speaking and writing.

  ◉ *Encourage students to try out the use of special focus words* throughout the day, through our modeling and with our support, in conversations and in writing.

  ◉ *Use vocabulary word walls in the content areas*—science, social studies, history, math, music, and so on—to post key words with definitions written with students that we expect them to reference, read, and write. For example, when Daria Orloff and her fourth graders explored the causes and "cures" for a polluted local lake (see pages 264–265), words such as *eutrophication* and *phosphorous* became an expected part of their speaking, writing, and spelling.

  ◉ *Feature a "vocabulary word of the day,"* with an explanation that students can understand. Some days we can choose the word; other days a student chooses.

These unique words and their meaning can be compiled into a classroom vocabulary notebook.

- **Make a daily commitment to vocabulary development.**
  - *Provide explicit vocabulary instruction.* Important keywords and definitions must be directly taught in order for students to grasp their meanings. Use explanations, demonstrations of use, physical involvement, prior knowledge, and as many senses as possible to make word meanings comprehensible.
  - *Advocate for extensive reading.* Many words used in literature and informational pieces are not ordinarily part of everyday spoken language; so again, the only way to learn them is through extensive reading in a wide variety of genres.
  - *Connect independent reading time to vocabulary growth.* On occasion, ask students to pick out and talk about one or two new words whose meanings they figured out.
  - *Make it smart to ask about interesting words* whose meanings we don't know. For example, we can say, "Thomas asked what *solution* means. That's what successful learners do so they can understand more."
  - *Point out interesting words and how they are used when reading aloud* to the class. Check with a librarian for more books like *Miss Alaineus: A Vocabulary Disaster* by Debra Frasier and *Donavan's Word Jar* by Monalisa DeGross that make vocabulary work fun and engrossing.

- **Weave explicit word study into daily teaching.**
  - *Teach word patterns.* Instead of focusing on rules, "help children focus on the sound-letter pattern."[34] Highlight common patterns, such as *-ake* in *make*, *take*, and *brake* during shared writing and shared reading, guided reading, and writing time. For word walls in primary grades, post only one word that fits a particular pattern, but highlight (for example, with transparent colored tape) the letters that form the consistent pattern (*-ake*).
  - *Use individual whiteboards to have all students quickly write and read featured words.* Include challenge words. In the aforementioned kindergarten restaurant reviews, *pizza* was our challenge word, and almost every student—midyear in a high-needs, half-day kindergarten class—spelled it correctly! They could all read *pizza* too.
  - *Expect students to self-check spelling* by using room resources such as charts and word walls, checking with peers, consulting student dictionaries, and looking at familiar texts.

- *Create with students, from the reading and writing we are doing, charts that conform to the word study in process*—for example, a chart of "ee" words or an important vowel combination students must know, or words with specific prefixes or suffixes or important roots. Students can use sticky notes to attach words to the chart and, if they are correctly spelled, add them to the chart.
- *Highlight features of words in familiar texts*—using a document camera or on charts, and so on. Use a sliding mask to feature a word and to blend word parts.
- *Evaluate everything we are teaching in word work.* One quick and reliable way is to take a familiar text, such as a class-authored one (for example, our restaurant review), and give each student a word-processed copy. Read through the text as a whole. Afterward, direct students to circle designated words, turn their papers over and write those words, and then self-check and correct for accuracy. Send home such papers weekly and have students read the text to their family and talk about the text and their word-work learning.

Observe an Excellent Kindergarten Teacher

Some years ago, our school district got a group of K–12 teachers together to determine a coherent literacy plan across the grades. I still recall the shock of secondary teachers, after several days of cross-grade-level collaboration, as they shifted their views of kindergarten teachers from "cut-and-paste teachers" to deep respect for "smart and savvy colleagues." They, along with many of us, had no idea how much it takes to be an expert kindergarten teacher. In my forty-plus years of teaching in many diverse schools, I have found that kindergarten teachers are often the most knowledgeable. They are usually well grounded in theory, practice, management, pacing, relationships, and the importance of play for learning and socializing. They seamlessly integrate music, drama, movement, and the arts into all they do. Although corners such as a vet clinic or a grocery store, building with blocks, painting on easels, and dress-up have sadly disappeared from many kindergarten classrooms as the push for academics trickles down, determined and wise kindergarten teachers have managed to hold on to sacred play time and to integrate explicit teaching into authentic writing and reading activities throughout the day. (See photo, page 371.)

Invite your superintendent and middle and high school principals to observe an exemplary kindergarten teacher in action. In my experience, such a visit works wonders for raising expectations for what's possible at every grade level. Just like the secondary teachers in the preceding paragraph, administrators are shocked at what our youngest learners are capable of achieving. Renowned educator Deborah Meier asks us to see kindergarten as the model for how our schools could be and to "use the principles of a good kindergarten as the basis for running a good high school."[35] Sage advice indeed.

 ## Take Action

* **Do everything possible to ensure that kindergarten teachers have high enough expectations and get high results.** With expert literacy teaching, almost all students can leave kindergarten as emerging and beginning readers and writers, which, in turn, raises achievement possibilities for the whole school. Richard Allington states, "Better-trained kindergarten teachers can solve the reading problems of at-risk students at the same rate as expert tutorial programs."[36]

* **Advocate for putting more resources into kindergarten** and ensuring that kindergarten teachers are highly proficient, that class size is small, and that all-day kindergarten becomes a reality everywhere. With excellent first teaching for all students, we prevent literacy problems before they occur, increase educational opportunities for more students, and save money in the long run.

Endnote

It's inequitable not to hold high expectations for all children or to fail to create opportunities that make it possible and probable to tap into their potential. Equity is about expert teaching that gives all kids the opportunity to learn and to want to learn in a school culture of empowerment.

One student I will never forget is first grader Alexia. I was told that she was a "selective mute," and on the firm recommendation of her psychologist she was not to be pushed to do anything she didn't want to do. How odd, I privately thought, to give a young child permission to opt out of learning. She was the only student in the class who turned in a blank sheet of paper while the rest of the class wrote about a best friend. After we had celebrated the writing of every student the next day in public writing conferences, I held up Alexia's blank paper and kindly said, "I'm sad we're not able to celebrate your writing, Alexia. I know you have lots of interesting things to say about your friend, and we'd love to hear them. I hope we can celebrate your writing tomorrow."

I had no idea what she would choose to do. But here's the thing. Every child wants to opt into learning. Alexia wrote a full, legible page titled "Tess and Me." Her use of language and thought were stirring and poetic; observing teachers were flabbergasted at what this child could do. Once a child does high-quality work and recognizes what she has accomplished—even when the process has been a struggle—nothing is the same. Alexia went on to become a writer. Once she and we found a way in, she was fully launched as a learner.

EQUITY 2

Reaching *All* Learners

Students who are engaged and enthusiastic learners believe their teachers know them, consider their interests, make the work meaningful, give them useful feedback, and treat them fairly and respectfully—all crucial for learning across the grades and across the disciplines. That statement is true for all students—high-performing students and those students who struggle.

Students are willing to work through challenging ideas they do not yet understand if teachers value questions and support students' struggle and failure as a normal part of learning. A high school student told me her "best" teachers encourage and enable her and her peers to make a full-out effort every day by respectfully answering all their questions, being available for ongoing support, and providing opportunities to revise work to make it better. By contrast, when a teacher rewards only final performance, deems some questions too insignificant to answer, and expects students to get it "right" on a first attempt, effort in that class is diminished. When students are made to feel "less than," it's difficult to reach them.

If we truly want all students to have the opportunity to learn deeply and joyfully, they require patient and kind teachers who demonstrate curiosity and ongoing determination to persist even when the learning does not come easily. This chapter will discuss actions, dispositions, and resources that can lead all students to succeed. I deliberately use the word *learner* in the title of this chapter to include not just students, but all of us educators—teachers, coaches, specialists, principals, and leaders at all levels.

Instill Determination to Learn

After years of work in diverse schools and classrooms, a crucial question persists for me: Why do teachers, students, and principals in some schools succeed in raising and sustaining achievement for our underserved students while so many do not? We graduate the easiest-to-reach students but do less well with those who struggle. It often seems to come down to a determination to learn—that is, a steadfast, unwavering commitment to getting better and learning more—no matter what it takes. For us educators, having such determination means recognizing where we need to improve, not accepting the status quo, and becoming professionally knowledgeable and highly skilled at our craft. It also means not letting challenging constraints, especially those over which we often have no control, demoralize us. Without intense, lifelong determination, we simply cannot make a critical and lasting difference for our students. Here is where an intellectual, collaborative culture of trust, shared beliefs, and shared values is crucial. Such a culture, as discussed in the Engagement section, serves as the sturdy infrastructure that makes expert teaching and learning against the odds possible and likely.

For our students, beginning in preschool, instilling a determination to learn is as vital as any literacy or content skills we teach them. It may, in fact, be the greatest gift we can give them. Kids have to believe in themselves in order to learn. Instead of giving up when a task or lesson gets frustrating and difficult, we demonstrate how, work with them, and support them to attain the necessary know-how and persistence that makes eventual success likely. We provide effective and timely instruction, thoughtful questions, guided practice, and useful feedback so they learn that hard-fought efforts lead to gratification, deep learning, and growing confidence.

Making a determined effort has to be taught. Students accustomed to praise and rewards for performance, as well as those accustomed to negative comments for not measuring up, need to experience—with our guidance and support—the internal satisfaction and reward that come from making a full-out effort.

Research has repeatedly shown that rewarding performance can have possible negative consequences and work against collaboration and intrinsic motivation. But rewarding persistence and hard work with specific, timely, and honest feedback sends the message that we value effort and that it is sustained effort that leads to lasting learning and success. Research by Carol Dweck showed that students who were told their success was due to their hard work were much more likely to challenge themselves as learners and to take more risks than those who were told their success was due to being smart.[1]

For students with learning issues, the situation is often dire. Here's a disturbing fact: while the overall high school graduation rate in the United States has improved, many states graduate less than 70 percent of students who are from low-income families, are English language learners, or are Hispanic or African American; for students with disabilities, that number is often much lower.[2] When we provide a relevant and engaging curriculum, teach with a sense of urgency and joy, respectfully invite everyone into the conversation, and celebrate strengths and small victories, then weaknesses, deficits, and behavioral problems can be greatly reduced—and in some cases disappear. We must also show through our own and others' examples that continuing determination to learn can help overcome hardships and setbacks. Easier said than done. We can't expect students to have a positive attitude about school if they are always failing. (See also pages 352–353.)

Students accustomed to a lifetime of failure—frequently interconnected with extreme poverty and hardships—often project an outward "I don't care" attitude to mask an "I can't do it" inner belief that inhibits asking for help and sabotages any chance for success.[3] However, until we raise our own expectations for what students can achieve and walk the walk with them so they are willing to go on after they stumble, their academic success will remain elusive. High expectations and determination to learn go hand in hand, and instilling determination to learn must become one of our highest teaching and leading priorities.

 ## Take Action

- **Listen to students and get to know them.** If students are to develop determination to learn, we have to help them find their self-worth. We can't help our students if we know them only through their test scores. We need to show we care by listening to them, talking with them, and knowing them. One way third-grade teacher Kyle Schwartz gets to know her students better and create a more open and supportive classroom is to have them finish the sentence "I wish my teacher knew _____."[4]

- **Welcome all students.** Greet each student personally each day with a smile. Ask students about their day. Give them some choices—in seating, group work, form of final product. Adopt a mind-set of "our classroom"; have them "design" how the classroom might be organized and work. Inspire them with your enthusiasm for being their teacher. View the three-minute, welcome-to-school video rap song by an excited first-year teacher, Dwayne Reed.[5]

◆ **Honor students' names.** Our names are our identity, and calling students by their correct or preferred name is an act of respect for their individuality, culture, and language. Especially for students new to our schools, English language learners, refugees and students from other countries, students who are homeless or otherwise struggling in their lives, and students who feel they don't belong, honoring their names is an important first step to validating who they are. Not only that, when we say students' names correctly it lets them know we care about them, that we see them and value them. For some students, honoring their names helps them adjust to school and avoid potential behavior issues because they no longer feel invisible.

◉ *Listen carefully to how students pronounce their names,* and verify with them we are pronouncing their names correctly. It's a sensitive area for most of us. I tell students:

> *Correctly pronouncing each of your names is very important to me, so if I mispronounce your name, please tell me right away. My name is Regie (Ree gee), and it is often mispronounced as Reggie, which always bothers me; so I want to be sure to get your name right.*

◉ *Help students feel proud of their names.* Some students, because they want to fit into the school's culture or for specific personal reasons, seek to change their names to gain a clearer identity or peer acceptance. Regardless of the age of your students, read and discuss the inspiring picture book *Thunder Boy Jr.* by Sherman Alexie, with illustrations by Yuyi Morales, to help students come to terms with their names.[6] See also "My Name, My Identity," a national campaign that celebrates students' names and pronouncing them correctly.[7]

◉ *Get to know the person behind the name.* Start by telling and then writing, in front of your students, your own story, "What I Want You to Know About Me." Have students do the same, first with a partner and then on paper. Or, if the number of students is manageable, sit down and talk with each one individually. Your students will never forget that personal time you devoted to getting to know them. (See also the story "Being Known," pages 287–289.)

Here are some possible conversation starters: "What's something you like to do when you have spare time?" "What do you like to do with your friends?" "What's your greatest strength?" "What's a goal you have for yourself?" "Who is someone you admire a lot?" "When was a time you felt broken?"[8]

◉ *Dispense with labels that stigmatize.* Labels, such as "dyslexic" or "reading disabled," can unintentionally serve to disenfranchise and brand students as less capable. Refer to a student as a learner first, such as "student with learning disabilities," rather than "learning-disabled student." Seek to use more positive terms. A group of middle school students recently petitioned the White House to request that the term "English language learners" be changed to "multilingual students."[9] Instead of ELL, Canada uses EAL, "English as an additional language," which seems to me a more respectful term.

- *Use a name word wall in kindergarten* with a photo of each student next to his or her name. It's a great way for students to read and write one another's names. Use the letter and sound combinations and chunks when teaching phonics, spelling, and writing. For example, highlight "ch" in Charles, "an" in Cassandra, and other common letter-sound patterns. (See also page 277.)

- ◆ **Inspire life and learning passions.** A passion is what we love, what we want to know everything about, what we are inspired by, and what brings us joy—not just for ourselves but for others as well. Our passion makes us relentless in our pursuit of excellence.

  - *Share our own passions.* For me it's teaching, collaborating in underserved schools, reading, writing, cooking and baking, and loving my family and friends. I bring those stories—including my inquiry questions and research—into the classroom. Find out what your students' passions are and nourish them as best you can.

  - *Provide opportunities for students to "find" their passion.* Equity cannot exist without opportunity to learn and thrive. Share the inspirational life story of Ryan Speedo Green, an internationally known and gifted opera singer, with middle and high school students.[10] It was a teacher who provided him a life-changing opportunity. (See page 67 for that story.)

  - *Implement "Genius Hour,"* giving students sustained time each week to explore their interests and burning questions through designing their own learning, in much the same way as Google promotes similar creative time for its workers.[11] In that vein, occasionally use your literacy block or class period throughout the school year for each student to investigate one or two passion projects in depth—student's choice. See *The Genius Hour Guidebook* and "6 Principles of Genius Hour in the Classroom" for specifics and recommendations.[12]

- ◆ **Embrace our mistakes.** Students and colleagues need to see us "mess up" and acknowledge our struggle, which builds a culture of trust and risk taking for students. When things are not going well during a lesson, I say something like this: "I've noticed that many of you are struggling with understanding such and such. I didn't give you enough time for ____, or do a good enough job explaining ____. Let's back up and ____." Giving our students and ourselves permission to regroup and change course helps students and us persevere. As well, our own honest example may help many students eventually believe that struggle and failure are a normal part of the learning process. (See more on pages 352–353.)

◆ **Help students believe they can succeed.** Determination to learn comes from knowing you can do the work, and that if and when you stumble, you can get support. Survey your students: "Do you believe intelligence is fixed?" Many of our low-performing students and students from low-income families are not optimistic about their chances for success. Share and discuss the research with them that effort and practice lead to higher achievement.[13] Let students know through our instruction and actions that we will do all we can to help them succeed and that we value them and their hard-fought efforts.

◆ **Present information using a variety of approaches and strategies** to ensure we reach learners with diverse needs. For example, move beyond traditional stand-and-deliver teaching to incorporate more shared reading, shared writing, multimedia, illustrations and visuals, collaborative group work, and opportunity for movement, music, and the arts.

◆ **Give credit to students' problem-solving and thinking processes** as well as to the final product or "right answer." Be sure to value steadfast effort and thoughtful responses in whole-class discussion, one-on-one conferences, revision work, small-group work, and homework in determining a student's grade. Value students' determination. Invite students to hand in not just their final paper, project, or homework but also all the notes, drafts, attempts, and evidence of problem solving that led to that end result.

◆ **Value group thinking.** When students collaborate in small groups, require a joint written response that shows evidence of their collaborative thinking and explanations—for example, the various solutions they attempted in figuring out a math problem.

◆ **Share stories of challenging experiences in which making a hard-fought effort eventually led to success.** Begin by sharing a personal story. Then encourage similar storytelling with a partner and within small groups. Also, read and discuss stories of adversity in which unrelenting effort led to success.[14]

◆ **Value students' stories** and try to ensure no one feels invisible in our classrooms. All of us want to be known, understood, and accepted. When students trust us and we create space to hear and value their life stories, they are more likely to feel respected and determined to learn. (See more on storytelling on page 171 and also page 173 for StoryCorps.)

STORY ❖ Being Known

How heartbreaking it is to be invisible, to be near the end of your life and not be known. We live our lives with the hope we will be kindly remembered and that our lives will have mattered. But what if no one knows our stories, our history, our family and friends, our joys and sorrows? What happens then?

A few months ago, a birthday card I had mailed to Ruth, a treasured friend, was returned to me. The stamped message on the envelope said something like "No such person at this address. No known forwarding address," which alarmed me. My friend Ruth, in her late 60s, lived independently in a beautiful home in southeastern Florida, where she intended to stay. I had spoken to her a couple of months prior, and although she was a bit confused once or twice in our conversation, she was mostly her usual intelligent, insightful self—telling interesting life stories and cracking jokes.

Truth be told, it had been getting harder to stay in contact with her. Sometimes it would take weeks for her to return my call, and that would be after I had left a few voicemail messages. I worried that if something happened to her, there would be no way for me to find out, so I asked her to give me the name and contact information of a nearby neighbor or friend. She gave me two names and phone numbers, and I tucked them away. After the birthday card was returned, I called one of them. She explained that after seeing newspapers piled up by Ruth's front door, she alerted the police, who found Ruth hallucinating and dehydrated. She was taken by ambulance to the local hospital, where it was determined she had suffered a stroke. She was moved to a nursing home, which is where I called her.

A nurse told me Ruth was unable to talk by phone. When I asked what had happened to her, she said legally she couldn't give me any information. I asked if she could just answer "yes" or "no" to my questions, which is how I learned Ruth had dementia, would be staying permanently at the nursing home, and had not had any visitors. "What do you know about her?" I asked the nurse. She and the other nurses said they didn't know anything about her. I felt shaken and heart-shattered. My friend Ruth, a remarkable woman, was a complete stranger to her caretakers. I knew Ruth had no living family members, but I mistakenly assumed that "someone" would step in to tell her stories, to show who she was and how she had lived her life.

"I need to tell you about her." I felt a sense of urgency to ensure Ruth would be known as the remarkable person she was. My sadness and guilt overwhelmed me. If I hadn't been so busy and preoccupied with my own life, wouldn't I have noticed and heeded some warning signs that Ruth was struggling? Why hadn't I reached out to Ruth more often? Why hadn't I been a better friend? I sat down and wrote a one-page letter about Ruth's life and sent it to the nursing home with the request that anyone who cared for her be given a copy. Some excerpts follow:

> Ruth has lived a full and rich life, one that has involved both a kind heart and a brilliant mind. She has been a generous, loving, and loyal friend to many and a close friend and colleague to me for twenty-five years. She was in a forty-year close and loving marriage with Walter, the man she adored and who adored her right back. They were inseparable until he died.
>
> She has been devoted to teaching, leading, and literacy all her life—at the local college level as well as at state, national, and international levels. In her community, she has served on the board of directors of several organizations devoted to civic responsibility and worked tirelessly to make lives better and more equitable for children and adults.
>
> As her dear friend of many years, please look beyond the diminished person she has become through no fault of her own and try to see a vibrant, loving, kind woman who has been loved and admired by all who have known her. Not to be minimized, her sense of humor was unrivaled and appreciated by all who knew her. Nobody enjoyed telling or hearing a good story or joke as much as she did.

Although Ruth and I live on opposite sides of the country, which makes it difficult to visit, I do keep in contact by calling the nursing home to see how she's doing and writing letters—with the request that the nurses read those aloud to her. On a recent call, when I gave my name as Ruth's friend and inquired how she was, the nurse said, "Are you the one who wrote the letter about Ruth? Everyone here has read it, and I believe it's made our job taking care of her more meaningful for us and for her." My hope is that, despite Ruth's *limited ability to communicate, the nurses will raise their expectations in how they speak and interact with her. She's still Ruth, and she still has sparks of astuteness and humor. Sometimes, the nurses tell me, she remembers who I am and smiles when they tell her I've called.*

So what does all this mean for our students and us? For many of our students, especially those who don't believe their lives sufficiently matter, it's up to us to validate them—to honor their cultures, respect their families, encourage them to speak their truths, and to seek out and value their stories. We need to know and really "see" the students we interact with every day.

We teachers can do that, but we have to make it a priority—over standards, test scores, and prescribed curriculum. I believe we all learn better and achieve more in a culture where people know and esteem us. Although our son, Peter, had many fine teachers over the years, the one who most won our hearts was the teacher who fondly spoke of what a unique and talented individual "our boy, Pete" was and how much she appreciated having him in her class. Peter blossomed that year, not just as a reader and writer but also as a confident thinker, learner, and leader. What he remembers most about his year with that extraordinary teacher is not what she taught him academically but that "she took the time to get to know me, and she believed in me."

Slow down, teach less but go deep, listen to your students, and take the time to get to know them. You will have touched their lives forever.

Ensure Excellent Instruction Right from the Start

I view excellent instruction as differentiated instruction, or what I prefer to call *responsive teaching*—that is, meeting the needs and interests of all students regardless of their instructional level. By putting the Optimal Learning Model into action (see pages 136–146), our instruction, assessment, resources, technology support, and all we do and say are designed to ensure students successfully progress in their learning. Excellent instruction requires deep knowledge, flexibility, and doing whatever it takes so all students succeed. (See "Ten Key Factors for Excellence," pages 102–103.) Interconnected with excellent teaching are indispensable literacy essentials, which include but are not limited to the following:

Critical Literacy Essentials

- Establish a schoolwide intellectual culture of trust and a collaborative, joyful learning environment.

- Engage students in a real-world curriculum that includes interesting literature, content worth knowing, and choice within structure.

- Ensure deep reading, writing, listening, and discussion of whole, meaningful, relevant texts and concepts across the curriculum.

- Make useful feedback and formative assessment integral to daily instruction.

- Recognize and respect every student's language, culture, background, and strengths.

All students deserve the best we have to offer. Expert first teaching is our best course of action to ensure equal educational opportunity for all. When we put most of our efforts into universal, exemplary instruction for all students, we can substantially reduce the number of students who need intervention.

 ## Take Action

- ◆ **Assume all students are intelligent.** Through our body language, tone of voice, choice of words, willingness to be supportive, and explicit and purposeful instruction, we can convey a "you can do it" message to every student.

- ◆ **Advocate for practices and resources that serve all students well.** For example, rely on first-rate texts and primary sources, not just published core programs. Also, study the research and results behind new program adoptions before a purchase is made. When the program seems inappropriate for the student body, join with colleagues to get involved, ask pertinent questions, speak up, and suggest alternatives.

- ◆ **Plan instructional opportunities for sustained and meaningful reading, writing, speaking, and listening** across the curriculum. Underperforming students get more "stuff" and isolated skills and activities that do not increase learning and achievement. In fact, excessive teaching and testing of isolated skills (part-to-whole instruction instead of whole-part-whole instruction as described on pages 273–274) limits and compromises students' time and opportunities for deeper learning and comprehension.

♦ **Ensure that classroom management and independent work facilitate and enhance learning.** This is a critical issue. We can waste a lot of students' time with tasks that aren't worth doing. For example, caution is needed when it comes to "seat work" or workstations where K–3 students can spend up to an hour a day independently working without teacher support or any follow-up assessment, typically during guided reading when the teacher is with a small group. A research study on the use of workstations indicates that especially for more challenged readers, that time is often unproductive and confusing.[15]

♦ **Be cautious about programs that impede opportunities to learn,** such as tracking, removing students from the classroom, limiting collaboration, having students complete worksheets on isolated skills, and covering so much that nothing is learned in depth.

♦ **Make sure viewing and sharing exemplary work is doable for the learner.** Students—and new teachers, too—who receive guidance and coaching far beyond where they are at a particular moment can feel discouraged, overwhelmed, and not capable. Tailor teaching and coaching to demonstrations and actions in which the learner is likely to feel that what is being shown is within reach with reasonable effort, support, and practice.

♦ **Put students before schedules.** Endeavor to establish practices and schedules that prioritize the needs of students, not the educational specialist. Work to make sure that a school's and district's policies and master schedule do not disadvantage students—for example, pulling students out for support during a rich language arts class. (See also page 294.)

♦ **Consider not reading students' files before they enter our classrooms.** Not reading their files makes it more likely that we will see all students as capable of learning at high levels.

♦ **Value productive group work.** Students engage more, interact more, and achieve more when they have opportunities to work and converse with others. Of course, check to be sure students understand the task before engaging in the group work.

Reduce the Need for Intervention

Take a close look at the number of students being identified as requiring intervention. When the percentages are high and most of the identified students qualify for free and reduced-cost meals, are African American, are Hispanic, or are English language learners, then we need to pause, reflect, and ask some hard questions:

Intervention Matters: Self-Evaluate

- Are we resorting to intervention before offering all students an equal opportunity to experience and engage in the same excellent content and instruction we offer our gifted students?

- Are we making full-out efforts to be responsive (differentiating instruction) to the needs and interests of every student?

- Have students had sufficient time and support to master what they are attempting to learn?

- Are our classrooms learning-focused or intervention-focused?

- Do we see all our students as capable?

Response to Intervention (RTI) was meant to be the great equalizer, with expert instruction meeting the needs of 80 percent of students, but it has not worked out that way. In fact, large numbers of students are targeted for intervention as soon as they begin to struggle even though many may be better off remaining in the classroom with an expert teacher. When I work in a school, I insist that all students, even those who would ordinarily not be in the classroom at that time, be included. Amazing things can and do happen. With support, students can and do achieve at levels that we, and they, did not know was possible. One example follows.

When I ask the principal and teachers about pressing literacy needs while planning for a schoolwide residency, the first thing that often comes up is how to deal with difficult student behaviors. As a typical example, in a school where most of the students are from low-income families and are receiving free and reduced-cost meals, I learn that as much as a quarter of the students are on medications for various reasons—hyperactivity, posttraumatic stress, depression, and more. Some of these students are apparently unable to function without an aide who has been assigned to them. As always, I insist all students be present for the residency and that I don't want to know anyone's label. By week's end, every student is fully participating, and it's impossible to pick out the labeled ones.

When we offer excellent, relevant teaching to all students, we effectively reduce our special education population. In one such elementary school that moved to intervention as a last resort, the percentage of students receiving special education services went from 18 percent to 3 percent over a three-year period, saving the school more than $100,000 per year, as the services of two full-time special education teachers were no longer required.

We must be sure any intervention program is truly evidence-based and suitable for the population we serve. Reading Recovery, a one-on-one intervention program for first graders, is one of the few rigorously studied, early-literacy intervention programs that yields significant positive results in reading growth.[16] As a former Reading Recovery teacher, I know that impact also extends to writing. Part of the reason our long-term initiative to improve the teaching of writing in high-needs schools in Winnipeg, Canada, has been so successful is the fact that each participating school has a Recovery teacher, who in many cases also serves as a literacy expert in the school.[17]

Although the right intervention can be life changing, we presently view too many students as needing to be on life support. An equitable literacy focus across a whole school requires ongoing, embedded professional learning (see pages 105–110), a positive mind-set that believes in focusing on the universal level first, and our collaborative advocacy for first-rate instruction for all.

Also very important, the success of many interventions for low-income students diminishes over time.[18] Sustaining and increasing gains depends on the learning environment the child returns to. I noticed that reality as a Reading Recovery teacher. The students who maintained their growth and continued to steadily improve returned to a classroom where the teacher's beliefs and instructional practices aligned with Reading Recovery principles and where the teacher treated those students as cognitively capable.

Take Action

◆ **Re-examine intervention policies and actions.** Research suggests that many interventions do not lead to improved student achievement. For example, in a study of more than 20,000 students in thirteen states, first graders reading below grade level who received interventions performed worse than peers who did not.[19] Again, but important enough to be restated, keep in mind that excellent first teaching is our best intervention for most students.

◆ **Ensure assessments used to identify students are equitable.** In states that use tests that give heavy weight to decoding nonsense words to determine reading levels—tests such as the FAST test, DIBELS, and mCLASS—as many as 50 percent of students can wind up in special education (see e-mail, page 374). Teachers are caught in a trap; they are forced to give a test they know does not inform them about their students or help them to teach better. Policy makers and big business rule, and inequitable practices continue. Know the research and the politics behind it. See the superb article by educator and equity advocate Michael Ford, "To DIBELS or Not to DIBELS," in this book's "References and Resources" for wise perspectives and excellent information on what we need to know and do about this contentious assessment. See also http://regieroutman.com/teachingessentials/DIBELS.asp for research on DIBELS, and use it to advocate for sane practices that put students—not noncredible research and big-profit sales—first, and see page 378 for one teacher's reflection on dealing with this issue.

◆ **Reconsider independent work practices.** What other students are doing while we're with a small group or conferring one-on-one with a student can augment learning or be a waste of time. Many students, especially those in low-performing schools or those referred for intervention, spend hours a day doing worksheets or frivolous activities—many of which never get evaluated for what the student is actually learning. (See page 221 on management.)

◆ **Rethink how we use support specialists.** Ensure our beliefs match research-based practices; for example, push-in models are proven to be more effective than pull-out models in many cases. If we believe that the classroom or content area teacher has the main responsibility for teaching the student, advocate for having support specialists work with their students in the classroom, alongside the teacher. Prioritize students' needs over specialists' schedules.

◆ **Use the principal's office as a safe haven, not a holding place.** I can often tell a lot about a school's culture and discipline policy by how many students are in—or waiting to enter—the principal's office for inappropriate behaviors. Part of ensuring that every student receives expert daily instruction is making sure students are present in the classroom. When students are disruptive, co-construct a discipline policy and help them understand how their behaviors affect their learning and others. Work as a staff to have the principal's office be seen and used as a safe, supportive space, not a punitive one. All of that said, there are students whose behavioral disruptions are so severe that removal from the classroom is necessary for the disrupter and for the rest of class to go on learning.

For information and specific ideas, research, and approaches on reducing the need for intervention, see my book *Read, Write, Lead: Breakthrough Strategies for Schoolwide Literacy Success* (2014), pages 137–180.

Provide Feedback That Supports the Learner

I have deliberately placed the topic of feedback within this "Reaching All Learners" chapter because the language and actions we use with students can be the main determinant for whether or not they move forward. Helpful feedback has been proven to be one of the most powerful strategies for accelerating student learning.[20] For students accustomed to failure, our feedback has the power to give them their first glimmer of hope or to demoralize them further. Take to heart the words of Dylan Wiliam, an internationally recognized expert on formative assessment: "Feedback is only successful if students use it to improve their performance."[21]

Feedback, to be useful, must use carefully crafted language that helps the learner improve the quality of the work or effort. The learner must also be ready to receive the constructive suggestions. That is why celebration, which we have already discussed (see page 25–27), is a necessary precursor to feedback. Feedback, thoughtfully delivered, gives the learner agency and energy to move forward. Finally, feedback needs to be immediate to be most helpful to the learner. Whether or not our feedback is well received and successfully applied is ultimately up to the learner and has a lot to do with trust and readiness. Being sensitive to the needs and interests of the learner influences how our feedback is received and utilized. The following story illustrates that point.

I will never forget walking into a primary-grades teacher's classroom and her enthusiastically saying, "What do you think of my word wall?" It filled the entire length of her classroom and had more than 200 words on it. "What do you want to know?" I asked her. She went on to talk about how carefully she had designed the wall and how proud of it she was. It was clear from her comments and demeanor that what she wanted was praise and validation for her hard work. We did not know each other well, so I wanted to be sure to choose my words very carefully but also to be honest. I said, "It's very colorful and beautiful. I can tell you've put a lot of effort into it. It's the first thing I noticed when I entered your room." She beamed.

A year later, when I was back in her classroom and we had established a level of trust, she asked me again, "What do you think of my word wall?" and again, I responded, "What do you want to know?" This time she said, "I think I may have way too many words up for the kids, and some of the words are placed so high I'm wondering if students can access them." Now she was ready to improve the quality of the word wall and see it as a useful literacy tool. So I told her, "Your word wall is beautiful, but it does seem like you have too many words up. I worry about kids who will be overwhelmed by how many words are there. Also, I wonder if you've thought about just having one word to represent a common rime, such as *-ake*, for example, and just having the word *make* up there and color coding *-ake* to let students know that if they know *make* they can figure out *take* and *wake*. Also, for those keywords that everyone can read and spell, you might consider taking those down." I did feel she needed to lower the word wall to be at eye level for most of the students, but I focused my feedback on what seemed easily doable and, most important at this time, to help her improve the word wall without overwhelming her. At a later date, I could add the other suggestion.[22]

Giving feedback can be risky business, so we've got to become expert at it. Easier said than done. In my experience, most of us educators have had no professional learning or practice on how to give effective feedback. Be cautious about student-to-student feedback, as much of that feedback is wrong or unhelpful.[23] Realistically, even with practice, most of our students cannot provide the depth and sensitive feedback language on, for example, improving the craft of writing an essay, that expert teachers can.

 # Take Action

Regardless of the literacy focus, subject matter, grade level we teach, and type of student conference or group work, the language and actions of effective feedback apply to everything we do. "If our feedback doesn't change the student in some way, it has probably been a waste of time."[24]

- **Focus first on the learner and second on the learning that might be needed.** Be thinking: "What is the most important thing I can say to this learner that will empower him to move forward and give him the energy to do the work?" Keep the following self-evaluation questions in mind when giving feedback:
  - Is it necessary?
  - Is it useful?
  - Is it kind and respectful?
  - Is it timely?
  - Does it move the learner forward?

- **Give positive feedback on what the learner has done well before making suggestions.** Learners first need to hear at least several positive statements focused on specific behaviors, actions, and efforts.

- **Limit comments to the task at hand.** Be thinking: "What is the learner ready and willing to hear now to improve the work?" As an example, see the specific language to the teacher in the earlier story about the word wall.

- **Give feedback in specific language the learner can understand.** Be thinking: "How can I say this in a way that is positive, comprehensible, and useful?"

- **Use language that will encourage the learner to take action.** For example, we might say something like "Carlos, let's review what we both agree you can do on your own. When you go back to your writing, carefully reread and refer to the brief comments we put on the sticky notes to remind you of actions to take and words to use. I'll be by after a while to check on how you're doing."

- **Check to be sure the learner has understood the feedback.** Have the learner say back what he or she has just heard. This recommendation applies to us educators-as-learners as well.

- **Evaluate feedback language.** Invite a trusted colleague to observe you give students feedback. Have the colleague script your language without judgment. Discuss together if your feedback met the self-evaluation questions in the first "Take Action" bullet. If not, what are your next steps for improvement and guided practice?

- **Involve students in the feedback process.** Esteemed high school teacher and author Cris Tovani notes that making students partners in the feedback process improved her teaching. She quotes John Hattie: "It was only when I discovered that feedback was most powerful when it was from the student to the teacher that

I started to understand it better."[25] One way to get such feedback is to periodically ask students to evaluate our feedback to them (see page 167 for one example). Or perhaps ask students, "What part of the feedback I just gave you is useful to your work?" or "What else would be helpful for moving forward?"

◆ **Seek to develop students' ability to self-critique** and give themselves useful feedback to advance their learning. The ultimate goal is for students—and teachers—to successfully self-assess to improve and enhance their own work. (See more in "Developing Self-determining Learners," pages 335–355.)

Support English Language Learners

As students learning English continue to make up one of the fastest-growing population segments of our schools, it's crucial we serve them well, which is often not the case. Many of our beliefs and actions about English language learners from pre-K through high school are not mandated but are rather business-as-usual actions based on old habits, ingrained beliefs, and past behaviors. For example, too many educators hold the belief that children who speak a different language are somehow less capable. Low expectations and dumbed-down practices commonly accompany that belief. A glaring example is the commonly perceived need for a separate—often scripted—curriculum for ELLs, which marginalizes what's possible and limits potential for deep thinking and discussion on important world-related matters. A positive sign that beliefs and practices may be changing is the November 2016 vote supporting bilingual education in California. That is, fluency in a student's first language and access to high-level academic content will be an integrated part of a student's instructional model while English language skills are developing. (See supportive research on page 300.)

Another misguided belief and practice is not allowing students to use their first language with their same-language peers; doing so can help them understand directions and work more effectively. *"Multi-language abilities are a resource for all students* (emphasis in original). Instead of viewing students who do not speak English as a first language as deficient, we should help students develop both first-language skills and English skills."[26] Fortunately, multilingualism is now beginning to be seen as "a sign of intellectual achievement and sophistication." A student's first language "is a source of self-knowledge, a form of cultural capital" that makes students smarter.[27]

What English Language Learners Need

All ELLs need to have high-level curriculum with expert scaffolding and sustained time to apply what they are learning, all done in a meaningful and relevant manner. Part of the problem is that many teachers are unsure about how to teach ELLs. First and foremost, ELLs need to know the learning goals—what they're learning, why it matters, and the evidence that proves they've learned the material. Those learning goals need to be posted; written in student-friendly language; read and discussed before, during, and after the lesson; and assessable by both students and teachers.

The majority of instruction needs to be delivered through meaningful conversations and teaching that involve showing and gesturing instead of just telling, the use of total physical response (TPR), real objects, and comprehensible input. Students must be doing at least 50 percent of the work—the thinking, speaking, reading, writing, discussing, and producing. At least three learning modalities (kinesthetic, auditory, visual) need to be included in all instruction. As well, granting students more time is especially crucial for deep understanding, application of academic language and content vocabulary, transfer of new learning to other content areas, and doing well on tests.[28]

By anticipating and addressing the learning challenges of ELLs, effective teachers design explicit instruction to ensure that the content is accessible and manageable. By engaging ELLs—and all students—in meaningful content and giving them sufficient demonstrations, time, support, and extended opportunities for guided practice to process and apply the information, students experience success as learners. Here is where incorporating the Optimal Learning Model is crucial. Also, for all learners, but especially for second-language learners and learners who struggle, we must connect whole-part-whole instruction with meaning and interesting content and embed most skills work within that context. We must also examine the predominance of pull-out models, which often marginalize students to a lesser curriculum and cause students to miss out on high-level classroom learning.

An English Language Learner Story

Jason was a second-language learner who was struggling mightily in all aspects of literacy. As was the policy for his school and district, he was pulled out of the classroom for ELL support each day. As a result, there was a disconnect between his classroom instruction and the pull-out support he received, and there was scant time for in-depth communication or collaboration with the classroom teacher. Gradually, with daily professional conversations and ongoing, high-quality professional development in her school, Jason's ELL teacher shifted her beliefs and practices from part-to-whole teaching to whole-part-whole teaching. As she witnessed firsthand the greater academic growth that accompanied meaningful instruction, she successfully lobbied her principal to shift to a push-in model for all ELL students. That push-in model built on the same excellent classroom instruction and content all students were receiving. That is, the inclusive model provided all learners the high-level, individualized support they deserve. The new model was so successful and joyful that it was replicated throughout the district. Not only that, but many non-ELL students who were also lacking in language skills benefited.

We are all learning language all the time, and what applies to ELLs also applies universally. We learn language and concepts best through genuine "need to know," meaningful use, supported practice, and relevant interaction (see also "Promote Oral Language Development," pages 304–309, and "Advocating for Students," pages 357–385.)

 ## Take Action

"Good instruction for students in general tends to be good instruction for ELLs in particular."[29]

+ **Build upon students' knowledge, experiences, culture, and interests** to bridge the divide between home and school and to build background knowledge for reading, writing, thinking, and talking in all literacy and content areas. Let students know through our words and actions that we value their literacy in their first language and see it as a strength and a bridge for high-level thinking and learning in an additional language.

+ **Value bilingualism and biliteracy** and know the difference between the two. Students who are bilingual can speak fluently in more than one language, but students who are biliterate can speak, read, and write in more than one language, which gives them a competitive edge. Most employers and industries favor hiring bilingual, and especially biliterate, candidates.[30]

+ **Apply whole-part-whole teaching,** which is a big shift in thinking and beliefs for many ELL teachers. Breaking learning into small pieces makes it harder for ELLs to understand. The parts make most sense in the context of a meaningful whole text or global concept. Of course, we must explicitly teach skills and strategies and ways of thinking, but we should temporarily separate these out and then put them back into context. For example, we explicitly teach vocabulary words including academic vocabulary every day, but the vocabulary words are in service to understanding a text, a concept, or an idea and are not part of an isolated list. (For more on whole-part-whole teaching, see pages 271–275.)

◆ **State clearly the language goals and purpose for the instruction.** State all objectives and directions succinctly and unambiguously; check to make sure students understand the learning goals for the content and language. Say something like "At the end of the lesson, we're going to check and find evidence of what we've learned."

◆ **Ask significant questions** (see pages 165–166). Separate language ability from content knowledge. Although ELLs may not yet be able to read and write at the highest levels, they can think at high levels if we expect it, scaffold our teaching so that the language and content are comprehensible, and ask important questions. One way we do that is by asking tiered questions—that is, we ask questions about content that match the student's language-acquisition stage. An early-tier question might begin with "Show me ____" or "Where is ____," and a more advanced tier might be "Explain ____" or "Why do you think ____."[31]

◆ **Involve as many senses as possible.** The more comprehensible we make the input, the easier it is to learn. ELLs need to hear it, see it, experience it, feel it, talk about it, and have physical involvement, wherever possible. For example, a class of kindergarten students wrote and performed their own raps for learning phonics rimes, such as *i-n-g*: "See me jumping—i-n-g. When am I doing it? Right now!" Raps were performed and celebrated schoolwide. In the past, the ELL teacher in this story would have told her students, "We're working on present-tense verbs." Now she says, "We're going to write a rap in order to learn about action words, also called *verbs*, which we do 'right now.'"

◆ **Advocate for principled practices.** Current research shows that second-language learners benefit most from dual-language programs[32] and intentional, real-world instruction. As well, ". . . teaching ELLs to read in their first language and then in their second language, or in their first and second languages simultaneously . . . compared with teaching them to read in their second language only, boosts their reading achievement *in the second language*" (emphasis in original quote). Also noteworthy, ELLs acquire much vocabulary incidentally when they read fiction they enjoy and find interesting.[33] Additionally, high school students are more likely to engage with meaningful content and conversation—and learn English quickly—when they work collaboratively with students who speak different first languages. The shared experience of everyone as a language learner builds students' confidence, language risk taking, and pride in their bilingualism.[34]

◆ **Include more nonfiction.** The content of nonfiction is often easier for ELL students to comprehend than fiction. Nonfiction is also a powerful vehicle for teaching academic vocabulary and building knowledge.

◆ **Provide necessary resources and books.** Accommodate, enhance, and accelerate students' learning experiences with visual, audio, and multimedia supports; student-friendly dictionaries, thesauruses, and word banks; dual-language texts; and additional time. Ensure classrooms and libraries offer culturally relevant books and dictionaries in multiple languages. Poetry is a great place to begin; a longtime personal favorite and great writing model for elementary through high school students is *My Name Is Jorge on Both Sides of the River: Poems in English and Spanish.*[35] Through shared writing, write your own books and create your own bilingual resources as needed.

◆ **Reevaluate the school's and district's English language learning program.** Advocate to push in and co-teach rather than pull out, when possible, so students maximize language-learning experiences. Again, but important enough to be restated, teach whole-part-whole with explicit skills and language objectives embedded into meaningful content, which accelerates language learning and makes the language and content more accessible, relevant, and enjoyable for all students.

Check to be sure most English language learners are being "reclassified" and moving beyond the ELL designation to "English-proficient." Too many ELLs stall in their learning and never get reclassified, which makes high school graduation more elusive. Mostly, these high school students can speak English well enough, but they lack the "academic language know-how" needed for school success. Strongly advocate for designing and offering classes for long-term English learners.[36]

Twelve Essential Actions to Help English Language Learners Succeed

1. **Celebrate successes.** Notice and name learners' specific strengths and efforts before focusing on what needs improvement.

2. **Set up and sustain a safe environment for taking risks.** Students who are learning a second language need to be assured their ideas and thinking matter and are respected, even when attempted responses are incomplete. As well, honor the silent period many newcomers learning a second language need; even if they are not yet speaking, they are processing comprehensible input.[37]

3. **Include ELLs in rich conversations.** Give students time to show evidence for their thinking; support and scaffold to help them clarify, define, and revise their thinking; and find useful resources to support their thinking. (See much more in next section, "Promote Oral Language Development.") Also, promote more collaborative learning that allows those who know English to translate for those learning it.

4. **Teach whole-part-whole, not part-to-whole.** Begin with whole, excellent texts in reading and writing. Avoid teaching isolated skills and embed most skills work within meaningful contexts in order to maximize comprehension.

5. **Rely on the reading-writing connection to maximize engagement and learning.** Starting in kindergarten, it is through daily writing for authentic audiences and purposes—and rereading their writing—that many ELLs learn to read, slow down and cement their letter-sound and word knowledge, and become proficient writers.

6. **Do daily reading aloud of fiction, nonfiction, and poetry—across the curriculum.** As you read, provide necessary background knowledge, say aloud your reactions to what's happening; explain how you figure out what certain words and phrases mean, including academic vocabulary; comment on the rhythm and flow of the language; and suggest how students might try out in their own writing a technique the author used. Include interactive read-aloud, as well, in which students also share their own thinking.

7. **Encourage the ELL specialist to work in the classroom** alongside the classroom teacher and as a co-teacher to support ELLs to comprehend the same high-level curriculum all students are receiving.

8. **Offer daily, shared language experiences that are engaging, culturally relevant, and challenging.** As the teacher, take the lead to shape the actual reading and writing of content, but encourage and accept the ideas and voices of all students. Ensure that student understanding and application of academic vocabulary, which we need to explicitly teach in each content area, is a priority. (See "Incorporate scaffolded conversations," pages 305–309.)

9. **Provide constant, comprehensible input to authentic, purposeful work.** Use multimedia, physical objects, role playing, and all modalities to ensure vocabulary, concepts, and language are understood.

10. **Do more small-group work and work with peers.** Flexible small groups and partner work provide more opportunities for interactively grappling with ideas through meaningful talk and collaboration. The more opportunities ELLs have to listen and talk with peers and to share their thinking around challenging and relevant curriculum and ideas, the more sophisticated their thinking and language will become.

11. **Advocate for best research-based practices for ELLs.** A strong body of research confirms valuing and teaching in a student's home language at the same time the student is learning a second language. (See research on page 120.)

12. **Give assessments in students' native language,** when possible. Such assessments value bilingual education, highlight ELLs' optimal comprehension and content knowledge, and do not penalize students' limitations in English proficiency.[38]

Promote Oral Language Development

Begin literacy instruction with rich and meaningful oral language. This includes the literary and informational language of books and texts we read aloud and discuss, the stories we tell, the texts we create together, and the rich vocabulary and curriculum in which we immerse students. Students who grow up in poverty—many of whom are also English language learners—often enter our schools with limited academic oral language, which makes learning to read and write more difficult. Research has shown that oral-language proficiency and high-level literacy development are interconnected, which makes it mandatory that we focus on developing speaking and listening skills—especially crucial for our English language learners.[39] (For information on teaching listening, speaking, and questioning, see pages 149–167.)

Although we cannot make up for the fewer words and conversations some students may have experienced, we must ensure their school experiences immerse them in a flood of rich, relevant, and explicit language throughout the day—in significant conversations, opportunities to ask questions and try out new words, reading and writing text after text, small-group work, and whatever it takes early on and throughout their school day. A highly skilled English language development teacher put it this way: "My sole purpose is to make sure our students, all of them, become master language manipulators in order to communicate in whatever format they are using."[40]

Incorporate scaffolded conversations, providing appropriate language support to assist learners in meeting their goal. Teachers are often surprised when I support students' oral language facility by explicitly suggesting possibilities—that is, I put the language in their ears, which pays big dividends. For example, instead of asking questions when the child is silent or reluctant to speak, I prompt his thinking by offering various possibilities: "You could say ____," or "You might want to say something like ____," or "Notice how this author worded that. How might you put that in your own words?" With our verbal support, the quality of the work the student produces is likely to be higher than when we leave all the thinking to the student.

In the scaffolded conversation, the child verbalizes his ideas on a topic the teacher has already demonstrated, perhaps through her own writing or through leading a discussion. Through back-and-forth conversation and guided questioning, we encourage and prompt the student to clarify and elaborate his thoughts in a meaningful and engaging manner. As noted, we also suggest language the child might want to try out.

Many of these scaffolded conversations are done publicly at the front of the class in a conference, with one student or a small group, with the whole class looking on. In that way, all students benefit and get ideas for their own writing or literature discussion of a book or curriculum topic. A caution: avoid *underscaffolding*, an approach in which we just keep asking questions, the child is mostly silent, and we ask more questions; and *overscaffolding*, also ineffective, because we do almost all the talking.

Effective scaffolded conversations are an essential part of the "we do it" phase in the Optimal Learning Model (pages 138–139). I include scaffolded conversations in this chapter on "Reaching All Learners" because these supported conversations are crucial to the success of English language learners, students who struggle, and all those who yet lack the confidence, know-how, and practice to independently speak and write connected and interesting thoughts. In my experience, scaffolded conversations are one of the most effective techniques my colleagues and I employ for ensuring all K–12 students succeed. (See the link to the three-minute video of Liam's scaffolded conversation, referenced in "Videos," page R21, and the student work that followed, below.)

> Name: Liam
> Dedicate to MRS.Routman
> Date: Tues, March 3rd
>
> What are some Important Facts.
>
> polar bears are good swimmers.
>
> Polar bears use their back legs and front legs to swim. Polar bears like to swim in the water. Polar bears can swim up to 60 miles. Polar bears are drawning because there are little bit of ice chunks and polar bears can't hold the breath that long

Liam's writing following a scaffolded conversation where he was initially silent.

Take Action

- **Communicate clearly with families.** Check to ensure families feel comfortable with our means of communication, the content, and the delivery. Translated materials and conversations, when necessary and possible, go a long way toward effectively communicating and promoting inclusivity. (See also "Make Parents Partners," pages 19–22.)

- **Invite students to tell the stories of their lives**—with our scaffolding and encouragement—through talk, illustrations, photos, dictation, writing, video, dramatization, and music with lyrics (such as raps) and then to publish, read, and perform many of these texts. Valuing students' stories and cultures helps to diminish the boundaries between home and school, which makes it more likely that students will engage and flourish as literacy and language learners. (See also pages 77 and 173.)

Name: Liam   Date: Tues, march. 3rd 201.

What are some Important Facts

Baby polar bears are very small

Baby polar bear is 30cm to 35cm. Baby polar bears are long as a class room ruler. They are big as a coloured tile bin.

Going beyond requirements: Liam, feeling successful and competent, choosing to independently write a second piece

◆ **Use a child's oral language to create readable texts,** and make some of these bilingual. Often a student's first reading may be her own written text. Our residency work shows that young students who write daily for authentic audiences and purposes readily learn phonemic awareness, all letters and sounds, and spelling of high-frequency words, and they develop a growing facility with language that extends to both reading and writing.

◆ **Promote avid reading.** The only way to "catch up" and learn the myriad concepts and vocabulary students must know to be "college and career ready" is to read widely in a variety of genres on a wide range of topics.

◆ **Do more partner work, turn and talk, and small-group work.** Make sure many of these structures are heterogeneous so that emerging and struggling language learners have excellent language models to learn from. Frequent speaking opportunities are especially important for developing oral language capacities.

◆ **Suggest specific language to the student.** There is no script for a scaffolded conversation, and it's not just "Tell me more." Imagine we are having a conversation with a fascinating individual. What do we want to know? How can we help that person tell his story or express his thoughts and ideas more fully? To a student writing a personal narrative, we might say something like the following:

  ◉ "What did you say to your dad after that happened? Did you say something like 'Dad, how you could you do that?' Or did you say _____?" (To promote the use of dialogue and in-the-moment writing)

  ◉ "What were you thinking? Just put us back in that moment when _____. How did you feel? Were you surprised, scared, or worried?" (To slow down the writing and encourage elaboration and detail)

  ◉ "Let's go back to the text. Where does the author say that? Let's look at page _____. Here the author says _____, but I'm thinking that means _____ because of the previous paragraph _____." (To promote the use of close reading before analyzing an author's message)

◆ **Help the student recall unique language.** We want the student to use the interesting words and phrases that emerge orally in the scaffolded conversation in their writing and speaking. So that the student and we can recall the actual language, write those words on a sticky note and give it to the student to affix to his writing. In that way, we let the student know that we value the unique language and encourage its use. We also have now preserved that language for reference when we confer with the student.

◆ **Go deep, and take sufficient time.** Hold fewer scaffolded conversations, but make them worthwhile. Two in-depth public conversations (see pages 233–234) will teach students, including those who may be observing, more than many quick ones that skim the surface.

Endnote

Finally, and important enough to be restated, we can't truly reach our students—or our colleagues—if we don't know them or attempt to know them. There's so much we may never know about the complicated life issues they face. Especially if students have given up on themselves, we may be their best hope for some success and respite from their daily struggle. We need to give them the benefit of the doubt and be empathetic, kind, and understanding. And we need to celebrate their strengths. A story brings home that final point.

Walter was a fifth-grade student who didn't talk much or make eye contact, and I didn't know anything about him. When I called him up for a public writing conference and celebrated his story and how he had used language that "sounds like a published author in a book I might read," he quietly beamed. His writing—on the topic of ways we've made an important difference for others—was about how he swept the snow off the steps and walk at the shelter he was now living in, in order to make it safer for everyone. His pride in doing an important job well was evident in his writing. His teacher later told me something shifted for him after that conference. He began to write more and to speak out more. I suspect, just like the rest of us, he became more comfortable and confident once we knew him better and celebrated his accomplishments.

Applying Responsible Assessment

I n Finland, known for its national education system, there's no Finnish word for "accountability," and there are no standardized tests. Instead, the assessment mind-set is "responsibility," which is as it should be. We act responsibly and equitably to ensure all students learn and are well served. "The best school systems are the most equitable—students do well regardless of their socio-economic background."[1] My many decades of work in diverse schools confirm that statement.

As knowledgeable and caring educators, we must engage all students in meaningful and appropriately challenging literacy and curricular pursuits across the curriculum. At the same time, we need to continually check to ensure students are learning and adjust our daily instruction, resources, and actions as needed. Quality assessment becomes a systematic and beneficial process of monitoring learning that is seamlessly and responsibly interwoven into our daily teaching.

Unfortunately, the use of quality assessments is not commonplace. Societally, we don't believe teachers are capable of creating and applying "responsible," classroom-based, quality assessments in part because we don't sufficiently prepare teachers to do so. The larger issue, I believe, is lack of trust in teachers, which has led to an obsession with standardized tests and holding teachers "accountable." Another big issue is that standardized tests are big business, with publishers lobbying hard for their adoption.

A societal blind spot has been created by the common belief that standardized test results are the only truly acceptable evidence of student achievement. If the evidence comes from the teacher and the classroom, applies to just one group of students, and doesn't yield comparable results beyond that context, then it's deemed untrustworthy.[2]

Despite the fact that standardized testing does not improve schools and that we have evidence of the negative effects of test-based accountability,[3] we are generally powerless to act for needed change. Learned helplessness, exhaustion, time, fear for our jobs, pressure from administrators, and more keep us from actively engaging in changing our harmful testing culture. Other unintended consequences of a testing culture include tampering with test scores, wide-scale cheating, and unfair teacher assessments tied to test scores.

Our overreliance on standardized test results has often led to irresponsible assessment and results. For example, we knowingly ignore the wide body of research that confirms that test scores primarily reflect family income, with students from affluent families—many including college-educated parents—scoring high. In addition, the appalling amount of time devoted to mandatory testing, test preparation, and progress monitoring narrows the curriculum and crowds out music and the arts, inquiry learning, and teaching for depth. Not to be minimized, an overemphasis on isolated skills, teaching-to-the-test, often crowds out teaching for understanding. Perhaps most important, over-testing and overreliance on tests destroy joy and competency in teaching and learning and create a culture of fear, embarrassment, and even harassment.

We must do whatever we feasibly can to bring sanity into assessment practices. Keep the following in mind and share widely: "There is no correlation between time spent testing and improved math and reading scores."[4] Our assessment mind-set needs to be this: instruction and assessment must go hand in hand, and they must improve the quality of teaching and learning. *Question any assessment that does not ultimately benefit the learner.* Our negative testing culture is destroying the morale of teachers and students. The financial, societal, and human costs of high-stakes testing are enormous.

Take whatever action you can to ensure assessments are both reliable and valid. That is, any worthwhile test must measure what it was intended to measure, and a repeated test must yield the same results (reliability). Also, and perhaps most important, the findings must be credible and genuine (validity).

Continue to question the validity of mandated assessments:

- Are these findings applicable to our student population and our teaching and learning goals?

- Is this assessment a valid predictor of our students as learners—readers, writers, mathematicians, thinkers?

- Can this assessment be credibly used to meaningfully improve student learning?

For example, common standardized reading tests such as DIBELS, FAST, and mCLASS yield reliable results on what they purport to measure—decoding, isolated skills, fluency—but those results are not valid for assessing the full measure of a student's reading process and progress, especially in reading comprehension. Inequity reigns. (See more on pages 294 and 374.)

To be valid and reliable also means, at least to my mind, that the assessment must be fair to all students in content and method and must yield results that help us to teach more effectively. For example, giving a speed-reading test as the student reads aloud for a correct-words-per-minute score is not and should never be seen as a valid indicator of reading for understanding or even fluency. Genuine fluency goes beyond speed and word accuracy to include expression and smoothness. These last two qualities are harder to measure and to assign a fixed number, which may be why such qualities are not included. Yet, narrowly defined results are routinely used as stand-alone measures of student growth in reading and to screen for students who need intervention. Those interventions then tend to overfocus on the narrow skills that were assessed without ever getting at the deep comprehension that is at the heart of successful reading.

Overzealous attention to speed reading and decoding—too often the main diet in high-poverty schools—will lead to better speed readers and decoders but not necessarily to comprehending, successful readers. The more common result will be students who dislike reading and who never get the intervention that could make them successful, passionate, comprehending readers. We therefore shortchange our students most in need, an egregious equity issue. As well, according to recent research, we further disadvantage low-performing students when they have to take written exams via computer; they score higher when they can use paper and pencil.[5] Also, for assessing reading, it's common sense that an online reading format, increasingly being used in our testing culture, would disadvantage those students who have not had regular access to and practice with reading on a screen. Most often, these are students from low-income families and rural areas.

We also "assess student performance way too early in the change process without looking at changes in the adults first."[6] Our students are unlikely to learn more if their teachers are still stuck in an old instructional model that did little to improve student engagement and learning, such as teaching reading as decoding. Also, deep learning, transfer of learning, and application to new contexts all take time, diligence, and patience. When we assess, for example, English language learners too soon, we may draw the wrong conclusions from the results.

Finally, we are not yet able to assess with integrity such significant factors as creativity, imagination, curiosity, and determination to learn. Such multifaceted attributes of intelligence and ingenuity defy easy measurement, so they are not generally factored into the full picture of a child's potential and achievement. Formative assessment, done well, is one powerful way to encourage equity and the development of those important, hard-to-measure qualities that cannot be fairly or accurately assessed with a number.

Rely on Formative Assessment

Quality formative assessments have the potential to create equal opportunities to learn for all students. "Formative assessment is a planned process in which teachers or students use assessment-based evidence to *adjust what they're currently doing*" (emphasis in original).[7] The most useful assessments are formative; they are ongoing and based on students' present needs and interests. Such formative assessments have the potential to reliably inform and enhance our daily instruction as well as to improve student learning, engagement, and motivation.

When expertly done, formative assessment has one of the highest impacts on student learning compared with other practices.[8] Perhaps most significant, formative assessment done well has the greatest effect on low-performing students.[9] Formative assessments empower students by enabling them to be increasingly successful and productive. As partners in the learning-assessing process, students learn how to become more responsible, self-regulating, and effective learners. Perhaps most important, "Good formative assessment keeps students believing that success is within reach if they keep trying."[10] Determination to learn (see pages 282–283) is a byproduct of excellent formative assessment.

Teachers who skillfully practice formative assessment observe, question, and respond to students' needs and interests as they teach, minute by minute and day by day. They use these assessments to *inform* instruction and adjust it as needed. Teachers who seamlessly integrate formative assessments into the daily life of the classroom are able to use ongoing assessments to modify, fine-tune, differentiate, and accelerate instruction for all learners—often on the spot.

Formative assessments might include, but are not limited to, the following:

- Probing questions and student responses to those questions.

- Oral and written information through quick-writes, responses to reading and multimedia, and explanations of thinking.

- Observations of small-group collaboration and individual thinking through—for example, informal notes, anecdotal records, running records, conferences (one-on-one, public, roving), short videos, and audio recordings.

- On-demand writing.

- Rubrics, appropriately constructed and used.

- Teacher-constructed quizzes.

- Quality of questions raised by students.

- Self-assessments and reflections by individual students and small groups, oral or written.

Formative assessments also include assessing the choices students make. That is, the teacher who becomes skilled at meaningful formative assessment will likely be one who believes students are more engaged and achieve more when they have some real choice in topics of study, books to read and discuss, audiences with whom to communicate, and presentation of learning—for example, creating final products that include multimedia and unique formats and styles that demonstrate learning.

Think about formative assessment as a fluid and continuous process that occurs before, during, and after teaching, although most of it generally takes place while the learning is happening. Much of formative assessment relies on astute teacher observation, which is why professional learning is so critical. Although summative and interim assessments, which typically include school-based exams and district and state tests, are important for accountability purposes—often for the wider community—their use is limited for analyzing or making responsible instructional decisions for individual students' growth. More important, summative tests are often high-stakes affairs, with accompanying sanctions and negative consequences, which often lead to overzealous attention to test preparation.

 ## Take Action

- **Cultivate and act upon a formative assessment mind-set.** Such a mind-set depends on being professionally knowledgeable, flexible, and perceptive so we can do the in-the-moment, inner self-questioning before, during, and after instruction to guide our next moves. Be thinking:
  - *What are the purposes and goals for this lesson?*
  - *What do students already know about _____?*
  - *What demonstrations and shared experiences will they need to understand and apply _____?*
  - *Are we building in enough frontloading and guided practice time?*
  - *What's our evidence that students are learning what we are teaching?*
  - *What are our next steps?*

- **Note trends and needs,** and reteach, provide more shared experiences, regroup, or instruct and further assess, as necessary, to meet the needs of all students. One way to notice student engagement in reading is to have a student lead the class in a familiar shared reading, leaving us free to observe the participation and behaviors of every student.

- **Integrate assessment with teaching.** Think of assessment as an integral part of all effective instruction, including what we ask students to do when they are working independently. We cannot assume that students are learning more without an assessment.

- **Provide quality feedback to the learner.** Assessment, to be effective, must help the learner, whether it's a teacher or a student, learn more. Effective feedback is not praise or criticism. It is carefully chosen language and actions that propel the learner forward (see more on feedback on pages 246–248 and 295–298). The learner's receptivity to feedback depends on a culture of trust and risk taking.

◆ **Incorporate more formative assessments.** The most useful assessment is the meaningful probing, nudging, and thoughtful questions we ask—in the act of teaching—to let us know what students are thinking and learning and where we need to adjust our instruction. Such assessment is part of responsive teaching, in which we listen and observe carefully and change course on our lessons—or not—based on learners' responses. (See *Regie Routman in Residence* for exactly what that assessment-as-part-of-teaching looks and sounds like: www.regieroutman. com/inresidence/default.aspx.)

◆ **Do more one-on-one conferring.** The word *assessment* comes from the Latin word *assidere*, which means "to sit by." Especially for improving achievement in reading and writing, meeting one-on-one with students is crucial. Some of these conferences are roaming conferences, done quickly, on-the-run, during literacy blocks; most take place with the teacher sitting right beside a student or, in other cases, a small group (see "Embrace Public Writing Conferences," page 243, and "Rely on One-on-One Reading Conferences," page 222).

Finally, we did not become teachers and leaders to chase test scores. Beware of easy-to-score tests that are unable to accurately discern deep comprehension. As well, tests that evaluate vital attributes of successful people, such as flexibility, innovative thinking, listening abilities, judgment, and common sense, cannot be accurately scored. Evaluating those qualities requires an astute teacher.

Resist Teaching to the Test

There is no credible evidence that indicates excessive test prep and testing lead to higher achievement. High test scores are a byproduct of a thriving school culture. (See page 9 and Appendix B.) Still, due to the extreme pressure on teachers, principals, and schools to raise test scores, many of us feel a need to prioritize teaching to the test. This is especially true for summative tests, which are often high-stakes, standardized state tests given annually to large groups of students for accountability purposes.

We want to do what's best, and we don't want to let anyone down—not the school, the students, their families, or ourselves. Here's one sobering truth: the side effects of excessive test prep can be extremely harmful. Scores might go up, but students do not necessarily learn more. In fact, what they and their teachers do learn may actually set them back. What follows is a cautionary tale.

Panic was evident on the faces of the conscientious teachers of the fourth grade—the high-stakes-testing grade—on the very first day of a writing residency. My best efforts to calm teachers down had little impact. I told them something like "The interim writing assessments we just did indicate that fourth graders are, typically, more than two years below grade level. We can't make that up in one year. So focus on excellent teaching of writing, not test prep. Remember that having fourth graders do well on the test is the responsibility of the whole school, not just the fourth-grade team."

The fourth-grade teachers tried to take my advice, but they didn't yet believe that spending most of their time on highly effective teaching was the surest route to raising achievement. Their beliefs about teaching writing were still evolving, and, for now, they believed that intensive test prep offered the best chance for improved writing scores. It would take more than a year for the teachers to come to believe and to put into practice: If we focus on the process, the product will improve.

At the end of the school year, most fourth graders had made minimal test gains, and their attitudes about writing had become negative. (See next page, a poem written by a class on why they hated the test and test prep.) In an interview with the teachers and the students, almost every student indicated that because of the constant attention to the test-prep writing and the ongoing focus on directed-writing prompts, they had lost enthusiasm for writing. The joy of writing, which we had experienced when we all worked together in the fall, was gone. Not only that, but students' everyday writing overall showed no improvement from fall to spring. It would take months of soul-searching by the teachers for that joy to return, along with improved quality of student writing. The excessive test-prep focus came with a high cost.

Standards and the tests that accompany them have also led to ineffective, part-to-whole teaching and time-wasting activities. Across various districts, teachers have been expected to deconstruct the standards as a first requirement. Such parsing of standards has not been shown to improve teaching and learning. In one district I worked in, test prep for writing in grade four focused on fifteen to twenty minutes of daily grammar exercises in isolation. But fourth graders did not yet have basic grammar, spelling, and handwriting under control. In another school, test prep centered on once-a-week prompt-writing that included having all students write on paper with a designated number of lines—the same number of lines that would be on the state test. Because test prep was, in fact, the school's writing curriculum, writing did not begin to improve until the whole school made an ongoing, professional learning commitment to improving the teaching of writing. That meant rethinking beliefs and moving to whole-part-whole instruction (see pages 271–275) through writing for real-world audiences and purposes. (For much more on standards, see pages 269–271.)

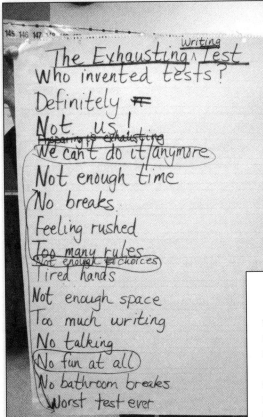

Above: Students sharing their frustration over a mandated state writing test through a class-authored (shared writing) draft with revisions

Right: Final published poem on "The Exhausting Writing Test"

The Exhausting Writing Test

Who invented tests?
Definitely
Not us!

Not enough time
Not enough space
Not enough choices

Feeling rushed
Tired hands
Too much writing
Worst test ever

No breaks
No talking
No fun at all

WE CAN'T TAKE IT
ANYMORE!

The hard working worn out students
In Mrs. T's class

Take Action

- ◆ **Keep testing and test prep to a minimum.**

  - ◉ *First of all, do what you can to reduce the number of tests students take.* Students in the United States are vastly over-tested and take too many redundant tests, leading to a loss of valuable instructional time. Also quite troubling, test results can take months to come in. Very disturbing, tests are sometimes used to evaluate teachers, an egregious use for which they were not designed.[11] At the very least, vigorously advocate for scaling back mandated testing and "progress monitoring," which are primarily used for accountability purposes and not as instructional tools.

  - ◉ *Recognize that the best test prep is expert teaching* in whole, real-world, meaningful contexts. For example, integrate test prep into daily teaching of all subjects "by making overt connections between what students need to know to be successful writers [or readers or mathematicians] to what is tested on their standardized tests."[12]

  - ◉ *Familiarize students with the test format* about a month before a standardized test. Teach test-taking strategies, and guide them through some practice test exercises, which will build their confidence. Demonstrate and practice with them strategies for how to answer different types of questions—for example, to ask themselves, "What do I already know that can help me figure that out?"

  - ◉ *Show students the rubric,* in a student-friendly version, that the district or state uses to score tests. Have students self-evaluate their practice tests with our guidance and set goals for improvement, if needed.

- ◆ **Maintain focus on expert teaching.** Keep in mind that students and schools can raise their test scores on standardized assessments, but that does not necessarily mean the school is of high quality or that students have improved in critical-thinking abilities.[13]

  Connect test taking with our meaningful work in the classroom. As an example, related to teaching transitions in writing to young children, I might say something like "Today, when we heard Maria read her piece, we noticed how she let the reader know when she was changing topics. She said, 'Here's what we do next.' We call that guidance to the reader a 'transition.' In your own writing, and when you take the state test, be sure to use transitions when needed."

◆ **Keep any test-prep process equitable.** Due to pressure to raise test scores, especially for students who greatly lag behind, teachers and interventionists are often forced to spend disproportionate amounts of time with what are sometimes called the "bubble kids" (those deemed closest to passing) or "nearly ready" kids in order to make the data "look good." Kids in the "far from ready" group, those deemed unable to pass the test, are sometimes warehoused in classrooms where they waste time on worksheets. Sadly, teachers who decry this outrageously unfair test process are often helpless to change it. Although test scores for the "bubble kids" may go up in year one, they often fall again by year two. Part-to-whole test prep and instruction that emphasize skills in isolation severely limit students' meaningful achievement in the long run.

◆ **Employ interim tests responsibly.** Interim assessments, or benchmark assessments, are standardized tests usually given a couple of times a year, and they are primarily used to see how a school or district is progressing in a particular domain. When used well, such tests have the potential to improve instruction—in writing, for example—across a whole school and district. The schools I collaborate with to improve the teaching of writing administer an interim writing assessment in the fall and spring.[14] As a whole school, we analyze the results. That is, first at grade levels and then across grade levels—and sometimes across the whole district or province—we read and analyze coded papers (without students' or teachers' names) to assess schoolwide and/or districtwide strengths and needs, and to determine next steps for improvement.

◆ **Inform parents.** *Let families know that any standardized test is just one measure of their child's progress.* Let them know that even if their child does not do well on a test or taking tests, ". . . qualities such as industriousness, perseverance, and leadership measured in young people later influenced wages just as much as years of education, IQ, and parental socioeconomic status."[15] Give parents a balanced picture of their child. Emphasize the child's efforts and strengths—for example, leadership and relationship qualities—not just academics.

Frequently share day-to-day formative assessments so families have a complete literacy and learning picture and can put high-stakes tests in perspective. For example, every week in the primary grades, send home a class-authored shared writing, whether it's a couple of sentences, a paragraph, or a complete explanation of learning. Expect students to read and talk about the writing—which has been reread and practiced in school—to their families.

On the reverse side of the shared-writing sheet, before it goes home, have students independently spell high-frequency or challenge words, share new vocabulary learned, or extend the shared writing further on their own. For older students, be sure that some work—whether it's writing, a reflection of learning, or a proposed thesis—makes it home and is shared with families. Regularly informing parents goes a long way toward ensuring there are no surprises for students or families when report cards are issued.

Use Data with Integrity

"Data" continues to be a hot-button issue with varying interpretations—some useful, some harmful. The very word scares and worries many of us—and often with good reason. How *data* is defined, analyzed, and applied affects how and what we teach and can even determine the trajectory of a child's future. So it's crucial that data application be equitable and sane and used in a manner that augments teaching and learning in beneficial ways for all learners—students and educators alike.

I define *data* as all the information and evidence we collect and analyze for the purposes of celebrating, improving, and accelerating meaningful and joyful learning. The inclusion of the word *joyful* is intentional; data focus must not just be about "needs improvement" and raising tests scores. Data can be applied to a system, such as a whole school or district or province, or to individual students; but the key is the data must ultimately lead to improving learning, which is no easy matter.

Take the lead in your school, and do what you can to ensure data gathering is accompanied by data analysis focused on meaningful student learning. "Data-driven decision making is not a particularly helpful approach. What is needed instead is a commitment to decision-driven data collection."[16] (See also "Advocate for Equitable Practices," pages 373–379.) Too often a flood of data overwhelms us, and data analysis becomes the main event rather than a vehicle for actual improvement of teaching and learning. Some data-team meetings wind up looking at and discussing how students perform on isolated standards or skills, which does nothing to advance meaningful learning in the long run. One frustrated teacher wrote me, "My administrator doesn't understand reading and relies heavily on the scores from a simple and quick reading test. Rather than considering and analyzing all the variables, we are expected to create a rigid flow map. None of this makes sense."[17]

As well, schools are often expected, without much training or experience, to take data-as-information and translate it to application of instructional practices that will improve learning for every student. "Educators are told the targets they must achieve but then are left largely on their own to figure out how actually to hit those targets."[18] Connected to those targets, we must upend our mind-set from data-driven to student-driven and create an assessment culture beyond test scores and reading levels to the specific strengths and needs of the particular students behind the numbers. Students may have similar test scores, but their strengths and weaknesses vary. Sheila Valencia and Marsha Riddle Buly found in their award-winning research study analyzing results on state reading tests that students fail tests for a variety of reasons, and, therefore, caution is needed to avoid overgeneralizing test results to one-size-fits-all instruction.[19]

Finally, we need to be sure to triangulate the data—that is, to have two or more reliable sources that, when taken together, give full and accurate evidence about the learner. Those sources for cross-verification might be, but are not limited to, student work samples, formative assessments, attitude surveys, anecdotal evidence from conferences and observations, test scores, conversations with students and families, student self-assessments and self-evaluations, portfolios, reflections, and more.

A continuous and deep look at a variety of data has the potential to lead to higher achievement. Keep these general questions in mind:

Thinking About Learning with Data in Mind

- What do we want to know?
- How will we find it out?
- How might we analyze the data?
- Are the data and data analysis valid, reliable, and useful?
- How might we use those results to improve student learning?
- What is our biggest priority?
- Is what we are prioritizing most important for increased student learning?
- Will our actions lead to more effective and joyful teaching and learning?

Take Action

- **Begin with a clearly focused, meaningful big question** that is specific to areas we are looking to assess for strengths and weaknesses and their root causes. For example, *How are our students doing in reading for understanding? Why is one group of students succeeding while others are failing? What teaching practices are working best? What are our next steps for improving instruction?* Without a clear focus and deep knowledge, educators can waste a lot of time examining massive amounts of data or examining data superficially—or both.

  For example, if we primarily view and "measure" reading for understanding as moving through levels and our teaching focus is directed there, we may see numbers move up in the short run and assume students are comprehending; but in the long run, as reading demands increase, we are likely to be disappointed. Here is where ongoing, high-level professional learning—beginning with discussing and challenging schoolwide beliefs and assumptions (pages 113–118)—is crucial for considering multiple points of view and how they relate to best-evidence practices. Professional *Literacy* Communities (see page 107) are a necessity for moving forward in a productive and equitable manner.

- **See the students behind the numbers.** Easy-to-read, numerical data can make some administrators feel they are being accountable and doing their job. However, data gathering without accompanying examination of the real person or group of people behind the data has little meaning and serves no useful purpose. For example, *What is causing the success or failure of this student or this particular group of students? What's working well, and how do we continue to build on that success? Why are some students underperforming, and what actions do we need to take to change that? What are our next steps?*

- **Be cautious with "data walls."** A data wall is a visual tool for representing student achievement. Often a data wall is used to notice, compare, track, and discuss whole-school and individual progress, trends, or interventions in reading or writing. On the positive side, having a data wall has the potential to help schools and teachers move from a mind-set of "my students" to "our students" when conversations, professional learning, and actions are centered on how to best instruct, guide, and support all students in the school to learn more. At the same time, we need to stay watchful that our data-wall discussions are not narrowly fixated on moving to higher scores and reading levels. Also, of crucial importance, any data wall needs to be in a private space, such as the teachers' lounge or a staff professional development meeting, and not in a public place where it has the potential to shame and stigmatize students, their teachers, and their families. Even if names are not used and data are coded, when a data wall can be publicly viewed, many students easily figure out who and where they are on the charts.

◆ **Ensure that grading practices are equitable.** *Grading should help, not harm, student learning.* The data that lead to the grade must be more than test scores and checklists and represent the student's true and full achievement. The kinds of information used to determine the grade, along with the weight given each type of data, needs to be known in advance to students and families and include multiple factors—for example, effort, homework, participation in class, group work, tests, work samples, and so on. I also firmly believe that a final grade should take into account opportunities we have provided students—at least on some occasions—to redo, revise, and retest to do better. Also, occasionally consider having students write their own narrative report cards so parents get a fuller picture of their child's progress and efforts.[20]

Let's keep grading in balance for our students. An eighth grader urged, "I wish teachers would do less grading, in general, and just make sure everyone understands what's being taught. My best teachers—very little was graded. Class was so interesting, everyone wanted to learn."[21]

◆ **Present any data analysis clearly and succinctly.** If educators, students, and their families cannot easily access and use the data in a format and language that helps all stakeholders understand and value students' progress, strengths, needs, and next steps in a productive manner, the data gathering is pretty much a waste of time.

Use Student-Friendly Rubrics

Think of a rubric as a detailed road map for moving students toward an expected destination, whether that desired end point is exemplary behaviors or specific achievements in literacy, math, or another content area. A rubric is not a curriculum; it is an evaluation tool, a continuum of learning that defines and describes desired traits or qualities—often attached to an escalating numerical scale—to let learners gauge how they are doing on their journey to excellence and where they need to improve. A rubric gives us the expected guidelines and requirements for meeting a standard of excellence. It is only meaningful and useful if the learner has first seen, examined, and understood the "whole" of what excellence looks like—an essay, a completed project, a public talk, a completed video, and so on.

Rubrics, when they are well done and appropriately used, take the mystery out of what an excellent product or process "looks like" and "sounds like." Accompanied by actual exemplars, which students examine and discuss with teacher guidance, students and teachers get a clear picture of what they and we are aiming for. The best rubrics, in terms of use and equity, are co-constructed with students *before* students begin "the work" but *after* students have examined, discussed, and understood the purpose, content, and audience for "the work." That is, whether it's a writing or reading assignment or an inquiry project, we co-create expected criteria in student-friendly language. Our "I can" statements, discussed on page 238, can also serve as an additional, co-constructed rubric that specifies qualities and actions the learner is expected to include in "the work." Of course, the more meaningful and relevant the work is, the more useful the rubric is likely to be.

For young students, having a clear and easy-to-follow rubric-as-checklist, including expectations for the work, is often key to their success, even with first attempts. For example, in a combined grade two–three class where we were writing stories about unlikely friendships for what would become a class book, I thought aloud as I wrote my own story in front of the class, and then we created a simple three-part rubric based on what I had included: (1) What happened? (2) What was the kindness that helped promote the friendship? (3) What was the lesson learned? After we had done sufficient frontloading (see pages 129–131), each student completed a draft within thirty minutes.

All twenty-three students were successful! Everyone included a satisfying lead, an elaboration on the kindness that changed their thinking, and a closure that delineated the lesson learned. The biggest advantage was the pride every student felt at having been successful. The conferences were joyful and gave energy rather than taking it away! Another huge advantage was that because there was little revision to do, students were willing to assume responsibility for the hard work of editing.

Still, there is a caution with all rubrics; they can be hazardous if inappropriately used. The biggest issue I have with rubrics is the parsing of work into predetermined categories, which can make teaching and learning more difficult. For example, when I read or write I am not thinking of specific traits, such as organization or voice, but rather of the impact words can have on the reader. Thomas Newkirk says it best: "The very authoritative language and format of rubrics, their pretense to objectivity, hides the human act of reading. The key qualities of good writing (organization, detail, a central problem) are represented as something the writing *has*—rather than something the writing *does*" (emphasis in original).[22]

Especially in writing, descriptors on the rubric often become the main instructional focus, and moving to higher levels becomes the main goal. Well-intentioned teachers who are not yet sufficiently knowledgeable about effective teaching of writing sometimes take the indicators or traits on the rubric and use them as separate teaching points, embracing part-to-whole teaching, such as teaching strategies or traits in isolation.

As an example, an entire writing conference with a student might center on examining each part of a student's writing against a rubric and giving feedback that is aligned with one or more of the rubric's descriptors. Rather than focusing first on the student and the whole piece of writing, including the writer's purpose and intended audience, the rubric takes center stage. The student leaves the conference with the goal of moving up on the rubric scale in a particular area or areas. Often the goal here is test preparation for high-stakes testing. However, writing progress and test scores in schools that misuse rubrics in this manner remain mostly stagnant and lackluster, as do students' attitudes about and abilities in writing.

Finally, rubrics can be given too much or incorrect weight when determining a student's grade. As a middle school principal and former language arts teacher noted, "Correcting student work with a rubric drives me crazy; the criteria is generally vague; most students only care whether or not the holistic score is a passing grade, and many get by without giving their best."[23] However, when we determine with students—on a rubric they have co-created—how much weight each trait or quality is worth, grading can become easier and fairer, and even enjoyable. Have students grade themselves on the completed work (after first demonstrating and practicing with them), and only change their grade if they cannot show evidence that validates their self-assessment.

 ## Take Action

◆ **Develop criteria and rubrics *with* students** for most significant work. Be sure students see and understand what exemplary work looks like and sounds like and that the criteria are written in language students and families can understand. Criteria need to be established with students before a project or unit is undertaken, and students need to clearly understand the purpose of the rubric. That said, take caution not to overuse or overemphasize rubrics.

◆ **Create clear guidelines.** Sometimes we complicate activities by making rubrics too complex—for example, by writing them in adult language or using rubrics written by publishers. Make sure the rubric's language and directions are student friendly and can be easily understood by both students and families. Save exemplars of student work, with permission from previous students, so students see the whole of what we're after in quality work, not just the parts. Be sure to also share rubrics with parents, so they know what their child is expected to be able to do in various areas.

- **Allow for flexibility.** One of the problems with rubrics is that their format and content can stifle and undervalue creativity, unique craft, and the full purpose of what the learner is attempting to convey. If a rubric is mostly about correctness and rigid requirements or if the rubric constrains students' thinking and choice, we discourage students to seek original approaches. I love what one student proposed: that "all rubrics should have a row labeled 'Surprise' to acknowledge new ways of thinking about an assignment."[24]

- **Stay focused on the meaningful whole.** Rubrics—by their nature of evaluating predetermined, weighted parts—discourage reading and judging the work as a complete entity.

- **Simplify.** Because I want students to aim for excellence and typical rubrics often contain so much information, I generally view and focus only on a one- or two-point rubric at the highest level(s)—usually a 4 or 5—and urge students to do the same. For younger students, I stick with a three-point criteria rubric, most often without numbered values attached, as noted on page 326.

- **Expect students to redo unacceptable work** and work toward a score of 3, as a minimum, on a five-point scale.[25] Consider, even, leaving out levels 1 and 2. Let students know we value persistent effort. Encourage students by noting strengths before weaknesses and setting reasonable goals with them.

- **Expect students to self-evaluate.** Teach students how to use rubrics as a way to monitor and assess their own progress. For example, do not confer with students until they have shown that they have met all the criteria on the agreed-upon rubric (for solving a problem, conducting research, reading, writing a draft, editing, and so on).

- **Be judicious in the use of rubrics.** We don't need rubrics for every lesson, activity, and piece of writing. Eventually we want students to internalize, for example, what effective writers and researchers do, without the need for a rubric. That outcome occurs—even when taking a test—when most of students' time has been devoted to sustained reading and writing of meaningful texts. Only a mind-set that views a rubric as an evaluation tool, not a curriculum, makes that outcome possible.

Finally, and most important, keep the focus on the students—and what they are trying to do—not the rubric.

Teach Self-Assessment

Self-assessment, which we teachers need to demonstrate, guide, expect, and practice with students, begins the day students enter our schools and classrooms. Self-assessment is a type of formative assessment, and it can be applied to all aspects of learning—from working well with peers to knowing how and what to improve as an effective reader, writer, and communicator.

Successful self-assessment by students requires that they can:

- Understand the goals of the lesson or learning target.
- Articulate and envision the criteria for success.
- Accurately judge and critique the quality of work-in-process.
- Apply a rubric—agreed-upon criteria—to clarify and augment the level of quality and completeness of their work.
- Notice and name their strengths.
- Improve and revise the work as needed.

Of course, the assessment is only worth doing if the work and its outcome benefit student learning in ways that matter.

Becoming an effective self-assessor depends a lot on the type of scaffolding and support we provide the learner. It's a delicate balance. Following the Optimal Learning Model (see pages 137–139), we want to give a "just right" amount of support—enough so learners can successfully problem-solve and strategize with minimal assistance but not so much that students continue to look to us every time they encounter a challenge. Determination to learn comes from knowing you can do the work, and that competence and confidence largely come from expert teaching and scaffolding. "If, after the lesson, readers are no better equipped to encounter a similar text without our scaffolding, then we haven't given them much that can transfer."[26] (See also scaffolded conversations, pages 305–309.)

Transfer of learning to new contexts is a necessary skill for independently navigating a task or a test, and successful transfer depends on students' ability to self-assess their work. Here's an example. Teachers are sometimes shocked and disappointed when their students don't do well on standardized tests. One teacher told me, "His writing in class is so much better than what he did on that test." Maybe. Yet, often the issue is that the classroom writing or reading is better because of all the support we give our students. We often tell students what needs improvement, fix spelling and grammar errors, and do much of the work for them. A common example is in guided reading, in which teachers supply most of the words students can't read. Not being expected to problem-solve and self-assess as they go along, students often falter when they have to think and work on their own.

Even our youngest learners can be taught to self-check and take more responsibility for monitoring their reading and writing. Ask, "Is it right?" "How do you know?" "Where can you find out?" "Where does it tell you that?" (See examples of self-assessment in kindergarten, pages 178–179 and 276.) Also, students can be taught and guided to write "I can" literacy statements that match a school's beliefs and practices and then to back up these statements with proof from their work. (See one class's examples of a few "I can" statements for writing on page 238.)

"Self-assessment is a major contributor to reading development, and doing well at self-assessment has significant cognitive and affective benefits."[27] In reading, one easy way to encourage student self-assessment is to have students review their reading records (monthly recording of books read with genre listed; see pages 195–196) and ask themselves questions similar to the ones I ask myself.

Self-Assessment: Voluntary Reading

- Have I done enough reading this month? (quantity)

- Am I sufficiently varying the type of reading I do? (genre)

- What have I learned and enjoyed? (new information, story, author's craft, different perspectives)

- Am I sometimes challenging myself? (new authors and genres, unfamiliar nonfiction topics)

- What are my goals? (books to read next, authors, genres, topics to study or learn more about)

In writing, whether it's at grade levels, in content areas, or as a whole school, come to agreement on how all writing will be dated, organized, and housed so students can easily manage and access the system and so that they, we, and their families can review and assess for quantity, quality, and growth over time. Then, make it a regular practice, with our demonstration and guidance, to have students self-assess by doing some version of the following practices.

Go back to a piece of writing from earlier in the school year. Self-assess for strengths, needs, and next steps for such qualities as organization and flow, leads, closure, word choice, spelling, and so on. Perhaps rewrite (choose a section if it's a long piece) to make it better. Set new goals for writing in the form of "I can" statements, such as "I can write a lead that engages the reader and sets the stage for what's to come" or "I can spell almost all high-frequency words correctly." Then, have students date, using evidence from their writing collection, where those "I can" statements can be verified.

Finally, as mentioned earlier, consider having students write their own narrative report cards to accompany the required school report card that goes to families. (See Routman, *Literacy at the Crossroads* [1996], pages 159–163, for procedures and examples of report cards authored by students.) You'll be amazed. Students can write reports on their strengths and needs that are so professional, it can be hard to tell who wrote them—the student or the teacher.

Take Action

- Employ more self-assessments, after first applying the OLM, demonstrating and explaining our expectations and guiding students through:
  - *Oral or written self-evaluations* by small groups or individual students.
  - *Portfolios*—collections of student work over time to show evidence of learning; chosen by the student, at first with teacher modeling and guidance. These can be digital or a combination of digital, print, and multimedia.
  - *"I can" statements*, backed up with evidence from students' work.
  - *Conferences* in which students restate their strengths and needs or write learning goals after those have been jointly set with the teacher.
  - *Questions generated by students* to demonstrate deep understanding of a topic.
  - *Practice tests* in which students self-score against a student-friendly rubric.
  - *Self-checks and self-corrections* for accuracy in word work in reading and for ensuring reading with understanding.

Endnote

When I work for at least a few days in a classroom, I expect all students—even those in primary grades—to fill out an "Evaluation of Student Learning." I explain the purpose—that I want to know what they learned, what they enjoyed, and any suggestions they might have for me. I tell them I am a learner, and I am always looking to improve my teaching. By telling students the audience and purpose for the writing, they take these evaluations seriously. This on-demand writing, done without teacher assistance, serves not only as a self-reflection but also as an assessment of student writing abilities—content, organization, fluidity, voice, legibility, spelling, and so on—both for individual students and as a whole class. (Examples from two students follow.) We also save and use these writing samples as one indicator of schoolwide growth from year to year.

Second grader Rein filling out his Evaluation of Learning after a three-day writing residency

Evaluation of Writing Residency

March 2016

Strathmillan School, Winnipeg, Manitoba

Name (optional) _Rein_____ Grade _3_____

Write down your thoughts on this week's writing residency. Please include insights, strengths, anything you took away from demonstrations, shared writing, conferences, coaching, conversations, things that you tried in your classroom, lingering questions, or anything that seems important to you.

I Was geting inSpird by uthr Kis.

to haw mrs. Roytman Seldrated my wrting.

I was in→Sbiring uthr Kis.

It is a Nice inSbiring tuthr Kis

Rein's thoughts on what he took away from the writing residency:

I was getting inspired by other kids.
How Mrs. Routman celebrated my writing.
I was inspiring other kids.
It is nice inspiring other kids.

Evaluation of Student Learning

March 2015

Strathmillan School, Winnipeg, Manitoba

Name _Julia_   Grade _4_

Write down your thoughts on what you learned this week about writing, editing, reading, thinking, speaking, listening, conferring, or anything that seems important to you.

I had A great week! I learned So Much about editing, revision, writing ect. I Also learned how important it is for me as a writer to relize how my writting is a lot better than I think it is! And that it's not all about suggestions and how to improve when we do conferences infront of the class, you taught me that their ment for mostly celebrating! My writting has improved so much! My favourite part was the letters to our parents! This was a great experience for me I'm glad that Our class got chosen. I LOVE reading and before I never relized that reading and writting were conected! I also never thought about writting for the readers prospective. I think that that helped me improve A lot as well! I am very exited to continue writting with the new tips you taught Me and I will definitly think about getting my writting into A children's Magizine! It was A pleasure to have you in our classroom! I will miss you!

    Thanks Again!,

        Julia

■ ■ Learning insights on writing and reading from Julia, a fourth grader, after
■ ■ a four-day writing residency. (Note increased awareness of audience and
       purpose as well as joy in reading and writing.)

Being able to accurately assess ourselves is a necessity for moving forward as continuing learners—not just for students but also for us teachers, leaders, and coaches. Self-assessment is a precursor and benchmark for becoming and being a self-determining learner, which is the focus of the next section.

Developing Self-determining Learners

L et's dare to do things a bit differently and inspire our students to do the same. Let's create a learning culture that champions questions, choices, and multiple ways of knowing, seeing, and doing. Rule followers and rigid programs have not advanced world progress much. Those who become innovators, big thinkers, and risk takers are the ones who create more livable and equitable communities. These are the self-determining learners among us, those who know how to learn and who use their knowledge and passion to make the world a better place—whether that world is a classroom, a school, a playground, or a neighborhood. It's difficult to teach and inspire our students to learn in ways that are foreign to us. Let's strive to become self-determining learners one and all! Let's examine what that means and how we might get there.

Self-determining learners are readers, writers, and thinkers in all disciplines who can use what they know and apply it to different contexts for their own meaningful purposes. (One example is applying the qualities of effective writing to all genres and forms. See Appendix G: 12 Writing Essentials for All Grade Levels.) Self-determining learners—students, teachers, and leaders at all levels—self-direct, self-reflect, and self-teach on an ongoing basis. These learners possess the qualities that excellent teachers possess, as described on pages 102–103. Very important, these learners constantly self-assess, and much of that self-assessment is through deep inner questioning to determine what supports, feedback, resources, approaches, and next steps are needed to move forward.

Self-determining learners set their own worthwhile goals; they continually work on getting better at something that's important; they self-monitor their literacy behaviors, attitudes, and actions; and they self-regulate their learning. Daniel Pink, in his fascinating book *Drive: The Surprising Truth About What Motivates Us*, has written about the three essential elements of self-determination: autonomy (exercising control over our own lives), mastery (becoming competent at something that matters), and purpose (setting meaningful goals that often go beyond self-interest).[1]

I believe becoming a self-determining learner also requires that we possess and act upon a disposition and conviction in which we:

- Trust ourselves to achieve a specific goal.
- Get better with ongoing, deliberate practice.
- Seek targeted and expert guidance, resources, and feedback as needed.
- "Reframe difficulty as opportunity."[2]
- Achieve excellence in an area that's important to us or others.

I further believe that becoming a self-determining learner means that the learner possesses such competencies as fierce determination to learn, ongoing curiosity, ability to think critically, relatedness with others, a sense of humor, and the ability to see struggle and setbacks as opportunities to self-reflect and move forward—all of which we can and must foster in our students, including our youngest learners.

Of course, developing a culture of self-determining learners does not exclude explicit guidelines, high standards, and curriculum requirements, which are a necessity for ensuring that all students receive an equitable education. However, application of requisites must allow for and encourage considerable flexibility and autonomy in implementation and assessment. As well, the goals and work must be worthwhile, enjoyable, and stretch our thinking—a necessity for us as well as our students.

Think about reconsidering the commonly used term and goal "independent learner." Keep in mind that just because we can do something on our own, such as following explicit directions in a guide or correctly completing a worksheet or task, doesn't mean we are on our way to becoming lifelong, self-sustaining learners. Students and we educators waste a lot of time in school on "stuff" we can do independently but that doesn't matter very much. In fact, such tasks do harm by fostering compliance and lack of enthusiasm for learning.

Regardless of college or career path, to be successful and fulfilled, today's students will need to be intrinsically motivated to continue to learn. They will need to be self-determining, empowered learners, and much of that depends on knowing how to learn and having the capacity for self-teaching. Fareed Zakaria, a prolific writer and political thinker, writes about how he learned to acquire knowledge on his own through a strong liberal arts education:

> *I learned how to read an essay closely, search for new sources, find data to prove or disprove a hypothesis, and detect an author's prejudices. I learned how to read a book fast and still get its essence. I learned to ask questions, present an opposing view, take notes, and, nowadays, watch speeches, lectures, and interviews as they stream across my computer. And most of all, I learned that learning was a pleasure—a great adventure of exploration.*[3]

Economists predict that half of the jobs that exist today will not exist in the future and that most people will need to change jobs often to stay viable. Linda Darling-Hammond states that access to twenty-first-century learning is the real equity challenge. She notes that providing access to jobs of the future will require students who can make sense of complex information, think creatively, work collaboratively in cross-cultural settings, and effectively incorporate many forms of media and data.[4] To successfully meet that challenge will require resilient students who are self-determining learners, able to rethink, retool, and reimagine possibilities as they work to solve real-world problems. This section will elaborate on actions and dispositions we can promote in our schools and classrooms to encourage self-determination in learning.

Balance the Power in the Classroom

Many of our students feel powerless; that is, they believe and behave as if they have little control over their challenging lives. Although it's not likely we can change their life circumstances, while they are in our schools we can at least adjust the power structure so their voices are heard and respected, they have some choice in the work they do, and they help determine how the classroom operates. When we relinquish some control and offer unwavering support, it's more likely that our students will feel valued and be willing to engage in challenging work.

Invite and encourage your students to give input and to set up guidelines for "our classroom." For example, seek input for organizing the classroom library, housing student writing, welcoming new students, establishing expected behaviors with a substitute teacher, resolving conflict, deciding what goes up on classroom walls, and so on. Although we may have the final say, when students know they have some decision-making power, they are more likely to be engaged and empowered learners, not just compliant ones. Perhaps most important in balancing the power structure is ensuring we hear and respect all students' voices—especially crucial for those who feel their voices don't matter or that their voices have been silenced. There can be no equity if freedom to speak our minds belongs only to those in authority.

It's often been said that the person who does the most talking does the most learning. "People with more power are used to talking more. People with less power have gotten used to talking less."[5] In our classrooms, teachers control 80 percent of the talking.[6] To be clear, by "talking" we mean lecturing, asking all or most of the questions, and controlling the dialogue. Conversation in the classroom is different and less common. In a conversation, we hear and encourage the sharing of many voices, without a hidden agenda. That is, as teachers, we see ourselves as listeners and learners who can benefit from our students' ideas and questions; we are not just acting as experts dispensing information. Not to be minimized: "Balancing the power in the room leads to a better power balance outside the room."[7] Students who have opportunities throughout the school day to voice their ideas and opinions without fear of retribution and to engage in true conversation are more likely to respectfully consider others' ideas—in and out of the classroom—with an open mind. The same is true for us teachers and leaders.

Make student self-efficacy part of our classroom and school culture. When we hold high expectations for every student and teach and guide students in how to self-monitor, self-direct, and self-evaluate their work and learning, they become more confident, competent, and self-reliant as learners. As such, they are more likely to take responsibility to problem-solve, revise their writing, reread when meaning is unclear, seek out a helpful resource, ask for help after they have made a genuine effort, and set their own worthwhile goals. Perhaps most important, empowered students come to believe they have agency in their lives, that they have the ability to implement positive change for themselves and others.

 ## Take Action

+ **Examine our rules of engagement.** Self-evaluate as a staff, or individually, our classroom and school values, regulations, and procedures to assess whether they are fair, respectful, and helpful. Also, consider having students anonymously submit a similar evaluation along with suggestions for improvement. Assure students we will take their views and suggestions seriously and that their honesty will not bring negative consequences. Also, include students' input in creating class and schoolwide beliefs and goals.

◆ **Check that students are clear about a lesson's purpose and learning goals** (see also pages 344–346). Too often students wind up, through no fault of their own, in a "gotcha" situation. When we fail to clearly explain our intentions, lesson purpose, and goals—and don't post them in student-friendly language—we disadvantage our students and their families too, who want to be supportive but don't know what's expected. As well, we need to check to be sure students clearly understand the task at hand and are sufficiently prepared before we send them off to do it. This is also very important for homework, when we unwittingly disadvantage some students whose families may not have adequate time, knowledge, or resources to provide sufficient help.

Use such questions as the following to check in with students and the class:

- ◉ Where do you think we are now in our study?
- ◉ What do you most need from me in the time we have today?
- ◉ How can I help you _____?
- ◉ Do you feel sufficiently prepared to _____?

◆ **Save exemplars from former students and classes.** Show exemplary student work, not just teacher models or examples from commercial texts, to make expectations visible for an expected final product. Follow an Optimal Learning Model to demonstrate and discuss why selected pieces are considered exemplary.

◆ **Be a generous listener.** Listen more than talk; encourage all voices to be heard and respected; self-monitor to ensure our teacher/leader voice is not the loudest one in the room. (For much more on listening, see pages 149–153.)

◆ **Be open to student feedback on lessons and actions.** We endear our students to us when they know we genuinely seek and value their feedback, and that we will act upon it in a positive manner. Some students find it difficult to speak up; they might be introverted, reluctant to speak publicly, or worried about how their question or response will be received. Have forms and a box in the classroom where students can anonymously (or not) leave information on academic and social-emotional matters, such as "Today's lesson would have been easier for me if _____," "I need help understanding why _____," "I'm struggling with _____," "It really helps me learn when you _____," and so on.

◆ **Do more shared writing** (see pages 142–144), which encourages all students' voices. Encourage participation and help shape the language of students' contributions without judgment. In a risk-taking, trusting environment, students feel safe to make their thoughts and voices public.

◆ **Have more student-directed, small-group conversations.** Use a fishbowl experience to show how that works. (See the bullet item "Demonstrate how productive groups work together" on page 349 for "fishbowl" explanation.) Then, with guidance, put students in charge of problem-solving classroom issues, literature conversations, and more.

◆ **Employ choice within structure** as much as possible. When students have some choice in a required task they are about to undertake, they are more likely to engage, put forth full effort, and self-monitor and self-direct their learning. (See "Provide More Choice Within Structure," pages 90–93.)

◆ **Share responsibility for what gets posted on walls and in hallways.** Give yourself a break for the first few weeks of school. Have only one welcoming bulletin board "done." Consider saying something like "This is *our* classroom this school year. Let's talk about what we might want to post on the walls." Certainly give some suggestions, such as "students as writers," favorite books and authors, and procedures and rules of behavior to follow; but do try to give students some choice and increased responsibility for what's on the walls inside and outside classrooms. Show photos from a previous year's class to spark ideas and thinking. While in the organization process, consider posting signs such as "Bulletin board under construction by ＿＿＿" or "Coming soon, amazing work on ＿＿＿ by the students of ＿＿＿."

◆ **Implement student-led conferences.** Beginning in kindergarten, demonstrate, practice with, and support students in conducting their own student-led conferences, an extremely effective and enjoyable way for students to showcase their learning. See *Literacy at the Crossroads* for guidelines, specifics, and samples of conference evaluations by the student and also the parents/caregivers in attendance.[8] Powerful stuff! As well, some schools have had great success using a portfolio process—physical or digital—often led by students, to make students' progress over time visible.

Establish Routines and Rituals Together

Closely connected to balancing the power in the classroom are the daily routines and actions that contribute to making a classroom or school feel like a safe, nurturing, and connected community. Predictable routines students can count on are especially important for our most vulnerable students. A daily greeting as simple as making eye contact, smiling, and saying "I'm so glad to see you today" can uplift students and give them the will to engage with learning.

Daily routines also include the way the class operates—for example, acceptable behaviors, procedures and norms for group work and conversations, organization of resources, problem solving, and so on. The better we are at teaching, guiding, and expecting students to self-manage behaviors and activities, the more we empower them as learners and collaborators.

Daily routines ground me and enable me to approach the tasks of the day with a sense of stability and optimism. For example, my husband, Frank, and I enjoy a breakfast ritual, which provides a tranquil start to our day. Frank cooks a delicious breakfast of eggs, pancakes, or oatmeal with all the trimmings, but not before handing me a steaming, perfect cup of Seattle's finest coffee. He knows I appreciate the indulgence and can barely speak or function without that morning brew. Then, over a leisurely breakfast, I read the *New York Times* (the actual paper version) while he reads the *Seattle Times* (paper as well). We do have some conversation about the news and politics, but mostly it's a peaceful, unhurried time that fortifies me with the energy, calm, and resolve to begin the messy, hard work of writing each day. While I realize that no longer having a daily job makes that morning routine possible, even when I was teaching every day in the classroom, I got up an hour earlier than needed in order to savor some quiet time before the rush of the day.

When I am writing a book, I also depend on a predictable routine and structure to be productive. Although I know a scholarly writer who writes every morning in his pajamas, I have to shower first and be fully dressed as if heading off for work. My desk also needs to have my writing tools at the ready—MacBook, notes, book outline, rough drafts, sharpened pencils, highlighter pens, sticky notes—and be free of papers unrelated to what I am working on. I aim for three hours of sustained quiet time every morning, which is my best thinking and writing time. My goal during that time is to draft a minimum of 500 words—hopefully meaningful ones. I turn off e-mail and Twitter, and usually it's still early enough that I am not interrupted with phone calls, deliveries, or other distractions. If my routine gets sidelined, I lose my focus, calm, and energy to do the work and do not meet my writing goal for the day.

Daily routines and rituals provide our students and us with a sense of calm and stability, knowing there are predictable things we can count on throughout the day. Knowing what to expect creates an order and a comfort that make it easier for students and us to focus on our work, meet our goals, and positively respond to the inevitable changes that occur in the unpredictable life of the classroom and school. Daily routines also help build stamina for learning (see pages 350–354) and create a sense of order that may be missing from some of our students' lives.

Homelessness, poverty, refugee status, abuse, constant failure, and other traumas render many students powerless to take any control over their lives. Inviting all students to help establish a stable classroom culture is a small but significant step in helping them to feel "I belong here. I am safe here. My opinions count. My teacher sees me."

 ## Take Action

- **Develop daily routines and rituals with students.** A routine or ritual may be as simple as students having reading choices before school officially begins or as complex as knowing how to self-direct a literature conversation group. What is important is that students have some say in the matter, and that teachers are not dictating how "my" classroom operates. Students are more apt to enjoy and take routines and operating procedures seriously when they have input in an environment that signals "our" classroom.

    Some daily routines and rituals might include, but are not limited to:

    - *Greeting each other daily.* Whether it's smiles, high-fives, or "How are you doing?," such gestures create a welcoming expectation.
    - *Establishing procedures* for how the classroom operates—jobs, bathroom use, approaches for problem-solving classroom issues that arise, guidelines for how we treat and speak to and with each other, guidelines for small-group work, recess rules and permitted games, guidelines for substitutes and visitors, and so on.
    - *Maintaining the classroom library* with students—sign-out procedures, organization, book return, adding new texts and categories.
    - *Coming to agreement on activities*—before-school and end-of-day.

- **Hold students accountable for following routines,** procedures and rituals, which have been established with input. When those activities do not go as they have been set up—including procedures and solutions for dealing with routine problems and behaviors (not the extreme ones)—place responsibility on them before intervening with suggestions and solutions. Ask questions: "What might you do differently next time so that _____?" "What can you do now to begin to correct this situation?"

"What's something else you might try now?" "What help do you need from me so you can ____?" (See related writing story, pages 58 and 82–83.)

♦ **Create predictable, daily structures.**

- **Start with a meaningful yet calm and predictable routine** in the morning or afternoon or even after recess, which can set the tone for the rest of the day. These transition times can be tricky for everyone. It's important that students be able to independently start the morning or class with a routine activity while the teacher greets students or reviews any messages from families.

  - One possibility for elementary classrooms is to start the first ten minutes of class with a daily math problem-solving activity that students can complete independently or with a partner. For those who finish early, have them create their own math problem or choose a book to read.
  - For middle and high school, consider—at least occasionally—having students begin with a five-to-ten-minute open-ended quick-write or prompt. (Linda Rief's classic *100 Quickwrites* is an excellent resource for ideas and procedures.[9]) Use that time to greet students, check homework, and do brief conferring.

- **Examine daily schedules** and work with the principal, grade-level colleagues, and specialists to ensure key subject-area times are not fragmented, which causes students to lose concentration and time on task. Middle school and high school schedules that allow sustained time for reading and writing are a challenge to create. One workable solution is to have at least several days in a row or a couple of weeks in succession devoted solely to reading or to writing so that sustained practice and deep learning are possible.

- **Try to schedule writing at the same time every day,** so students come to depend on it, anticipate it, and are ready to write. Especially for our youngest students, think about scheduling writing in the morning, when their energy and concentration are highest.

- **Work to minimize pull-outs** and to ensure all students are present for rich literacy and language activities. Research on RTI indicates that interventions have not raised achievement as expected.[10] Students who are pulled out might be better served by staying in the classroom with an expert teacher. (An exception would be students with emotional and behavioral disabilities too severe to be handled in the classroom.)

    Consider using the intervention or resource teacher's time by having him or her work with students on reading right in the classroom while the whole class is in small reading groups or doing independent reading. Or the teacher and resource teacher can co-teach during a writing lesson and then circulate during a writer's workshop. Just as an equity issue, pull-outs make many students feel stigmatized.

♦ **Include celebrations and appreciations** as part of the daily life of the classroom and school. Develop rituals for birthdays, special occasions, performances, notable accomplishments, hard-fought efforts, and so on. Show appreciation often! Simple statements, such as "Thank you for being present today. I know how hard it is for you to get here. You contribute so much to our classroom community," can go a long way toward letting students know we value them. The same is true for us teachers; principals who celebrate their staffs and show appreciation create happier school cultures.

Make Learning Intentions Clear and Attainable

Learning intentions—our goals and objectives—must consider not just required curriculum and standards but also students' interests and needs. As one middle school student told me, "Teachers need to mold lessons to kids; don't mold your kids to your lessons." Goal setting for and with students is crucial, but only if the goals we set are meaningful and lead to increased student learning, engagement, and even empowerment. Students need to see a connection between their effort and the learning outcome.

To that end, some educators now use the term *learning targets* with students to replace *learning objectives*, which were traditionally written for teachers. Regardless of your preferred terminology (I mostly use *learning goals*), ensure that the ultimate goal is for students to take responsibility for improving, assessing, and expanding their learning. Establish learning goals with students in student-friendly language and then tailor instruction and feedback to ensure students understand, value, and can accomplish these goals/targets with minimal support.

One of the most productive ways to use goal setting is through conferring and interacting with students one-on-one, in small groups, and as a whole class. In the course of everyday teaching, expert teachers continually notice and name what students are doing well and assess what demonstrations, shared experiences, and guided practice students need to productively move forward. That ongoing, formative assessment includes helpful and actionable feedback that learners use to reinforce existing goals, revise current goals, and independently set new goals. (See pages 246–248 and 295–298 for much more on feedback.)

A big caution: goal setting by itself can be a waste of time, especially if we set too many goals or the goals set are trivial and squander students' learning time. Some schools require that goals be posted in every classroom every day and that students be able to state these goals. However, just because goals are posted and correctly stated doesn't mean student learning will increase in any meaningful way. Our goals mirror our values and beliefs. For instance, if we believe students learn best through skills-in-isolation instruction, our goals and where we put our time and effort will reflect that priority, and student learning will not advance much. As well, too often we set goals because they can be easily measured, but easy measurement such as movement through book levels or higher scores on a test does not necessarily address purposeful student achievement.

Meaningful goal setting requires that we educators be highly knowledgeable and conversant with research-based practices, and that our beliefs and practices align schoolwide. As well, goal setting and school culture are interconnected. We and our students are more likely to achieve goals in an upbeat, positive, trusting culture where we feel safe, valued, and encouraged to raise questions, voice our opinions, and set our own worthy goals.

Ultimately, of course, we want students to be able to self-assess and set their own worthy goals. That outcome is more likely when students are driving their own learning and have some say and choice in what they are learning or being asked to do.[11]

 ## Take Action

Keep in mind that students need to know, visualize, and understand the learning targets/goals in order for our feedback or their own self-assessment to be useful or actionable.

The following guidelines assume that literacy and learning across the curriculum are about effective communication and interaction with real-world audiences through purposeful reading, writing, speaking, listening, and the arts. Use these guidelines as a self-evaluation for establishing your own goal setting, with input from students. That said, be sure to communicate goals and guidelines in a way that encourages and celebrates curiosity, exploration, and innovative thinking. We will not develop self-determining learners by prioritizing compliance and conformity.

• **Establish guidelines for setting and achieving purposeful learning goals.** Self-evaluate our process for determining learning goals and the content of those goals.

Purposeful Learning Goals

- *Goals and expectations are meaningful, clear, and transparent* and can be articulated by students as well as teachers.

- *Goals are often written with students* in student-friendly language.

- *Success criteria are defined and visible*, demonstrated, practiced, and discussed so that students know what the end goal "looks like" and "sounds like" and believe they can "get there."

- *Students examine and discuss examples of excellent work* (exemplars) and, with guidance, become familiar and practiced with the qualities of such work and the language of helpful critique.

- *Ongoing assessment is a vital part of a goal-setting culture* that is fluid, not fixed, and that includes giving students opportunities to revise work to improve it.

- *Goals include development of qualities such as stamina*, a positive mindset, collaborating well with peers, self-checking, and self-evaluating.

- *Useful, actionable feedback is essential,* and such feedback relates to the instructional goals and focuses first on strengths before needs.

- *Some student choice is provided within the required goals*; rigid requirements can take away learners' initiative and energy.

- *Excellence is included as a goal.* For example, when conducting reading and writing conferences with students, impart the message and mindset that being excellent at something means we are always seeking to improve our abilities.

Finally, we want goals to extend beyond a lesson plan, a standard, or a curriculum requirement. Ultimately, we want our instruction to lead to learners who think for themselves, fervently seek to learn more, and create new knowledge. Educator Susan Brookhart wisely notes: "Higher-order thinking happens when students engage with what they know in such a way as to *transform* it (emphasis in original). That is, this kind of thinking doesn't just reproduce the same knowledge; it results in something new."[12]

Make Students Less Dependent on Us

We teachers too often do for our students what they are capable of doing for themselves, making it less likely they can become self-determining learners. As a parent and a teacher, I'm as guilty as anyone. We're pressed for time, and it seems quicker and more efficient to do the task ourselves. That works in the short run for us, but in the long run we disadvantage and disable kids by thwarting and delaying the development of competencies that lead to growing self-confidence and self-reliance. Students develop self-regulation and self-sufficiency only when we teach for it and expect it. The following story illustrates that point.

A kind and caring intermediate-grades teacher complained that her students were always seeking her attention and help. It was getting harder to meet with small groups and to confer with students one-on-one. In fact, she had a long line of students at her desk on most days, especially during writing time. I suggested she tell her students that they could no longer seek her out while she was with another student or group and that from now on they would be expected to find misspellings, use resources, and do everything she had taught them how to do before she would agree to help them. She told the whole staff, "It was like a miracle. I didn't really believe it would work, but it did! I sternly told the kids, 'You can no longer approach me when I'm working with students. Find the help you need. You can quietly ask a friend, you can try everything you know, but you cannot come to me.' Amazingly, the room got quiet, everyone was working, and I could finally do my job. What a revelation!"

One of the best ways to develop self-determining, self-evaluating learners is through student-directed, small-group work. Having small, heterogeneous groups of three to five students working together is ideal for extending shared experiences; giving every student an opportunity to speak, discuss, and fully participate; and building confidence before students attempt a task on their own.

As noted on page 304, such grouping can pay big dividends for English language learners. Groups might be revising a class-authored shared writing, composing an introduction to a research report, holding a literature conversation, solving a problem in math, making scientific observations, and so on. Small-group work is the shared and guided practice stage of the Optimal Learning Model.

Once we have laid sufficient groundwork with students (how to establish norms for behaviors, conversations, problem solving, and so on, devised jointly with students), it's feasible and efficient to have multiple groups meeting at the same time—even in the primary grades. With students actively in charge of their learning, we are freed up to float among groups and take brief observational notes on strengths and needs or to join one or more groups who need more explanation and guidance. In self-directed, small-group work, students collaborate and try out or refine what we have been teaching, so our expectations and guidelines need to be very clear. As well, we need to have done enough frontloading so students are successful with minimum guidance from us.[13]

 Take Action

- **State clear and reasonable expectations** for students and expect them to meet them. We do need, first, to demonstrate exactly what those expectations look like and sound like in practice. It may also be advisable to have co-constructed written norms of behavior. Although initially it can take longer not to "fix" everything ourselves, it's a win–win situation in the long run—less work for us, and more responsibility and independence for our students, which is more productive and satisfying all around. (See the bullet item "Make expectations clear and prominent" on pages 58–59 for more.)

- **Guide students to assume responsibility for reaching their learning goals.** Ensuring that learning targets are clear, meaningful, and student friendly—and giving students useful feedback in their learning process—is crucial. Students need to be able to "understand their learning target, assess how close they are to the target, and then plan strategies for their own improvement."[14]

- **Give students the message that we value and reward their thinking,** backed up by evidence, over a "right" answer that we teachers hold in our heads. We can say something like "I'm not just interested in a correct answer. If you give me your best thinking and back it up, you can't be wrong."

- **Refrain from immediately giving students "the answer."** It's okay to say "I'm not going to tell you the answer. You can figure this out. We'll come back to this again later after you've had more time to think about it" or "Let's figure this out together."

- **Ask more questions that make students think for themselves,** such as the following:
  - Why do you think that?
  - I'm not sure I know what you mean. Say more about that.
  - What else might be the reason for _____?
  - How could you find out _____?

- What questions have you asked yourself (or what strategies have you tried) that might help you determine _____?

- **Teach students to ask and answer their own vital questions.** Demonstrate the difference between open questions, which encourage multiple responses, and closed questions, which usually have one right answer and shut down discussion. (See more on pages 164–165.)

- **Teach self-checking.** Rather than checking all answers and papers ourselves, set up systems that allow students to self-evaluate, self-monitor, and self-correct— beginning in kindergarten (see pages 178–179 for an example). Use group and individual self-reflections to assess the impact of collaborative group work.

- **Make sure students "hold the pen" when conferring with them,** and have them make any necessary adjustments, with our guidance, on their writing papers. Editing—especially spelling and punctuation—is one area where students can do much more on their own once we've applied the OLM. For example, when students turn in a "final" paper with errors in spelling of high-frequency words or basic editing expectations that we've charted together as a whole class, I say something like "In the first few lines, I notice several editing issues that we all agreed students would be responsible for. So I'm not going to read any further until you fix those. Also, carefully reread your paper a few more times to catch other editing errors." (See also page 240, in Excellence, "Teaching Writers.")

- **Rely on more partner and small-group work.** Once we have applied an Optimal Learning Model to our instruction and students know how and what to do, peers can effectively help each other with spelling, editing, reading, conferring, problem solving, and much more. Include procedures for expected behaviors, such as making eye contact, speaking politely and coherently, citing evidence to back up statements, respectfully adding on, agreeing with, or disagreeing with a speaker, and so on.

- **Demonstrate how productive groups work together.** Guide one student group while all other students look on. Use a fishbowl demonstration, taking on the role of group facilitator and leading the group to stay on task and ensure that every group member gets a chance to speak. Have onlookers jot down what they notice the facilitator and students doing well, which keeps students focused and also serves as our evaluation of the positive moves students take away from the observation. Also use the notes to create a rubric of student expectations. Hold each group member responsible for the collective "work."

- ◆ **Coach students on how to use the OLM.** Make the Optimal Learning Model (pages 138–140) explicit to students, and encourage them to apply the model when working with peers and younger students.

- ◆ **Have students regularly self-evaluate** their behaviors for working on their own or productively with a partner or group. Follow the OLM to gradually release responsibility to students as a group to orally (and eventually in writing) note their strengths, areas for improvement, and goals for next steps. Later do the same for students individually. As well, we can use students' self-evaluations to determine our own next steps.

- ◆ **Have useful resources available and accessible,** and teach students how to use them. Provide resources that encourage and support students to seek "answers"—books, texts, websites, and multimedia sources. Also, guide students in how to use classroom resources—for example, word walls, anchor charts, posted directions, student-friendly spelling resources, and peers—to find information and self-check their work.

Build Stamina and the Will to Learn

Stamina relates to having the energy, perseverance, and staying power to sustain mental and physical efforts. Stamina is a competency that has to be developed and nurtured; none of us are born with it. Look at any dazzling musician, dancer, artist, athlete, or inventor; a major share of their brilliance comes from their countless hours of practice and desire to excel. People with stamina are much more likely to reach their goals because they *want* to excel, not just for themselves but also for real-world audiences—the public, their families, their friends. If we really want to motivate students to learn deeply and become self-determining learners, we need to stop wasting their time with, among other things, speed-reading tests used to measure comprehension and high-stakes tests that disadvantage students who need more time than what's allotted. We develop stamina working on what we value, what we love, and what we believe we can achieve.

Writing is my passion, and my stamina for writing increases the more I write. That is, the more writing becomes a daily habit, the longer I can stay with the task and the more efficient and energetic I become as a writer. Building endurance depends on sufficient practice time, with something like an 80-to-20-percent ratio of practice to lesson. The amount of time deliberately practicing what has been taught in a lesson—whether it be writing, reading, researching, playing a sport, or playing an instrument—must be where most of students' time and effort are concentrated, not in our lesson or demonstration.

Stamina also requires that the underlying basics have been learned—for example, adequate handwriting skills for sustained writing, sufficient reading habits and strategies for independent reading, or the rudiments of playing an instrument for sustained practice. Stamina calls for sufficient know-how, determination, and resilience—all characteristics of successful people.

To be clear, although stamina and sticking with a task are necessary attributes for becoming a self-determining learner at any age, they only matter if the task is worth doing. Too often, students compliantly stick with activities that waste their time and their minds. Students only develop stamina and the will to learn when they value or understand the goal and how to reach it, when they are willing to invest mental and emotional efforts for sustained periods, and when they have developed an "I can do it" attitude. Straight talk with students who are struggling can help them develop stamina and the will to do better. What follows is a brief story that shows how telling the truth led a student to develop the stamina and will required for assuming more responsibility for higher achievement.

A Student Develops Stamina

Jordan was a fourth grader cruising though levels and reading two years below grade level. Neither she nor her teacher were holding her accountable for being a better reader, and Jordan seemed unaware of how far behind she was. In a one-on-one reading conference that made it clear that she was far more capable than her lackluster efforts indicated, I said something like "Jordan, I can tell from our conference that you're not reading much at home or in school. Because you read so slowly and finish very few books, it's not likely you're going to become a great reader. I can also tell you understand what you read, so that's great. But right now, you're just reading easy books that are at about a second-grade level and you're in fourth grade. If you want to do well in school and accomplish your dreams, you need to push yourself a lot harder, starting now. You need to do a lot more reading, and you need to challenge yourself more."

Back at her school a year later, Jordan, who was now a fifth grader, tracked me down and insisted on meeting with me. Here's part of what she proudly told me: "When you told me I was two years below where I should be, I was shocked! I couldn't believe it, so I started working harder and reading more. I read every night now, and my reading is a lot better." Jordan, through her own efforts and with her teacher's support, was now reading and understanding texts at her grade level. And her stamina for reading was amazing. The process of seeing continuing improvement gave her the will to keep going. Keep in mind there were no external rewards, which don't work in the long run, but the intrinsic reward of becoming a comprehending and joyful reader.

It was telling Jordan the truth that prompted her to begin to invest in the hard work of developing the reading stamina and will she needed to improve. Our students and their families have the right to know the achievement realities and possibilities and their role in improvement. If we are careful with the language and tone we use and are transparent and caring in our motives—whether the student is a struggling reader or writer or a gifted one—honesty really is the best policy. As part of stamina development and the will to learn, students also need to have sufficient support before they can assume more responsibility for their learning.

Students, as well as we educators, also need to believe and value that a steadfast effort, which requires stamina, leads to success and that failure is inherent—and even necessary—in order to achieve a worthy goal. We need to revise the conversation around failure from the constant reminder many learners receive that they don't measure up to talking about how failure can be an important part of learning. And we need to help students recover from failure and build resiliency. Jo Boaler, a Stanford University math professor, argues that "mistakes" actually make one's brain grow and that, without mistakes, we don't learn.[15]

Mary Beth Nicklaus, a thoughtful junior high school literacy interventionist and teacher-researcher, now shares her own failures with her students. She notes that when students who struggle hear only success stories—even inspiring ones—the stretch to success feels out of reach for many. "For students who are unfamiliar with agency in their own lives, a teacher can model it for them by sharing her own accounts of failure, and her own resiliency in the face of it."[16] She further notes, in relation to building stamina in her students:

> *In 8th and 9th grade at our school, we start seeing kids in reading intervention who never needed it before. This is the level where the need for reading stamina really begins to kick in. Students find themselves in shock because of higher-level vocabulary, larger amounts of reading in core area classes, and the inability to handle it all. When it comes to sink or swim, many of them just give up and flunk because they don't know how to get better at the skills they need. They feel helpless. I have to become a partner to the student. We work together to find the new tools to build that stamina they need to grow into an efficient, effective functional reader. Getting students involved in their own progress monitoring is one strategy that works well.*[17]

 ## Take Action

- **Let students know why stamina matters.** Say something like "Today I'm going to expect you to work in your groups (or read independently, continue writing, take notes, and so on) for thirty minutes. We've slowly been building up stamina. Stamina is being able to stick with something and give it your full effort. Stamina is very important for becoming an excellent student, a successful worker at a job, or a highly skilled athlete, musician, mathematician, dancer, scientist, writer, and so on." Talk about your own stamina for a passion or goal you have.

- **Favor "You haven't learned it *yet*" over "You haven't learned it."** This is where we lose new teachers and learners who struggle. They can become overwhelmed by so many expectations and requirements that they want to give up. Saying to them, "You haven't learned it *yet*, but you will learn it, and I will help you learn it" goes a long way toward keeping them willing to make a big effort. Help new teachers develop that important mind-set as well.

- **Start small.** Help students build up stamina slowly, day by day. For example, although young students may, at first, be able to read or write on their own—or stay focused in group time—for only five to ten minutes, incremental increases over time can add up to forty-five to sixty minutes a day.

◆ **Connect stamina to effort.** Increased stamina is easier to attain when the activity or task is purposeful to us and we can visualize the end results. When we value the lesson or activity, we are more likely to persist at it, even in the face of difficulty. It's hard to develop stamina at something we don't want to do. This is as true for us educators as it is for students. For example, it is the passion I have for promoting and increasing engagement, excellence, and equity for all learners, as well as how much I care about my readers, that drives me to generate the stamina I need to write a meaningful book.

◆ **Give feedback that values stamina and the will to learn.** Let students know when we notice their stamina increasing. For example, say something like "I noticed you were able to work on your own and figure out your own solutions for a full hour today. When you take the state reading test, you will need that kind of stamina, and now you have it."

◆ **Legitimize struggle and failure** as powerful learning tools. Competency, self-direction, and stamina do not develop quickly or automatically. We need to communicate through our words, feedback, actions, and our own stories that making mistakes and failing are all a normal part of the learning process. Build on students' strengths and knowledge. Be patient with their questions. Give students multiple opportunities to improve the quality of their work.

Finally, and important enough to be restated, we develop stamina for the things we ultimately enjoy and become expert at. Concentrating on tasks we love and that give us satisfaction make developing stamina and the will to learn certain. It's human nature that we are willing to make great efforts for the intrinsic rewards that come from seeking to learn more and develop greater expertise. It's what dedicated teachers do every day.

Endnote

Becoming a self-determining learner is not easy, but it's our best hope for developing students and teachers who challenge the status quo and are not afraid to ask and then to seek solutions to questions such as "Why does it have to be this way?" and "What can I do to ensure more equity for others?" When Larry Page and Sergey Brin, the cofounders of Google, were asked "whether having parents who were professors was key to their success, they both cited going to Montessori schools as a more important factor. 'I think it was part of that training of not following rules and orders, and being self-motivated, questioning what's going on in the world and doing things a little bit differently,'" Page contended.[18]

To be a self-determining learner takes the courage to venture beyond expected parameters. Courage, at least for me, is not about having the confidence to try something new but having the will and mental mind-set to be a positive outlier—to question the obvious, to see things differently, to follow our passions, to learn from failure, to become a change agent—all with the goal of learning more and being more, for ourselves and for others.

In the end, it is not technology but self-determining learners, innovative thinkers, and concerned citizens who will play the biggest role in resolving equity issues. Horace Mann, a nineteenth-century educational reformer who championed universal public education, once famously said, "Be ashamed to die until you've scored some victory for humanity." Do your part. Leave the world a little better off. Even having an impact on one child, by equalizing and providing excellent educational opportunities, is a victory.

Advocating for Students

A ccess to a good school can transform a child's life. "Talent is universal, but opportunity is not."[1] Every time we increase a child's access to a good education, we reduce inequity. Time and time again I've seen students whom teachers had given up on blossom once they were invited into the learning community as an equal member. That is, they were treated as capable, provided with excellent resources—including teachers—and given the explicit instruction, time, choice, respect, and deliberate practice needed to learn and succeed. We teachers can do that—ensure equal opportunity to learn, one student at a time. It's not easy, but it's possible.

Such change requires teaching with a sense of urgency and acquiring the knowledge, courage, and will to do better. It requires that each one of us advocate for our students by ensuring that decisions around implementing any programs, curriculum documents, standards, resources, technology, and professional development put students' learning—not test scores—first. Test scores will improve as a by-product of excellent and equitable instruction that is combined with formative assessment.

Disastrously for many of our children, as a society we lack the collective will, moral fiber, and commitment to educate everyone and see everyone's life as equally worthy of fulfillment. It's easier to look the other way, do what we can to advantage our own children, opt out of public schools, and hope that others will take some action. We are those "others"! Our society punishes kids who don't succeed in school—with suspension, prison, unemployment, poverty, and more—so equal opportunity to learn must become a birthright for every student.

Let me say straightaway here that I am a staunch and unapologetic supporter and defender of public schools. I believe that is where the best hope lies for students and for democracy. I am the product of integrated public schools, as are my children and grandchildren. I believe with all my heart that public schools are the lifeblood of any democracy and that they are a necessity for us to survive and thrive as a nation of caring, knowledgeable people. "If there is hope for a renewal of our belief in public institutions and a common good, it may reside in the public schools."[2]

I also believe as citizens we must each do all we can to make public schools viable and equitable for all students. For the past forty-five years, I have chosen to work almost exclusively in high-poverty schools. I work with students, teachers, principals, coaches, and leaders at all levels and consider this work a great privilege and joy. Collaborating with talented and committed colleagues, we have seen what can happen when we don't just talk about doing better for all kids but when we actually band together as a community and attempt to do so.

Still I understand the lure of charter schools, schools that are privately run but publicly funded. Some excellent charter schools have helped many students, the lucky ones who were accepted and prospered and went on to college or a successful career. For those students, charter schools have changed the potential of their lives. But for too many others, the promise of charters has not materialized. African American students account for the major enrollment in charter schools in the United States, which has too often meant "increased segregation and high rates of suspensions and expulsions for black students" as well as fiscal mismanagement and poor oversight.[3] Charter school practices have not, in general, improved learning outcomes for students. "Charters nationwide do not have significantly better test scores than public schools with similar populations."[4]

So if we truly believe in equity for all, our collective energy must go to better serving students in public schools, which includes recognizing and dealing with the realities of charter schools—especially important as political forces and special interests continue to push hard for more charter schools. Be informed!

The charter school process is often neither equitable nor transparent. Charters receive public money but are not regulated by the policies of traditional public schools. Choice is neither guaranteed nor a democratic process. Disgruntled and disillusioned parents, often lured by the for-profit companies that operate many charters, are persuaded by cash bonuses, laptops, and verbal assurances. Even where families have choice in where to send their children to school, the application process can be so overwhelming and, in some cases, unjust as to make real choice unavailable. Another issue working against equitable choice is that few charters enroll and retain equal numbers of special-needs students, compared to traditional public schools. "People had so much confidence in choice and choice alone to close the achievement gap. Instead we're replicating failure."[5]

And let's be honest. The accompanying voucher movement (subsidies given to parents for tuition at a school of their choice) was originally an outcome of desegregation efforts so that white students could attend white-only private schools.[6] Currently, even though vouchers have expanded school choice to include more students, too many vouchers wind up sending low-income students to private-sector schools that are poorly regulated and academically inferior. Pointedly, three comprehensive research studies confirm that voucher programs harm many students by placing them in low-quality private schools where, compared to their public school peers, their reading and writing achievement and test scores "decline drastically."[7] The false promise that vouchers often offer undermines the stability of public schools, which are attended by 90 percent of US students. In fact, the current federal push for vouchers would do irreparable harm to most school districts.[8] We must do whatever we can as educators, taxpayers, and responsible citizens to ensure our public schools are well funded, financially and structurally stable, and staffed with expert teachers for all students.

Even where attending a charter school leads to higher test scores and college attendance, there is no research yet that shows those gains are accompanied by higher earnings, as compared to earnings of students from public schools. That may be because an extreme focus on reading and math deprives students of exposure to such disciplines as art and history. That is, students' test scores are better, but their deep thinking and world knowledge might be lacking, and these are important competencies for doing well in the workplace.[9] Put another way, the combination of wide and deep experience is crucial to the creative, original thinking our new economy requires.

The bottom line is that all students deserve a first-rate education in an intellectual culture that ensures literacy as the foundation and route to personal achievement and fulfillment. Our public schools remain one of the truly democratic institutions of our society, and, as such, they and we have the moral obligation to ensure all children have learning opportunities that fully engage their hearts and minds, capitalize on their talents, and open up real possibilities for a promising and secure future.

At the same time, I wouldn't be honest if I didn't acknowledge reality. Some public schools, especially in low-socioeconomic areas, are so substandard that I would have a hard time enrolling my own child there. So I do understand why parents who can afford to or who qualify for financial aid might choose a private school. That said, I would urge such parents to continue to support their local public schools—through volunteering; working to equalize resources, including advocating for first-rate teachers; and expressing outrage that we so often leave poor and minority students behind. It's not the democratic way. In the aftermath of September 11, 2001, in the many hundreds of oral histories and interviews that came later, there was not one story of anyone saying they were abandoned or attacked. In times of disaster and deepest trouble, we seem hardwired for kindness and generosity and for behaving with grace and dignity.[10]

What's good for some must be available for all. An excellent education cannot be a privilege for the fortunate; it must be an inviolable right for all. Keep in mind that worldwide, the highest-performing countries invest heavily in their public school systems.[11] Public schools, staffed by expert teachers, are our best hope for sustaining a democracy of engaged, fully educated citizens who possess the thinking and creative skills to deal with an uncertain future.

Teaching is and has always been personal, political, and professional. It is an altruistic profession, and it requires our best selves in action. Advocacy for students means trying to ensure we collectively do the right things for the right reasons for every student. Such advocacy means that we employ mind-sets, behaviors, strategies, and actions that make it more likely that more students have equitable opportunities to learn. It means we do everything we can to prepare all students for success, not just in school but for their future lives. This chapter deals with some actions we can undertake to increase equitable opportunities for students in our classrooms, schools, or districts and provinces.

Equalize Resources

We have in our schools not just an economic gap but also an opportunity gap. Students from low-income families and, in particular, students of color receive fewer resources and experience fewer opportunities for intellectual learning, including immersion in the arts. It is well known that these same students are more likely to have a less-qualified teacher than students from high-income families. It is also more likely that students in high-poverty neighborhoods attend a school that would be considered unacceptable in terms of building quality and infrastructure compared to a school in a middle-class or affluent area. Literally, the poor get poorer—poorer teachers, poorer resources, lower-level skills, and fewer opportunities to interact and learn at high levels. Compared to other districts nationally, high-poverty districts in the United States receive $1,200 less per student from state and local sources, and those sources make up 90 percent of a school's revenue.[12] Yet we continue to expect high-poverty schools to do more with less, and we compare their achievement to that of schools in wealthy areas.

A troubling recent research finding from a massive database found that school districts with the most resources available to serve all students often have the worst inequities.[13] One might think that rich districts would share their resources in an attempt to lessen the achievement divide. But that is rarely the case. There is a "hyper-achievement orientation" in places where competition is high, and "resources matter even more than they do in places where you don't have that sort of achievement anxiety."[14]

Sadly, it has too often been the policy makers, politicians, and career reformers—often from outside a district—that wind up wielding the power in how money gets spent, especially in large urban districts. Their business-style management, test-based accountability, and a belief that money can fix all problems—often accompanied by hubris and a disregard for buy-in and input from parents and teachers—doom any chances for worthwhile and sustainable change. A blatant and tragic example is how the $100 million, well-intentioned gift by Facebook's Mark Zuckerberg to improve Newark, New Jersey's long-failing public schools was completely squandered. Five years later, there was little to show for good intentions.[15] A major part of the systemic failure was the failure to include and respect the voices and knowledge of teachers, families, and the local community in seeking, finding, and carrying out solutions. *Money matters, but how it's spent matters more.*

It's been well documented that we teachers are not primarily motivated by money; most of us are motivated by a moral commitment to do right by our students. We work hard because we care so much. Students of teachers who do not receive merit pay achieve as well as students whose teachers do receive the extra pay.[16] That said, how our school and district budgets are allocated speaks volumes about what we value and how and what we prioritize. We need to work together to ensure budgets in public schools are allocated equitably and efficiently to best serve all students. Otherwise we will continue to lose families and teachers to alternative schools.

One dedicated public school teacher's decision to move to a charter, which she hoped would be a temporary move, was based on a belief "not that charters were inherently better, but rather that they were structured to more easily deliver money to classrooms than was the district."[17] Her district's failure to get more money into classrooms and schools that need it most left her unable to provide the resources that her students needed, such as an in-class learning specialist working with small groups of children and access to a school social worker.

Resources and practices we employ must respect and dignify all the children and families we serve. Let's be honest here. The most important and equitable resource we can provide is an excellent teacher in every classroom. Until we put our strongest teachers in our neediest schools—and pay them more for undertaking that challenge—we will continue to be disappointed in achievement results. Yet the reality is that although politicians and voters say they want better schools and better-paid teachers, increasing school funding remains unpopular—despite the crucial fact that poor children are more likely to graduate from high school and have higher earnings if they attend schools where funding has increased by just 10 percent per student from kindergarten through grade twelve.[18] One hopeful sign is the Every Student Succeeds Act of 2015 (ESSA), which gives states and districts flexibility to use federal money they receive to equalize funding, support, and opportunity for poor and low-income students. Let's do our best to ensure those funds equitably make their way into our schools. More than that, we must be vigilant that such funds and resources are responsibly used to improve learning outcomes for underserved and marginalized students.

 ## Take Action

◆ **Reduce the book gap.** It's well known that kids from affluent homes may have up to hundreds of books in their home, while the poorest children may have only a few. What is less well known is that students from low-income families learn as much each year as middle-class students but suffer a summer reading setback because of lack of access to books. Not reading over the summer produces a huge learning gap over time for poor kids; by third grade they are a year behind, and by ninth grade they are three or more years behind. However, when these students are able to self-select free books to read over summer, setback is greatly reduced.[19]

Advocate to make it possible for all students to buy at least several new books to own—for example, at school book fairs and for summer reading. Also, take advantage of the Digital Public Library of America, which has launched Open eBooks, an app providing free school and home access to e-books for students from Title 1 schools and students served by teachers of special education. (See more ideas on page 174.)

◆ **Equalize library resources.** Do everything you can to ensure every school has a librarian (often called a library media specialist), which should be a guaranteed right in every school. Librarians are indispensable for finding culturally relevant titles, collaborating with us on curriculum and research, managing information, providing tech support, and assisting students to access, use, and evaluate resources—print and online—across the curriculum.

Work to ensure all classrooms have well-stocked libraries. Schools in poor neighborhoods do not receive the same funding as their richer counterparts. When budgets are underfunded and collections are out of date in high-income neighborhood schools, parent-teacher groups in those schools will work to make up the shortfall; PTAs in low-income neighborhoods are unable to do the same.[20]

Work with school librarians to lobby district officials and school boards to allocate sufficient and equal funding and services to all school libraries for books, programs, and other necessary items. Do what you can to decrease public library disparities in poorer neighborhoods. Advocate for extending school library hours—before school starts and at the end of the school day—to increase access and to provide Internet access for those who don't have it at home.

◆ **Ensure all students have required school supplies.** Students who qualify for free-or-reduced lunch, homeless students, or new immigrant and refugee families often don't have the money and time to buy needed supplies, which can cost up to several hundred dollars if you add in backpacks. See what you can do through local parent-teacher groups, donations, and fundraisers to guarantee that all students in your school and district have basic supplies when school starts and when new supplies are needed. My local newspaper, the *Seattle Times*, sponsors an annual fundraising drive that ensures thousands of students go back to school with new backpacks and needed supplies. Lobby your local newspaper to do the same in your community.

As well, look into bulk ordering of supplies to get the best prices. Consider having a steady and free supply of pencils on hand, available to all. Also, where budgets are tight for classroom supplies, check out crowdfunding sources as a way to raise money from a large number of people via the Internet. DonorsChoose.org is one such reputable site.

◆ **Seek to equalize funding in your district.** Although property taxes still account for most school funding, we can and must do better with securing and using funds more equitably. Lobby local and state representatives to ensure they are working to adequately fund and staff all schools.

- *Get on a budget committee.* Check how much state funding per pupil has dropped on average, nationally, even as enrollment expands and costs continue to rise. Find out how monies are being allocated in your school and district. Question big-money purchases, such as core reading programs and technology, which have generally not been proven to increase achievement. Make sure classroom libraries are well funded in every school *before* considering program and technology purchases. Urge school leaders to prioritize budgeting for first-rate books across the curriculum.
- *Advocate for more funding for professional learning.* Keeping in mind that the most effective professional learning is schoolwide and embedded into the culture, advocate for release time for teachers to collaborate with and coach one another and for occasional hiring of substitutes who rove to make that possible.
- *Advocate for more funding for libraries.* Start a letter-writing and social media campaign to support and equalize library funding. Show up at budget hearings and school board meetings. Perhaps wear T-shirts that say something like "Invest in our libraries."
- *Share the wealth.* If you teach in a middle-class or affluent school that raises money to avoid painful cuts or has a private foundation to ensure that music and art and other niceties are provided to students, reduce the inequity. Work to ensure that some percentage of money raised in your school goes to a district fund dedicated to providing more resources in schools unable to secure such funds from their community.

Finally, seek out community volunteers to enrich learning in your school—artists, writers, mathematicians, historians, businesspeople, and people with unique talents. When my son, Peter, wanted to give something back to his community—specifically, the local public school his daughters were attending—he volunteered to teach a math enrichment class. For one hour each week, before his work and the normal school day started, he taught math to any fourth grader who wished to participate. It was a win-win; he loved the experience, and all students, regardless of their math ability, had an opportunity to explore math in novel and challenging ways.

Use Technology Judiciously

"People, not technology, is the answer to resolving issues of equity in education."[21] We cannot outsource expert instruction to software companies or devices. I believe that the main purpose of technology use must be to promote and enhance deep thinking, problem solving, excellence, and equity in education. Additionally, I believe this: "Almost every digital tool, whether designed for it or not, was commandeered by humans for a social purpose: to create communities, facilitate communication, collaborate on projects, and enable social networking."[22] If we accept the reasoning of the previous statements, then we as knowledgeable and responsible educators—face-to-face with our students—are still the best tech tools we have.

As far as I can tell from a lot of reading, researching, teaching, and reflecting, the greatest benefit of technology hardware and software is increased access to online learning and information in general. However, that greater access, which has created the potential for more learning equity, has not, at least so far, yielded greater learning achievement.

A large international study by a highly respected organization conducted extensive field studies and analyzed how computer access in schools affects student learning. "Students who use computers very frequently at school do a lot worse in most learning outcomes, even after controlling for social background and student demographics."[23] This is critically important research as it relates to equity: ". . . perhaps the most disappointing finding in the report is that technology is of little help in bridging the skills divide between the advantaged and disadvantaged students."[24] These results need to give us pause because technology as the center of instruction and learning is often the go-to solution in schools, especially where students are underperforming and failing.

I believe this lackluster outcome from technology use is largely because much of the technology centers on drilling on isolated skills rather than on activities that deepen thinking. As a school improvement coach and adjunct university faculty adviser wrote me,

> Schools over-rely on computer driven reading/language arts programs to help improve achievement scores of low-performing students, which yield minimal results. What we found most effective for significant student gains was a 1:1 tutoring program modeled on Reading Recovery. We had sophomores and juniors, highly trained in reading and writing instruction, come into schools and work with one student for 30 minutes, 2–3 times a week for at least several weeks.[25]

Even in tech-savvy schools where technology use has been implemented thoughtfully, results are often uneven. For example, a study found that college students who were permitted to use laptops for final exams scored worse, and the smartest students were the ones most affected.[26] Matt Renwick, an elementary school principal and longtime technology champion, notes uneven results as well:

> *Even when schools attempt to integrate technology within instruction it too rarely moves the needle when it comes to the instructional impact on student learning. I know, because we assessed ourselves as a school last year on digital citizenship and the 4Cs. We were emerging in these areas, across the board. This is after multiple years of embedding digital tools into our teaching and learning with thoughtfulness and intention.[27]*

How any new technologies—or, for that matter, how any standards, programs, or instructional frameworks—are implemented ultimately determines the degree of learning success or failure. It's in the application stage where we often fall short as a profession. Training and implementation support are often insufficient. We need to become expert at teaching and applying exemplary instructional and assessment practices so we can effectively guide our students' use of technology as a tool that helps them learn and achieve more. At the same time, we need to ensure technology use actually enhances meaningful learning, as discussed on pages 93–98.

Be very cautious. Technology is big business, with big marketing and big sales. Technology is seductive; we can be easily lured into wanting the next "shiny new thing." Consider some sobering facts. The amount of money spent annually by US schools (nursery through high school) for computer devices, educational software, and digital content is more than $13 billion.[28] That enormous expenditure is likely to keep on growing as tech giants such as Apple, Google, Microsoft, and Amazon continue to produce and push their wares and educators flock to that marketplace. Those educators are many. The 2016 annual conference by ISTE, the International Society for Technology in Education, attracted about 16,000 educators.

Imagine if just a fraction of the billions of dollars going to technology went to ensuring every school had a librarian and a first-rate collection of books and resources in every classroom and school library. Imagine if every school had a functioning and beautiful building infrastructure. Imagine, most of all, if every school, regardless of its zip code, had an expert teacher in every classroom. Technology, at its best, is a tool to enhance learning intentions, ignite curiosity, and help students learn more. Make a point of checking that technology use is a supporting act and not the main event.

We're still in the infancy stages of seamlessly integrating technology in and out of school in a manner that improves teaching, learning, and living. Tread carefully.

In terms of equity, ensure that technology use will:

- Make it possible for all students to participate.
- Enhance the desired learning goals and outcomes.
- Facilitate and equalize access to information.
- Encourage transfer of learning to other contexts and subject areas.
- Support and increase competency and confidence for all learners.

Take Action

◆ **Be cautious with technology purchases.** Although there is a massive amount of hardware and digital educational materials to choose from—textbooks, apps, lessons, online courses, test prep, websites, and growing online education services of all kinds, to name just some—whether or not those materials work to improve and enhance student learning is often questionable. The Every Student Succeeds Act (ESSA) opens up new possibilities for districts to purchase more technology. It's our job to carefully examine the products and research behind any technology and to professionally determine what fits with our beliefs, practices, goals, and vision. (See Appendix D for recommended tech tools and apps.)

◆ **Invest first in teachers.** Invest most in professional learning for expert literacy teaching and leading. The right mix of teacher expertise and educational technology can positively affect student learning. For technology to facilitate and augment learning, an expert teacher needs to explicitly demonstrate reading, writing, and thinking strategies with the specific tool. Also, for technology use in the classroom to be successful, teachers need lots of support, both technical and professional. For example, technology breaks down; ensure you have a system in place that gives teachers the assistance they will need.

◆ **Value a print-rich classroom.** Although digital and online learning and paperless classrooms are increasing, there is scant evidence that student achievement has increased. Continue to prioritize books as well as paper and pen—old technologies that work beautifully in the hands of an expert teacher—and incorporate blogs, videos, podcasts, and multimedia into a print classroom. Also important, most students prefer paper textbooks to online ones; ensure e-textbooks are not the only option.[29]

◆ **Incorporate social media.** Social media matters to kids because they recognize the power and influence of their personal voice. However, income affects who uses social media and how it's used. In school we can help equalize the communication impacts of social media by teaching kids to respectfully text, tweet, and post on blogs in and out of school, and legitimize these forms as real writing. For example, one research study found that when students received several informative texts from their teacher per week and had the option to reply with a question or comment, they demonstrated greater learning gains than the control group who received no teacher texts.[30]

◆ **Equalize access.** The policy known as "BYOD" (bring your own device, such as a smartphone or tablet) is popular in many schools as a way for students to use personal mobile devices to respond to questions, take notes, complete assignments, and more. Although there may be great potential here for student engagement and equalizing access, if you go this route be sure to accommodate all learners; many low-income kids don't own smartphones. Also, there's scant research that indicates smartphones enhance learning.[31] The main issue seems to be that students, accustomed to using their phones for entertainment, often have a difficult time staying focused on the learning task. Here, as for most successful learning outcomes, teacher expertise is key.

For students who don't have their own devices, encourage sharing with peers, make school computers available (and ensure students know how to optimally use them to find and respond to information), and make paper an option for response. Because Internet usage and connectedness at home vary greatly—especially in poor and rural areas—let students and families know about free broadband access at libraries and community centers, on school buses, and more.

◆ **Teach digital citizenship,** including, but not limited to, digital etiquette, how to responsibly post messages online, and why and how plagiarism is a legal offense. Also, regulate time spent on digital devices. We disadvantage young children with too much screen time, which can limit their vocabulary development and take away precious time for creating and imagining.

◆ **Evaluate the impact of technology.** As responsible educators, we have to know if what we are doing is working and to gauge effectiveness—whether it's with technology, learning centers, or guided-reading groups. Assessment of learning must accompany any technology use, and that assessment must be more than clicking on an app to obtain a level, a number, or a test score.

Incorporate Music and the Arts

It's well known that music and the visual and performing arts have the potential to improve academic performance and student engagement, which is especially critical for students in our underperforming schools. By "the arts" we mean not just music and art but also drama, theater, dance, poetry, and more, including pop culture. Yet, sadly, the arts are routinely cut when budgets get slashed. Boston public schools are a rare but shining example of a system that's working to provide weekly arts education to all students from kindergarten through eighth grade.[32] Hopefully, with the passage of the Every Student Succeeds Act, which views music and the arts as core subjects, all students—regardless of their socioeconomic status—stand to benefit from an expanded education.

In many cases, it will be up to us to ensure a balanced curriculum. The national obsession in the United States with testing, beginning in kindergarten, has led to less time for nonacademic subjects. As kindergarten students now spend more of their time in school on literacy and math instruction, music and the arts receive much less attention.[33] For students who learn differently or who have had limited success with traditional school approaches, emphasizing the arts can positively and permanently affect their lives.

I still fondly remember Paul, one of the most disabled and talented students with whom I'd ever worked. As a nonreader in fourth grade, he had extraordinary artistic abilities, which we used as a way into his becoming a reader. Turning his deep knowledge about cars into a book—beginning with his remarkable and detailed drawings and then adding his own language through dictation to each illustrated page—we used his own artwork to jump-start his phonics learning and his reading abilities, and, as well, to boost his standing among his peers.

And, again, in a school in California where almost all the students qualified for free and reduced-cost meals, and most of whom were also English language learners, students had just attended their first classical music concert, which was to be the district's last because of budget constraints. The students were so affected by the "new music" they heard that we successfully lobbied the school board, through letters and personal communications, to continue this annual program for future classes. The students learned not only the power of persuasive and argumentative writing but also that they could have agency in their own lives.

On a personal level, the superb music education both my granddaughters continue to receive in the public schools they attend—from elementary through high school—has greatly enriched their lives. Our middle school granddaughter studies violin and plays in the strings orchestra; our high school granddaughter studies jazz piano and plays in the instrumental jazz band. What I love about attending their school performances is not just relishing their accomplishments but also delighting in seeing and hearing diverse students playing beautifully and joyfully together.

All students benefit from exposure to and experience with the arts. In fact, for some of our students, it's through the arts that we reach them and they reach us—all by honoring and tapping into their unique interests and talents. One fascinating point: Nobel Prize–winning scientists, as well as highly successful entrepreneurs and inventors, are "dramatically more likely" to be involved in the arts—for example, playing an instrument, painting, woodworking, writing poetry, or amateur acting—than their less-accomplished peers.[34]

We must take the long view, which includes educating for quality of life, and that includes equitable earning power. College and career readiness and well-rounded citizens who can think critically and innovatively depend on far more than reading and math performance. As well, we must ensure that the current promotion of STEM—science, technology, engineering, and math—does not crowd out not just the arts but also the humanities, such as literature, philosophy, and history. One hopeful sign is the STEAM movement—with A standing for "art." STEAM embraces artistic thinking, real-world project learning, design thinking, digital art, and other artistic pursuits as a way to maximize creativity, engagement, and productivity in STEM areas and beyond.[35]

 ## Take Action

- Become creatively subversive as needed. For example, in kindergarten do not accept the notion that we don't have time for dramatic play, music, and the arts. Young children still need painting easels, sand tables, blocks, and spaces to create and imagine. Completing mindless worksheets is disrespectful, a time waster, and a dangerous trend. Put a large "WRITING CENTER" sign over a classroom area devoted to integrating literacy through social and dramatic play, songs, and real-world reading and writing. Do not ask permission; just do it. Study and interact with engaging informational topics, such as taking pets to a veterinary clinic, shopping for groceries, and creating a museum (of dolls, trucks, and so on). You can teach young children literacy skills through authentic, engaging content.

Kindergartners setting up a veterinary clinic: authentically connecting literacy skills and purposeful play through reading, writing, discussing, negotiating, and constructing. Not seen in photo: designated areas with handwritten labels for waiting room, reception desk, examination table, and forms for making an appointment, giving information about the pet's health, and writing prescriptions for treatment.

- **Provide multiple ways for students to demonstrate their thinking and knowledge.** Encourage expressive forms, such as creating an original documentary, video, artwork, song, rap, dance, or prose poem to demonstrate content area learning.

- **Include popular culture.** Many students become more engaged in reading, writing, history, and critical thinking when they connect literacy to popular culture. "There's something about using hip-hop specifically because of the role that it plays in the world right now that leads to more developed understanding." Students have written longer, better-developed pieces and provided specific evidence for things they questioned and noticed.[36] Use the soundtrack and widespread love of *Hamilton*, the award-winning, mesmerizing hip-hop and rap musical by Lin-Manuel Miranda, to engage students in history and encourage them to try out similar music and language with other historical events. As well, consider using lyrics of songs by pop-culture singers, such as Adele, to teach close reading and language craft.

◆ **Act out stories.** Re-creating a story, either fiction or historical, can be done through pantomime, dance, and music. Have students collaborate to present their interpretation of a text or partial text and play the role of different characters. Share with a peer audience.

◆ **Integrate the visual and performing arts into all we do.** Explicitly teach and expose students to the work of artists, musicians, painters, performers, actors, dancers, and filmmakers, and connect the influence of the arts to content area studies and fully lived lives. For example, as noted earlier on page 176, elementary music teacher Randal Bychuk uses Modest Mussorgsky's *Pictures at an Exhibition* to incorporate music, art, and literacy. "The suite of music treats listeners to an orchestral experience of walking through an art gallery and viewing a series of 10 paintings—all very different."[37]

◆ **Invite local artists, musicians, and performing artists into schools.** Many artists are eager to give back to their communities and will do so without charge or for a minimal fee. Have students write persuasive letters of invitation for classroom visits, an evening program for families, daylong visits, or residency programs.

◆ **Include excellent texts about artists, musicians, dancers, and performers** in literature discussions, read-alouds, guided-reading groups, content areas, and classroom libraries. Some outstanding favorites that celebrate the power of the arts are *My Name Is Georgia: A Portrait* by Jeanette Winter (a picture book on painter Georgia O'Keeffe, for primary grades), *Sandy's Circus: A Story About Alexander Calder* by Tanya Lee Stone (a picture book for grades one through four on Calder's wire sculptures), *The Art of Miss Chew* by Patricia Polacco (a memoir and picture book for elementary grades), *To Dance: A Ballerina's Graphic Novel* by Siena Cherson Siegel (a graphic novel for upper-elementary through high school), and *This Land Was Made for You and Me: The Life and Songs of Woody Guthrie* by Elizabeth Partridge (biography for grades six and up).

◆ **Encourage unique descriptive arts** for storytelling, displaying content knowledge, and completing major projects; this may include offering wide options incorporating the visual, musical, and performance arts, such as original use of media, graphics, illustrations, photos, paintings, videos, audio tools, songs, dance, film, and more—which make it more likely all students can successfully participate and present information in a way that respects their talents, learning styles, and cultural diversity.

♦ **Make art and artists central to content study.** Use visuals and noteworthy art and artists for art appreciation and the study of history and culture, and as a way to reach all learners. Inspire students to learn about the life and work of internationally known artists who make a difference in our world. Two examples are Theaster Gates and Kal Barteski. Gates turned a shuttered bank in an underinvested part of Chicago's South Side neighborhood into a thriving, nonprofit center for the arts.[38] Through her magnificent paintings and ongoing advocacy, Kal Barteski of Churchill, Manitoba, is a strong voice for polar bears, who are severely affected by climate change. Also, when showing documentaries, highlight how these works and other multimedia presentations depend on photos, art, and visuals to both engage the audience and convey a message. Encourage original art to accompany student writing and presentations.

Advocate for Equitable Practices

Equality of educational opportunity is a social justice issue. It's up to us to ensure equitable practices in instruction, assessment, resources, and learning outcomes for all students. Too many students are receiving a substandard education, and most often these are students of color who are from low-income families. A distraught literacy coach wrote to me:

> *This issue is heavy on my heart. It's always hard when you can attach a name and face to the examples of injustice. I met a third grader last week who has been stuck on the same guided reading level since first grade, where she was retained. She receives no interventions even though she is in Tier 3. Her teacher came to me for help. She has been working with her on nonsense word fluency all year and hasn't seen any progress. This is a poor black child, who is sweet, quiet, and co-operative.*[39]

Implementing equitable practices is one area where we can and must do better! Even when we know we need to change practices that are not working, we commonly face an implementation challenge. That is, we often lack the individual and collective expertise—and sometimes the will—to fully understand the problem and marshal the know-how to take productive actions that will work to improve student learning. A common barrier is our high-pressure, hurry-up culture; we need results quickly even though we know deep learning takes time. Scholar and researcher Anthony

Byrk uses the term "solutionitis" for this phenomenon of "implementing fast and learning slow"; that is, we "see complex matters through a narrow lens," which "often leads decision makers into unproductive strategies."[40]

A glaring yet typical example of "solutionitis" is how some states, districts, and schools assess reading, interpret those results—which may or may not be valid—and then take questionable actions to "improve instruction," as the literacy coach quoted earlier points out. Even when common sense dictates the absurdity of it all, we are often helpless to change our test-crazed culture, the driver of many mandated "solutions."

One egregious example of a disturbing, state-mandated test is the FAST (Formative Reading Assessment System for Teachers) test, a high-stakes speed-reading test with terrible consequences for kids who fail it. The FAST test was all that teachers were talking about at a recent state conference; it made me want to weep. If a third grader fails that one test, he is automatically retained unless he attends a seventy-five-hour summer school class on—you guessed it—more phonics and decoding. As one parent told me, "It's enough to make a parent of a struggling reader want to move out of the state." Not only that: students come to hate reading, and some students who successfully read with understanding but read slowly are seen as failures. Learned helplessness and fear accompany these tests, one result of what happens when states overvalue testing and devalue education and educators. I hope parents, teachers, and principals start collectively pushing their legislators harder to reverse these damaging policies.

The mCLASS test in reading is another test that's easy to score and measure, but is it accurate or useful? A skillful, conscientious teacher wrote to me:

> *Some good readers are scoring really low because they can't write "appropriate" answers to the written comprehension questions. Their mClass instructional reading levels are coming out well below grade level, but if you look carefully you'll see some of these same students reading fluently with possibly 100% accuracy on much harder books. Then these students are being held back to ridiculously low guided reading levels.[41]*

I don't have the answers here, but too many students are suffering ill consequences because of harmful tests. (See also DIBELS, pages 294 and 313.) We must do what we can to keep the needs and interests of our students at the center of our conversations and our actions. Remember to triangulate the data and rely mostly on daily, formative teacher assessment. Continue to advocate for sane and useful practices!

And keep in mind that it is not just our students from high-poverty schools who are shortchanged. I have learned that all schools are high-needs schools in different ways. I will never forget teaching in an affluent school where test scores were high (attributed mostly to families' large incomes and high educational levels) but teachers' expectations were generally low, as was their literacy knowledge for highly effective teaching. I was surprised by the mediocre quality of the work. Because test scores were high, teachers were complacent, which resulted in students being academically underserved. At the end of the week of our work together, several students thanked me for the "gifted teaching," which stunned me because the high-level teaching was the same as what I strive for in all schools.

When we speak of equitable practices, we must include all students. We must not consider students in great need as just students from poverty. All students, including our most gifted ones, deserve expert teaching and a challenging and relevant curriculum. Also, just as all students are different and learn differently, there is no standard profile of a student who is gifted.

Seeing firsthand what students, teachers, and leaders are capable of accomplishing is a game changer; the "yes-buts" disappear and the "we can do its" rise up. Mind-sets, skills sets, relationships, achievements, and students' and teachers' lives are often transformed by living with what's possible. I learned that lesson early. My experience working and succeeding in a school where almost all students were African American and living in poverty changed me for life. Once failing students demonstrated they could learn to read and write as well as their white peers—by our moving away from core reading programs to teaching reading with children's literature—nothing was the same. I tell that hopeful story and describe its impact on the classroom, school, and district in *Transitions: From Literature to Literacy*.[42]

Excellent teachers don't complain without offering possible solutions. Nobody likes spending their days with a whiner, a naysayer, or a grump. Be part of the solution, and put equitable learning opportunities for all at the forefront of instruction, assessment, decision making, and feedback. Continually question and ask, "What might we do differently so everyone succeeds?"

 ## Take Action

- ◆ **Become an informed skeptic.** Question everything that doesn't make sense and that's not working. Gather as much data and information as you can on the issue; then follow your knowledgeable experiences, current research, and common-sense instincts to take credible action. Remember there is no one best way to teach or assess, and when someone tells us that there is, we need to question that premise. For example, if our schools and districts are pressuring us to act in ways that are harmful to students or that disadvantage them, we have a moral responsibility to make our voices heard and to suggest and lobby for alternative, beneficial approaches.

- **Make sure any research being touted is credible and reliable** and equitably applies to our population of students. Check the updated website of the What Works Clearinghouse (http://ies.ed.gov/ncee/wwc/) for reviews of high-quality, evidence-based research studies on educational programs, products, practices, and policies. The overhauled clearinghouse includes more information to help schools and districts make decisions about interventions, which is very significant, because ESSA (Every Student Succeeds Act) permits districts wide leeway on strategies they can implement to improve student achievement as long as there is accompanying strong evidence. "Visitors can search for particular studies based on the characteristics of their schools, from grade span or locale to the demographics of the students."[43] Use social media, such as Twitter, to publicize your findings.

- **Set priorities.** Equity is also about the choices we make. As one teacher told me, "It's up to us to change our practices to meet the needs of our learners, not our learners changing to meet our needs." Regardless of what we say, it's what we do and how we spend our time that shows what we most value. If we truly value giving students sustained time to read and discuss books with their peers, then we find a way to make time for it. Even in situations that may include unfair, non-negotiable requirements, there are ways to work around them to ensure more time for meaningful practices. Use the research and practices offered in this book to assist you. Focus on reading, writing, speaking, listening, and viewing to inform, persuade, enhance, and broaden students' knowledge, language, perspectives, and possibilities. (See also Appendix I: Quick Summary of Effective Practices That Promote Equity.)

- **Make homework policies equitable.** Know the research on homework: it's not very beneficial before middle and high school.[44] The best homework extends and solidifies the learning, builds good study habits, and helps students feel more competent and confident. In the elementary grades, I favor daily reading of a self-selected book or having students share with their parents class-authored writing (shared writing) and their own writing—including occasional self-evaluations.

    Advocate for homework practices that are equitable. For example, some high school teachers kindly forgo assigning homework in their content area for as long as a week when they know students have a major test that week in another subject. Related to reading, let's not require a parent's signature on nightly reading, number of pages, and so on—a common practice in the elementary grades—which turns kids off to reading. Also, keep in mind that when parents are short on time or don't understand the work or what's expected of students, or the family lacks connection to the Internet, we simply can't expect them to help their kids with homework.

◆ **Highlight and advocate for social and economic justice.** Be courageous in your school and district. Tackle contentious but important issues such as racism, justice, poverty, and prejudice through reading and discussing editorials, first-person accounts, videos, essays, and interviews. Combine reading and writing with current world issues and the responsibilities of citizenship. Teaching about democracy and how we protect and sustain it is our moral obligation. The 2016 US presidential election has made that abundantly clear. Fear and discrimination cannot coexist with hope and joy in living and learning in a free society. We must prepare the next generation to do better than we have done.

Combine social justice issues with literature in language arts classes, an approach that is especially fitting for middle and high school students. Read and discuss such landmark papers as "Letter from a Birmingham Jail," written by Martin Luther King in 1963, and the remarkable essays and poems in *The Fire This Time: A New Generation Speaks About Race.*[45]

For lessons, advice, and perspectives on social justice issues, see the websites of Teaching Tolerance, Rethinking Schools, Constitutional Rights Foundation Chicago, Interactive Constitution–National Constitution Center, and ReadWriteThink, to name several. Also, come to some agreement on how teachers select and use children's books, which play a crucial role in how students see themselves and their possibilities—or not—in the world. Ensure the reading and discussion of diverse texts that reflect the full human condition, not just an oppression narrative.

Seek to raise awareness of the need for more social services and counselors to deal with homelessness, social-emotional issues, life traumas, hunger, abuse, neglect, severe behavior issues, and more. Attempt to partner with an adjacent community health and well-being center that might be able to provide such services as counseling, clothing, food, and medical and dental care. Reduce hunger in your community through involvement with a nonprofit local or national organization. One such national organization is End 68 Hours of Hunger (http://www.end68hoursofhunger.org/), which provides backpacks filled with food at the end of every school week for those kids who don't have enough to eat over the weekend.

- **Attend a school board meeting and bring students and student work with you.** My experience has been that most school boards rubber-stamp what the superintendent proposes, and that board members rarely if ever get into actual classrooms. There is nothing like a reality check with real students showing and talking knowledgeably and enthusiastically about their work and ideas to make an impact on the decision making by the board of education. Seeing and hearing the evidence in front of them, from competent teachers and students, puts data in perspective. Speak respectfully, ask for what you want to happen, make sure it's within reason, and then be relentless in your pursuit of it.

- **Develop alternative assessments to accurately reflect students' achievement.** When Mary Beth Nicklaus, a conscientious junior high school reading interventionist, found she could no longer tolerate the discrepancy between the weekly mandated "progress monitoring" (focused on speed reading and fluency to determine comprehension) and the growth she actually observed in her students, she took action. Although she did the required "progress monitoring," she also began her own action research using students' free-choice writing—and publishing those stories—as a way to assess reading comprehension. Additionally, she began writing encouraging notes to her students on their journal entries. For one student, just writing to him "How is it going, Daniel?" kicked off an obsession to write to her about how it was going. One paragraph turned into a page, and then three pages a few days later. As students' overall writing became richer, their interest in reading and their reading comprehension grew. One student was pleasantly surprised when his grade in his English class went from a D to a B– two weeks after he began writing in his intervention class. (See also pages 352–353.)

- **Seek a waiver from required testing** when tests are injurious and unhelpful for moving students forward in productive ways. Expert teaching is the best revenge. High test scores are a result of a thriving intellectual culture of excellence. When your school's test scores are high due to expert teaching, request that your principal lobby the superintendent for a waiver and for permission to primarily use formative assessments to evaluate students.

◆ **Create a sense of urgency at the school level to reduce bias and inequities.** Examine discipline policies, homework policies, and in-school policies. Do not wait for districts and communities to set policies and expected behaviors that welcome all and treat all students equitably. We must be those change agents!

◆ **Improve school-home connections.** Get to know students and their families. Send a letter home to families with information about ourselves as teachers, family members, and caring professionals. Include a photo, cultural information, and an invitation to visit the classroom on days and times designated for that purpose. Communicate expectations in a manner that is nonthreatening and can be clearly understood by all families. Think about using Language Line, a phone translation service, for families for whom English is not their first language. Consider home visits, which are time consuming but go a long way toward making families of our students, especially those living in poverty—often refugees, immigrants, indigenous peoples, and other marginalized groups—feel safe, respected, and valued.

   Treat all students and families with dignity. Work to end toxic policies that prioritize following rigid rules before seeking any type of mediation or implementing sensible discipline. For example, we sometimes criminalize the behavior of kids with no previous history of egregious behavior, which can scar them for life. If at all possible, abolish most out-of-school suspensions, an approach that punishes the students who most need our help.

◆ **Help parents navigate the system,** whether it's access to a reputable counselor, financial aid, homework policies, the college application process, or how to give input into their child's Individual Education Plan. Especially for parents of students of poverty, school can be an intimidating place. Parents, like their students and most of us, sometimes can use some hand-holding to figure out the school's policies and expectations.

◆ **Do something to equalize educational opportunities,** no matter how small it might seem. Then ask yourself, "Have I done enough?" "What else might be possible?" "Am I hearing and honoring everyone's voice?" "Are my instructional practices fair and beneficial for all students?" Do everything you can to put into action practices that promote more equity in the classroom and that can help raise and sustain achievement, engagement, and enjoyment. Ensure that your classroom and school cultures are inclusive and fair to all. Strive to use the limited time you have more effectively. *Narrow your focus to things that matter most and then prioritize relentlessly.*

STORY ❖ Advocating for Students

It is late fall in a first-grade classroom where I am teaching students to tell, write, and publish important stories from their lives. I am having a public writing conference with Marco. He has written some random letters on his paper, and his teachers believe that is the best he can do. We soon learn that he is capable of much more. With lots of back-and-forth conversation and encouragement, Marco tells a story about falling off the monkey bars on the playground and hurting his back. Sitting side by side and gently questioning (How did that happen? Were you badly hurt? Then what did you do?), I guide him to write on his own and apply what he knows about letters and sounds. His classroom teacher immediately publishes his story by hand. She writes it on four pages, with one line per page. Marcos illustrates it and, with great pride, reads his very first book to his peers.

I later learn that Marco has an Individual Education Plan for reading, math, and speech and is "pulled out" of the classroom three times daily to receive support from three different specialists. When his conscientious classroom teacher asks the specialists what she can do to help him learn, she is advised to "have him copy words from a book." Sadly, it is all too common for students like Marco, many of whom come from poverty and are English language learners, to have kind, well-intentioned teachers who expect little from them.

When the classroom teacher and I speak a couple of months later, she reports that test results indicate that Marco has made no demonstrable progress. Despite five months of daily support, nothing of significance has changed for this child. I advise her to advocate for him and take more responsibility for teaching him. Rather than having fidelity to the program or specialist, we teachers need to have fidelity to the child and to restore common sense to any support plan. We need to ask ourselves: What do my experiences with the child tell me? What would I want to happen if this were my child? What does this child most need, and what is the best way to provide it? How can all available support services in a school be reconfigured so that more children benefit?

I am constantly stunned and saddened at how often we teachers unwittingly put the child last. Exhausted by having to implement yet another new program and deal with testing demands and mandates, teachers become victims of learned helplessness. I am sympathetic to my fellow teachers, but I am heartbroken for the child. Who will advocate for our children if we do not?

Marco is fortunate. His caring classroom teacher has begun to take action by meeting with the principal and specialists to craft a plan to accelerate his learning. Her advocacy gives him a chance to become a learner; his learning gives him a chance to fulfill his personal and professional dreams.

Put Energy Where Results Are Most Likely

"My advice is to fight for the things that you care about, but do it in a way that will lead others to join you. . . . Don't ask them to go too far too fast, or you'll lose what you might have won."[46] I love this quote from Ruth Bader Ginsburg because to be successful at advocacy efforts we may need to step out of our comfort zones and respectfully employ common sense as an equity measure.

When I first started working as a literacy coach in schools, I was equitable about how I spent my time. I believed in trying to get every single teacher "on board" with our literacy vision. The same was true when I began doing teaching and coaching residencies. In fact, in my first residencies, the host teacher, in whose classroom I did demonstration teaching and coaching for observing teachers, was often a weak teacher. I initially had to spend so much time on management that I wasn't able to teach with a sense of urgency or demonstrate all I had planned. More important, the host teacher wasn't strong enough to move forward after the residency, on her own, let alone mentor others.

Here's what I've learned: we can exhaust ourselves trying to work with colleagues who, for various reasons, are very slow to change. My husband, Frank, helped me shift my thinking. He said, "You know how we both love to eat pistachio nuts. Well, when you come across that nut that's hard to crack, you can either break your fingernails trying to crack it or set it aside and move on. There's a whole bowl waiting for you." Now, I ask the principal and superintendent to place me with the strongest teachers and principals or with those demonstrating high potential. In that way, we can maximize our teaching, leading, and learning time for educators and students. I coach the host teachers and principals to take on what they've learned and practiced and to share that learning with willing colleagues through collaborating, co-teaching, and co-leading in their classrooms and schools.

Along the same lines, we must use caution and common sense about how much time we put into learning how to use and apply new district-mandated programs, standards, resources, and technology. All the time and energy it takes to learn new techniques and approaches must be worth our investment and the students'. The new resources must align with our beliefs, practices, and curriculum and not the other way around.

With our students, of course, it's our responsibility to reach and teach every one. To get great results, we need first-rate resources, expert teaching skills, additional support, and more. We also need to acknowledge that there is no quick fix in making the transition to more effective practices and that, in fact, it can take several years to see full benefits. Some needed support in accelerating literacy achievement can come from peers or students in upper grades, such as when an upper-grades class partners weekly with a primary-grades class in reading. "Each one, teach one" is a great philosophy as long as the person doing the teaching is knowledgeable and able to work well with others. We have only so much time and energy, and we must apportion it wisely and where it does the most good. Not only that, but also staying positive and optimistic about our daily work is essential to our overall effectiveness and well-being.

Do whatever you can to level the playing field for all students. Although there will always be things we have no control over, we can at least make our voices heard. Advocate for more equitable distribution of funding and resources (see pages 360-364); schedules that serve students first and make it possible for teachers to teach deeply, reducing the need for intervention and ensuring the intervention fits the child's need; and expert, research-based, schoolwide practices supported by shared beliefs.

 ## Take Action

- **Advocate for long-term leadership.** Strong, visionary principals need to remain in a school for at least five years. I know. That sounds unfathomable, but here's the inconvenient truth. In my forty-plus years working in schools, I have never seen achievement gains sustained when successful leadership is moved too soon, usually by the superintendent, to a needier school. The best intentions here—to equalize resources across a district to improve achievement—mostly go unrealized.

- **Become a teacher-leader.** In addition to daily teaching of students, consider becoming a teacher-leader and part of a school leadership team. Teacher-leaders take on the role of partnering with the principal to build trusting relationships and to plan and facilitate professional learning—all with the end goal of improving student learning. I have yet to see a school sustain achievement gains without a strong leadership team or some similar structure firmly in place.[47]

- **Integrate new teachers into the school culture.** Take great care as a staff to have a coordinated and realistic plan for supporting and mentoring new teachers and teachers new to the school. Typically, new teachers receive either too little or too much support. First-year teacher Morgan Manns confesses to receiving so much kind and well-intentioned support, she was overwhelmed. It took some time to move from feeling "I should do this . . ." to "I could do this. . ." and to realize that all those great suggestions didn't need to be implemented right away.[48] Do reassure new teachers that becoming an expert is a journey that takes time. Check in with them regularly to ensure they are feeling more successful than challenged.

  Ensure, also, that any mentor teacher is a good fit, not just socially-emotionally, but also academically. That is, the experience-knowledge gap between the new teacher and mentor must not be so great that the new teacher feels overpowered. Sometimes the best mentor might be a competent teacher just a bit further along on the teaching-learning journey than the new teacher.

- **Present a balanced-assessment process to families.** Be sure families see a comprehensive and varied assessment of their student's progress. Beware of value-added assessment data (a statistical method that uses standardized test scores to isolate the impact of a teacher on an individual's student growth), which can distort students' progress and demoralize educators.

- **Examine and adjust school schedules for equity.** A frustrated teacher wrote me:

  My schedule isn't working and with three other teachers coming into my room to provide special ed and ELL push-in, I feel like everyone needs to "get their minutes." This chunks my day into 20 min. segments where kids are going from teacher to teacher, leaving hardly any time for whole group instruction, individual conferences, or time to just read books.[49]

  If schedules—classroom, interventionist, coaching—do not have a positive impact on student learning, advocate for adjusting schedules so students' needs come first. Then take action. A savvy primary-grades teacher told me, "In spite of the district's rigid literacy-framework schedule, I basically just do what I need to for my kids." (See also pages 291 and 294.)

◆ **Abandon practices that aren't worth the time they take.** Put students first! If you are mandated to use a program that doesn't serve your students' needs and interests, skip the parts you can or adjust so meaning comes first, eliminating time-wasters such as focusing on isolated bits and pieces. Literacy educator and researcher Nell Duke suggests abandoning the following "less-than-optimal practices" that are not supported by research: looking up a list of vocabulary words and writing their definitions, giving prizes as reading incentives, weekly spelling tests, independent reading time unaccompanied by instruction and coaching, and punishing students by taking away recess.[50]

◆ **Use resources judiciously.** Rather than following a program or resource lock-step, employ that program as a framework. Choose and use what matches our curriculum, standards, beliefs, practices, and students' needs and interests. Don't be afraid to change the order of recommended activities or texts so they make more sense or to skip and set aside activities, worksheets, and texts that aren't relevant, appropriate, or worth our time.

◆ **Watch your workload.** Question projects, learning centers, test prep, or any activity that takes so much preparation and monitoring that we wind up exhausted. Complicated work does not mean a better result. Simplify. Keep in mind this well-known quote from Steve Jobs: "That's been one of my mantras—focus and simplicity. Simple can be harder than complex: You have to work hard to get your thinking clean to make it simple. But it's worth it in the end because once you get there, you can move mountains."

◆ **Apply common sense.** Common sense in teaching is not based on blind intuition or a gut feeling; it is knowing how to act in a sensible manner based on reason, deep knowledge, wide experience, data analysis, and knowing the students in front of us. Applying common sense requires competence, confidence, and a strong desire to do right by our students.

Endnote

Slow down; breathe; listen to students; respond to their strengths. Believe not only that *all* students can succeed but that we as teachers can succeed as well. We have to. Our students are counting on us. I leave the last words to a student.

In talking recently with a high school junior, she couldn't stop raving about a "really great" science teacher.

I didn't even realize how much I was learning. She was super-attentive to every student, constantly reassuring us we could do the work, even when we thought we couldn't. She was patient with everyone. She took time to explain things until we understood them. She gave us time to talk and work in small groups. In other classes, I felt like I was sometimes bothering the teacher when I asked a question, but not with Mrs. B. She never, not even once, made anyone feel stupid for asking a question, even if it was an obvious one. There was no sarcasm, no targeting or blaming a student for not knowing. She would patiently explain whatever was being asked. She made sure everyone understood. I never had a teacher who did that before. I remember right before finals she gave us a talk. She said: "I care way more about you as people than what your grades are." She helped me feel connected to her way beyond just being a student in her class trying to get a good grade. I didn't realize until months after school was over how much I'd learned from her and what a great teacher she was. But now I know, and I'll never forget her.[51]

That high school student speaks to the power and obligation we have to ensure that each of our students is treated with dignity, respect, and intelligence and that we advocate for engagement, excellence, and equity for all. This student also reminds us that we teachers matter in ways that we cannot always know. Our caring, our fairness, our expertise, and our kindness are not forgotten.

The Need for Civic Engagement

As I was completing the writing of this book, another US presidential election had just ended, which underscored—once again—the significance of civic rights and responsibilities. Democracy was on the ballot, as it always is. And yet. Less than half of the citizens eligible to vote exercised their constitutional right and duty, demonstrating, among other factors, complacency, distrust, disgust, or a lack of knowledge and sense of urgency about why their vote matters.

I still recall teaching some years ago in a fifth-grade classroom in a high-needs school where students were failing to successfully learn to read and write. While deciding on an authentic writing topic to engage their hearts and minds, we learned most of the students were living in fear of their undocumented parents being sent back to Mexico. Students, encouraged to tell their stories, ultimately wound up sharing their hopes and dreams for themselves and their families through *Dreams: Listen to Our Stories*.

It was the publication and distribution of their book to local, state, and national officials that gave students their first sense that their voices mattered and could give them agency in their own lives. (See sten.pub/literacyessentials for a complete copy of *Dreams* as well as recent quotes from the student authors as high school seniors.)

These students' school lives had been focused on basic literacy skills and raising test scores. There had been no space for nurturing their natural curiosity about the

Dreams: Listen to Our Stories

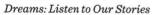

Dreams: Listen to Our Stories

world and their role in it as informed citizens. It was through the oral storytelling and discussion *before* students wrote that we learned they had scant knowledge of history and how democracy and our government work. *How can we expect students to care about and fight for the core issues that democracy stands for when many of them have no idea we have a constitution, three branches of government, voting rights, and laws to protect people?*

Once those fifth graders moved from learning isolated skills in a void to reading and writing with real-world audiences and purposes, they found their calling and their voices, and their lives changed forever. With the help of a community-created mentorship program and scholarship fund, many went on to become the first in their family to graduate high school and to attend college. Their hopes and dreams are reflected in how they see their future. Here are just a few of their many comments:

> Back in fifth grade, my main goal was to go back to my home in Mexico and be able to "wake up with a kiss or hug from my family in Mexico." As a senior in high school now, I see things from a whole different perspective. Being the first member of my family to graduate from high school and getting a degree in psychology are my main priorities. (Lourdes, 2014)

> My Dream has always been to attend college but my major has shifted. I wanted to study graphics and design to create video game art. Now, I want to use my bilingual skills for a career in international business. I push myself to be the best I can be to make my mother's life easier and to put a smile on her face. (German, 2014)

> Looking back at my life since fifth grade, countless things have changed but not my belief that people who are born in America and people who are not can both be just as good at making America a better place. I have broadened my Dreams of how I can help my community by becoming a translator for those who do not have the advantage of being bilingual. My family is undocumented, so I was not optimistic about my future. When I received a letter that approved me for Deferred Action, it opened up a new world of possibilities. I now have a bright future and opportunities to make my dreams come true. (Yessica, 2014)

As educators, we need to ensure we are instructing students beyond basic skills and passing tests, that we are honoring their stories, families, and cultures, and that we are celebrating their strengths. To help students envision promising futures, we must strive to build a sacred trust with them and their families that includes the guarantee that we are teaching, practicing, and applying the rights, responsibilities, and duties of citizens each and every day. Renowned educator and scholar Deborah Meier reminds us that the dispositions of *informed skepticism*—"a willing suspension of prior belief"—and *informed empathy* are necessary for an open society and urges us to put developing those dispositions at the heart of a democratic education, starting in kindergarten and going all the way through school.[1]

To foster those qualities in our students, we must begin by treating all people with dignity, fairness, and respect. We must begin by creating civic-minded classrooms and schools where free and open dialogue on important topics and study—and historical and scientific events and their consequences—are based on in-depth, first-rate resources, varying viewpoints, honest debate, and established norms for civil discourse. We must also begin with us as knowledgeable citizens modeling how each of us is obligated to participate in our messy and fragile democracy in order to keep it invigorated and workable for all. That is, we stay informed, vote, make our voices heard, advocate for justice and inclusivity, and speak up for the vulnerable when they cannot.

Getting our students ready to be citizens—preparing each of them to become engaged, committed, and intelligent participants in a democracy—may be our most crucial responsibility of all. It's no exaggeration to say that the survival of any republic depends on it. "An ignorant people can never remain a free people."[2] It's not enough to hope for citizen-ready students. Hope is only a beginning. It must be accompanied by deliberate and thoughtful action. "Not everything that is faced can be changed, but nothing can be changed until it is faced," said author and activist James Baldwin. Gather up your courage. Seek to become the best teacher, leader, and citizen you can be. Savor the small victories. Persevere despite the setbacks. You are not alone. So many of us are walking beside you and cheering you on.

Appendices

A downloadable version of all appendix forms, along with additional materials, can be found online at sten.pub/literacyessentials.

If you get the culture right, everything else can follow. If you don't get the culture right, nothing else will matter.

▶ *Characteristics of a thriving, empowering, achieving culture*

Trusting

- ◆ Safety—physical and emotional
- ◆ All voices heard and respected
- ◆ Organization, schedules, procedures, routines
- ◆ Instructional walks and feedback—focused first on strengths

Collaborative

- ◆ Coaching, co-teaching, sharing lessons, "our students"
- ◆ Leadership team at school, district/provincial levels
- ◆ Common times to plan and work together; ongoing mentorship

Intellectual

- ◆ Level of questions, conversations, quality of feedback
- ◆ Professional *Literacy* Communities
- ◆ Shared beliefs and common language connected to "best" practices
- ◆ Challenging curriculum connected to real-world issues

Responsible

- ◆ Assessment—balanced, used to improve student learning
- ◆ Literacy plan—workable, improves student learning
- ◆ Initiatives, limited

Equitable

- ◆ Resources (includes technology)
- ◆ Opportunities

Joyful

- ◆ Celebrations
- ◆ Appreciations
- ◆ Positive mind-set

| Appendix B | **A Healthy and Thriving School Culture** |

▶ *High achievement and good test scores are a by-product*

Self-Evaluation: 1 = Not yet; 2 = On the way; 3 = Getting there; 4 = Achieving;
5 = Thriving

- ◆ **Solid Infrastructure**—physical, mental, and emotional operating system
  - ☐ High trust levels—personal and professional; safe, risk-taking climate
  - ☐ Shared beliefs that align with research-based literacy practices
  - ☐ Exemplary leadership—principals, teachers, administrators; leadership team
  - ☐ Efficient and effective use of schedules, resources, technology, time, management
  - ☐ Challenging and viable curriculum with alignment across the grades
  - ☐ Deep engagement with community and families—welcoming school
  - ☐ Celebration and joy in reading, writing, thinking, creating, learning

- ◆ **Cohesive Professional Learning**—relevant and ongoing, not "random acts of professional development"
  - ☐ Collaboration and mentoring—daily
  - ☐ Intellectual environment of inquiry and high-level questioning
  - ☐ Well-planned professional learning in both vertical and horizontal teams; strong leadership team
  - ☐ Continuous learning, with practical application to the classroom leading to greater student learning

- ◆ **Focus on Student Learning**—student-based, not standards-based; equitable
  - ☐ High expectations for all learners
  - ☐ Responsive teaching
  - ☐ Data used to move student learning forward
  - ☐ Smart and sane reading and writing priorities
  - ☐ Balanced assessment, mostly formative
  - ☐ Self-determining learners

- ◆ **Important Conversations**—focus and priorities
  - ☐ Important questions being asked (success depends on asking the "right" questions—about data, learning, students, curriculum, texts—with appropriate smart answers); *What if? How might we? Why not try?*
  - ☐ Useful feedback to students, to teachers
  - ☐ Open communication—opportunities to hear all the voices; speaking and listening; self-directed conversations
  - ☐ Instructional walks ongoing (see Routman 2014), not just teacher evaluations
- ◆ **Authenticity**—Real-world audience and purpose for writing and reading
  - ☐ Whole-part-whole instruction
  - ☐ Choice within structure
  - ☐ First-rate resources, programs, curriculum, texts; smart use of technology
  - ☐ Personal and cultural relevance of "the work"

(See sten.pub/literacyessentials for entire lesson plan framework)

▶ *Topic: Endangered Animals, Environmental Stewardship, and Sustainability*
Strathmillan School, grade two-three class, Winnipeg, Manitoba, Canada

Note: Content in italics and the four big focus questions on page A6 can be adapted to any curricula study of importance, such as human rights and the rights of the child, refugee crisis, immigration, endangered environments, the role of government, and much more.

Overarching Goals and Outcomes

Uppermost in our planning, teaching, and assessing: focus in depth on real-life issues and questions so significant, relevant, and fascinating that students' literacy and learning lives would be permanently and positively affected. We looked at the curriculum for the big ideas, overlap between subject areas, and content worth knowing for a lifetime.

Specific Goals/Learning Outcomes

The following goals and outcomes align with teaching for deep understanding, integrating the language arts (reading, writing, speaking, and listening, as well as the arts) and standards into the actual science and social studies curriculums, and connecting "the work" to real-world issues, audiences, and purposes.

- ◆ *Understand* the importance and impact of sustainability, stewardship, and the relationship between people and the land as connected to protecting endangered species.

- ◆ *Recognize* that a sustainable environment is essential to human and animal life (in this case the polar bear, the first animal added to the endangered species list due to global warming).

- ◆ *Assess* the impact of human interaction and climate change on our environment.

- ◆ *Advocate* for needed environmental change, propose solutions, and live in ways that respect principles of environmental stewardship and sustainability.

- *Create* informative/explanatory/persuasive texts to examine an important and relevant topic/problem/issue (in this case, endangered polar bears).

- *Communicate* information clearly in a variety of texts and online formats (such as video, blogs, podcast, song, rap, display, chart, brochure, letter, editorial, commentary, interview, booklet, picture book for students, pamphlet, advertisement, oral presentation, school bulletin board, and so on).

Big Focus Questions

- *What do we know about* polar bears and their current habitats?

- *What are the issues* polar bears are facing and their causes?

- *Why does it matter?*

- *What can we do* to make a difference?

Planning for Engagement, Excellence, and Equity: Considerations

- *Immersion in topic with first-rate resources*—literature, video, podcasts, websites, primary sources such as news articles, speakers, teacher-librarian

- *Skills to teach*—read and view nonfiction resources in multiple mediums, recognize and apply text features, determine main ideas with important supporting details, take notes in own words

- *Supportive classroom environment*—charts, resources, and pertinent information readily available and accessible to all students—for example, books on topic that accommodate a variety of reading levels

- *Connections to other subject areas*—math, art, writing

- *Audience and purpose to make writing meaningful and authentic*—critical if we expect students to invest full efforts in writing craft, revision, editing, and so on

Lesson Plan Framework/Overview (continued)

◆ *Choice within structure*—within required framework, students have choices (see sign-up chart photo on page 91)

◆ *Scaffolding and sufficient guided practice*

◆ *Conferring and public conferencing*

◆ *Publishing options*

Let the Frontloading Begin!

◆ *Read, study, and discuss multiple examples and characteristics of the genre*, in this case nonfiction related to our study.

   ◻ *Allow sufficient time to go deep*; in this study it was three weeks.
   ◻ *Discuss with students purpose of study and the frontloading.*
   ◻ *Read aloud* throughout the week a variety of excellent nonfiction texts.
   ◻ *Discuss what we notice and chart responses.* (See charts on increasing knowledge about content and format in online lesson plan.)
   ◻ *Notice text features*: titles, subtitles, illustrations and pictures, labels, diagrams, maps, charts, fun facts, table of contents, glossary, fonts and use of bold type.
   ◻ *Emphasize vocabulary*: teach and post essential words to understand.
   ◻ *Apply the Optimal Learning Model* (see page 136–146 and visuals).

◆ *Constantly check for understanding as you go along*—formative assessment in action—and adjust instruction to meet students' needs and interests.

   ◻ *Turn and talk with a partner*
   ◻ *Small-group work*
   ◻ *Examining notes students are taking*
   ◻ *Information gathering on charts—accuracy, depth, content, vocabulary*
   ◻ *Quality of student talk, engagement, and efforts*

Appendix D	Technology Tools That Help Support Schoolwide Literacy Learning

By Trish Richardson

Note: Asterisks indicate my favorite apps, websites, or technology tools that I use on an ongoing basis.

Technology in the classroom can be used to meet a variety of learners' needs; it can support and enhance reading and writing in the classroom; it can increase audience and showcase creativity; and it can help connect students, families, and staff members throughout the school and community. Here are apps and programs that support authentic, purposeful reading and writing in the classroom and school.

Simple but Powerful Uses of Technology Tools

Simple technology can sometimes be the most purposeful.

Smartphone camera*—Using the camera on your phone to photograph student learning can be powerful. Photographs could include students in action or a simple photo of a favorite quote or title that inspires writing and reading. These can be shared with the class as you reflect at the end of class or saved to share with families.

Video*—Create videos to share knowledge. When students can publish their writing through video, it allows for a different level of creativity by thinking beyond the lines of the paper. Video allows for students with different needs and learning styles to share their thinking easily. Students can record book talks and book reviews. Try green-screen presentations to allow student videos to be set in faraway locations. Increase the audience by uploading these videos to **YouTube**. Turn on the **dictate** function on your device. Most tablets and iPads allow you to talk to your device while it converts your words into text. This can be helpful as a way for students who are reluctant writers to get their ideas out quickly.

Technology Tools and Apps for Collaboration and Audience

Creating digital spaces for both staff and students of all ages to take part in online learning communities is a powerful use of technology. Teaching students to communicate and take part in online communities is important as they learn to become digital citizens. Increasing the audience allows for greater purpose, ownership, and pride for writers of all ages.

Appendix D	**Technology Tools That Help Support Schoolwide Literacy Learning (continued)**

Padlet* or **TodaysMeet*** are virtual walls where you can share ideas or questions on a specific topic. A free account can easily be set up, as well as a variety of different pages on different topics. These can be accessed with a URL. Pages can be saved or added to blogs. They can also be used at staff meetings to collect reflections and questions. Both **Padlet** and **TodaysMeet** allow you to control privacy settings for who has access and who can add to these virtual walls.

Twitter is a form of social media or networking categorized as "microblogging." It is easy to use and to connect with a community of online educators. Educators can create a classroom Twitter account and share daily and weekly events with families about learning. In higher grades it is a great way to encourage collaboration and sharing of ideas, answering questions, and writing short reflections or recaps. Use hashtags such as #edchat and #engchat to connect with other educators.

Google Drive* allows you to keep photos, writing, and videos in an online storage space that can be accessed from a variety of devices. You can keep it private, but it can be highly effective for collaborating and sharing a document with others. Staff members or students can work on or view the same document with a unique link and see the changes being made as they are working.

Skype* allows you to make Internet calls via your computer, television, or phone. Skype paired with a webcam allows you to have video calls with people in faraway locations. It's a wonderful way to bring the world into your classroom.

Technology Tools for Sharing Learning and Ideas

Technology expands the possibilities for the traditional classroom newsletter and other communications. Students can be a big part of the sharing, reflecting, and learning. Many of these technology tools increase the audience for the writing, allowing families to comment on and participate in the learning the same day the learning happens.

Blogger is a blog-publishing service. Blogs are great ways to share your class's learning. Teachers can blog pictures and updates about the class, and students can be involved in writing and publishing on a blog. **Kidblog (kidblog.org)** is a safe, kid-friendly, and simple way to set up a class set of blogs for your younger students.

Technology Tools That Help Support Schoolwide Literacy Learning (continued)

Instagram* is an online photo-sharing network service. Create a classroom Instagram account and post short videos or photographs about what is happening in the classroom or at the school. It is an effective way to communicate and share with families.

iTunes U is a free app for all Apple devices. You can search and have access to a variety of digitized courses and information at a variety of levels. If your school district has an iTunes U site, you have access to create, edit, and manage your own courses. Schools or divisions can create a course and share information and articles with staff on a variety of topics, including literacy beliefs.

QR codes* (Quick Response) are machine-readable codes that can be scanned by a smartphone or tablet. They are easy to create and are useful for sharing Internet links. This is one of my favorite things to create, either for sharing a great website with students or for sharing a link to a presentation the class created on a bulletin board or in a newsletter. There are a variety of free QR-code generators that can be easily found online. Try using **Google's web link shortener** by going to goo.gl. One of the features of Google shortener is that it allows you to create QR codes for free.

Remind is a free service that enables teachers and administrators to send out quick texts to parents and students. Texts can be preset and scheduled to be sent at specific times. It can be used to send out reminders of upcoming events or assignment due dates. Some teachers also use it to send out links to interesting articles.

Technology Tools and Apps for Creative Multimedia Presentations

Introducing and modeling using a variety of technology tools enhances projects and allows you to address different learning styles and needs. Before beginning a project, always consider the audience and how best to share your project. Technology should be used to raise awareness, change minds, and make a difference.

Book Creator* is a child-friendly app for tablets that allows students and teachers to easily create e-books. A voice-dictation feature allows the child to speak into the device, and the dictation is then converted into digital text. This is very useful for reluctant writers or students who require extra support in writing. Pictures, photographs, video, and audio recordings can be added to the book. Class books or individually created books can be made into e-books or printed easily. Book Creator can also be used as a digital portfolio. Uploading the book to SlideShare allows you to share easily on the **SlideShare** site or embed the book on other sites, allowing for a greater audience.

Comic Life is a tool that allows you to create your own comics. You can easily add photos of friends or your own drawings into the comics. Students can create their own graphic novels, comic strips, how-to guides, flyers, or storyboards. It can be used on a tablet or desktop computer.

GarageBand is software that turns your iPad, computer, or iPhone into a collection of instruments, allowing you to record and make music in a variety of settings. Students can record themselves reading their own writing or a favorite piece of text and layer in sound effects.

Haiku Deck is an easy way to create beautiful online slide presentations from a tablet or smartphone.

Popplet is an app that can be used to create graphic organizers such as webs, timelines, and other visual organizers.

ThingLink is an interactive online media platform that allows you to layer and add links, photos, and videos to presentations. It can be used with photographs, posters, maps, and family albums. For example, students can add links with more information onto a map or a picture of a community that they are studying.

iMovie* is a very student-friendly way for students to create films or Hollywood-style trailers. A variety of interesting templates can be used to create videos for sharing student learning. You can create book trailers or educational videos on a topic being studied in class.

SketchBook Express* is a digital drawing app for a tablet that includes a great variety of drawing tools and the ability to layer images. Text can also be added, which is useful for adding labels or text to artwork. Photographs can be added to and drawn on as well. It can be used for art creation and creative note-taking.

TypeDrawing, **WordFoto**, and **Patext** are apps that allow you to use typography to create artwork. Students can type in their own words or poems and then use these to draw with, turning poems and lists into visually poetic artwork.

Appendix D	**Technology Tools That Help Support Schoolwide Literacy Learning (continued)**

Word-Processing Tools and Note-Taking Tools

Effective word-processing tools allow you to collaborate, add photos and videos, and even use a stylus or a finger to write directly into your notes. If using iPads or tablets, consider investing in a set of **styluses** for the class to use for drawing, notetaking, printing, and handwriting. A stylus is a pen-shaped instrument similar to a pen that can be used on touchscreen devices.

Evernote* is an app for collecting notes in a paperless way. Notes can be accessed from a variety of devices using a log-in. Students can use it to create a digital portfolio, including photos and videos.

Notability is a great way to collect notes and information. It can combine handwriting, drawings, photos, audio, and type. Teachers or older students can use it to collect notes and add rubrics for assessment in a paperless way. Files and subfiles are easily created, allowing for a very efficient organizational system.

Wonderopolis* is a website that asks and answers "wonders" and questions. There is a new wonder every day. You can send in your own wonders, search previous wonders, or explore the wonder wall—and so much more!

Trish Richardson is an early-years and multiage teacher and visual artist in Winnipeg, Manitoba. Her teaching career has spanned kindergarten through grade five. She currently teaches at the St. James-Assiniboia School Division in a multiage grade two–three class. Her passions are writing, reading, art, and technology.

Appendix E	**Talk Moves to Support Classroom Discussion**

Revoicing *"So you're saying . . ."*	• Repeat some or all of what the student has said, then ask the student to respond and verify whether or not the revoicing is correct. Revoicing can be used to clarify, amplify, or highlight an idea.
Repeating *"Can you repeat what she said in your own words?"*	• Ask a student to repeat or rephrase what another student said. • Restate important parts of complex ideas in order to slow the conversation down and dwell on important ideas.
Reasoning *"Do you agree or disagree, and why?"* *"Why does that make sense?"*	• After students have had time to process a classmate's claim, ask students to compare their own reasoning to someone else's reasoning. • Allow students to engage with each other's ideas. • Student: "I respectfully disagree with that idea because . . ."; "This idea makes sense to me because . . ."
Adding On *"Would someone like to add on to this?"*	• Prompt students, inviting them to participate in the conversation or to clarify their own thinking. • Student: "I'd like to add on . . ."
Wait Time *"Take your time . . ."*	• Wait after asking a question before calling on a student. • Wait after a student has been called on to give the student time to organize his or her thoughts. • Student: "I'd like more time . . ."
Turn and Talk *"Turn and talk to your neighbor . . ."*	• Circulate and listen to partner talk. Use this information to choose whom to call on. • Allow students to clarify and share ideas. • Allow students to orient themselves to each other's thinking.
Revise *"Has anyone's thinking changed?"* *"Would you like to revise your thinking?"*	• Allow students to revise their thinking as they have new insights. • Student: "I thought . . . But now I think . . . because . . ." "I'd like to revise my thinking."

Source: Elham Kazemi and Allison Hintz, *Intentional Talk: How to Structure and Lead Productive Mathematical Discussions* (Portland, ME: Stenhouse, 2014), p. 21.

1. **Provide more time and choice to read every day**—first priority (nonfiction, fiction, graphic texts, comics, news articles, series books, texts in various genres, etc.).

2. **Provide easier access** (classroom library of culturally relevant literature, not leveled, including e-books).

3. **Require less writing** (in response to reading).

4. **Encourage more book talk** (student, self-directed conversations; book clubs, not just whole class).

5. **Give more time to sustained silent independent reading** (mainstay of reading program; includes monitoring through conferring—especially one-on-one to ensure students deeply understand what they read; more likely with other nine factors in place).

6. **Put guided reading in its rightful place** (temporary scaffold, students doing most of the work).

7. **Do more reading aloud** (great way to introduce new books, authors, and series, notice author's craft, and build vocabulary).

8. **Ensure fluency for youngest readers** (natural-language texts, rereading, partner reading, Readers Theatre).

9. **Do more shared reading** (especially of student and class-authored texts).

10. **Demonstrate reading processes** (teacher as a reader—thinking aloud, choosing books, figuring out vocabulary, reading closely, self-monitoring, rereading, questioning, strategizing, applying what we know, inferring meaning from text and life experiences).

| **12 Writing Essentials for All Grade Levels**

Teach these essentials well in any genre or content area; with guidance and sustained practice, students can adapt and transfer their use to all real-world writing.

1. *Writing with a specific reader in mind* and a clearly understood purpose

2. *Reading deeply, with a writer's perspective*

3. *Choosing an appropriate topic* (choice within structure) and narrowing the focus; deciding what's most important to include for the reader

4. *Applying agreed-upon writing criteria* to the particular writing piece

5. *Organizing the writing* in a logical, easy-to-follow style (prewriting, putting like information together; elaborating with pertinent details, explanations, and evidence to express main ideas; knowing when and what information, words, and visuals to include; paragraphing; using transitions to make it easier for the reader)

6. *Communicating clearly* in an efficient, effective, and even elegant manner

7. *Applying author's craft* and playing around with language to engage, enchant, persuade, and educate the reader (includes composing satisfying lead and closure)

8. *Writing with a personal style* that illuminates the writer's personality (may include dialogue, humor, point of view, writing stance)—writer's unique voice

9. *Rereading, thinking, and rethinking in act of composing* (includes revising and editing along the way, assessing, self-evaluating, writing as a recursive process)

10. *Employing correct conventions* (spelling, punctuation, capitalization, grammar, legibility)

11. *Ensuring accuracy in facts*, analysis, sources, visuals, websites consulted, etc.

12. ***Taking responsibility for producing effective writing*** (immersion in particular genre, drafting, revising, organizing, using technology wisely, proofreading, sustaining the writing effort, editing, self-evaluating, and doing whatever is necessary to ensure the text is meaningful and clear to the reader as well as accurate and engaging)

These essentials are applicable in grades K–12 and beyond. The actual writing skills we teach across the grades are similar, which precludes the need for a separate list of skills for every grade level. What changes are the depth, complexity, length, and variety of texts students compose and the amount of writing support and practice students require. Also, although students do need to know and understand the particular attributes that define each genre and content area, successful writing in a specific genre or content domain involves being able to apply the writing essentials that are part of all effective writing.

(Adapted from Regie Routman, *Writing Essentials*, Portsmouth, NH: Heinemann, 2005)

College and Career Readiness Anchor Standards for Reading

Note: We accessed the standards for reading and writing at, respectively, http://www.corestandards.org/ELA-Literacy/CCRA/R/ and http://www.corestandards.org/ELA-Literacy/CCRA/W/.

The grades K–12 standards on the following pages define what students should understand and be able to do by the end of each grade. They correspond to the College and Career Readiness (CCR) anchor standards below by number. The CCR and grade-specific standards are necessary complements—the former providing broad standards, the latter providing additional specificity—that together define the skills and understandings that all students must demonstrate.

Key Ideas and Details

1. Read closely to determine what the text says explicitly and to make logical inferences from it; cite specific textual evidence when writing or speaking to support conclusions drawn from the text.

2. Determine central ideas or themes of a text and analyze their development; summarize the key supporting details and ideas.

3. Analyze how and why individuals, events, or ideas develop and interact over the course of a text.

Craft and Structure

4. Interpret words and phrases as they are used in a text, including determining technical, connotative, and figurative meanings, and analyze how specific word choices shape meaning or tone.

5. Analyze the structure of texts, including how specific sentences, paragraphs, and larger portions of the text (e.g., a section, chapter, scene, or stanza) relate to each other and the whole.

6. Assess how point of view or purpose shapes the content and style of a text.

Integration of Knowledge and Ideas

7. Integrate and evaluate content presented in diverse formats and media, including visually and quantitatively, as well as in words.

8. Delineate and evaluate the argument and specific claims in a text, including the validity of the reasoning as well as the relevance and sufficiency of the evidence.

9. Analyze how two or more texts address similar themes or topics in order to build knowledge or to compare the approaches the authors take.

Range of Reading and Level of Text Complexity

10. Read and comprehend complex literary and informational texts independently and proficiently.

Literacy Essentials: Engagement, Excellence, and Equity for All Learners by Regie Routman.
Copyright © 2018. Stenhouse Publishers.

College and Career Readiness Anchor Standards for Writing

Text Types and Purposes

1. Write arguments to support claims in an analysis of substantive topics or texts using valid reasoning and relevant and sufficient evidence.

2. Write informative/explanatory texts to examine and convey complex ideas and information clearly and accurately through the effective selection, organization, and analysis of content.

3. Write narratives to develop real or imagined experiences or events using effective technique, well-chosen details, and well-structured event sequences.

Production and Distribution of Writing

4. Produce clear and coherent writing in which the development, organization, and style are appropriate to task, purpose, and audience.

5. Develop and strengthen writing as needed by planning, revising, editing, rewriting, or trying a new approach.

6. Use technology, including the Internet, to produce and publish writing and to interact and collaborate with others.

Research to Build and Present Knowledge

7. Conduct short as well as more sustained research projects based on focused questions, demonstrating understanding of the subject under investigation.

8. Gather relevant information from multiple print and digital sources, assess the credibility and accuracy of each source, and integrate the information while avoiding plagiarism.

9. Draw evidence from literary or informational texts to support analysis, reflection, and research.

Range of Writing

10. Write routinely over extended time frames (time for research, reflection, and revision) and shorter time frames (a single sitting or a day or two) for a range of tasks, purposes, and audiences.

Literacy Essentials: Engagement, Excellence, and Equity for All Learners by Regie Routman.
Copyright © 2018. Stenhouse Publishers.

| Appendix I | **Quick Summary of Effective Practices That Promote Equity** |

◆ Highly knowledgeable, experienced teachers

◆ Valuing and validating students' and families' stories and culture

◆ Shared writing and shared reading

◆ Scaffolded conversations

◆ More face-to-face time with teacher, less technology

◆ Small-group work

◆ Emphasis on oral language and vocabulary

◆ Asking high-level questions

◆ Optimal Learning Model (OLM)—responsive teaching in action, differentiation, whole-part-whole teaching

◆ Hearing all the voices—lots of opportunities for conversations

◆ Not giving the "right answer"—expecting students to figure it out

◆ Seeing failure as a learning tool

◆ Extensive libraries—diverse collections with easy access

◆ Choice within structure

◆ Schedules that promote integration and large blocks of uninterrupted time

◆ Interventionist working in classroom; students not removed

◆ Reading aloud literature that reflects students' cultures

◆ More student choice

◆ Respectful language

◆ Flexible grouping (heterogeneous, cross-racial, short term)

◆ Cutting back on tracking; at least in ninth grade, doing away with honors English and history

◆ Bilingual and dual-language programs

◆ Ensuring physical and psychological safety

◆ Adequate funding

◆ First-class resources

Literacy Essentials: Engagement, Excellence, and Equity for All Learners by Regie Routman.
Copyright © 2018. Stenhouse Publishers.

ENGAGEMENT

Introduction

1. Flow has been best described and researched by Hungarian psychologist Mihaly Csikszentmihalyi, beginning in the 1960s, when he sought to discover how some artists became so immersed in their work that they disregarded everything else going on around them. You can hear and see Csikszentmihalyi on YouTube, including his presentation at the February 2004 TED conference: https://www.ted.com/talks/mihaly_csikszentmihalyi_on_flow.

Engagement 1: Developing Trusting Relationships

1. David L. Kirp, *Improbable Scholars: The Rebirth of a Great American School System and a Strategy for America's Schools* (New York: Oxford University Press, 2013), p. 45, citing research by Anthony Bryk and Barbara Schneider in their book *Trust in Schools: A Core Resource for Improvement* (New York: Russell Sage, 2005).

2. Regie Routman, "Creating a Culture of Trust," March 2015, http://www.regieroutman.org/files/1014/2508/7728/creating-culture-trust.pdf.

3. Trish Richardson shared this idea with me in January 2016, in a personal communication. She teaches grades two–three at the Strathmillan School in Winnipeg, Manitoba, Canada.

4. For an example, see the three-minute video "Sharing Our Stories" at http://www.regieroutman.com/inresidence/cnctn/samples.aspx.

5. The ideas in this paragraph come from an *Edutopia* article by Lisa Currie, "Why Teaching Kindness in Schools Is Essential to Reduce Bullying," first published on October 17, 2014. https://www.edutopia.org/blog/teaching-kindness-essential-reduce-bullying-lisa-currie?utm_source=twitter&utm_medium=socialflow; and from a *Mind/Shift* article by Linda Flanagan, "How Making Kindness a Priority Benefits Students," published June 6, 2017. https://ww2.kqed.org/mindshift/2017/06/06/how-making-kindness-a-priority-benefits-students/.

6. I describe the bullying study in greater detail in Chapter 2 of *Read, Write, Lead: Breakthrough Strategies for Schoolwide Literacy Success* (Alexandria, VA: ASCD, 2014).

7. For more suggestions on books and other resources, see Routman, 2014, p. 314, endnote 23.

8. Currie, October 17, 2014.

9. The quote from the parent leader is from "Response from Shane Safir" and appeared in a January 23, 2016, blog post by Larry Ferlazzo, "Response: How Can We Best Engage Families? Seeing Families as 'Co-Creators' of Our Schools," http://blogs.edweek.org/teachers/classroom_qa_with_larry_ferlazzo/2016/01/response_seeing_families_as_co-creators_of_our_schools.html. The entire blog is an excellent source for ideas on engaging families.

10. For more information on how to teach students to conduct their own conferences and the benefits of doing so, see Regie Routman, *Literacy at the Crossroads: Crucial Conversations About Reading, Writing, and Other Teaching Dilemmas* (Portsmouth, NH: Heinemann, 1996), pp. 153–159.

Engagement 2: Celebrating Learners

1. For more on instructional walks, see Regie Routman, *Read, Write, Lead* (Alexandria, VA: ASCD, 2014), pp. 197–216.

2. Marie Clay, *Reading Recovery: A Guidebook for Teachers in Training* (Portsmouth, NH: Heinemann, 1993).

3. See Carol Dweck's pioneering work *Mindset: The New Psychology of Success* (New York: Random House, 2006); the article "Commentary: Carol Dweck Revisits the 'Growth Mindset," *Education Week,* September 22, 2015; and "The Journey to a Growth Mindset," Dweck's general session keynote address at the 2016 ASCD Annual Conference, Atlanta, Georgia, April 3.

4. For more on this residency work, see the video-based literacy series *Regie Routman in Residence: Transforming Our Teaching* (Portsmouth, NH: Heinemann, 2008, 2013) and my book *Read, Write, Lead: Breakthrough Strategies for Schoolwide Literacy Success.*

5. John Hattie, *Visible Learning for Teachers: Maximizing Impact on Learning* (New York: Routledge, 2012), p. viii.

6. For a powerful example, see the video interview of a former special education student and nonreader at http://regieroutman.com/inresidence/overview.aspx.

7. Arthur C. Brooks, "Choose to Be Grateful. It Will Make You Happier," *The New York Times,* November 22, 2015, Sunday Review, SR5, nytimes.com/2015/11/22/opinion/sunday/choose-to-be-grateful-it-will-make-you-happier.html?_r=0.

8. This tradition is described by Ayelet Waldman in her foreword to *Loving Learning: How Progressive Education Can Save America's Schools*, by Tom Little and Katherine Ellison (New York: W. W. Norton, 2015), pp. 10–11.

9. Brooks, 2015.

10. Jeanne Marie Laskas, "To Obama with Love, and Hate, and Desperation," *The New York Times Magazine,* January 17, 2017, https://www.nytimes.com/2017/01/17/magazine/what-americans-wrote-to-obama.html?_r=0. A print version, titled "The Mail Room," appeared in the magazine on January 22, 2017, pp. 30–39.

11. The quote is from Mary Yuhas, former first-grade teacher at Ardmore Elementary School in Bellevue, Washington.

12. Steven Wolk, "Joy in School," *Educational Leadership,* September 2008, pp. 8–15, http://www.ascd.org/publications/educational-leadership/sept08/vol66/num01/Joy-in-School.aspx.

13. Trish Richardson shared this memory in a personal communication in January 2016.

Engagement 3: Creating a Thriving Learning Environment

1. Stuart McNaughton, *Designing Better Schools for Culturally and Linguistically Diverse Children* (New York: Routledge, 2011), p. 31.

2. Lynn Allyson Matczuk, "A Comparative Examination of Outcomes of a Longitudinal Professional

Development Experience in Writing Instruction in Schools for Kindergarten to Grade 3," unpublished dissertation, University of Manitoba, Winnipeg, Canada, 2016, p. 134.

3.　John Hattie, *Visible Learning for Teachers: Maximizing Impact on Learning* (New York: Routledge, 2012), p. 78.

4.　For specifics on environmental walks, see Regie Routman, *Read, Write, Lead* (Alexandria, VA: ASCD, 2014), pp. 89–90.

5.　For ideas on how to work with your students to organize the library, see Regie Routman, *Reading Essentials: The Specifics You Need to Teach Reading Well* (Portsmouth, NH: Heinemann, 2003), pp. 74–80.

6.　Two sources that cite multiple studies on this topic are Evie Blad, "Positive School Climates May Shrink Achievement Gaps," *Education Week*, November 15, 2016, p. 9, http://www.edweek.org/ ew/articles/2016/11/16/positive-school-climates-may-shrink-achievement-gaps.html; and Eric Schaps, "Student Health, Supportive Schools, and Academic Success," Chapter 3 in *The Role of Supportive School Environments in Promoting Academic Success: Getting Results, Developing Safe and Healthy Kids: Update 5*. (Sacramento: California Department of Education, 2005), https:// www.collaborativeclassroom.org/research-articles-and-papers-the-role-of-supportive-school- environments-in-promoting-academic-success.

7.　Brooke Benmar shared this observation with me during a personal conversation on August 15, 2016.

8.　Katrina Schwartz, "Why Group Work Could Be the Key to English Learner Success," *Mind/Shift*, February 23, 2017, https://ww2.kqed.org/mindshift/2017/02/23/why-group-work-could-be-the- key-to-english-learner-success/.

9.　Sandra Figueroa offered this advice during a conference session at the California Reading Association Annual Professional Development Institute in Visalia, California, on November 5, 2016.

10.　Amanda Ripley, *The Smartest Kids in the World and How They Got That Way* (New York: Simon and Schuster, 2013), p. 199.

11.　Allison Flood, "Book Up for a Longer Life: Readers Die Later, Study Finds," *The Guardian*, August 8, 2016, https://www.theguardian.com/books/2016/aug/08/book-up-for-a-longer-life-readers- die-later-study-finds.

12.　Colum McCann, *Thirteen Ways of Looking: A Novella and Three Stories* (New York: Random House, 2015).

13.　Jacqueline Woodson, *Another Brooklyn* (New York: HarperCollins, 2016).

14.　I gathered these quotes from Jacqueline Woodson at her book talk at Elliott Bay Book Company in Seattle, Washington, on September 21, 2016.

15.　Daniel Bergner tells the story of Ryan Speedo Green in his book *Sing for Your Life: A Story of Race, Music, and Family* (New York: Lee Boudreaux Books, 2016).

16.　Ryan Speedo Green was interviewed by Tavis Smiley on *The Tavis Smiley Show*, Public Radio International, November 19, 2016.

17.　Links to current articles and archived articles dating from 2013 are available at Kelly Gallagher's website: http://www.kellygallagher.org/article-of-the-week/.

18.　Regie Routman, *Transitions: From Literature to Literacy* (Portsmouth, NH: Heinemann, 1988).

19.　John Hattie, *Visible Learning for Teachers: Maximizing Impact on Learning* (New York: Routledge, 2012).

20.　Matt Renwick, *5 Myths About Classroom Technology: How Do We Integrate Digital Tools to Truly Enhance Learning?* (Alexandria, VA: ASCD, 2016), p. 7.

21.　Katie Egan Cunningham, S*tory: Still the Heart of Literacy Learning* (Portland, ME: Stenhouse, 2015).

22. Linda Flanagan, "How Teens Can Develop and Share Meaningful Stories with 'The Moth,' *Mind/Shift*, June 19, 2017, https://ww2.kqed.org/mindshift/2017/06/19/how-teens-can-develop-and-share-meaningful-stories-with-the-moth/. See also Jim Dillon, "Stories Stick with Students," *SmartBrief*, June 7, 2017, http://www.smartbrief.com/original/2017/06/stories-stick-students.

23. Steven Wolk, "Joy in School," *Educational Leadership,* September 2008, pp. 8–15, http://www.ascd.org/publications/educational-leadership/sept08/vol66/num01/Joy-in-School.aspx; Regie Routman, "To Raise Achievement, Let's Celebrate Teachers Before We Evaluate Them," *Reading Today*, June/July 2013, pp. 10-12, http://www.regieroutman.org/files/4813/7842/4350/Reading_Today-6-13.pdf; Judy Wallis, "Teachers, Don't Forget Joy," *Education Week,* October 16, 2013, http://www.edweek.org/ew/articles/2013/10/16/08wallis.h33.html.

Engagement 4: Teaching with Purpose and Authenticity

1. Nell K. Duke, Samantha Caughlan, Mary M. Juzwik, and Nicole M. Martin, "Teaching Genre with Purpose," *Educational Leadership*, March 2012, pp. 34–39.

2. Regie Routman, *Teaching Essentials: Expecting the Most and Getting the Best from Every Learner, K–8* (Portsmouth, NH: Heinemann, 2008), companion website: http://regieroutman.com/teachingessentials/default.asp; *Regie Routman in Residence: Transforming Our Teaching,* video-based literacy series (Portsmouth, NH: Heinemann, 2008, 2013).

3. Trish Richardson shared this experience in a personal communication in January 2016. She teaches grades two–three at the Strathmillan School in Winnipeg, Manitoba, Canada.

4. The excerpt is from a reflection by Daria Orloff on January 6, 2017. She teaches grade four at the Strathmillan School in Winnipeg, Manitoba, Canada.

5. Trish Richardson's reflection on planning is from June 2016.

6. For more on instructional walks, see Regie Routman, *Read, Write, Lead: Breakthrough Strategies for Schoolwide Literacy Success* (Alexandria, VA: ASCD, 2014), pp. 197–216.

7. Matt Renwick, "When Technology Isn't Necessary (and Maybe Not Even Nice)," *ASCD Edge* (blog), October 9, 2015, http://edge.ascd.org/blogpost/when-technology-isnt-necessary-and-maybe-not-even-nice.

8. Matt Renwick shared this information in an e-mail on January 23, 2016.

9. William Powers, *Hamlet's BlackBerry: A Practical Philosophy for Building a Good Life in the Digital Age* (New York: HarperCollins, 2010), p. 147.

10. Powers, p. 17.

11. The ideas in this paragraph, and the quote, are from Thomas Friedman, "From Hands to Heads to Hearts," *The New York Times*, January 4, 2017, Op-Ed, A21, http://www.nytimes.com/2017/01/04/opinion/from-hands-to-heads-to-hearts.html?_r=0.

12. Trish Richardson wrote this reflection on March 7, 2017.

EXCELLENCE

Excellence 1: Embedding Professional Learning

1. Regie Routman, "Teacher Education, Not Teacher Training," edCircuit, February 2016, http://www.edcircuit.com/teacher-education-not-teacher-training/.

2. Linda Darling-Hammond and Nikole Richardson, "Research Review/Teacher Learning: What Matters?" *Educational Leadership*, February 2009, pp. 46–53; Thomas R. Guskey and Kwang Suk Yoon, "What Works in Professional Development?" *Phi Delta Kappan*, March 2009, pp. 495-500.

3. Nancy Flanagan, "Professional Development Is Useless! Or Not," *Education Week Teacher* (blog), August 9, 2015, http://blogs.edweek.org/teachers/teacher_in_a_strange_land/2015/08/professional_development_is_useless_or_not.html.

4. Routman, February 2016.

5. Regie Routman, *Read, Write, Lead: Breakthrough Strategies for Schoolwide Literacy Success* (Alexandria, VA: ASCD, 2014). See Chapter 6, "Professional *Literacy* Communities," pp. 219–253, for guidelines and specifics.

6. Regie Routman, *Regie Routman in Residence: Transforming Our Teaching,* video-based literacy series (Portsmouth, NH: Heinemann, 2008, 2013), http://regieroutman.com/inresidence/cnctn/default.aspx.

7. Melissa Kirkland offered her reflection as part of an evaluation of a writing residency in March 2016.

8. Routman, 2014; Lynn Allyson Matczuk, "A Comparative Examination of Outcomes of a Longitudinal Professional Development Experience in Writing Instruction in Schools for Kindergarten to Grade 3," unpublished dissertation, University of Manitoba, Winnipeg, Canada, 2016.

9. Andy Hargreaves, "Why We Can't Reform Literacy and Math All at Once," *The Washington Post,* September 26, 2014, Answer Sheet by Valerie Strauss, https://www.washingtonpost.com/news/answer-sheet/wp/2014/09/26/why-we-cant-reform-literacy-and-math-all-at-once/.

10. Mike Schmoker, "It's Time to Restructure Teacher Professional Development," Commentary, *Education Week,* October 21, 2015, http://www.edweek.org/ew/articles/2015/10/21/its-time-to-restructure-teacher-professional-development.html.

11. Charles Duhigg, "Group Study," *The New York Times Magazine,* February 28, 2016, Work-Life issue, pp. 24, 72.

12. Regie Routman, *Transitions: From Literature to Literacy* (Portsmouth, NH: Heinemann, 1988).

13. Principal Matt Renwick shared his observation in an e-mail on January 8, 2016.

14. Stacey Wester is principal of Iola-Scandinavia Elementary School in Iola, Iowa. Before becoming a principal she was an intermediate classroom teacher for twenty-one years. She shared her thoughts in an e-mail on December 31, 2016.

15. See *Regie Routman in Residence: Transforming Our Teaching*, video-based literacy series, Session 3, for protocols and procedures: www.regieroutman.com/inresidence/default.aspx. For procedures, see also Routman, 2014, Appendix C: Examining Beliefs About Reading, p. 289.

16. The ideas here are slightly adapted from Allison Zmuda, 2015, "Personalized Learning," Chapter 7, pp. 135–154, in Alan M. Blankstein and Pedro Noguera, with Lorena Kelly, *Excellence Through Equity: Five Principles of Courageous Leadership to Guide Achievement for Every Student* (Alexandria, VA: ASCD, 2015), p. 135.

17. Nell K. Duke and Nicole M. Martin, "10 Things Every Literacy Educator Should Know About Research," *The Reading Teacher,* September 2011, p. 11.

18. Michael Fullan and Andy Hargreaves, *What's Worth Fighting for in Your School?* rev. ed. (New York: Teachers College Press, 1996).

19. Richard Allington, "What I've Learned About Effective Reading Instruction from a Decade of Studying Exemplary Elementary Classroom Teachers," *Phi Delta Kappan*, June 2002, pp. 740–747.

20. Barbara M. Taylor, Debra S. Peterson, P. David Pearson, and Michael C Rodriguez, "Looking Inside Classrooms: Reflecting on the 'How' as Well as the 'What' in Effective Reading Instruction," *The Reading Teacher*, November 2002, pp. 270–279.

21. Routman, 2014.

22. Peter Dewitz, Jennifer Jones, and Susan Leahy, "Comprehension Strategy Instruction in Core Reading Programs," *Reading Research Quarterly*, April–June 2009, pp. 102–126.

23. Richard Allington, "What At-Risk Readers Need," *Educational Leadership*, March 2011, pp. 40–45.

24. Steve Graham and Michael Hebert, *Writing to Read: Evidence for How Writing Can Improve Reading* (New York: Carnegie Corporation, 2010).

25. Nell K. Duke, Victoria Purcell-Gates, Leigh A. Hall, and Cathy Tower, "Authentic Literacy Activities for Developing Comprehension and Writing," *The Reading Teacher*, December 2006–January 2007, pp. 344–355.

26. Richard L. Allington, Kimberly McCuiston, and Monica Billen, "What Research Says About Text Complexity and Learning to Read," *The Reading Teacher*, April 2015, pp. 491–501.

27. Donald Murray, *Crafting a Life in Essay, Story, Poem* (Portsmouth, NH: Heinemann, 1996).

28. Nell K. Duke and V. Susan Bennett-Armistead, *Reading and Writing Informational Texts in the Primary Grades: Research-Based Practices* (New York: Scholastic, 2003).

29. George Hillocks, *The Testing Trap: How State Writing Assessments Control Learning* (New York: Teachers College Press, 2002).

30. Sheila Valencia, "Using Assessment to Improve Teaching and Learning," in *What Research Has to Say About Reading Instruction,* 4th ed., ed. S. Jay Samuels and Alan E. Farstrup (Newark, DE: International Reading Association, 2011), pp. 379–405.

31. Jill Barshay, "Using Computers Widens the Achievement Gap in Writing, a Federal Study Finds," *The Hechinger Report*, Education by the Numbers, January 11, 2016, http://hechingerreport. org/online-writing-tests-widen-achievement-gap/. See also related research on taking PARC tests: Benjamin Herold, "PARCC Scores Lower for Students Who Took Exams on Computers," *Education Week,* February 3, 2016, http://www.edweek.org/ew/articles/2016/02/03/parcc-scores-lower-on-computer.html.

32. John Hattie, *What Works Best in Education: The Politics of Collaborative Expertise* (London: Pearson, 2015), https://www.pearson.com/content/dam/corporate/global/pearson-dot-com/ files/hattie/150526_ExpertiseWEB_V1.pdf.

33. Ilana M. Umansky, Rachel A. Valentino, and Sean F. Reardon, "The Promise of Two-Language Education," *Educational Leadership,* February 2016, themed issue, "Helping ELLs Excel," pp. 10–17.

34. Kath Glasswell and Michael Ford, "Let's Start Leveling About Leveling," *Language Arts*, January 2011, pp. 208–216.

35. Liana Heitin, citing Steve Graham's 2007 research meta-analysis, in "Will the Common Core Step Up Schools' Focus on Grammar?" *Education Week,* February 23, 2016, http://www.edweek. org/ew/articles/2016/02/24/will-the-common-core-step-up-schools.html.

36. Stephen Krashen, "Research Supports Value of School Libraries," Letters to the Editor, *Education Week,* June 1, 2016, pp. 28–29.

37. Michigan Association of Intermediate School Administrators, General Education Leadership Network, Early Literacy Task Force, *Essential Instructional Practices in Early Literacy: Grades K to 3* (Lansing, MI: Authors, 2016), https://sites.google.com/a/umich.edu/nkduke/publications/ new-essentials-documents. The same task force also produced a pre-kindergarten document on essential instructional practices: http://www.gomaisa.org/sites/default/files/Pre-K%20 Literacy%20Essentials%203.2016.pdf.

38. Routman, 2014.

39. Andrew Hargreaves, Gábor Halász, and Beatriz Pont, "School Leadership for Systemic Improvement in Finland," Organization for Economic Cooperation and Development, 2007, https://www.oecd.org/edu/school/39928629.pdf; Hattie, 2012, *Visible Learning for Teachers*; and Hattie, 2015, "High-Impact Leadership."

40. Matczuk, 2016, p. 138.

41. See Routman, 2014, pp. 231–245, for specifics on establishing and sustaining an effective leadership team.

Excellence 2: Expert Teaching Through Frontloading

1.   The excerpt is from an evaluation of a writing residency written by teacher Trish Richardson on March 5, 2015.
2.   Terry Heick, "Are You Teaching Content or Teaching Thought?" *TeachThought: We Grow Teachers* (blog), February 27, 2014, http://www.teachthought.com/critical-thinking/teaching-content-or-teaching-thought/.
3.   Matthew Vaughn-Smith, "Stop Wasting Time: Be Intentional," *Mr. Vaughn-Smith's Literacy Corner* (blog), February 13, 2016, http://vsliteracycorner.weebly.com/literacy-in-action/stop-wasting-time-be-intentional.
4.   Regie Routman, *Reading Essentials: The Specifics You Need to Teach Reading Well* (Portsmouth, NH: Heinemann, 2003).
5.   P. David Pearson and Margaret C. Gallagher, "The Instruction of Reading Comprehension," *Contemporary Educational Psychology*, July 1983, pp. 317–344.
6.   MaryEllen Vogt made this observation in an e-mail on November 13, 2016.
7.   Jana J. Echevarria, MaryEllen J. Vogt, and Deborah J. Short, *Making Content Comprehensible for English Learners: The SIOP Model*, 5th ed. (Boston: Pearson, 2017), p. 130.
8.   Regie Routman, *Writing Essentials: Raising Expectations and Results While Simplifying Teaching* (Portsmouth, NH: Heinemann, 2005).
9.   For an example of what that looks like and sounds like in practice, see *Regie Routman in Residence: Transforming Our Teaching*, video-based literacy series (Portsmouth, NH: Heinemann, 2005).
10. See Routman, 2003, p. 173, for visuals and directions on making sliding masks in various sizes.
11. For much more on shared reading and shared reading aloud, see Routman, 2003, pp. 130–149; and Regie Routman, T*ransforming Our Teaching Through Reading to Understand*, video-based literacy series (Portsmouth, NH: Heinemann, 2013). For viewing a shared read-aloud lesson in a grade 5–6 class using a nonfiction picture book, see *Sixteen Years in Sixteen Seconds: The Sammy Lee Story* by Paula Yoo (New York: Lee & Low Books, 2005); see session 9.

Excellence 3: Listening, Speaking, and Questioning That Elevate Teaching and Learning

1.   Jonathan Kozol, December 22, 2015, "60 Seconds with Jonathan Kozol," YouTube video, https://www.youtube.com/watch?v=d_5tbTW2oOc&feature=youtu.be.
2.   Erik Palmer, *Teaching the Core Skills of Listening and Speaking* (Alexandria, VA: ASCD, 2014), p. 22, citing the National Association of Colleges and Employers (2012) and a Stanford Business School study. Palmer's entire book is excellent for learning how to effectively teach speaking and listening. See also Palmer's excellent book *Well Spoken: Teaching Speaking to All Students* (Portland, ME: Stenhouse, 2011).
3.   John Hattie, *Visible Learning for Teachers: Maximizing Impact on Learning* (New York: Routledge, 2012), p. 80, for second and third sentences of paragraph. John Goodlad, *A Place Called School*, 20th anniversary ed. (New York: McGraw-Hill, 2004), p. 229, for fourth and fifth sentences and quotes in same paragraph.
4.   Sherry Turkle, *Reclaiming Conversation: The Power of Talk in a Digital Age* (New York: Penguin Press, 2015), pp. 225–227, in the section "Seduced by Transcription: Putting Machines Aside," describing the work of Harvard Law School professor Carol Streiker.
5.   Turkle, 2015, p. 246.
6.   W. Dorsey Hammond and Denise D. Nessel, *The Comprehension Experience: Engaging Readers Through Effective Inquiry and Discussion* (Portsmouth, NH: Heinemann, 2011), p. 89.
7.   Hattie, 2012, p. 81.
8.   Jal Mehta and Sarah Fine, *The Why, What, Where, and How of Deeper Learning in American*

Secondary Schools, research report, Deeper Learning Research Series (Boston, MA: Jobs for the Future, December 2015), http://www.jff.org/sites/default/files/publications/materials/The-Why-What-Where-How-121415.pdf.

9. Charles Duhigg, "Group Study," *The New York Times Magazine,* Work-Life issue, February 28, 2016, p. 72.

10. Duhigg, 2016, p. 24.

11. Angela Watson, "8 Ways Teachers Can Talk Less and Get Kids Talking More," *The Cornerstone for Teachers* (blog), September 11, 2014, http://thecornerstoneforteachers.com/2014/09/8-ways-teachers-can-talk-less-get-kids-talking.html.

12. See Chapter 5, "Literature Conversations," in Regie Routman, *Conversations: Strategies for Teaching, Learning, and Evaluating* (Portsmouth, NH: Heinemann, 2000), pp. 171–204.

13. Elham Kazemi and Allison Hintz, *Intentional Talk: How to Structure and Lead Productive Mathematical Discussions* (Portland, ME: Stenhouse, 2014), p. 21.

14. David Carr, "A Writer's Last Word on Journalism, Aimed at Students," *The New York Times,* February 15, 2015, B1 and B3, http://www.nytimes.com/2015/02/16/business/media/david-carr-as-a-passionate-professor-shaping-the-future-of-journalism.html?_r=0.

15. See Regie Routman, *Read, Write, Lead: Breakthrough Strategies for Schoolwide Literacy Success* (Alexandria, VA: ASCD, 2014).

16. Chris Anderson, *TED Talks: The Official TED Guide to Public Speaking* (Boston: Houghton Mifflin Harcourt, 2016), p. xi.

17. Carmine Gallo, *Talk Like TED: The 9 Public-Speaking Secrets of the World's Top Minds* (New York: St. Martin's Press, 2014), p. 243.

18. Gallo, 2014, pp. 198–199.

19. The quote is from Anderson, 2016, pp. 245–246.

20. The quote is from a tweet from Penny Kittle, July 26, 2016. Michelle Obama's speech is available at https://www.youtube.com/watch?v=4ZNWYqDU948.

21. For detailed guidelines on student-led conferences, see Regie Routman, *Literacy at the Crossroads: Crucial Talk About Reading, Writing, and Other Teaching Dilemmas* (Portsmouth, NH: Heinemann, 1996), pp. 153–159.

22. Hattie, 2012, p. 83.

23. Susan M. Brookhart, *How to Design Questions and Tasks to Assess Student Thinking* (Alexandria, VA: ASCD, 2014).

24. Regie Routman, "What Reflects a Great School? Not Test Scores," Commentary, *Education Week,* October 21, 2014, http://regieroutman.org/files/9414/2051/7470/Regie_Routman_Education_Week_Commentary.pdf.

Excellence 4: Embracing the Reading-Writing Connection

1. National Governors Association Center for Best Practices and Council of Chief State School Officers, *Common Core State Standards for English Language Arts and Literacy in History/Social Studies, Science, and Technical Subjects* (Washington, DC: Author, 2010), p. 4.

2. Juhee Lee and Diane L. Schallert, "Exploring the Reading-Writing Connection: A Yearlong Classroom-Based Experimental Study of Middle School Students Developing Literacy in a New Language" (abstract), *Reading Research Quarterly,* April/May/June 2016, doi: 10.1002/rrq.132. This article also has a review of the extensive research base on reading-writing connections.

3. See my reading blogs at regieroutman.org for examples.

4. Regie Routman, *Read, Write, Lead: Breakthrough Strategies for Schoolwide Literacy Success* (Alexandria, VA: ASCD, 2014), pp. 143–150.

5. Katie Egan Cunningham, *Story: Still the Heart of Literacy Learning* (Portland, ME: Stenhouse, 2015), p. 89.

6. Alison Flood, "Short Story Vending Machines Press French Commuters' Buttons," *The Guardian,* November 13, 2015, https://www.theguardian.com/books/2015/nov/13/short-story-vending-machines-press-french-commuters-buttons.

7. http://regieroutman.com/teachingessentials/default.asp.

8. Sarah McKibben, "Pass the Mic: Teaching with Hip-Hop," *Education Update,* June 2016, p. 1.

9. Global Goals for Sustainable Development produced this brief video on girl power: https://www.youtube.com/watch?v=sZQ2RUFd54o.

10. Cunningham, 2015.

11. Amy Choi, "How Telling Stories Can Transform a Classroom," *TED-Ed* (blog), describing how to use StoryCorpsU Interviews, September 30, 2015, http://blog.ed.ted.com/2015/09/30/how-telling-stories-can-transform-a-classroom/.

12. David Bornstein cites a vast worldwide longitudinal study in "A Book in Every Home, and Then Some," *Opinionator* (blog), *The New York Times,* May 16, 2011, http://opinionator.blogs.nytimes.com/2011/05/16/a-book-in-every-home-and-then-some/?_r=0.

13. Bornstein, 2011.

14. Richard Allington, "What I've Learned About Effective Reading Instruction from a Decade of Studying Exemplary Elementary Classroom Teachers," *Phi Delta Kappan*, June 2002, pp. 740–747; Barbara M. Taylor, Debra S. Peterson, P. David Pearson, and Michael C. Rodriguez, "Looking Inside Classrooms: Reflecting on the 'How' as Well as the 'What' in Effective Reading Instruction," *The Reading Teacher*, November 2002, pp. 270–279.

15. Cathy Haruf, wife of renowned author Kent Haruf, contributed most of this entry, "Kent Haruf's *Our Souls at Night*: 'A Book About Us,'" on the Picador Books blog, June 4, 2015, http://www.picador.com/blog/may-2015/%E2%80%8Bkent-harufs-our-souls-at-night-a-book-about-us.

16. David Carr, "A Writer's Last Word on Journalism, Aimed at Students," *The New York Times,* February 15, 2015, B1 and B3, http://www.nytimes.com/2015/02/16/business/media/david-carr-as-a-passionate-professor-shaping-the-future-of-journalism.html?_r=0.

17. Liana Heitin, citing Steve Graham's 2007 research meta-analysis, in "Will the Common Core Step Up Schools' Focus on Grammar?" *Education Week,* February 23, 2016, http://www.edweek.org/ew/articles/2016/02/24/will-the-common-core-step-up-schools.html.

18. For instructions on how to make "zines," see John DePasquale, "Zine Making 101," Scholastic.com, April 29, 2016, https://www.google.com/search?q=zine+making+101+by+john+depasquale%2C+2015&ie=utf-8&oe=utf-8.

19. Roger Rosenblatt, "By the Book," *The New York Times*, January 10, 2016, Sunday Review, SR8.

20. Dwight Garner, "Review: Christopher Hitchens Expounds in 'And Yet,'" *New York Times,* November 24, 2015, Book Review, http://www.nytimes.com/2015/11/25/books/review-christopher-hitchens-expounds-in-and-yet.html.

21. Georgia Heard included this statement in her keynote address, "Writing Begins in Wonder," at the annual conference of the Colorado Council International Reading Association (CCIRA) in Denver, February 5, 2016.

22. Regie Routman, *Kids' Poems: Teaching Children to Love Writing Poetry;* series, separate volumes for kindergarten, grade 1, grade 2, and grades 3–4 (New York: Scholastic, 2000).

23. Linda Christensen and Dyan Watson, eds., *Rhythm and Resistance: Teaching Poetry for Social Justice* (Milwaukee, WI: Rethinking Schools, 2015), p. iv.

24. Regie Routman, *Kids' Poems: Teaching Third and Fourth Graders to Love Writing Poetry* (New York: Scholastic, 2000), pp. 30–34.

25. Christensen and Watson, 2015.

26. Kwame Alexander includes some great teaching ideas in his article "How Kwame Alexander Gets Teens Reading and Writing Poetry," *School Library Journal*, December 7, 2015 (originally published as an article in *School Library Journal*, November 2015), http://www.slj.com/2015/12/

teens-ya/how-kwame-alexander-gets-teens-reading-and-writing-poetry/#.

27. "Freedom Road," video, https://www.youtube.com/watch?v=bsCDwWepjFU. Created by Daria Orloff and Randal Bychuk with third- and fourth-grade students at Strathmillan School, Winnipeg, Canada.

28. For specifics, including "heart poems" lesson plans and students' published poems, see Regie Routman, *Writing Essentials: Raising Expectations and Results While Simplifying Teaching* (Portsmouth, NH: Heinemann, 2005), pp. 305–315, and the accompanying DVD with multiple student examples. See also *Heart Maps: Helping Students Create and Craft Authentic Writing* by Georgia Heard (Portsmouth, NH: Heinemann, 2016) for many examples of multi-genre heart maps, templates, and resulting poems by students.

Excellence 5: Teaching Readers

1. Giorgio Brunello, Guglielmo Weber, and Christoph Weiss, "Books Are Forever: Early Life Conditions, Education and Lifetime Earnings in Europe," *The Economic Journal*, April 25, 2016; cited in Jamie Doward, "Boys Who Live with Books 'Earn More as Adults,'" *The Guardian,* May 28, 2016, http://www.theguardian.com/education/2016/may/29/boys-books-earnings-adults.

2. Stephen Krashen, "Research Supports Value of School Libraries," Letters to the Editor, *Education Week,* June 1, 2016, pp. 28–29; Keith E. Stanovich, "Matthew Effects in Reading: Some Consequences of Individual Differences in the Acquisition of Literacy, *Reading Research Quarterly,* Fall 1986, pp. 380–382, http://people.uncw.edu/kozloffm/mattheweffect.pdf.

3. Ciara Nugent, "New Chapter for Classic Paris Bookstore: Books Printed on Demand in Minutes," *The New York Times,* June 13, 2016, Business Day, B1 and B3.

4. Naomi Baron, "Why Digital Reading Is No Substitute for Print," *The New Republic,* July 20, 2016, https://newrepublic.com/article/135326/digital-reading-no-substitute-print; Scholastic, *Kids and Family Reading Report,* 6th ed. (New York: Author, 2015), http://mediaroom.scholastic.com/kfrr.

5. Baron, 2016.

6. See Alison Flood, "Book Up for a Longer Life: Readers Die Later, Study Finds," *The Guardian,* December 15, 2016, https://www.theguardian.com/books/2016/aug/08/book-up-for-a-longer-life-readers-die-later-study-finds. Flood reported on a study by Avni Bavishi, Martin Slade, and Becca Levy from the Yale University School of Public Health, described in their paper "A Chapter a Day: Association of Book Reading with Longevity."

7. *New York Times* chief book critic Michiko Kakutani shared Obama's thoughts on reading based on her interview with him, as reported in "Obama's Secret to Surviving the White House Years: Books," *The New York Times*, January 16, 2017, A1 and A15, https://www.nytimes.com/2017/01/16/books/obamas-secret-to-surviving-the-white-house-years-books.html.

8. John Norton shared this information in an e-mail on June 6, 2016.

9. Stephen Krashen, "Learning to Read: There Is Nothing Magic About Grade 3," *SKrashen* (blog), May 7, 2016, http://skrashen.blogspot.com/2016/05/learning-to-read-there-is-nothing-magic.html. See also Stephen Krashen and Jeff McQuillan, "The Case for Late Intervention," *Educational Leadership*, October 2007, pp. 68–73.

10. Alice Ozma, *The Reading Promise: My Father and the Books We Shared* (New York: Grand Central Publishing, 2011).

11. Mem Fox, "What Next in the Read-Aloud Battle? Win or Lose?" *The Reading Teacher*, September 2013, pp. 4–8.

12. Sarah E. Peterson, "Using Storybooks to Enhance Literacy Development in Early Emergent Readers," *WSRA* [Wisconsin State Reading Association] *Journal*, Spring 2016, pp. 16–27.

13. Brian Dennis, Kirby Larson, and Mary Nethery, *Nubs: The True Story of a Mutt, a Marine, and a Miracle* (New York: Little, Brown, 2009). See also Larson and Nethery's excellent book, *Two Bobbies: A True Story of Hurricane Katrina, Friendship, and Survival* (New York: Walker, 2008).

14. Stephen Layne, *In Defense of Read-Aloud: Sustaining Best Practice* (Portland, ME: Stenhouse, 2015).

15. Perri Klass, "Turn the Page, Spur the Brain," *The New York Times,* August 18, 2015, Science Times, D6.

16. Peterson, 2016, p. 25.

17. Richard L. Allington, Kimberly McCuiston, and Monica Billen, "What Research Says About Text Complexity and Learning to Read," *The Reading Teacher*, April 2015, p. 495 (also citing other researchers); Stanovich, 1986, pp. 379–381.

18. Alexandra Spichtig, Elfrieda Hiebert, and others, "The Decline of Comprehension-Based Silent Reading Efficiency in the United States: A Comparison of Current Data with Performance in 1960," *Reading Research Quarterly,* April/May/June 2016, pp. 239–259.

19. Allington, McCuiston, and Billen, 2015, pp. 493–494.

20. Pernille Ripp, "6 Simple Ideas to Get Kids to Read," blog post, July 22, 2015, https://pernillesripp.com/2015/07/22/6-simple-ideas-to-get-kids-to-read.

21. Krashen, June 1, 2016.

22. All of the following sources cite multiple studies from reviews of the research: Stephen Krashen, "Free Voluntary Reading: New Research, Applications, and Controversies," paper presented at the RELC Conference, Singapore, April 2004, http://www.sdkrashen.com/content/articles/singapore.pdf; Regie Routman, *Reading Essentials: The Specifics You Need to Teach Reading Well* (Portsmouth, NH: Heinemann, 2003); Janice Pilgreen, *The SSR Handbook: How to Organize and Manage a Sustained Silent Reading Program* (Portsmouth, NH: Heinemann, 2000), http://www.teslej.org/wordpress/issues/volume4/ej16/ej16r14/?wscr.

23. Stanovich, 1986, as cited in Kath Glasswell and Michael Ford, "Let's Start Leveling About Leveling," *Language Arts,* January 2011, p. 213.

24. Stanovich, 1986, pp. 364–365, citing several researchers; Marie Clay, *Reading Recovery: A Guidebook for Teachers in Training* (Portsmouth, NH: Heinemann, 1993).

25. Stephen Krashen, "Learning to Read: There's Nothing Magic About Grade 3," *SKrashen* (blog), May 7, 2016, http://skrashen.blogspot.com/2016/05/learning-to-read-there-is-nothing-magic.html.

26. Stephen Krashen and Jeff McQuillan, "The Case for Late Intervention: Once a Good Reader, Always a Good Reader," in *Reconsidering a Balanced Approach to Reading,* ed. Constance Weaver (Urbana, IL: NCTE, 1998), Chapter 14, pp. 409–416, https://secure.ncte.org/library/NCTEFiles/Resources/Books/Sample/02344Chap14.pdf.

27. Trish Richardson shared her approach in an e-mail in July 2016.

28. The information about English language learners and the use of iPods comes from Megan Kowalski, "In Defense of Audio Books," *CRWP Teachers as Writers* (blog), January 18, 2016, http://chippewariverwp.org/blog/2016/01/18/in-defense-of-audio-books/.

29. Barbara A. Marinak and Linda Gambrell, *No More Reading for Junk: Best Practices for Motivating Readers* (Portsmouth, NH: Heinemann, 2016).

30. Shalina Chatlani, "Literary Fiction Here to Stay in Curriculum," *Education Dive,* October 4, 2016, http://www.educationdive.com/news/literary-fiction-here-to-stay-in-curriculum/427396/.

31. Charles McGrath, "Caution: Reading Can Be Hazardous," *New York Times,* December 8, 2013, Sunday Review, SR9, http://www.nytimes.com/2013/12/08/opinion/sunday/caution-reading-can-be-hazardous.html.

32. Mei Kuin Lai, Aaron Wilson, Stuart McNaughton, and Selena Hsiao, "Improving Achievement in Secondary Schools: Impact of a Literacy Project on Reading Comprehension and Secondary School Qualifications," *Reading Research Quarterly*, July–September 2014, pp. 305–306.

33. Steve Figurelli and Natalie Franzi, "Literacy in the Digital Age: Five Sites with High-Quality Informational Text," *Tchers' Voice* (blog), August 19, 2015, https://www.teachingchannel.org/blog/2015/08/19/literacy-in-the-digital-age-informational-text-sap/.

34. The information about teens becoming interested in science and the recommended titles—along with others—are from Deborah Farmer Kris, "14 Books That Connect Students with Valuable Scientists' Struggles," *Mind/Shift* (blog), May 26, 2016, https://ww2.kqed.org/mindshift/2016/05/26/14-books-that-connect-students-with-valuable-scientists-struggles/.

35. Peterson, 2016, p. 21.

36. Anne Niccoli, "Paper or Tablet? Reading Recall and Comprehension," *EDUCAUSEreview*, September 28, 2015, http://er.educause.edu/articles/2015/9/paper-or-tablet-reading-recall-and-comprehension.

37. Sean Cavanagh, "Demand for Print Persists Amid K–12 Digital Surge," *Education Week*, April 15, 2015, pp. 1 and 12, http://www.edweek.org/ew/articles/2015/04/15/k-12-schools-still-mix-print-and-digital.html.

38. Tom Newkirk, "Unbalanced Literacy: Reflections on the Common Core," *Language Arts*, March 2016, p. 305.

39. Heather Dean, "Creating Critical Readers: Connecting Close Reading and Technology," *The California Reader*, Summer 2017, Vol. 50, No. 4, pp. 8–11.

40. Niccoli, 2015.

41. W. Dorsey Hammond and Denise D. Nessel, *The Comprehension Experience: Engaging Readers Through Effective Inquiry and Discussion* (Portsmouth, NH: Heinemann, 2011), p. 39.

42. Jo Worthy and others, "What Are the Rest of the Students Doing? Literacy Work Stations in Two First-Grade Classrooms," *Language Arts,* January 2015, p. 184, citing Maloch and others, 2013, and Ford and Optiz, 2008.

43. Douglas Fisher, Nancy Frey, and John Hattie, *Visible Learning for Literacy, Grades K–12: Implementing the Practices That Work Best to Accelerate Student Learning* (Thousand Oaks, CA: Corwin, 2016), p. 162.

44. Kath Glasswell and Michael Ford, "Let's Start Leveling About Leveling," *Language Arts*, January 2011, pp. 211–212.

45. Peter Dewitz, Jennifer Jones, and Susan Leahy, "Comprehension Strategy Instruction in Core Reading Programs," *Reading Research Quarterly*, April–June 2009, pp. 102–126.

46. Allington, McCuiston, and Billen, 2015, p. 494.

47. Worthy and others, 2015, p. 183.

48. For detailed information on reading conferences, including viewing some examples, see Routman, 2003, pp. 100–111; and videos in Routman, 2008 and 2013, *Transforming Our Teaching Through Reading to Understand,* for procedures, questions to ask, and teaching points to make. To view a 17-minute conference with a fourth grader, see http://www.regieroutman.com/inresidence/rdg/samples.aspx. You can also view my videos of one-on-one conferences through a mini-course at Hein.pub/RoutmanOnDemand, 2017. For a blank Informal Reading Conference form, see *Reading Essentials* by Routman, 2003, Appendix H, p. A-9.

49. To view my interview with Kathy as a confident high school student, see http://regieroutman.com/inresidence/overview.aspx and click on "View Success Story."

Excellence 6: Teaching Writers

1. The quote is from a transcript of an interview of President Obama by chief *New York Times* book critic Michiko Kakutani: "Transcript: President Obama on What Books Mean to Him," *The New York Times*, January 16, 2017, https://www.nytimes.com/2017/01/16/books/transcript-president-obama-on-what-books-mean-to-him.html.

2. Carolyn Gregoire, "How to Think Like a Writer," *The Huffington Post*, May 15, 2014, http://www.huffingtonpost.com/2014/05/15/how-the-worlds-best-write_n_5331610.html.

3. Tom Newkirk, *Minds Made for Stories: How We Really Read and Write Informational and Persuasive Texts* (Portsmouth, NH: Heinemann, 2014), p. 19.

4. Douglas Martin, "William Zinsser, Author of 'On Writing Well,' Dies at 92" (obituary), *The New*

York Times, May 13, 2015, http://www.nytimes.com/2015/05/13/arts/william-zinsser-author-of-on-writing-well-dies-at-92.html?_r=0.

5.   Ta-Nehisi Coates, "Advice on Writing," video, *The Atlantic*, August 2015, https://www.facebook.com/TheAtlantic/videos/10153577188343487/.

6.   Regie Routman, "10 Surefire Ideas to Remove Writing Roadblocks," *MiddleWeb* (blog), January 2016, http://www.middleweb.com/26954/10-surefire-ideas-to-remove-writing-roadblocks/.

7.   Rusul Alrubail, "How to Use Social Media to Strengthen Student Writing," *Edutopia* (blog), February 13, 2016, http://www.edutopia.org/discussion/how-use-social-media-strengthen-student-writing.

8.   Scott Hamm, "Why Texting Should Be Part of Teaching," *EdTech,* March 30, 2015, http://www.edtechmagazine.com/k12/article/2015/03/why-texting-should-be-part-teaching.

9.   For many good ideas, see Steve Garbarino, "Five Practical Uses for a Vintage Manual Typewriter," *The Wall Street Journal,* December 26, 2014, http://www.wsj.com/articles/five-practical-uses-for-a-vintage-manual-typewriter-1419627431.

10.   Regie Routman, *Writing Essentials: Raising Expectations and Results While Simplifying Teaching* (Portsmouth, NH: Heinemann, 2005), pp. 112–118.

11.   You can view the video, "Freedom Road," on YouTube at https://www.youtube.com/watch?v=bsCDwWepjFU.

12.   Cathy Haruf, "Kent Haruf's *Our Souls at Night*: 'A Book About Us,'" *Picador Books* (blog), June 4, 2015, http://www.picador.com/blog/may-2015/%E2%80%8Bkent-harufs-our-souls-at-night-a-book-about-us.

13.   Matt Renwick shared this information in a tweet on July 25, 2016.

14.   Jay Matthews, "Writing Instruction in Our Schools Is Terrible. We Need to Fix It," *The Washington Post*, August 14, 2016, https://www.washingtonpost.com/local/education/writing-instruction-in-our-schools-is-terrible-we-need-to-fix-it/2016/08/14/a47b705e-6005-11e6-8e45-477372e89d78_story.html.

15.   For videos of editing conferences, see Regie Routman, *Regie Routman in Residence: Transforming Our Teaching* (Portsmouth, NH: Heinemann, 2008 and 2013), sessions 8, 9, and 10 in *Writing for Audience and Purpose*; see also the DVD that comes with Regie Routman, *Writing Essentials: Raising Expectations and Results While Simplifying Teaching* (Portsmouth, NH: Heinemann, 2005).

16.   Trish Richardson shared her experience in an e-mail on June 15, 2016.

17.   Carol Dweck, "The Journey to a Growth Mindset," general session keynote address, ASCD Annual Conference, Atlanta, Georgia, April 3, 2016.

18.   To view a public writing conference, see the sources in Note 15.

19.   Perri Klass, citing several research studies, in "Why Handwriting Is Still Essential in the Keyboard Age," *Well* (blog), *The New York Times,* June 20, 2016, http://well.blogs.nytimes.com/2016/06/20/why-handwriting-is-still-essential-in-the-keyboard-age/?_r=1.

20.   Eric Weiner, "In a Digital Chapter, Paper Notebooks Are as Relevant as Ever," National Public Radio, *Morning Edition,* May 27, 2015.

21.   This information comes from Steve Graham, professor of educational leadership and innovation at Arizona State University, reporting on long-term research, cited in Liana Heitin, "Why Don't the Common-Core Standards Include Cursive Writing?" *Education Week* (blog), October 10, 2016, http://blogs.edweek.org/edweek/curriculum/2016/10/why_dont_the_common-core_standards_include_cursive_writing.html?print=1.

22.   Pam A. Mueller and Daniel M. Oppenheimer, "The Pen Is Mightier Than the Keyboard: Advantages of Longhand over Laptop Note Taking," *Psychological Science*, June 2014, pp. 1159–1168. For easier access to that research, see James Doubek, "Attention, Students: Put Your Laptops Away" (transcript), National Public Radio, *Weekend Edition Sunday*, April 17, 2016, http://www.npr.org/2016/04/17/474525392/attention-students-put-your-laptops-away.

23. Lynn Allyson Matczuk, "A Comparative Examination of Outcomes of a Longitudinal Professional Development Experience in Writing Instruction in Schools for Kindergarten to Grade 3," unpublished dissertation, University of Manitoba, Winnipeg, Canada, 2016; Regie Routman, *Read, Write, Lead: Breakthrough Strategies for Schoolwide Literacy Success* (Alexandria, VA: ASCD, 2014).

24. Matczuk, p. 130.

25. Nicole Boudreau Smith, "A Principled Revolution in the Teaching of Writing," *English Journal*, May 2017, p. 71. For the term and explanation of *principled practices*, Smith acknowledges the work of Peter Smagorinsky in "Is It Time to Abandon the Idea of 'Best Practices' in the Teaching of English?" *English Journal*, June 2009, vol. 98, no. 6, pp. 15–22.

26. Stephen King, *On Writing: A Memoir of the Craft* (New York: Scribner, 2000), p. 236.

27. The quote from Jane Kenyon appears in Maria Popova, "Poet Jane Kenyon's Advice on Writing: Some of the Wisest Words to Create and Live By," Brainpickings.org, September 15, 2015, https://www.brainpickings.org/2015/09/15/jane-kenyon-advice-on-writing/.

EQUITY

Introduction

1. Pedro Noguera and Alan Blankstein, "Excellence Through Equity: Five Principles of Courageous Leadership to Guide Achievement for Every Student," second general session, a joint keynote address and presentation at the ASCD Annual Conference, Atlanta, Georgia, April 2, 2016.

2. Poverty and Race Research Action Council (PRRAC), "Annotated Bibliography: The Impact of School-Based Poverty Concentration on Academic Achievement and Student Outcomes," 2011, http://www.prrac.org/pdf/annotated_bibliography_on_school_poverty_concentration.pdf.

3. This statement comes from the research of Stanford University professor Sean Reardon, cited in Sarah D. Sparks, "Achievement Gaps and Racial Segregation: Research Finds an Insidious Cycle," *Education Week* (blog), April 29, 2016, http://blogs.edweek.org/edweek/inside-school-research/2016/04/achievement_gaps_school_segregation_reardon.html.

4. National Center for Children in Poverty, "Child Poverty," 2016, http://nccp.org/topics/childpoverty.html.

5. Sean F. Reardon, Jane Waldfogel, and Daphna Bassok, "The Good News About Educational Equality," *The New York Times,* August 28, 2016, Sunday Review, SR10, http://www.nytimes.com/2016/08/28/opinion/sunday/the-good-news-about-educational-inequality.html?_r=0.

6. Kate Zernike, "Heralded Choice Fails to Fix Detroit's Schools," *The New York Times*, June 29, 2016, A1.

7. Andrea Gabor, "The Myth of the New Orleans School Makeover," *The New York Times*, August 23, 2015, Sunday Review, SR3.

8. Regie Routman, *Read, Write, Lead: Breakthrough Strategies for Schoolwide Literacy Success* (Alexandria, VA: ASCD, 2014).

Equity 1: Making High Expectations an Instructional Reality

1. Douglas Fisher, Nancy Frey, and John Hattie, *Visible Learning for Literacy, Grades K–12: Implementing the Practices That Work Best to Accelerate Student Learning* (Thousand Oaks, CA: Corwin, 2016), p. 162.

2. Sheen S. Levine and David Stark, "Diversity Makes You Brighter," *The New York Times,* December 9, 2015, Op-Ed, A31, http://www.nytimes.com/2015/12/09/opinion/diversity-makes-you-brighter.html?_r=0.

3. The quote is from research by Teaching Tolerance, an educational project of the Southern Poverty Law Center, cited in Melinda D. Anderson, "When Black and White Children Grow

Apart," *The Atlantic,* June 14, 2016, http://www.theatlantic.com/education/archive/2016/06/interracial-friendships-fade/486902/.

4. Elizabeth A. Harris, citing Richard D. Kahlenberg, a senior fellow at the Century Foundation, a public policy research group, in "Small Steps, but No Major Push, to Integrate New York's Schools," The New York Times, July 6, 2016, A1, https://www.nytimes.com/2016/07/06/nyregion/new-york-city-schools-segregation-carmen-farina.html.

5. Anderson, 2016, citing two reports by the Century Foundation, a progressive policy and research think tank.

6. Emma Brown, "On the Anniversary of Brown v. Board, New Evidence That U.S. Schools Are Resegregating," *The Washington Post,* May 17, 2016, Education, https://www.washingtonpost.com/news/education/wp/2016/05/17/on-the-anniversary-of-brown-v-board-new-evidence-that-u-s-schools-are-resegregating/.

7. Claudia Rowe, citing comments by Seattle mayor Ed Murray at a local education summit, in "Garfield High Principal Wrestles with City's Divides," *The Seattle Times,* June 26, 2016, A1, A16, and A17.

8. Rowe, 2016, A17.

9. Justin Trudeau, "Justin Trudeau Explains the Power of Diversity," video, Davos, Switzerland, January 21, 2016, http://qz.com/602525/justin-trudeau-perfectly-articulates-the-value-of-diversity-in-childhood-not-just-in-the-workforce/.

10. Anderson, 2016, citing a research study by Elise Cappella, associate professor of applied psychology at New York University and lead author.

11. Amy Stuart Wells, Lauren Fox, and Diana Cordova-Cobo, *How Racially Diverse Schools and Classrooms Can Benefit All Students* (New York City and Washington, DC: The Century Foundation, February 9, 2016), p. 63.

12. See Lorna Collier, "No Longer Invisible: How Diverse Literature Helps Children Find Themselves in Books, and Why It Matters," *The Council Chronicle,* National Council of Teachers of English (NCTE), September 2016, p. 16; Jessica Lifshitz, "Having Students Analyze Our Classroom Library to See How Diverse It Is," *Crawling Out of the Classroom* (blog), May 7, 2016, "https://crawlingoutoftheclassroom.wordpress.com/2016/05/07/having-students-analyze-our-classroom-library-to-see-how-diverse-it-is/; and Jonda C. McNair, "#WeNeedMirrorsAndWindows: Diverse Classroom Libraries for K–6 Students," *The Reading Teacher,* November–December 2016, pp. 375–381.

13. Tammy Campbell, "Stereotyped at Seven? Biases in Teacher Judgment of Pupils' Ability and Attainment," *Journal of Social Policy*, July 2015, pp. 517–547, https://doi.org/10.1017/S0047279415000227.

14. Nikole Hannah-Jones, "Worlds Apart," *The New York Times Magazine*, June 12, 2016, p. 37, http://www.nytimes.com/2016/06/12/magazine/choosing-a-school-for-my-daughter-in-a-segregated-city.html.

15. Jason A. Grissom and Christopher Redding, "Discretion and Disproportionality: Explaining the Underrepresentation of High-Achieving Students of Color in Gifted Programs," *AERA Open,* January 19, 2016, http://www.aera.net/Newsroom/News-Releases-and-Statements/Does-Student-Race-Affect-Gifted-Assignment/Discretion-and-Disproportionality-Explaining-the-Underrepresentation-of-High-Achieving-Students-of-Color-in-Gifted-Programs.

16. Brown, 2016, citing data from the Government Accountability Office.

17. Regie Routman, *Read, Write, Lead: Breakthrough Strategies for Schoolwide Literacy Success* (Alexandria, VA: ASCD, 2014).

18. Terry Heick, "Are You Teaching Content or Teaching Thought?" *TeachThought: We Grow Teachers* (blog), February 27, 2014, http://www.teachthought.com/critical-thinking/teaching-content-or-teaching-thought/.

19. John Hattie, *Visible Learning for Teachers: Maximizing Impact on Learning* (New York: Routledge, 2012), p. 80.

20. William H. Parrett and Kathleen M. Budge, "5 Questions That Promote Student Success in High-Poverty Schools," *Edutopia: Education Equity,* June 15, 2016, http://www.edutopia.org/blog/high-poverty-schools-promote-student-success-william-parrett-kathleen-budge.

21. Daria Orloff's statements are part of a reflection she wrote on January 6, 2017.

22. Paige Cornwell, reporting on Mehta's findings, in "Deeper Learning: More Crucial Than Ever, Yet Too Rare," *The Seattle Times*, May 11, 2016, *Education Lab,* B2, http://www.seattletimes.com/education-lab/a-deep-dive-into-deeper-learning/.

23. David Kirp, "How to Nudge Students to Succeed," *The New York Times,* October 30, 2016, Sunday Review, SR2, http://www.nytimes.com/2016/10/30/opinion/nudges-that-help-struggling-students-succeed.html?_r=0.

24. Society for Research in Child Development, reporting on a study led by David S. Yeager at the University of Texas at Austin, in "For Youth of Color, Losing Trust in Teachers May Mean Losing the Chance to Make It to College," *Science Daily,* February 8, 2017, https://www.sciencedaily.com/releases/2017/02/170208094432.htm.

25. Jinnie Spiegler, "Turning Current Events Instruction into Social Justice Teaching," *Edutopia* (blog), January 6, 2016, http://www.edutopia.org/blog/current-events-social-justice-teaching-jinnie-spiegler. The author is the director of curriculum at the Anti-Defamation League. Her blog post includes excellent ideas for instruction.

26. Michael Fullan and Joanne Quinn, *Coherence: The Right Drivers in Action for Schools, Districts, and Systems* (Thousand Oaks, CA: Corwin, 2016), p. 111, paraphrasing the work of Richard Elmore.

27. Jay Matthews, "Writing Instruction in Our Schools Is Terrible. We Need to Fix It," *The Washington Post*, August 14, 2016, https://www.washingtonpost.com/local/education/writing-instruction-in-our-schools-is-terrible-we-need-to-fix-it/2016/08/14/a47b705e-6005-11e6-8e45-477372e89d78_story.html.

28. Nancy Boyles, "Pursuing the Depths of Knowledge," *Educational Leadership*, October 2016, p. 46.

29. Diane Ravitch, "Renouncing the Common Core," *The New York Times,* July 24, 2016, Sunday Review, SR9, http://www.nytimes.com/2016/07/24/opinion/sunday/the-common-core-costs-billions-and-hurts-students.html?_r=0.

30. Tom Loveless, "The 2012 Brown Center Report on American Education: How Well Are American Students Learning?" (Washington, DC: Brookings Institution, 2012), https://www.brookings.edu/wp-content/uploads/2016/07/0216_brown_education_loveless.pdf.

31. Jeff Anderson, "Zooming In and Zooming Out: Putting Grammar in Context into Context," *English Journal*, May 2006, p. 29. This is the best article I've read on teaching grammar.

32. Meghan D. Liebfreund, "Success with Informational Text Comprehension: An Examination of Underlying Factors," *Reading Research Quarterly,* October/November/December 2015, pp. 387–392.

33. Stephen Krashen, "Reading for Pleasure Can Close 'Vocabulary Gap' at Any Age," Letters to the Editor, *Education Week*, May 13, 2015, p. 24, citing a study by Alice Sullivan and Matt Brown of the Center for Longitudinal Studies at the University of London.

34. Meghan K. Block and Nell K. Duke, "Preschool Through Grade 3: Letter Names Can Cause Confusion and Other Things to Know About Letter-Sound Relationships," *Young Children,* March 2015, p. 85.

35. Deborah Meier, "How Our Schools Could Be," *Phi Delta Kappan*, January 1995, p. 371.

36. Richard Allington, "What At-Risk Readers Need," *Educational Leadership*, March 2011, p. 41.

Equity 2: Reaching All Learners

1. Carol Dweck, *Mindset: The New Psychology of Success* (New York: Random House, 2006).
2. Christina Samuels, citing a report from America's Promise Alliance, in "Special Education Graduation Disparities Highlighted in New Report," *Education Week, On Special Education* (blog), January 21, 2016, http://blogs.edweek.org/edweek/speced/2016/01/special_education_graduation_d.html.
3. Nadia Lopez, with Rebecca Paley, *The Bridge to Brilliance: How One Principal in a Tough Community Is Inspiring the World* (New York: Viking, 2016), p. 246 (phrases in quotes are my own).
4. Donna De La Cruz, "What Kids Wish Their Teachers Knew," *The New York Times*, August 31, 2016, http://www.nytimes.com/2016/08/31/well/family/what-kids-wish-their-teachers-knew.html. See also #iwishmyteacherknew on Twitter.
5. Dwayne Reed, "Welcome to the Fourth Grade," video rap song, https://www.youtube.com/watch?v=XBLcuGunRxU&feature=youtu.be.
6. Sherman Alexie and Yuyi Morales, *Thunder Boy Jr.* (New York and Boston: Little, Brown, 2016).
7. Corey Mitchell, "Mispronouncing Students' Names: A Slight That Can Cut Deep," *Education Week* (blog), May 10, 2016, http://www.edweek.org/ew/articles/2016/05/11/mispronouncing-students-names-a-slight-that-can.html?cmp=SOC-SHR-twitter.
8. The last question is from Nadia Lopez, 2016, p. 228.
9. Corey Mitchell, "Does the Term 'English-Language Learner' Carry a Negative Connotation?" *Education Week* (blog), February 1, 2016, http://blogs.edweek.org/edweek/learning-the-language/2016/02/does_the_term_english-language.html.
10. Daniel Bergner, *Sing for Your Life: A Story of Race, Music, and Family* (New York: Lee Boudreaux Books, 2016).
11. Denise Krebs and Gallit Zvi, *The Genius Hour Guidebook: Fostering Passion, Wonder, and Inquiry in the Classroom* (New York and London: Routledge, 2016).
12. Krebs and Zvi, 2016; Terry Heick, "6 Principles of Genius Hour in the Classroom," *TeachThought: We Grow Teachers* (blog), September 28, 2014, http://www.teachthought.com/learning/6-principles-of-genius-hour-in-the-classroom/.
13. Dweck, 2006.
14. For picture book examples, see the *Teaching Essentials* website at www.regieroutman.com/teachingessentials/default.asp. Click on "Text Resources" and "I Can Do It! A Selected Book List to Inspire Hope."
15. Jo Worthy and others, "What Are the Rest of the Students Doing? Literacy Work Stations in Two First-Grade Classrooms," *Language Arts,* January 2015, pp. 173–186.
16. What Works Clearinghouse, http://ies.ed.gov/ncee/wwc/; and Henry May, Philip Sirinides, Abigail Gray, and Heather Goldsworthy, *Reading Recovery: An Evaluation of the Four-Year i3 Scale-Up,"* research report (Philadelphia: Consortium for Policy Research in Education, University of Pennsylvania; and Newark, DE: Center for Research in Education and Social Policy, University of Delaware, March 2016), http://www.cpre.org/sites/default/files/reading_recovery_final_report.pdf.
17. Regie Routman, *Read, Write, Lead: Breakthrough Strategies for Schoolwide Literacy Success* (Alexandria, VA: ASCD, 2014). In same text, also see Chapter 4, "Reducing the Need for Intervention," pp.137–180, for ideas and strategies (available at http://www.ascd.org/publications/books/113016/chapters/Reducing-the-Need-for-Intervention.aspx).
18. Sarah Sparks, "Focus on Fade-Out (Part 2): What We Learn from Lost Effects in Education," *Education Week* (blog), January 20, 2016, http://blogs.edweek.org/edweek/inside-school-research/2016/01/fade-out_2_faltering_education.html.

19. Sarah Sparks, "RTI Practice Falls Short of Promise, Research Finds," *Education Week*, November 11, 2015, pp. 1 and 12, http://www.edweek.org/ew/articles/2015/11/11/study-rti-practice-falls-short-of-promise.html.

20. John Hattie, *Visible Learning* (New York: Routledge, 2009). This superb text comprises a meta-analysis of educational research; that is, the author has analyzed the results of multiple studies to draw his conclusions.

21. Dylan Wiliam, "The Secret of Effective Feedback," *Educational Leadership*, April 2016, p. 10, http://www.ascd.org/publications/educational-leadership/apr16/vol73/num07/The-Secret-of-Effective-Feedback.aspx.

22. This word wall story is adapted from Regie Routman, *Teaching Essentials: Expecting the Most and Getting the Best from Every Learner, K–8* (Portsmouth, NH: Heinemann, 2008), p. 44.

23. Hattie, 2009, p. 174, citing research of Graham Nuthall, *The Hidden Lives of Learners* (Wellington, NZ: New Zealand Council for Educational Research Press, 2007).

24. Wiliam, 2016, p. 11.

25. Hattie, 2009, p. 173.

26. Joe Levitan, "Bilingual Students Need Support in Their Native Language," Commentary, *Education Week*, May 12, 2015, http://www.edweek.org/ew/articles/2015/05/13/bilingual-students-need-support-in-their-native.html.

27. Both quotes are from Héctor Tobar, "The Spanish Lesson I Never Got at School," *The New York Times*, November 15, 2016, Op-Ed, A27, http://www.nytimes.com/2016/11/15/opinion/the-spanish-lesson-i-never-got-at-school.html?_r=0.

28. The ideas in this paragraph come from Sandra Figueroa, a participant in a conference session at the California Reading Association Annual Professional Development Institute, November 5, 2016, Visalia, California.

29. Claude Goldenberg, "Teaching English Language Learners: What the Research Does—and Does Not—Say," *American Educator*, Summer 2008, p. 15 for quote on teaching reading, and p. 17 for sentence on vocabulary acquisition. An excellent, comprehensive resource.

30. The statements about biliteracy are based on James Cohen, Sadie McCarthy, and John Evar Strid, "Why Should a Monolingual English Speaking Reading Teacher Advocate for Biliteracy of English Learners?" *Illinois Reading Council Journal*, Spring 2016, pp. 20–27.

31. The suggestions related to tiered questions are from Jane Hill, "Engaging Your Beginners," *Educational Leadership*, themed issue, "Helping ELLs Excel," February 2016, pp. 18–23.

32. Ilana M. Umansky, Rachel A. Valentino, and Sean F. Reardon, "The Promise of Two-Language Education," *Educational Leadership*, February 2016, themed issue, "Helping ELLs Excel," pp. 10–17.

33. Barry Lee Reynolds, "A Mixed-Methods Approach to Investigating First- and Second-Language Incidental Vocabulary Acquisition Through Reading of Fiction," *Reading Research Quarterly*, January/February/March 2015, pp. 111–127.

34. Katrina Schwartz, "Why Group Work Could Be the Key to English Learner Success," *Mind/Shift*, February 23, 2017, https://ww2.kqed.org/mindshift/2017/02/23/why-group-work-could-be-the-key-to-english-learner-success/.

35. Jane Medina, *My Name Is Jorge on Both Sides of the River: Poems in English and Spanish* (Honesdale, PA: WordSong, 1999).

36. The ideas in this paragraph are from Alyson Klein, "Teaching America's English-Language Learners: For Stalled ELL Students, Graduation Is Often an Elusive Goal," *Education Week*, May 11, 2016, http://www.edweek.org/ew/articles/2016/05/11/for-stalled-ell-students-graduation-is-often.html.

37. Wayne E. Wright, "Let Them Talk!" *Educational Leadership*, February 2016, themed issue, "Helping ELLs Excel," p. 27.

38. This twelve-point list, slightly adapted here, first appeared in Larry Ferlazzo, "Response: Teach English-Language Learners by Meeting Them 'Where They Are,'" *Education Week Teacher* (blog), October 24, 2015, http://blogs.edweek.org/teachers/classroom_qa_with_larry_ferlazzo/2015/10/response_teach_english_language_learners_by_meeting_them_where_they_are.html.

39. Wright, 2016.

40. The quote is from an e-mail from Sharline Markwardt, July 2013.

Equity 3: Applying Responsible Assessment

1. Pasi Sahlberg, "Learning from Finland: How One of the World's Top Educational Performers Turned Around," *Boston Globe,* December 27, 2010, Op-Ed, http://archive.boston.com/bostonglobe/editorial_opinion/oped/articles/2010/12/27/learning_from_finland/.

2. Rick Stiggins, "Improve Assessment Literacy Outside of Schools Too," *Phi Delta Kappan*, October 2014, p. 68.

3. Linda Darling-Hammond tweeted the following on July 2, 2014: "Test-based accountability produced no gains from 2000–2012 on PISA. Time for a new approach?" https://twitter.com/ldh_ed/status/484388825645326337.

4. Denisa R. Superville, "Students Take Too Many Redundant Tests, Study Finds," *Education Week,* October 24, 2015, http://www.edweek.org/ew/articles/2015/10/28/students-take-too-many-redundant-tests-study.html.

5. Benjamin Herold, "PARCC Scores Lower for Students Who Took Exams on Computers," *Education Week,* February 3, 2016, p. 1, http://www.edweek.org/ew/articles/2016/02/03/parcc-scores-lower-on-computer.html.

6. Carol Ann Tomlinson and Michael Murphy, *Leading for Differentiation: Growing Teachers Who Grow Kids* (Alexandria, VA: ASCD, 2015), p. 150.

7. W. James Popham, *Transformative Assessment* (Alexandria, VA: ASCD, 2008), p. 16.

8. John Hattie, "High-Impact Leadership," *Educational Leadership*, February 2015, pp. 36–40; and John Hattie, *Visible Learning* (New York: Routledge, 2009).

9. Paul Black and Dylan Wiliam, "Inside the Black Box: Raising Standards Through Classroom Assessment," *Phi Delta Kappan*, October 1998, pp. 139–144, http://www.rdc.udel.edu/wp-content/uploads/2015/04/InsideBlackBox.pdf. The authors present the results of a meta-analysis—i.e., analysis of the results of multiple studies; this is a terrific article for understanding and applying formative assessment.

10. The quote is from Rick Stiggins, in Catherine Gewertz, "Q and A: Misconceptions About Formative Assessment," November 9, 2015, *Education Week*, http://www.edweek.org/ew/articles/2015/11/11/qa-misconceptions-about-formative-assessment.html.

11. Superville, 2015, for statements on over-testing and redundancy, the lag in getting results, and use of tests for teacher evaluation. The article reports on a review of testing in sixty-six urban districts.

12. Jeff Anderson, "Zooming In and Zooming Out: Putting Grammar in Context into Context," *English Journal*, May 2006, p. 33. The words in brackets are mine.

13. Al Churchill, citing a recent study by psychologists at Harvard, Brown, and the Massachusetts Institute of Technology, in "Put Down Your No. 2 Pencils: Too Much Testing in Public Schools," Guest Commentary, Bridge: The Center for Michigan, May 20, 2016, http://bridgemi.com/2016/05/put-down-your-no-2-pencils-too-much-testing-in-public-schools/.

14. See Regie Routman, *Read, Write, Lead: Breakthrough Strategies for Schoolwide Literacy Success* (Alexandria, VA: ASCD, 2014), Appendix F, pp. 294–295, for test directions and analysis.

15. Anya Kamenetz, *The Test: Why Our Schools Are Obsessed with Standardized Testing—But You Don't Have to Be* (New York: Public Affairs, 2015), p. 135.

16. Dylan Wiliam, "Assessment: The Bridge Between Teaching and Learning," *Voices from the Middle*, December 2013, p. 17.
17. Lori Johnson shared these thoughts in an e-mail in May 2016.
18. Anthony S. Byrk, "Accelerating How We Learn to Improve," 2014 AERA Distinguished Lecture, *Educational Researcher*, December 2015, p. 468.
19. Sheila Valencia and Marsha Riddle Buly, "Behind Test Scores: What Struggling Readers *Really* Need," in *Reading Assessment Principles and Practices for Elementary Teachers*, 2nd ed., ed. Shelby J. Barrentine and Sandra M. Stokes (Newark, DE: International Reading Association, 2005), pp. 134–146.
20. See Regie Routman, *Literacy at the Crossroads: Crucial Talk About Reading, Writing, and Other Teaching Dilemmas* (Portsmouth, NH: Heinemann, 1996), pp. 159–163, for guidelines and student examples.
21. Brooke Benmar offered these comments in a conversation in August 2016.
22. Thomas Newkirk, "A Mania for Rubrics," Commentary, *Education Week*, September 13, 2000, http://www.edweek.org/ew/articles/2000/09/13/02newkirk.h20.html.
23. Dennis Kafalas, "Working and Conferencing with a Rubric: Easy Tweaks for Effort + Quality," *The Cornerstone for Teachers* (blog), September 10, 2015, https://www.google.com/search?q=the+cornerstoneforteachers.com%2F2015%2F09%2Feasy-rubric-tweaks.html&ie=utf-8&oe=utf-8.
24. Matt Glover and Ellin Oliver Keene, eds., citing Dennie Palmer Wolf, in *The Teacher You Want to Be: Essays About Children, Learning, and Teaching* (Portsmouth, NH: Heinemann, 2015), p. 188.
25. Kafalas, 2015.
26. Jan Burkins and Kim Yaris, *Who's Doing the Work? How to Say Less So Readers Can Do More* (Portland, ME: Stenhouse, 2016), p. 5.
27. Peter Afflerbach, "Self-Assessment and Reading Success," *Reading Today*, November/December 2014, pp. 29–31.

Equity 4: Developing Self-Determining Learners

1. Adapted from Daniel Pink, *Drive: The Surprising Truth About What Motivates Us* (New York: Riverhead Books, 2009), pp. 207–208.
2. Jan Burkins and Kim Yaris, *Who's Doing the Work? How to Say Less So Readers Can Do More* (Portland, ME: Stenhouse, 2016), p. 6.
3. Fareed Zakaria, *In Defense of a Liberal Education* (New York: W. W. Norton, 2015), p. 78.
4. Linda Darling-Hammond, "Now We Confront the Real Equity Challenge: Providing Access to 21st Century Learning," *Learning Policy Institute* (blog), December 11, 2015, https://learningpolicyinstitute.org/blog/now-we-confront-real-equity-challenge-providing-access-21st-century-learning.
5. Gloria Steinem, interview, *The Tavis Smiley Show*, National Public Radio, November 2, 2015.
6. John Hattie, *Visible Learning* (New York: Routledge, 2009).
7. Steinem, 2015.
8. Regie Routman, *Literacy at the Crossroads: Crucial Talk About Reading, Writing, and Other Teaching Dilemmas* (Portsmouth, NH: Heinemann, 1996), pp. 153–155.
9. Linda Rief, *100 Quickwrites: Fast and Effective Freewriting Exercises That Build Students' Confidence, Develop Their Fluency, and Bring Out the Writer in Every Student* (New York: Scholastic, 2003).
10. Sarah Sparks, "RTI Practice Falls Short of Promise, Research Finds," *Education Week*, November 11, 2015, pp. 1 and 12, http://www.edweek.org/ew/articles/2015/11/11/study-rti-practice-falls-short-of-promise.html.

11. The text here is adapted from my response to the question "How can we use goal setting with our students?" See Larry Ferlazzo, "Response: 'Provide "Voice" and "Choice" When Students Set Goals,'" *Education Week Teacher* (blog), January 17, 2017, http://blogs.edweek.org/teachers/classroom_qa_with_larry_ferlazzo/2017/01/response_provide_voice_choice_when_students_set_goals.html.

12. Susan M. Brookhart, *How to Design Questions and Tasks to Assess Student Thinking* (Alexandria, VA: ASCD, 2014), p. 2.

13. To view detailed information on self-directed groups, see *Regie Routman in Residence: Transforming Our Teaching,* video-based literacy series (Portsmouth, NH: Heinemann, 2008, 2013). See *Transforming Our Teaching Through Reading/Writing Connections,* Session 7, "Shared Writing to Reading," for self-directed, small-group revision on a class-authored writing.

14. Susan M. Brookhart and Connie M. Moss, "Leading by Learning," *Phi Delta Kappan*, May 2013, p. 17.

15. Jo Boaler, "Mistakes Grow Your Brain," Youcubed at Stanford University, 2015, https://www.youcubed.org/think-it-up/mistakes-grow-brain/. The article includes a music video featuring enthusiastic middle school students at a "mistake-friendly" summer math camp.

16. Mary Beth Nicklaus, "Gloom, Despair, and Strawberry Pop Tarts: Failure Stories and Their Effect on Agency During the Bad Days in the Reading Intervention Classroom," *WSRA* [Wisconsin State Reading Association] *Journal*, Spring 2016, pp. 69–70.

17. Mary Beth Nicklaus shared these observations in an e-mail on November 1, 2016. Nicklaus's teacher-research involves encouraging writing and publication as a way to increase reading skills.

18. The quote is from an interview with Larry Page and Sergey Brin conducted by Barbara Walters of *ABC News* on December 8, 2004, and cited in Walter Isaacson, *The Innovators: How a Group of Hackers, Geniuses, and Geeks Created the Digital Revolution* (New York: Simon and Schuster, 2014), pp. 451–452.

Equity 5: Advocating for Students

1. Nicholas Kristof, "From Somaliland to Harvard," *The New York Times,* September 13, 2015, Sunday Review, SR1, https://www.nytimes.com/2015/09/13/opinion/sunday/nicholas-kristof-from-somaliland-to-harvard.html.

2. Nikole Hannah-Jones, "Have We Lost Sight of the Promise of Public Schools?" *The New York Times Magazine*, February 26, 2017, p. 15, https://www.nytimes.com/2017/02/21/magazine/have-we-lost-sight-of-the-promise-of-public-schools.html?_r=0.

3. Arianna Prothero, "Charter Schools Aren't Good for Blacks, Civil Rights Groups Say," *Education Week,* August 30, 2016, http://www.edweek.org/ew/articles/2016/08/31/charter-schools-arent-good-for-blacks-civil.html.

4. Michael Mulgrew, "The Essence of Wrongheaded School 'Reform,'" Commentary, *Education Week,* December 9, 2015, p. 21. Mulgrew is president of the United Federation of Teachers in New York City.

5. Kate Zernike, quoting Amber Areliano, executive director of the Education Trust Midwest, in "Heralded Choice Fails to Fix Detroit's Schools," *The New York Times*, June 29, 2016, A14.

6. Hannah-Jones, 2017, p. 15.

7. Kevin Carey, "Dismal Results from Vouchers Surprise Researchers," *The New York Times*, February 24, 2017, A20, https://www.nytimes.com/2017/02/23/upshot/dismal-results-from-vouchers-surprise-researchers-as-devos-era-begins.html?_r=0.

8. Andrew Ujifusa, "Nationwide Voucher Program Could Cripple Most Districts, Report Argues," *Education Week, Charters and Choice* (blog), March 6, 2017, http://blogs.edweek.org/edweek/charterschoice/2017/03/report_nationwide_voucher_program_could_cripple_vast_majority_of_districts.html?cmp=soc-edit-tw.

9. The observations in this paragraph are based on Arianna Prothero, "Does Graduating from a Charter Help or Hinder Future Earnings?" *Education Week,* September 13, 2016, http://www.edweek.org/ew/articles/2016/09/14/does-graduating-from-a-charter-help-or.html.

10. Rebecca Solnit, *Hope in the Dark: Untold Histories, Wild Possibilities* (Chicago: Haymarket Books, 2016), pp. 118–120, for comments on September 11 and related behavior.

11. Andy Hargreaves, "The Iniquity of Inequality: And Some International Clues About Ways to Address It," in Alan M. Blankstein and Pedro Noguera, with Lorena Kelly, *Excellence Through Equity: Five Principles of Courageous Leadership to Guide Achievement for Every Student* (Alexandria, VA: ASCD, 2016), p. 284.

12. Kevin Carey, "The Uproar Over Trying to Help Poor Schoolchildren," *The New York Times,* May 19, 2016, The Upshot, A3, https://www.nytimes.com/2016/05/18/upshot/why-poor-districts-receive-less-government-school-funding-than-rich-ones.html.

13. Sarah D. Sparks, "Achievement Gaps and Racial Segregation: Research Finds an Insidious Cycle," *Education Week* (blog), April 29, 2016, http://blogs.edweek.org/edweek/inside-school-research/2016/04/achievement_gaps_school_segregation_reardon.html.

14. Sean Reardon and other researchers, quoted in Sparks, April 29, 2016.

15. Dale Russakoff, *The Prize: Who's in Charge of America's Schools?* (New York: Houghton Mifflin Harcourt, 2015).

16. Mulgrew, 2015, p. 21.

17. Russakoff, 2015, p. 217.

18. *New York Times* Editorial Board, "Schoolchildren Left Behind," editorial, November 12, 2016, A24, http://www.nytimes.com/2016/11/12/opinion/schoolchildren-left-behind.html?_r=0.

19. Information about the reading setback is from Richard Allington and Anne McGill-Franzen, "Won't Read Much If I Don't Have Any Books: Access to Books, and the Rich/Poor Reading Achievement Gap," *Heinemann* (blog), May 22, 2014, http://www.heinemann.com/blog/wont-read-much-if-i-dont-have-any-books-poverty-access-to-books-and-the-richpoor-reading-achievement-gap/.

20. Paige Cornwell, "Seattle's School Libraries: A Stark Example of Rich and Poor," *The Seattle Times,* May 8, 2016, Education Lab, A1 and A8, http://www.seattletimes.com/seattle-news/education/librarians-urging-equality-in-school-libraries/.

21. Kanoe Namahoe, "Disrupting Our Default Settings," SmartBrief, September 16, 2016, http://www.smartbrief.com/original/2016/09/disrupting-our-default-settings. The quote paraphrases comments made by sociologist and Princeton University assistant professor Ruha Benjamin in her keynote address to the 2016 Conference of the International Society for Technology in Education.

22. Walter Isaacson, *The Innovators: How a Group of Hackers, Geniuses, and Geeks Created the Digital Revolution* (New York: Simon and Schuster, 2014), p. 485.

23. Anya Kamenetz, "Caution Flags for Tech in Classrooms," *nprED* (blog), National Public Radio, August 11, 2016, https://www.google.com/search?q=Kamenetz%2C+Anya.+August+11%2C+2016.+%E2%80%9CCaution+Flags+for+Tech+in+Classrooms.%E2%80%9D+National+Public+Radio&ie=utf-8&oe=utf-8. Kamenetz is quoting from the findings of a report by the Organization for Economic Co-operation and Development (OECD), which administers the international PISA test.

24. Kamenetz, August 11, 2016, again quoting the OECD report.

25. Barb Ide shared her thoughts in an e-mail on March 15, 2015.

26. Jeff Guo, "Why Smart Kids Shouldn't Use Laptops in Class," *Wonkblog* (blog), *The Washington*

Post, May 16, 2016, https://www.washingtonpost.com/news/wonk/wp/2016/05/16/why-smart-kids-shouldnt-use-laptops-in-class/.

27. Matt Renwick, "Why I am #NotatISTE16," *Reading by Example* (blog), June 25, 2016, https://readingbyexample.com/2016/06/25/why-i-am-notatiste16/. The four Cs, as identified by the Partnership for 21st Century Learning, are creativity, critical thinking, collaboration, and communication.

28. Natasha Singer, "Amazon to Pursue Education Technology with a Marketplace for Teachers," *The New York Times*, June 28, 2016, B8, https://www.nytimes.com/2016/06/28/technology/amazon-unveils-online-education-service-for-teachers.html.

29. Alex Lenkei, citing a research study by Naomi Baron and a study by Scholastic, in "Students Prefer Print: Why Are Schools Pushing Digital Textbooks?" *Education Week, BookMarks* (blog), March 7, 2016, http://blogs.edweek.org/edweek/bookmarks/2016/03/students_prefer_print_schools_pushing_digital_textbooks.html.

30. Scott Hamm, "Why Texting Should Be Part of Teaching," *EdTech,* March 30, 2015, http://www.edtechmagazine.com/k12/article/2015/03/why-texting-should-be-part-teaching.

31. Paul Barnwell, "Blended Learning: Will Giving Greater Student Access to Smartphones Improve Learning?" *The Hechinger Report*, April 27, 2016, http://hechingerreport.org/will-giving-greater-student-access-smartphones-improve-learning/.

32. Lisa Stark, "Boston Brings the Music Back by Boosting Arts Education," *PBS NewsHour*, September 27, 2016, http://www.pbs.org/newshour/bb/boston-brings-music-back-boosting-arts-education/.

33. *Education Week*, reporting on a research study comparing views and experiences of kindergarten teachers in 1998 and 2010, in "Kindergarten Today: Less Play, More Academics," February 10, 2016, http://www.edweek.org/ew/section/multimedia/kindergarten-less-play-more-academics.html.

34. Adam Grant, *Originals: How Non-Conformists Move the World* (New York: Viking, 2016), pp. 46–47.

35. Anna Feldman, "STEAM Rising: Why We Need to Put the Arts into STEM Education," *Slate,* June 16, 2015, http://www.slate.com/articles/technology/future_tense/2015/06/steam_vs_stem_why_we_need_to_put_the_arts_into_stem_education.htm.

36. Elisha McNeil, "English Teachers' Hip-Hop Curriculum Gets Students Writing," *Education Week Teacher*, June 20, 2016, http://www.edweek.org/tm/articles/2016/06/20/english-teachers-hip-hop-curriculum-gets-students-writing.html. The quote is from English teacher and author Lauren Leigh Kelly.

37. Randal Bychuk made this statement in an e-mail, September 11, 2016.

38. Christopher Jobson, "Artist Theaster Gates Bought a Crumbling Chicago Bank for $1 and Turned It into a World-Class Arts Center," *Colossal* (blog), October 13, 2015, http://www.thisiscolossal.com/2015/10/stony-island-arts-bank/.

39. Literacy coach Lori Johnson shared her experience in an e-mail in January 2016.

40. Anthony S. Byrk, "Accelerating How We Learn to Improve," 2014 AERA Distinguished Lecture, *Educational Researcher*, December 2015, p. 468.

41. Lori Johnson shared this observation in an e-mail on January 8, 2016.

42. Regie Routman, *Transitions: From Literature to Literacy* (Portsmouth, NH: Heinemann, 1988).

43. Sarah D. Sparks, "New 'What Works Clearinghouse' Aims to Help Districts Find Research for ESSA," *Education Week* (blog), September 12, 2016, http://blogs.edweek.org/edweek/inside-school-research/2016/09/what_works_clearinghouse_ESSA_overhaul.html. (Note updated website for What Works Clearinghouse: http://ies.ed.gov/ncee/wwc/.)

44. Harris M. Cooper, *The Battle Over Homework: Common Ground for Administrators, Teachers, and Parents* (Thousand Oaks, CA: Corwin, 2007).

45. Jesmyn Ward, ed., *The Fire This Time: A New Generation Speaks About Race* (New York: Scribner, 2016).

46. Ruth Bader Ginsburg, quoted in Irin Carmon, "Justice Ginsburg's Cautious Radicalism," *The New York Times*, October 25, 2015, Sunday Review, SR3, http://www.nytimes.com/2015/10/25/opinion/sunday/justice-ginsburgs-cautious-radicalism.html?_r=0.

47. See p. 231 in Regie Routman, *Read, Write, Lead: Breakthrough Strategies for Schoolwide Literacy Success* (Alexandria, VA: ASCD, 2014).

48. Morgan Manns, "I Could Walk on the Silver Line: A Reflection of a First Year Teacher," *The Silver Line Blog: Reflections of a Nearly New Teacher* (blog), August 23, 2016, http://silverlineteacher.weebly.com/home/i-could-walk-on-the-silver-line-a-reflection-of-a-first-year-teacher.

49. Beth Tadlock shared her concerns in an e-mail on December 25, 2014.

50. Nell K. Duke, "What Doesn't Work: Literacy Practices We Should Abandon," *Edutopia* (blog), June 3, 2016, http://www.edutopia.org/blog/literacy-practices-we-should-abandon-nell-k-duke.

51. Katie Benmar shared her experience in a personal interview on July 11, 2016.

Afterword

1. Deborah Meier, "Supposing That . . . ," *Phi Delta Kappan*, December 1996, pp. 271–276, https://deborahmeier.files.wordpress.com/2012/02/1996supposingthat.pdf.

2. David Souter, "Former Supreme Court Justice Souter on the Danger of America's 'Pervasive Civic Ignorance'," *PBS NewsHour*, September 17, 2012. A video excerpt is available at https://www.youtube.com/watch?v=rWcVtWennr0. Be sure to view and discuss with intermediate through college students the powerful 7.40-minute video excerpt from the interview by PBS reporter Margaret Warner with Justice Souter discussing the crucial need for civic education for maintaining any democracy. The first three minutes of the video are for us educators and citizens. Four minutes in, when Souter says, "What I worry about . . . ," his comments are prescient for today's times. I believe those last three minutes should be required viewing for teaching civics.

Author note: Due to the large number of issues addressed in *Literacy Essentials* and text limits, no attempt has been made at a comprehensive research review. Many of these references came my way through reliable Twitter sites, blogs, newspapers, and educational journals. Whenever possible, accompanying URLs are provided. (See online References for easy retrieval of those web links and all videos referenced in text.) Use those URLs to selectively access articles, blogs, research, and related links to further your professional learning. Reading and discussing current research and practices with your colleagues is one excellent way to improve upon and reflect on pertinent educational issues and practices. For permission to photocopy and for online and electronic access, contact the publisher.

Afflerbach, Peter. 2014. "Self-Assessment and Reading Success." *Reading Today* 32 (3) (November/ December): 29–31.

Alexander, Kwame. 2015. "How Kwame Alexander Gets Teens Reading and Writing Poetry." *School Library Journal*, December 7. http://www.slj.com/2015/12/teens-ya/how-kwame-alexander-gets-teens-reading-and-writing-poetry/#. Great teaching ideas!

Allington, Richard L. 2002. "What I've Learned About Effective Reading Instruction from a Decade of Studying Exemplary Elementary Classroom Teachers." *Phi Delta Kappan*, 83 (10) (June): 740–747.

_____.2011. "What At-Risk Readers Need." *Educational Leadership*, March, 40–45.

Allington, Richard L., Kimberly McCuiston, and Monica Billen. 2015. "What Research Says About Text Complexity and Learning to Read." *The Reading Teacher* 68 (7) (April): 491–501. doi: 10.1002/ trtr.1280.

Allington, Richard, and Anne McGill-Franzen. 2014. "Won't Read Much If I Don't Have Any Books: Access to Books, and the Rich/Poor Reading Achievement Gap." *Heinemann* (blog). May 22. http://www.heinemann.com/blog/wont-read-much-if-i-dont-have-any-books-poverty-access-to-books-and-the-richpoor-reading-achievement-gap/.

Alrubail, Rusul. 2016. "How to Use Social Media to Strengthen Student Writing." *Edutopia* (blog). February 13. http://www.edutopia.org/discussion/how-use-social-media-strengthen-student-writing.

_____.2016. "Equity for English-Language Learners." *Edutopia* (blog). July 7. http://www.edutopia. org/blog/equity-for-english-language-learners-rusul-alrubail.

Anderson, Chris. 2016. *TED Talks: The Official TED Guide to Public Speaking.* Boston: Houghton Mifflin Harcourt.

Anderson, Jeff. 2006. "Zooming In and Zooming Out: Putting Grammar in Context into Context." *English Journal* 95 (5) (May): 28–34. The best article I've read on teaching grammar.

Anderson, Melinda D. 2016. "When Black and White Children Grow Apart." *The Atlantic*, June 14. http://www.theatlantic.com/education/archive/2016/06/interracial-friendships-fade/486902/.

Barnwell, Paul. 2016. "Blended Learning: Will Giving Greater Student Access to Smartphones Improve Learning?" *The Hechinger Report*, April 27. http://hechingerreport.org/will-giving-greater-student-access-smartphones-improve-learning/.

Baron, Naomi. 2016. "Why Digital Reading Is No Substitute for Print." *The New Republic,* July 20. https://newrepublic.com/article/135326/digital-reading-no-substitute-print.

Barshay, Jill. 2016. "Using Computers Widens the Achievement Gap in Writing, a Federal Study Finds." *The Hechinger Report*, Education by the Numbers, January 11. http://hechingerreport.org/online-writing-tests-widen-achievement-gap/.

Benmar, Katie. 2015. "My Favorite Teachers Use Social Media: A Student Perspective." Commentary. *Education Week,* April 22, 22–23. http://www.edweek.org/ew/articles/2015/04/22/my-favorite-teachers-use-social-media-a.html.

Berger, Warren. 2014. *A More Beautiful Question: The Power of Inquiry to Spark Breakthrough Ideas.* New York: Bloomsbury.

Black, Paul, and Dylan Wiliam. 1998. "Inside the Black Box: Raising Standards Through Classroom Assessment." *Phi Delta Kappan* 80 (2) (October): 139–144. http://www.rdc.udel.edu/wpcontent/uploads/2015/04/InsideBlackBox.pdf. (The results of a meta-analysis, i.e., analysis of the results of multiple studies; a terrific article for understanding and applying formative assessment.)

Blad, Evie. 2016. "Positive School Climates May Shrink Achievement Gaps." *Education Week*, November 15, 9. http://www.edweek.org/ew/articles/2016/11/16/positive-school-climates-may-shrink-achievement-gaps.html.

Blankstein, Alan M., and Pedro Noguera, with Lorena Kelly. 2015. *Excellence Through Equity: Five Principles of Courageous Leadership to Guide Achievement for Every Student.* Alexandria, VA: ASCD.

Block, Meghan K., and Nell K. Duke. 2015. "Preschool Through Grade 3: Letter Names Can Cause Confusion and Other Things to Know About Letter-Sound Relationships." *Young Children* 70 (1) (March): 84–91.

Boaler, Jo. 2015. "Mistakes Grow Your Brain." Youcubed at Stanford University. https://www.youcubed.org/think-it-up/mistakes-grow-brain/.

Bornstein, David. 2011. "A Book in Every Home, and Then Some." *Opinionator* (blog). *The New York Times,* May 16. http://opinionator.blogs.nytimes.com/2011/05/16/a-book-in-every-home-and-then-some/?_r=0.

Boyles, Nancy. 2016. "Pursuing the Depths of Knowledge." *Educational Leadership,* October, 46–50.

Bridges, Lois, ed. 2014. *Open a World of Possible: Real Stories About the Joy and Power of Reading.* New York: Scholastic. More than 100 well-known educators and authors of children's literature share their personal reading stories. Available as a free e-book from Scholastic.

Brookhart, Susan M. 2014. *How to Design Questions and Tasks to Assess Student Thinking.* Alexandria, VA: ASCD.

Brookhart, Susan M., and Connie M. Moss. 2013. "Leading by Learning." *Phi Delta Kappan* 94 (8) (May): 13–17.

Brooks, Arthur C. 2015. "Choose to Be Grateful. It Will Make You Happier." *The New York Times,* November 22, Sunday Review, SR 5. nytimes.com/2015/11/22/opinion/sunday/choose-to-be-grateful-it-will-make-you-happier.html?_r=0.

Brown, Emma. 2016. "On the Anniversary of Brown v. Board, New Evidence That U.S. Schools Are Resegregating." *The Washington Post,* May 17, Education. https://www.washingtonpost.com/news/education/wp/2016/05/17/on-the-anniversary-of-brown-v-board-new-evidence-that-u-s-schools-are-resegregating/.

Brunello, Giorgio, Guglielmo Weber, and Christoph Weiss. 2016. "Books Are Forever: Early Life Conditions, Education and Lifetime Earnings in Europe." *The Economic Journal* 127 (600) (April 25): 271–296. doi: 10.1111/ecoj.12307.

Burkins, Jan, and Kim Yaris. 2016. *Who's Doing the Work? How to Say Less So Readers Can Do More.* Portland, ME: Stenhouse.

Byrk, Anthony S. 2015. "Accelerating How We Learn to Improve." 2014 AERA Distinguished Lecture. *Educational Researcher* 44 (9) (December): 467–477.

_____.2016. "Fidelity of Implementation: Is It the Right Concept?" *Carnegie Commons* (blog). Carnegie Foundation for the Advancement of Teaching, March 17. http://www.carnegiefoundation.org/blog/fidelity-of-implementation-is-it-the-right-concept/.

Campbell, Tammy. 2015. "Stereotyped at Seven? Biases in Teacher Judgment of Pupils' Ability and Attainment." *Journal of Social Policy* 44 (3) (July): 517–547. https://doi.org/10.1017/S0047279415000227.

Carey, Kevin. 2016. "The Uproar Over Trying to Help Poor Schoolchildren." *The New York Times,* May 19, The Upshot, A3. https://www.nytimes.com/2016/05/18/upshot/why-poor-districts-receive-less-government-school-funding-than-rich-ones.html.

_____.2017. "Dismal Results from Vouchers Surprise Researchers." *The New York Times*, February 24, A20. https://www.nytimes.com/2017/02/23/upshot/dismal-results-from-vouchers-surprise-researchers-as-devos-era-begins.html?_r=0.

Carmon, Irin. 2015. "Justice Ginsburg's Cautious Radicalism." *The New York Times,* October 25, Sunday Review, SR3. http://www.nytimes.com/2015/10/25/ opinion/sunday/justice-ginsburgs-cautious-radicalism.html?_r=0.

Carr, David. 2015. "A Writer's Last Word on Journalism, Aimed at Students." *The New York Times,* February 15, B1 and B3. http://www.nytimes.com/2015/02/16/business/media/david-carr-as-a-passionate-professor-shaping-the-future-of-journalism.html?_r=0.

Cavanagh, Sean. 2015. "Demand for Print Persists Amid K–12 Digital Surge." *Education Week*, April 15, 1, 12–13. http://www.edweek.org/ew/articles/2015/04/15/k-12-schools-still-mix-print-and-digital.html.

Chatlani, Shalina. 2016. "Literary Fiction Here to Stay in Curriculum." *Education Dive*. October 4. http://www.educationdive.com/news/literary-fiction-here-to-stay-in-curriculum/427396/.

Chen, Alice. 2016. "How to Inspire a New Generation of Writers Through Blogging." *KQED Education* (blog). September 13. https://ww2.kqed.org/learning/2016/09/13/how-to-inspire-a-new-generation-of-writers-through-blogging/.

Choi, Amy. 2015. "How Telling Stories Can Transform a Classroom." *TED-Ed* (blog). September 30. http://blog.ed.ted.com/2015/09/30/how-telling-stories-can-transform-a-classroom/.

Christensen, Linda, and Dyan Watson, eds. 2015. *Rhythm and Resistance: Teaching Poetry for Social Justice*. Milwaukee, WI: Rethinking Schools.

Churchill, Al. 2016. "Put Down Your No. 2 Pencils: Too Much Testing in Public Schools." Guest Commentary. Bridge: The Center for Michigan. May 20. http://bridgemi.com/2016/05/put-down-your-no-2-pencils-too-much-testing-in-public-schools/.

Clay, Marie. 1993. *Reading Recovery: A Guidebook for Teachers in Training.* Portsmouth, NH: Heinemann.

Coates, Ta-Nehisi. 2015. "Advice on Writing" (video). *The Atlantic,* August. https://www.facebook.com/TheAtlantic/videos/10153577188343487/.

Cohen, James, Sadie McCarthy, and John Evar Strid. 2016. "Why Should a Monolingual English Speaking Reading Teacher Advocate for Biliteracy of English Learners?" *Illinois Reading Council Journal* 44 (2) (Spring): 20–27. http://www.luc.edu/media/lucedu/education/pdfs/languagematters/Sp16_Cohen-et-al_article_why_should_monolingual_teachers_advocate_biliteracy.pdf.

Collier, Lorna. 2016. "No Longer Invisible: How Diverse Literature Helps Children Find Themselves in Books, and Why It Matters." *The Council Chronicle.* National Council of Teachers of English (NCTE), September, 13–17.

Cooper, Harris M. 2007. *The Battle Over Homework: Common Ground for Administrators, Teachers, and Parents.* Thousand Oaks, CA: Corwin.

Cornwell, Paige. 2016. "Seattle's School Libraries: A Stark Example of Rich and Poor." *Seattle Times,* May 8, Education Lab, A1, A8. http://www.seattletimes.com/seattle-news/education/librarians-urging-equality-in-school-libraries/.

———.2016. "Deeper Learning: More Crucial Than Ever, Yet Too Rare." *Seattle Times,* May 11, Education Lab, B2. http://www.seattletimes.com/education-lab/a-deep-dive-into-deeper-learning/.

Cunningham, Katie Egan. 2015. *Story: Still the Heart of Literacy Learning.* Portland, ME: Stenhouse.

Currie, Lisa. 2014. "Why Teaching Kindness in Schools Is Essential to Reduce Bullying." *Edutopia,* October 17. https://www.edutopia.org/blog/teaching-kindness-essential-reduce-bullying-lisa-currie?utm_source=twitter&utm_medium=socialflow.

Darling-Hammond, Linda. 2014. "Test-based accountability produced no gains from 2000-2012 on PISA. Time for a new approach." Tweet. July 2. https://twitter.com/ldh_ed/status/484388825645326337.

———.2014. "The Common-Core Standards Offer a Guide, Not a Straitjacket." *Education Week,* October 15, Letters to the Editor, 24.

———.2015. "Now We Confront the Real Equity Challenge: Providing Access to 21st Century Learning. *Learning Policy Institute* (blog). December 11. https://learningpolicyinstitute.org/blog/now-we-confront-real-equity-challenge-providing-access-21st-century-learning.

Darling-Hammond, Linda, and Nikole Richardson. 2009. "Research Review/Teacher Learning: What Matters?" *Educational Leadership*, February, 46–53.

Datnow, Amanda. 2015. "Data Use—For Equity." *Educational Leadership,* February, 49–54.

Dean, Heather. 2017. "Creating Critical Readers: Connecting Close Reading and Technology." *The California Reader* 50 (4): 8–11.

De La Cruz, Donna. 2016. "What Kids Wish Their Teachers Knew." *The New York Times,* August 31. http://www.nytimes.com/2016/08/31/well/family/what-kids-wish-their-teachers-knew.html.

DePasquale, John. 2016. "Zine Making 101." Scholastic.com. April 29. https://www.google.com/search?q=zine+making+101+by+john+depasquale%2C+2015&ie=utf-8&oe=utf-8.

Dewitz, Peter, and Michael Graves. 2014. "Teaching for Transfer in the Common Core Era." *The Reading Teacher* 68 (2) (October): 149–158.

Dewitz, Peter, Jennifer Jones, and Susan Leahy. 2009. "Comprehension Strategy Instruction in Core Reading Programs." *Reading Research Quarterly* 44 (2) (April–June): 102–126. dx.doi.org/10.1598/RRQ.41.2.1.

Dillon, Jim. 2017. "Stories Stick with Students." SmartBrief, June 7. http://www.smartbrief.com/original/2017/06/stories-stick-students.

Domonoske, Camila. 2016. "Students Have 'Dismaying' Inability to Tell Fake News from Real, Study Finds." National Public Radio, *The Two-Way,* November 23. http://www.npr.org/sections/the-two-way/2016/11/23/503129818/study-finds-students-have-dismaying-inability-to-tell-fake-news-from-real?utm_source=twitter.com&utm_medium=social&utm_campaign=npr&utm_term=nprnews&utm_content=2054.

Donald, Brooke. 2016. "Stanford Researchers Find Students Have Trouble Judging the Credibility of Information Online." Report by the Stanford History Education Group (SHEG). Stanford, CA: Stanford Graduate School of Education. November 22. https://ed.stanford.edu/news/stanford-researchers-find-students-have-trouble-judging-credibility-information-online.

Doubek, James. 2016. "Attention, Students: Put Your Laptops Away" (transcript), National Public Radio, *Weekend Edition Sunday,* April 17. http://www.npr.org/2016/04/17/474525392/attention-students-put-your-laptops-away.

Doward, Jamie. 2016. "Boys Who Live with Books 'Earn More as Adults.'" *The Guardian,* May 28, Education. http://www.theguardian.com/education/2016/may/29/boys-books-earnings-adults.

Duhigg, Charles. 2016. "Group Study." *The New York Times Magazine,* February 28, Work-Life issue, 20–26, 72, and 75.

Duke, Nell K. 2016. "What Doesn't Work: Literacy Practices We Should Abandon." *Edutopia* (blog). June 3. http://www.edutopia.org/blog/literacy-practices-we-should-abandon-nell-k-duke.

Duke, Nell K., and V. Susan Bennett-Armistead. 2003. *Reading and Writing Informational Texts in the Primary Grades: Research-Based Practices*. New York: Scholastic.

Duke, Nell K., Samantha Caughlan, Mary M. Juzwik, and Nicole M. Martin. 2012. "Teaching Genre with Purpose." *Educational Leadership,* March, 34–39.

Duke, Nell K., and Nicole M. Martin. 2011. "10 Things Every Literacy Educator Should Know About Research." *The Reading Teacher* 65 (1) (September): 9–22.

Duke, Nell K., Victoria Purcell-Gates, Leigh A. Hall, and Cathy Tower. 2006–2007. "Authentic Literacy Activities for Developing Comprehension and Writing." *The Reading Teacher* 60 (4) (December–January): 344–355.

Dweck, Carol. 2006. *Mindset: The New Psychology of Success*. New York: Random House.

_____.2015. "Commentary: Carol Dweck Revisits the 'Growth Mindset.'" *Education Week,* September 22, 20, 24. http://www.edweek.org/ew/articles/2015/09/23/carol-dweck-revisits-the-growth-mindset.html.

_____.2016. "The Journey to a Growth Mindset." General session keynote address, ASCD Annual Conference, Atlanta, Georgia, April 3.

Echevarria, Jana J., MaryEllen J. Vogt, and Deborah J. Short. 2017. *Making Content Comprehensible for English Learners: The SIOP Model*. 5th ed. Boston: Pearson.

Education Week. 2016. "Kindergarten Today: Less Play, More Academics." February 10. http://www.edweek.org/ew/section/multimedia/kindergarten-less-play-more-academics.html.

Feldman, Anna. 2015. "STEAM Rising: Why We Need to Put the Arts into STEM Education." *Slate,* June 16. http://www.slate.com/articles/technology/future_tense/2015/06/steam_vs_stem_why_we_need_to_put_the_arts_into_stem_education.htm.

Ferlazzo, Larry. 2015. "Response: Teach English-Language Learners by Meeting Them 'Where They Are.'" *Education Week Teacher* (blog). October 24. http://blogs.edweek.org/teachers/classroom_qa_with_larry_ferlazzo/2015/10/response_teach_english_language_learners_by_meeting_them_where_they_are.html.

_____.2016. "Response: How Can We Best Engage Families: Seeing Families as 'Co-Creators' of Our Schools." *Classroom Q&A with Larry Ferlazzo* (blog). January 23. http://blogs.edweek.org/teachers/classroom_qa_with_larry_ferlazzo/2016/01/response_seeing_families_as_co-creators_of_our_schools.html.

_____.2016. "Response: Reading Digitally vs. Reading Paper." *Education Week Teacher* (blog). May 28. http://blogs.edweek.org/teachers/classroom_qa_with_larry_ferlazzo/2016/05/response_reading_digitally_vs_reading_paper.html. Information is from "Response from Daniel Willingham," who shares results of several studies on this issue.

_____.2017. "Response: Provide 'Voice' and 'Choice' When Students Set Goals." *Education Week Teacher* (blog). January 17. http://blogs.edweek.org/teachers/classroom_qa_with_larry_ferlazzo/2017/01/response_provide_voice_choice_when_students_set_goals.html.

Figueroa, Sandra. 2016. California Reading Association Annual Professional Development Institute. Conference session, Visalia, California, November 5.

Figurelli, Steve, and Natalie Franzi. 2015. "Literacy in the Digital Age: Five Sites with High-Quality Informational Text." *Tchers' Voice* (blog). August 19. https://www.teachingchannel.org/blog/2015/08/19/literacy-in-the-digital-age-informational-text-sap/.

Fisher, Douglas, Nancy Frey, and John Hattie. 2016. *Visible Learning for Literacy, Grades K–12: Implementing the Practices That Work Best to Accelerate Student Learning.* Thousand Oaks, CA: Corwin.

Flanagan, Linda. 2016. "How Teachers Are Using 'Hamilton' the Musical in the Classroom." *Mind/Shift*, March 14. https://ww2.kqed.org/mindshift/2016/03/14/how-teachers-are-using-hamilton-the-musical-in-the-classroom/.

_____.2017. "How Making Kindness a Priority Benefits Students." *Mind/Shift*, June 6. https://ww2.kqed.org/mindshift/2017/06/06/how-making-kindness-a-priority-benefits-students/.

_____.2017. "How Teens Can Develop and Share Meaningful Stories With 'The Moth.'" *Mind/Shift*, June 19. https://ww2.kqed.org/mindshift/2017/06/19/how-teens-can-develop-and-share-meaningful-stories-with-the-moth/.

Flanagan, Nancy. 2015. "Professional Development Is Useless! Or Not." *Education Week Teacher* (blog). August 9. http://blogs.edweek.org/teachers/teacher_in_a_strange_land/2015/08/professional_development_is_useless_or_not.html.

Flood, Alison. 2015. "Short Story Vending Machines Press French Commuters' Buttons." *The Guardian,* November 13. https://www.theguardian.com/books/2015/nov/13/short-story-vending-machines-press-french-commuters-buttons.

_____.2016. "Book Up for a Longer Life: Readers Die Later, Study Finds." *The Guardian,* August 8. https://www.theguardian.com/books/2016/aug/08/book-up-for-a-longer-life-readers-die-later-study-finds.

Ford, Michael P. 2017. "To DIBELS or Not to DIBELS? Answering Questions About Fluency-Based Measures in the Era of Response to Intervention." *WSRA Journal* 54 (2): 32–41.

Ford, Michael P., and Michael F. Optiz. 2008. "A National Survey of Guided Reading Practices: What We Can Learn from Primary Teachers." *Literacy Research and Instruction* 47 (4): 309–331.

Fox, Mem. 2013. "What Next in the Read-Aloud Battle? Win or Lose?" *The Reading Teacher* 67 (1) (September): 4–8. doi: 10.1002/TRTR.1185.

Friedman, Thomas L. 2017. "From Hands to Heads to Hearts." *The New York Times,* January 4, Op-Ed, A21. http://www.nytimes.com/2017/01/04/opinion/from-hands-to-heads-to-hearts.html?_r=0.

Fullan, Michael, and Andy Hargreaves. 1996. *What's Worth Fighting for in Your School?* Rev. ed. New York: Teachers College Press.

Fullan, Michael, and Joanne Quinn. 2016. *Coherence: The Right Drivers in Action for Schools, Districts, and Systems.* Thousand Oaks, CA: Corwin.

Gabor, Andrea. 2015. "The Myth of the New Orleans School Makeover." *The New York Times,* August 23, Sunday Review, SR3.

Gallagher, Kelly. 2013–present. "Article of the Week." Current and archived articles. http://www.kellygallagher.org/article-of-the-week/.

Gallo, Carmine. 2014. *Talk Like TED: The 9 Public-Speaking Secrets of the World's Top Minds.* New York: St. Martin's.

Garbarino, Steve. 2014. "Five Practical Uses for a Vintage Manual Typewriter." *The Wall Street Journal,* December 26. http://www.wsj.com/articles/five-practical-uses-for-a-vintage-manual-typewriter-1419627431.

Garner, David. 2015. "Review: Christopher Hitchens Expounds in 'And Yet.'" *New York Times,* November 24, Book Review. http://www.nytimes.com/2015/11/25/books/review-christopher-hitchens-expounds-in-and-yet.html.

Gewertz, Catherine. 2015. "Q and A: Misconceptions About Formative Assessment," in "Understanding Formative Assessment." *Education Week,* November 9. http://www.edweek.org/ew/articles/2015/11/11/qa-misconceptions-about-formative-assessment.html.

Glasswell, Kath, and Michael Ford. 2011. "Let's Start Leveling About Leveling." *Language Arts* 88 (3) (January): 208–216.

Global Goals for Sustainable Development. 2016. Brief video on girl power. July 5. https://www.youtube.com/watch?v=sZQ2RUFd54o. Appropriate and inspiring for high school students.

Global Read Aloud: One Book to Connect the World. https://theglobalreadaloud.com/. See website for information, book choice suggestions, sign-up, and procedures.

Glover, Matt, and Ellin Oliver Keene, eds. 2015. *The Teacher You Want to Be: Essays About Children, Learning, and Teaching.* Portsmouth, NH: Heinemann.

Goldenberg, Claude. 2008. "Teaching English Language Learners: What the Research Does—and Does Not—Say." *American Educator* 32 (2) (Summer): 8–23, 42–44. https://www.aft.org/sites/default/files/periodicals/goldenberg.pdf.

Goodlad, John I. 2004. *A Place Called School.* 20th anniversary ed. New York: McGraw-Hill.

Graham, Steve, and Michael Hebert. 2010. *Writing to Read: Evidence for How Writing Can Improve Reading.* New York: Carnegie Corporation.

Grant, Adam. 2016. *Originals: How Non-Conformists Move the World.* New York: Viking.

Green, Ryan Speedo. 2016. Interview with Tavis Smiley. *The Tavis Smiley Show.* Public Radio International. November 19.

Gregoire, Carolyn. 2014. "How to Think Like a Writer." *The Huffington Post,* May 15. http://www.huffingtonpost.com/2014/05/15/how-the-worlds-best-write_n_5331610.html.

Grissom, Jason A., and Christopher Redding. 2016. "Discretion and Disproportionality: Explaining the Underrepresentation of High-Achieving Students of Color in Gifted Programs." Overview: Abstract, *AERA Open.* January 19. http://www.aera.net/Newsroom/News-Releases-and-Statements/Does-Student-Race-Affect-Gifted-Assignment/Discretion-and-Disproportionality-Explaining-the-Underrepresentation-of-High-Achieving-Students-of-Color-in-Gifted-Programs.

Guo, Jeff. 2016. "Why Smart Kids Shouldn't Use Laptops in Class." *Wonkblog* (blog). *The Washington Post*, May 16. https://www.washingtonpost.com/news/wonk/wp/2016/05/16/why-smart-kids-shouldnt-use-laptops-in-class/.

Guskey, Thomas R., and Kwang Suk Yoon. 2009. "What Works in Professional Development?" *Phi Delta Kappan* 90 (7) (March): 495–500.

Hamm, Scott. 2015. "Why Texting Should Be Part of Teaching." *EdTech*, March 30. http://www.edtechmagazine.com/k12/article/2015/03/why-texting-should-be-part-teaching.

Hammond, W. Dorsey, and Denise D. Nessel. 2011. *The Comprehension Experience: Engaging Readers Through Effective Inquiry and Discussion*. Portsmouth, NH: Heinemann.

Hannah-Jones, Nikole. 2016. "Worlds Apart." *The New York Times Magazine*, June 12, 34–39, 50–53, and 55. http://www.nytimes.com/2016/06/12/magazine/choosing-a-school-for-my-daughter-in-a-segregated-city.html.

———. 2017. "Have We Lost Sight of the Promise of Public Schools?" *The New York Times Magazine*, February 26, 13–15. https://www.nytimes.com/2017/02/21/magazine/have-we-lost-sight-of-the-promise-of-public-schools.html?_r=0.

Hargreaves, Andrew, Gábor Halász, and Beatriz Pont. 2007. "School Leadership for Systemic Improvement in Finland: A Case Study Report for the OECD Activity, Improving School Leadership." Paris, France: Organization for Economic Cooperation and Development. https://www.oecd.org/edu/school/39928629.pdf.

Hargreaves, Andy. 2014. "Why We Can't Reform Literacy and Math All at Once." *The Washington Post,* September 26, The Answer Sheet by Valerie Strauss. https://www.washingtonpost.com/news/answer-sheet/wp/2014/09/26/why-we-cant-reform-literacy-and-math-all-at-once/.

———. 2015. "The Iniquity of Inequity: And Some International Clues About Ways to Address It." In *Excellence Through Equity: Five Principles of Courageous Leadership to Guide Achievement for Every Student*, ed. Alan Blankstein and Pedro Noguera, with Lorena Kelly. Alexandria, VA: ASCD.

Harris, Elizabeth A. 2016. "Small Steps, but No Major Push, to Integrate New York's Schools." *The New York Times*, July 6, A1. https://www.nytimes.com/2016/07/06/nyregion/new-york-city-schools-segregation-carmen-farina.html.

Haruf, Cathy. 2015. "Kent Haruf's *Our Souls at Night*: 'A Book About Us.'" *Picador Books* (blog). June 4. http://www.picador.com/blog/may-2015/%E2%80%8Bkent-harufs-our-souls-at-night-a-book-about-us.

Hattie, John. 2009. *Visible Learning*. London and New York: Routledge. This text comprises a meta-analysis of educational research; that is, the author has analyzed the results of multiple studies to draw his conclusions.

———. 2012. "Know Thy Impact: Feedback for Learning." *Educational Leadership,* September, 18–23.

———. 2012. *Visible Learning for Teachers: Maximizing Impact on Learning*. London and New York: Routledge.

———. 2015. "High-Impact Leadership." *Educational Leadership,* February, 36–40.

———. 2015. *What Works Best in Education: The Politics of Collaborative Expertise*. London: Pearson. https://www.pearson.com/content/dam/corporate/global/pearson-dot-com/files/hattie/150526_ExpertiseWEB_V1.pdf.

Heard, Georgia. 2016. "Writing Begins in Wonder." Keynote address at annual CCIRA conference, Denver, Colorado, February 5.

———. 2016. *Heart Maps: Helping Students Create and Craft Authentic Writing*. Portsmouth, NH: Heinemann.

Heick, Terry. 2014. "Are You Teaching Content or Teaching Thought?" *TeachThought: We Grow Teachers* (blog). February 27. http://www.teachthought.com/critical-thinking/teaching-content-or-teaching-thought/.

_____.2014. "6 Principles of Genius Hour in the Classroom." *TeachThought: We Grow Teachers* (blog). September 28. http://www.teachthought.com/learning/6-principles-of-genius-hour-in-the-classroom/.

Heitin, Liana. 2016. "Will the Common Core Step Up Schools' Focus on Grammar?" *Education Week,* February 23. http://www.edweek.org/ew/articles/2016/02/24/will-the-common-core-step-up-schools.html.

_____.2016. "Why Don't the Common-Core Standards Include Cursive Writing?" *Education Week* (blog). October 10. http://blogs.edweek.org/edweek/curriculum/2016/10/why_dont_the_common-core_standards_include_cursive_writing.html?print=1.

Herold, Benjamin. 2016. "PARCC Scores Lower for Students Who Took Exams on Computers." *Education Week,* February 3. http://www.edweek.org/ew/articles/2016/02/03/parcc-scores-lower-on-computer.html.

Higgins, John. 2016. "Q & A with Walter Parker, the UW Professor Who Reinvented AP Government." *Seattle Times,* May 13, Education Lab. http://www.seattletimes.com/education-lab/q-a-with-walter-parker-the-uw-prof-who-reinvented-ap-government/.

Hill, Jane. 2016. "Engaging Your Beginners." *Educational Leadership,* February (themed issue, "Helping ELLs Excel"), 18–23.

Hillocks, George. 2002. *The Testing Trap: How State Writing Assessments Control Learning.* New York: Teachers College Press.

Isaacson, Walter. 2014. *The Innovators: How a Group of Hackers, Geniuses, and Geeks Created the Digital Revolution.* New York: Simon and Schuster.

Jensen, Ben, Julie Sonnemann, Katie Roberts-Hull, and Amélie Hunter. 2016. "Beyond PD: Teacher Professional Learning in High-Performing Systems." Washington, DC: National Center on Education and the Economy.

Jobson, Christopher. 2015. "Artist Theaster Gates Bought a Crumbling Chicago Bank for $1 and Turned It into a World-Class Arts Center." *Colossal* (an art, design, and culture blog). October 13. http://www.thisiscolossal.com/2015/10/stony-island-arts-bank/.

Kafalas, Dennis. 2015. "Working and Conferencing with a Rubric: Easy Tweaks for Effort + Quality." *The Cornerstone for Teachers* (blog). September 10. https://www.google.com/search?q=the+cornerstoneforteachers.com%2F2015%2F09%2Feasy-rubric-tweaks.html&ie=utf-8&oe=utf-8.

Kakutani, Michiko. 2017. "Obama's Secret to Surviving the White House Years: Books." *The New York Times,* January 16, A1 and A15. https://www.nytimes.com/2017/01/16/books/obamas-secret-to-surviving-the-white-house-years-books.html.

Kamenetz, Anya. 2015. *The Test: Why Our Schools Are Obsessed with Standardized Testing—But You Don't Have to Be.* New York: Public Affairs.

_____.2016. "Caution Flags for Tech in Classrooms." *nprED* (blog). National Public Radio, August 11. https://www.google.com/search?q=Kamenetz%2C+Anya.+August+11%2C+2016.+%E2%80%9CCaution+Flags+for+Tech+in+Classrooms.%E2%80%9D+National+Public+Radio&ie=utf-8&oe=utf-8.

Kazemi, Elham, and Allison Hintz. 2014. *Intentional Talk: How to Structure and Lead Productive Mathematical Discussions.* Portland, ME: Stenhouse.

King, Stephen. 2000. *On Writing: A Memoir of the Craft*. New York: Scribner.

Kinzler, Katherine. 2016. "Bilinguals' Superior Social Skills." *The New York Times,* March 13, Sunday Review, SR10. http://www.nytimes.com/2016/03/13/opinion/sunday/the-superior-social-skills-of-bilinguals.html?_r=0.

Kirp, David L. 2013. *Improbable Scholars: The Rebirth of a Great American School System and a Strategy for America's Schools.* New York: Oxford University Press.

_____.2016. "How to Make Pre-K a Success." *The New York Times*, February 14, Sunday Review, SR6. https://www.nytimes.com/2016/02/14/opinion/sunday/how-new-york-made-pre-k-a-success.html.

_____.2016. "How to Nudge Students to Succeed." *The New York Times,* October 30, Sunday Review, SR2. http://www.nytimes.com/2016/10/30/opinion/nudges-that-help-struggling-students-succeed.html?_r=0.

Kittle, Penny. 2016. Tweet regarding inspirational speech by Michelle Obama. July 26. Speech available at https://www.youtube.com/watch?v=4ZNWYqDU948.

Klass, Perri. 2015. "Turn the Page, Spur the Brain." *The New York Times*, August 18, Science Times, D6.

_____.2016. "Why Handwriting Is Still Essential in the Keyboard Age." *Well* (blog). *The New York Times,* June 20. http://well.blogs.nytimes.com/2016/06/20/why-handwriting-is-still-essential-in-the-keyboard-age/?_r=1.

Klein, Alyson. 2016. "Teaching America's English-Language Learners: For Stalled ELL Students, Graduation Is Often an Elusive Goal." *Education Week,* May 11. http://www.edweek.org/ew/articles/2016/05/11/for-stalled-ell-students-graduation-is-often.html.

Knapp, Michael, Patrick Shields, and Brenda Turnbull. 1995. "Academic Challenge in High-Poverty Classrooms." *Phi Delta Kappan* 76 (10) (June): 770–776.

Kowalski, Megan. 2016. "In Defense of Audio Books." *CRWP* [Chippewa River Writing Project] *Teachers as Writers* (blog). January 18. http://chippewariverwp.org/blog/2016/01/18/in-defense-of-audio-books/.

Kozol, Jonathan. 2015. "60 Seconds with Jonathon Kozol." Video clip. December 22. https://www.youtube.com/watch?v=d_5tbTW2oOc&feature=youtu.be.

Krashen, Stephen. 2004. "Free Voluntary Reading: New Research, Applications, and Controversies." Paper presented at the RELC Conference in Singapore, April. http://www.sdkrashen.com/content/articles/singapore.pdf.

_____.2015. "Reading for Pleasure Can Close 'Vocabulary Gap' at Any Age." *Education Week,* May 13, Letters to the Editor, 24.

_____.2016. "Learning to Read: There Is Nothing Magic About Grade 3." *SKrashen* (blog). May 7. http://skrashen.blogspot.com/2016/05/learning-to-read-there-is-nothing-magic.html.

_____.2016. "Research Supports Value of School Libraries." *Education Week,* June 1, Letters to the Editor, 28–29.

Krashen, Stephen, and Jeff McQuillan. 1998. "The Case for Late Intervention: Once a Good Reader, Always a Good Reader," in *Reconsidering a Balanced Approach to Reading,* ed. Constance Weaver. Urbana, IL: National Council of Teachers of English. https://secure.ncte.org/library/NCTEFiles/Resources/Books/Sample/02344Chap14.pdf.

Krebs, Denise, and Gallit Zvi. 2016. *The Genius Hour Guidebook: Fostering Passion, Wonder, and Inquiry in the Classroom.* New York and London: Routledge.

Kris, Deborah Farmer. 2016. "14 Books That Connect Students with Valuable Scientists' Struggles." *Mind/Shift* (blog). May 26. https://ww2.kqed.org/mindshift/2016/05/26/14-books-that-connect-students-with-valuable-scientists-struggles/.

Kristof, Nicholas. 2015. "From Somaliland to Harvard." *The New York Times,* September 13, Sunday Review, 1 and 11. https://www.nytimes.com/2015/09/13/opinion/sunday/nicholas-kristof-from-somaliland-to-harvard.html.

_____.2016. "America the Unfair?" *The New York Times,* January 21, Op-Ed, A23.

Lai, Mei Kuin, Aaron Wilson, Stuart McNaughton, and Selena Hsiao. 2014. "Improving Achievement in Secondary Schools: Impact of a Literacy Project on Reading Comprehension and Secondary School Qualifications." *Reading Research Quarterly* 49 (3) (July–September): 305–334.

Laskas, Jeanne Marie. 2017. "To Obama with Love, and Hate, and Desperation." *The New York Times Magazine,* January 17, 30–39. https://www.nytimes.com/2017/01/17/magazine/what-americans-wrote-to-obama.html?_r=0.

Layne, Steven. 2015. *In Defense of Read-Aloud: Sustaining Best Practice.* Portland, ME: Stenhouse.

Lee, Juhee, and Diane L. Schallert. 2016. "Exploring the Reading-Writing Connection: A Yearlong Classroom-Based Experimental Study of Middle School Students Developing Literacy in a New Language." *Reading Research Quarterly* 51 (2) (April/May/June): 143–164. doi: 10.1002/rrq.132. See this article for a review of the extensive research base on reading-writing connections.

Lenkei, Alex. 2016. "Students Prefer Print: Why Are Schools Pushing Digital Textbooks?" *BookMarks* (blog). *Education Week,* March 7. http://blogs.edweek.org/edweek/bookmarks/2016/03/students_prefer_print_schools_pushing_digital_textbooks.html.

Levine, Sheen S., and David Stark. 2015. "Diversity Makes You Brighter." *The New York Times,* December 9, Op-Ed, A31. http://www.nytimes.com/2015/12/09/opinion/diversity-makes-you-brighter.html?_r=0.

Levitan, Joe. 2015. "Bilingual Students Need Support in Their Native Language." *Education Week,* May 12, Commentary. http://www.edweek.org/ew/articles/2015/05/13/bilingual-students-need-support-in-their-native.html.

Liebfreund, Meghan D. 2015. "Success with Informational Text Comprehension: An Examination of Underlying Factors." *Reading Research Quarterly* 50 (4) (October/November/December): 387–392. doi:10.1002/rrq.109.

Lifshitz, Jessica. 2016. "Having Students Analyze Our Classroom Library to See How Diverse It Is." *Crawling Out of the Classroom* (blog). May 7. https://crawlingoutoftheclassroom.wordpress.com/2016/05/07/having-students-analyze-our-classroom-library-to-see-how-diverse-it-is/.

Little, Tom, and Katherine Ellison. 2015. *Loving Learning: How Progressive Education Can Save America's Schools.* New York and London: W. W. Norton.

Lopez, Nadia, with Rebecca Paley. 2016. *The Bridge to Brilliance: How One Principal in a Tough Community Is Inspiring the World.* New York: Viking.

Loveless, Tom. 2012. *The 2012 Brown Center Report on American Education: How Well Are American Students Learning?* Washington, DC: Brookings Institution. https://www.brookings.edu/wp-content/uploads/2016/07/0216_brown_education_loveless.pdf. The report includes sections on predicting the effect of the Common Core State Standards, achievement gaps on the two NAEP tests, and misinterpreting international test scores.

Maloch, Beth, Jo Worthy, Angela Hampton, Michelle Jordan, Holly Hungerford-Kresser, and Peggy Semingson. 2013. "Portraits of Practice: A Cross-Case Analysis of Two First-Grade Teachers and Their Grouping Practices." *Research in the Teaching of English* 47 (3) (February): 277–312.

Manns, Morgan. 2016. "I Could Walk on the Silver Line: A Reflection of a First Year Teacher." *The Silver Line Blog: Reflections of a Nearly New Teacher.* August 23. http://silverlineteacher.weebly.com/home/i-could-walk-on-the-silver-line-a-reflection-of-a-first-year-teacher.

Marinak, Barbara A., and Linda Gambrell. 2016. *No More Reading for Junk: Best Practices for Motivating Readers.* Portsmouth, NH: Heinemann.

Martin, Douglas. 2015. "William Zinsser, Author of 'On Writing Well,' Dies at 92" (obituary). *The New York Times,* May 13. http://www.nytimes.com/2015/05/13/arts/william-zinsser-author-of-on-writing-well-dies-at-92.html?_r=0.

Matczuk, Lynn Allyson. 2016. "A Comparative Examination of Outcomes of a Longitudinal Professional Development Experience in Writing Instruction in Schools for Kindergarten to Grade 3." Unpublished dissertation, University of Manitoba, Winnipeg, Canada.

Matthews, Jay. 2016. "Writing Instruction in Our Schools Is Terrible. We Need to Fix It." *The Washington Post,* August 14. https://www.washingtonpost.com/local/education/writing-instruction-in-our-schools-is-terrible-we-need-to-fix-it/2016/08/14/a47b705e-6005-11e6-8e45-477372e89d78_story.html?utm_term=.69df06d6d188. Article reporting on research on school assignments in middle schools.

May, Henry, Philip Sirinides, Abigail Gray, and Heather Goldsworthy. 2016. *Reading Recovery: An Evaluation of the Four-Year i3 Scale-Up* (research report). Philadelphia: Consortium for Policy Research in Education, University of Pennsylvania; and Newark, DE: Center for Research in Education and Social Policy, University of Delaware. http://www.cpre.org/sites/default/files/reading_recovery_final_report.pdf.

McGrath, Charles. 2013. "Caution: Reading Can Be Hazardous." *New York Times*, December 8, Sunday Review, SR9. http://www.nytimes.com/2013/12/08/opinion/sunday/caution-reading-can-be-hazardous.html.

McKibben, Sarah. 2016. "Pass the Mic: Teaching with Hip-Hop." *Education Update* 58 (6) (June): 1, 4, and 5.

McNair, Jonda C., ed. 2016. "#WeNeedMirrorsAndWindows: Diverse Classroom Libraries for K–6 Students." *The Reading Teacher* 70 (3) (November/December): 375–381. doi: 10.1002/trtr.1516.

McNaughton, Stuart. 2011. *Designing Better Schools for Culturally and Linguistically Diverse Children.* New York and London: Routledge.

McNeil, Elisha. 2016. "English Teachers' Hip-Hop Curriculum Gets Students Writing." *Education Week Teacher*, June 20. http://www.edweek.org/tm/articles/2016/06/20/english-teachers-hip-hop-curriculum-gets-students-writing.html.

McQuillan, Jeff. 1998. *The Literacy Crisis: False Claims, Real Solutions.* Portsmouth, NH: Heinemann.

Mehta, Jal, and Sarah Fine. 2015. *The Why, What, Where, and How of Deeper Learning in American Secondary Schools.* Research report (part of Deeper Learning Research Series). Boston: Jobs for the Future. http://www.jff.org/sites/default/files/publications/materials/The-Why-What-Where-How-121415.pdf.

Meier, Deborah. 1995. "How Our Schools Could Be." *Phi Delta Kappan* 76 (5) (January): 369–373.

———. 1996. "Supposing That . . . ." *Phi Delta Kappan* 78 (4) (December): 271–276. https://deborahmeier.files.wordpress.com/2012/02/1996supposingthat.pdf.

Michigan Association of Intermediate School Administrators, General Education Leadership Network, Early Literacy Task Force. 2016. *Essential Instructional Practices in Early Literacy: Grades K to 3.* Lansing, MI: Authors. https://sites.google.com/a/umich.edu/nkduke/publications/new-essentials-documents. There is also a prekindergarten document on essential instructional practices from the same task force, available at http://www.gomaisa.org/sites/default/files/Pre-K%20Literacy%20Essentials%203.2016.pdf.

Minkel, Justin. 2015. "Putting Books Back into Reading." *Education Week Teacher,* December 29. http://www.edweek.org/tm/articles/2015/12/29/putting-books-back-into-reading.html.

Mitchell, Corey. 2016. "Does the Term 'English-Language Learner' Carry a Negative Connotation?" *Education Week* (blog). February 1. http://blogs.edweek.org/edweek/learning-the-language/2016/02/does_the_term_english-language.html.

_____.2016. "Mispronouncing Students' Names: A Slight That Can Cut Deep." *Education Week* (blog). May 10. http://www.edweek.org/ew/articles/2016/05/11/mispronouncing-students-names-a-slight-that-can.html?cmp=SOC-SHR-twitter.

Mueller, Pam A., and Daniel M. Oppenheimer. 2014. "The Pen Is Mightier Than the Keyboard: Advantages of Longhand over Laptop Note Taking." *Psychological Science* 25 (6) (June): 1159–1168. For easier access to this research, see James Doubek, 2016.

Mulgrew, Michael. 2015. "The Essence of Wrongheaded School 'Reform.'" *Education Week,* December 9, Commentary, 21. (Mulgrew is president of the United Federation of Teachers in New York City.)

Murray, Donald. 1996. *Crafting a Life in Essay, Story, Poem.* Portsmouth, NH: Heinemann.

Namahoe, Kanoe. 2016. "Disrupting Our Default Settings." SmartBrief, September 16. http://www.smartbrief.com/original/2016/09/disrupting-our-default-settings.

National Center for Children in Poverty. 2016. "Child Poverty." New York: Columbia University. http://nccp.org/topics/childpoverty.html.

National Governors Association Center for Best Practices, and Council of Chief State School Officers. 2010. *Common Core State Standards for English Language Arts and Literacy in History/Social Studies, Science, and Technical Subjects.* Washington, DC: Authors.

National School Reform. Harmony Education Center, Bloomington, IN. https://www.nsrfharmony.org/free-resources/protocols.

Newkirk, Thomas. 2000. "A Mania for Rubrics." *Education Week*, September 13, Commentary. http://www.edweek.org/ew/articles/2000/09/13/02newkirk.h20.html.

_____.2014. *Minds Made for Stories: How We Really Read and Write Informational and Persuasive Texts.* Portsmouth, NH: Heinemann.

_____.2016. "Unbalanced Literacy: Reflections on the Common Core." *Language Arts* 93 (4) (March): 304–311.

New York Times Editorial Board. 2016. "Schoolchildren Left Behind." *The New York Times*, November 12, Editorial, A24. http://www.nytimes.com/2016/11/12/opinion/schoolchildren-left-behind.html?_r=0.

Niccoli, Anne. 2015. "Paper or Tablet? Reading Recall and Comprehension." *EDUCAUSEreview,* September 28. http://er.educause.edu/articles/2015/9/paper-or-tablet-reading-recall-and-comprehension.

Nicklaus, Mary Beth. 2016. "Gloom, Despair, and Strawberry Pop Tarts: Failure Stories and Their Effect on Agency During the Bad Days in the Reading Intervention Classroom." *WSRA Journal* [Wisconsin State Reading Association] 53 (2) (Spring): 67–71.

Noguera, Pedro, and Alan Blankstein. 2016. "Excellence Through Equity: Five Principles of Courageous Leadership to Guide Achievement for Every Student." Second general session, ASCD Annual Conference, Atlanta, Georgia, April 2.

Nugent, Ciara. 2016. "New Chapter for Classic Paris Bookstore: Books Printed on Demand in Minutes." *The New York Times*, June 13, Business Day, B1 and B3.

Ohanian, Susan. 1997. "Some Are More Equal Than Others." *Phi Delta Kappan* 78 (6) (February): 471–474.

Ozma, Alice. 2011. *The Reading Promise: My Father and the Books We Shared.* New York: Grand Central Publishing.

Palmer, Erik. 2011. *Well Spoken: Teaching Speaking to All Students.* Portland, ME: Stenhouse.

_____.2014. *Teaching the Core Skills of Listening and Speaking.* Alexandria, VA: ASCD. This is an excellent source for learning how to effectively teach speaking and listening. See also Palmer's excellent book *Well Spoken* (above).

Parrett, William H., and Kathleen M. Budge. 2012. *Turning High-Poverty Schools into High-Performing Schools*. Alexandria, VA: ASCD.

_____.2016. "5 Questions That Promote Student Success in High-Poverty Schools." *Edutopia: Education Equity,* June 15. http://www.edutopia.org/blog/high-poverty-schools-promote-student-success-william-parrett-kathleen-budge.

Pearson, P. David, and Margaret C. Gallagher. 1983. "The Instruction of Reading Comprehension." *Contemporary Educational Psychology* 8 (3) (July): 317–344. https://doi.org/10.1016/0361-476X(83)90019-X.

Peterson, Sarah E. 2016. "Using Storybooks to Enhance Literacy Development in Early Emergent Readers." *WSRA Journal* [Wisconsin State Reading Association] 53 (2) (Spring): 16–27.

Pilgreen, Janice. 2000. *The SSR Handbook: How to Organize and Manage a Sustained Silent Reading Program*. Portsmouth, NH: Heinemann. http://www.teslej.org/wordpress/issues/volume4/ej16/ej16r14/?wscr.

Pink, Daniel. 2009. *Drive: The Surprising Truth About What Motivates Us*. New York: Riverhead Books.

Popham, W. James. 2008. *Transformative Assessment*. Alexandria, VA: ASCD.

Popova, Maria. 2015. "Poet Jane Kenyon's Advice on Writing: Some of the Wisest Words to Create and Live By." *Brainpickings,* September 15. https://www.brainpickings.org/2015/09/15/jane-kenyon-advice-on-writing/.

Poverty and Race Research Action Council (PRRAC). 2011. "Annotated Bibliography: The Impact of School-Based Poverty Concentration on Academic Achievement & Student Outcomes." Washington, DC: Author. http://www.prrac.org/pdf/annotated_bibliography_on_school_poverty_concentration.pdf.

Powers, William. 2010. *Hamlet's BlackBerry: A Practical Philosophy for Building a Good Life in the Digital Age*. New York: HarperCollins.

Prothero, Arianna. 2016. "Charter Schools Aren't Good for Blacks, Civil Rights Groups Say." *Education Week*, August 30. http://www.edweek.org/ew/articles/2016/08/31/charter-schools-arent-good-for-blacks-civil.html.

_____.2016. "Does Graduating from a Charter Help or Hinder Future Earnings?" *Education Week,* September 13. http://www.edweek.org/ew/articles/2016/09/14/does-graduating-from-a-charter-help-or.html.

Ravitch, Diane. 2016. "Renouncing the Common Core." *The New York Times,* July 24, Sunday Review, 9. http://www.nytimes.com/2016/07/24/opinion/sunday/the-common-core-costs-billions-and-hurts-students.html?_r=0.

Reardon, Sean F., Jane Waldfogel, and Daphna Bassok. 2016. "The Good News About Educational Equality." *The New York Times,* August 28, Sunday Review, 10. http://www.nytimes.com/2016/08/28/opinion/sunday/the-good-news-about-educational-inequality.html?_r=0.

Reed, Dwayne. 2016. "Welcome to the Fourth Grade." Video rap song. August 20. https://www.youtube.com/watch?v=XBLcuGunRxU&feature=youtu.be.

Remillard, Janine T. 2016. "How to Partner with Your Curriculum." *Educational Leadership,* October, 34–38.

Renwick, Matt. 2015. "When Technology Isn't Necessary (and Maybe Not Even Nice)." *ASCD Edge* (blog). October 9. http://edge.ascd.org/blogpost/when-technology-isnt-necessary-and-maybe-not-even-nice.

_____.2016. *5 Myths About Classroom Technology: How Do We Integrate Digital Tools to Truly Enhance Learning?* Alexandria, VA: ASCD.

_____.2016. "Technology for the Sake of Technology: Consider the Why and the How." *Reading by Example* (blog). January 23. https://readingbyexample.com/2016/01/23/technology-for-the-sake-of-technology-consider-the-why-and-the-how/.

_____.2016. "Why I am #NotatISTE16." *Reading by Example* (blog). June 25. https://readingbyexample.com/2016/06/25/why-i-am-notatiste16/.

Reynolds, Barry Lee. 2015. "A Mixed-Methods Approach to Investigating First- and Second-Language Incidental Vocabulary Acquisition Through Reading of Fiction." *Reading Research Quarterly* 50 (1) (January/February/March): 111–127. doi:10.1002/rrq.88.

Rief, Linda. 2003. *100 Quickwrites: Fast and Effective Freewriting Exercises That Build Students' Confidence, Develop Their Fluency, and Bring Out the Writer in Every Student.* New York: Scholastic.

Ripley, Amanda. 2013. *The Smartest Kids in the World and How They Got That Way.* New York: Simon and Schuster.

_____.2016. "What the U.S. Can Learn from Other Nations' Schools." *The New York Times,* December 8, The Upshot. http://www.nytimes.com/2016/12/06/upshot/what-america-can-learn-about-smart-schools-in-other-countries.html?_r=0.

Ripp, Pernille. 2015. "6 Simple Ideas to Get Kids to Read." *Pernille Ripp* (blog). July 22. https://pernillesripp.com/2015/07/22/6-simple-ideas-to-get-kids-to-read.

Robinson, Ken, and Lou Aronica. 2015. *Creative Schools: The Grassroots Movement That's Transforming Education.* New York: Viking Penguin.

Rosenblatt, Roger. 2016. "By the Book." *The New York Times,* January 10, Sunday Review, SR8.

Rothstein, Dan, and Luz Santana. 2011. *Make Just One Change: Teach Students to Ask Their Own Questions.* Cambridge, MA: Harvard Education Press.

Routman, Regie. 1988. *Transitions: From Literature to Literacy.* Portsmouth, NH: Heinemann.

_____.1996. *Literacy at the Crossroads: Crucial Talk About Reading, Writing, and Other Teaching Dilemmas.* Portsmouth, NH: Heinemann.

_____.2000. *Conversations: Strategies for Teaching, Learning, and Evaluating.* Portsmouth, NH: Heinemann.

_____.2000. *Kids' Poems: Teaching Children to Love Writing Poetry.* New York: Scholastic. Separate volumes for kindergarten, grade 1, grade 2, and grades 3–4.

_____.2003. *Reading Essentials: The Specifics You Need to Teach Reading Well.* Portsmouth, NH: Heinemann.

_____.2005. *Regie Routman in Residence: Transforming Our Teaching Through Reading/Writing Connections.* Video-based series. Session 7, "Shared Writing to Reading." Portsmouth, NH: Heinemann.

_____.2005. *Writing Essentials: Raising Expectations and Results While Simplifying Teaching.* Portsmouth, NH: Heinemann.

_____.2008, 2013. *Regie Routman in Residence: Transforming Our Teaching.* Video-based literacy series. Portsmouth, NH: Heinemann. See sessions 8, 9, and 10 in *Writing for Audience and Purpose* for videos of content and editing conferences. See http://www.regieroutman.com/inresidence/rdg/samples.aspx from *Reading for Understanding* for 17-minute video of an informal reading conference.

_____.2008. *Teaching Essentials: Expecting the Most and Getting the Best from Every Learner, K–8.* Portsmouth, NH: Heinemann. Companion website: http://regieroutman.com/teachingessentials/default.asp. See http://regieroutman.com/teachingessentials/DIBELS.asp for research on DIBELS.

_____.2012. *Literacy and Learning Lessons from a Longtime Teacher.* Newark, DE: International Reading Association.

_____.2013. "To Raise Achievement, Let's Celebrate Teachers Before We Evaluate Them." *Reading Today* (June/July): 10–12. http://www.regieroutman.org/files/4813/7842/4350/Reading_Today-6-13.pdf.

_____.2014. *Read, Write, Lead: Breakthrough Strategies for Schoolwide Literacy Success.* Alexandria, VA: ASCD. Chapter 4, "Reducing the Need for Intervention", pages 137–180, is available at http://www.ascd.org/publications/books/113016/chapters/Reducing-the-Need-for-Intervention.aspx.

_____.2014. "What Reflects a Great School? Not Test Scores." *Education Week,* October 21, Commentary. http://regieroutman.org/files/9414/2051/7470/Regie_Routman_Education_Week_Commentary.pdf.

_____.2015. "Creating a Culture of Trust." http://www.regieroutman.org/files/1014/2508/7728/creating-culture-trust.pdf.

_____.2016. "10 Surefire Ideas to Remove Writing Roadblocks." *Middleweb* (blog). January 10. https://www.middleweb.com/26954/10-surefire-ideas-to-remove-writing-roadblocks/. Includes an embedded video on telling the story—in this case, a memoir snippet—before writing it.

_____.2016. "Teacher Education, Not Teacher Training." *edCircuit,* February 1. http://www.edcircuit.com/teacher-education-not-teacher-training/.

_____.2017. *Transforming Our Teaching: On-Demand Mini-Courses.* Portsmouth, NH: Heinemann. "Reading to Understand K–6" at Hein.pub/RoutmanOnDemand. "Reading/Writing Connections K–1" at Hein.pub/RoutmanSingleSession.

Rowe, Claudia. 2016. "Garfield High Principal Wrestles with City's Divides." *The Seattle Times,* June 26, A1, A16 and A17.

Russakoff, Dale. 2015. *The Prize: Who's in Charge of America's Schools?* New York: Houghton Mifflin Harcourt.

Sahlberg, Pasi. 2010. "Learning from Finland: How One of the World's Top Educational Performers Turned Around." *Boston Globe,* December 27, Op-Ed. http://archive.boston.com/bostonglobe/editorial_opinion/oped/articles/2010/12/27/learning_from_finland.

Samuels, Christina. 2016. "Special Education Graduation Disparities Highlighted in New Report." *Education Week: On Special Education* (blog). January 21. http://blogs.edweek.org/edweek/speced/2016/01/special_education_graduation_d.html.

Schaps, Eric. 2005. "Student Health, Supportive Schools, and Academic Success." In *The Role of Supportive School Environments in Promoting Academic Success: Getting Results, Developing Safe and Healthy Kids: Update 5.* Sacramento: California Department of Education. https://www.collaborativeclassroom.org/research-articles-and-papers-the-role-of-supportive-school-environments-in-promoting-academic-success.

Schmoker, Mike. 2015. "It's Time to Restructure Teacher Professional Development." *Education Week,* October 21, Commentary. http://www.edweek.org/ew/articles/2015/10/21/its-time-to-restructure-teacher-professional-development.html.

Scholastic. 2015. *Kids and Family Reading Report.* 6th ed. New York: Scholastic. http://mediaroom.scholastic.com/kfrr.

Schwartz, Katrina. 2017. "Why Group Work Could Be the Key to English Learner Success." *Mind/Shift,* February 23. https://ww2.kqed.org/mindshift/2017/02/23/why-group-work-could-be-the-key-to-english-learner-success/.

Shanahan, Timothy, and Cynthia R. Shanahan. 2015. "Disciplinary Literacy Comes to Middle School." *Voices in the Middle* 22 (3) (March): 10–13.

Shen, Danxi. 2016. "Quick Write." ABLConnect (online repository). Boston: Harvard University, Graduate School of Education. September 20. http://ablconnect.harvard.edu/quick-write.

Sibberson, Franki, and Karen Szymusiak. 2016. *Still Learning to Read: Teaching Students in Grades 3–6.* 2nd ed. Portland, ME: Stenhouse.

Simmons, Andrew. 2014. "Why Teaching Poetry Is So Important." *The Atlantic,* April 8. http://www.theatlantic.com/education/archive/2014/04/why-teaching-poetry-is-so-important/360346/.

Singer, Natasha. 2016. "Amazon to Pursue Education Technology with a Marketplace for Teachers." *The New York Times,* June 28, B8. https://www.nytimes.com/2016/06/28/technology/amazon-unveils-online-education-service-for-teachers.html.

Smith, Nicole Boudreau. May 2017. "A Principled Revolution in the Teaching of Writing." *English Journal* 106(5): 70–75.

Society for Research in Child Development. 2017. "For Youth of Color, Losing Trust in Teachers May Mean Losing the Chance to Make It to College." *Science Daily,* February 8. https://www.sciencedaily.com/releases/2017/02/170208094432.htm.

Souter, David. 2012. "Former Supreme Court Justice Souter on the Danger of America's 'Pervasive Civic Ignorance.'" *PBS NewsHour,* discussion moderated by Margaret Warner. September 17. Video excerpt: https://www.youtube.com/watch?v=rWcVtWennr0.

Sparks, Sarah D. 2015. "RTI Practice Falls Short of Promise, Research Finds." *Education Week,* November 11, 1 and 12. http://www.edweek.org/ew/articles/2015/11/11/study-rti-practice-falls-short-of-promise.html.

_____.2016. "Focus on Fade-Out (Part 2): What We Learn from Lost Effects in Education." *Education Week* (blog). January 20. http://blogs.edweek.org/edweek/inside-school-research/2016/01/fade-out_2_faltering_education.html.

_____.2016. "Achievement Gaps and Racial Segregation: Research Finds an Insidious Cycle." *Education Week* (blog). April 29. http://blogs.edweek.org/edweek/inside-school-research/2016/04/achievement_gaps_school_segregation_reardon.html.

_____.2016. "New 'What Works Clearinghouse' Aims to Help Districts Find Research for ESSA." *Education Week* (blog). September 12. Retrieved at http://blogs.edweek.org/edweek/inside-school-research/2016/09/what_works_clearinghouse_ESSA_overhaul.html. (Note updated website for What Works Clearinghouse: http://ies.ed.gov/ncee/wwc/.)

Spichtig, Alexandra, Elfrieda Hiebert, Christina Vorstius, Jeffrey Pascoe, P. David Pearson, and Ralph Radach. 2016. "The Decline of Comprehension-Based Silent Reading Efficiency in the United States: A Comparison of Current Data with Performance in 1960." *Reading Research Quarterly* 51 (2) (April/May/June): 239–259. doi: 10.1002/rrq.137.

Spiegler, Jinnie. 2016. "Turning Current Events Instruction into Social Justice Teaching." *Edutopia,* January 6. http://www.edutopia.org/blog/current-events-social-justice-teaching-jinnie-spiegler. Author is the director of curriculum, Anti-Defamation League. Blog post includes some excellent ideas.

Stanovich, Keith E. 1986. "Matthew Effects in Reading: Some Consequences of Individual Differences in the Acquisition of Literacy." *Reading Research Quarterly* 21 (Fall): 360–406. http://people.uncw.edu/kozloffm/mattheweffect.pdf.

Stark, Lisa. 2016. "Boston Brings the Music Back by Boosting Arts Education." *PBS NewsHour,* September 27. http://www.pbs.org/newshour/bb/boston-brings-music-back-boosting-arts-education/.

Steinem, Gloria. 2015. Interview. *The Tavis Smiley Show.* National Public Radio, November 2.

Stiggins, Rick. 2014. "Improve Assessment Literacy Outside of Schools Too." *Phi Delta Kappan* 96 (2) (October): 67–72. doi: 10.1177/0031721714553413.

Superville, Denisa R. 2015. "Students Take Too Many Redundant Tests, Study Finds." *Education Week,* October 24. http://www.edweek.org/ew/articles/2015/10/28/students-take-too-many-redundant-tests-study.html.

Taylor, Barbara M., Debra S. Peterson, P. David Pearson, and Michael C. Rodriguez. 2002. "Looking Inside Classrooms: Reflecting on the 'How' as Well as the 'What' in Effective Reading Instruction." *The Reading Teacher* 56 (3) (November): 270–279.

Tobar, Héctor. 2016. "The Spanish Lesson I Never Got at School." *The New York Times,* November 15, Op-Ed, A27. http://www.nytimes.com/2016/11/15/opinion/the-spanish-lesson-i-never-got-at-school.html?_r=0.

Tomlinson, Carol Ann, and Michael Murphy. 2015. *Leading for Differentiation: Growing Teachers Who Grow Kids.* Alexandria, VA: ASCD.

Tovani, Cris. 2012. "Feedback Is a Two-Way Street." *Educational Leadership,* September, 49–51.

Trudeau, Justin. 2016. "Justin Trudeau Explains the Power of Diversity." Talk in Davos, Switzerland, January 21. Video. http://qz.com/602525/justin-trudeau-perfectly-articulates-the-value-of-diversity-in-childhood-not-just-in-the-workforce/.

Tucker, Mark. 2016. "Professional Development Transformed." *Education Week* (blog). January 14. http://blogs.edweek.org/edweek/top_performers/2016/01/professional_development_transformed.html?cmp=SOC-SHR-TW.

Turkle, Sherry. 2015. *Reclaiming Conversation: The Power of Talk in a Digital Age.* New York: Penguin Press.

Turner, Julianne, and Scott G. Paris. 1995. "How Literacy Tasks Influence Children's Motivation for Literacy." *The Reading Teacher* 48 (8) (May): 662–673.

Ujifusa, Andrew. 2017. "Nationwide Voucher Program Could Cripple Most Districts, Report Argues." *Education Week, Charters and Choice* (blog). March 6. http://blogs.edweek.org/edweek/charterschoice/2017/03/report_nationwide_voucher_program_could_cripple_vast_majority_of_districts.html?cmp=soc-edit-tw.

Umansky, Ilana M., Rachel A. Valentino, and Sean F. Reardon. "The Promise of Two-Language Education." *Educational Leadership,* February (themed issue, "Helping ELLs Excel"), 10–17.

Valencia, Sheila. 2011. "Using Assessment to Improve Teaching and Learning." In *What Research Has to Say About Reading Instruction* (4th ed.), ed. S. Jay Samuels and Alan E. Farstrup. Newark, DE: International Reading Association.

Valencia, Sheila, and Marsha Riddle Buly. 2005. "Behind Test Scores: What Struggling Readers *Really* Need." In *Reading Assessment Principles and Practices for Elementary Teachers* (2nd ed.), ed. Shelby J. Barrentine and Sandra M. Stokes. Newark, DE: International Reading Association.

Vaughn-Smith, Matthew. 2016. "Stop Wasting Time: Be Intentional." *Mr. Vaughn-Smith's Literacy Corner* (blog). February 13. http://vsliteracycorner.weebly.com/literacy-in-action/stop-wasting-time-be-intentional.

Wallis, Judy. 2011. "Practical Solutions for Complex Leadership Issues." Session at CESA 6, Literacy and Leadership Institute, Milwaukee, Wisconsin, June.

———. 2013. "Teachers, Don't Forget Joy." *Education Week,* October 16. http://www.edweek.org/ew/articles/2013/10/16/08wallis.h33.html.

Watson, Angela. 2014. "8 Ways Teachers Can Talk Less and Get Kids Talking More." *The Cornerstone for Teachers* (blog). September 11. http://thecornerstoneforteachers.com/2014/09/8-ways-teachers-can-talk-less-get-kids-talking.html.

Weiner, Eric. 2015. "In a Digital Chapter, Paper Notebooks Are as Relevant as Ever." *Morning Edition.* National Public Radio, May 27.

Wells, Amy Stuart, Lauren Fox, and Diana Cordova-Cobo. 2016. *How Racially Diverse Schools and Classrooms Can Benefit All Students.* New York City and Washington, DC: Century Foundation.

What Works Clearinghouse. Institute of Educational Sciences. Washington, DC: U.S. Department of Education. https://ies.ed.gov/ncee/wwc/.

Wilhelm, Jeffrey D., and Michael W. Smith. 2017. *Diving Deep into Nonfiction, Grades 6–12: Transferable Tools for Reading ANY Nonfiction Text.* Thousand Oaks, CA: Corwin.

Wiliam, Dylan. 2013. "Assessment: The Bridge Between Teaching and Learning." *Voices from the Middle* 21 (2) (December): 15–20.

_____.2016. "The Secret of Effective Feedback." *Educational Leadership,* April, 10–15. http://www.ascd.org/publications/educational-leadership/apr16/vol73/num07/The-Secret-of-Effective-Feedback.aspx.

Wolk, Steven. 2008. "Joy in School." *Educational Leadership,* September, 8–15. http://www.ascd.org/publications/educational-leadership/sept08/vol66/num01/Joy-in-School.aspx.

Woodson, Jacqueline. 2016. *Another Brooklyn.* Book talk at Elliott Bay Book Company, Seattle, Washington, September 21.

Worthy, Jo, Beth Maloch, Becky Pursley, Holly Hungerford-Kresser, Angela Hampton, Michelle Jordan, and Peggy Semingson. 2015. "What Are the Rest of the Students Doing? Literacy Work Stations in Two First-Grade Classrooms." *Language Arts* 92 (3) (January): 173–186.

Wright, Wayne E. 2016. "Let Them Talk!" *Educational Leadership,* February (themed issue, "Helping ELLs Excel"), 24–29.

Zakaria, Fareed. 2015. *In Defense of a Liberal Education.* New York: and London: W. W. Norton.

Zernike, Kate. 2016. "Heralded Choice Fails to Fix Detroit's Schools." *The New York Times,* June 29, A1, A14, and A15.

Zmuda, Allison. 2015. "Personalized Learning." In *Excellence Through Equity: Five Principles of Courageous Leadership to Guide Achievement for Every Student,* ed. Alan M. Blankstein and Pedro Noguera. Alexandria, VA: ASCD.

Literature Cited

Alexander, Kwame. 2014. *The Crossover.* Boston, MA: Houghton Mifflin Harcourt.

_____.2016. *Booked.* Boston, MA: Houghton Mifflin Harcourt.

Alexie, Sherman. 2007. *The Absolutely True Diary of a Part-Time Indian.* New York: Little, Brown.

Alexie, Sherman (author), and Yuyi Morales (illustrator). 2016. *Thunder Boy Jr.* New York and Boston: Little, Brown.

Applegate, Katherine (author), and Patricia Castelao (illustrator). 2015. *The One and Only Ivan.* New York: HarperCollins.

Austen, Jane. 1813. *Pride and Prejudice.* London: Thomas Egerton.

Barnes, Julian. 2011. *The Sense of an Ending.* London: Alfred A. Knopf.

Benedict, Elizabeth, ed. 2013. *What My Mother Gave Me: Thirty-one Women on the Gifts That Mattered Most.* Chapel Hill, NC: Algonquin Books of Chapel Hill.

Bergner, Daniel. 2016. *Sing for Your Life: A Story of Race, Music, and Family.* New York: Lee Boudreax Books.

Berne, Jennifer. 2013. *On a Beam of Light: A Story of Albert Einstein.* San Francisco: Chronicle Books.

Bronte, Charlotte. 1847. *Jane Eyre.* London: Smith, Elder.

DeGross, Monalisa. 1998. *Donavan's Word Jar*. New York: HarperCollins.

Dennis, Brian, Kirby Larson, and Mary Nethery. 2009. *Nubs: The True Story of a Mutt, a Marine, and a Miracle*. New York: Little, Brown.

Frasier, Deborah. 2007. *Miss Alaineus: A Vocabulary Disaster*. Boston: Houghton Mifflin Harcourt.

Green, John. 2005. *Looking for Alaska*. New York: Dutton Books.

_____ .2012. *The Fault in Our Stars*. New York: Penguin Books.

Hesse, Karen. 1997. *Out of the Dust*. New York: Scholastic Press.

Holland, Jennifer. 2011. *Unlikely Friendships: 47 Remarkable Stories from the Animal Kingdom*. New York: Workman.

Hopkins, Joseph H., and Jill McElmurry. 2013. *The Tree Lady*. New York: Beach Lane Books.

Hosseini, Khaled. 2003. *The Kite Runner*. New York: Riverhead Books.

Ignotofsky, Rachel. 2016. *Women in Science: 50 Fearless Pioneers Who Changed the World*. New York: Ten Speed Press.

Jahren, Hope. 2016. *Lab Girl*. New York: Random House.

Jeffers, Oliver, and Sam Winston. 2016. *A Child of Books*. Somerville, MA: Candlewick Press.

King, Martin Luther. 1963. "Letter from a Birmingham Jail."

Kuntz, Doug, and Amy Shrodes (authors), and Sue Cornelison (illustrator). 2017. *Lost and Found Cat: The True Story of Kunkush's Incredible Journey*. New York: Crown Books for Young Readers.

Larson, Kirby, and Mary Nethery. 2008. *Two Bobbies: A True Story of Hurricane Katrina, Friendship, and Survival*. New York: Walker Publishing.

Levy, Debbie (author), and Elizabeth Baddeley (illustrator). 2016. *I Dissent: Ruth Bader Ginsburg Makes Her Mark*. New York: Simon and Schuster.

Ludwig, Trudy. 2005. *My Secret Bully*. Berkeley, CA: Tricycle Press.

_____ .2006. *Sorry!* Berkeley, CA: Tricycle Press.

Magoon, Scott. 2014. *Breathe*. New York: Simon and Schuster.

Martin, Jacqueline Briggs (author), and Mary Azarian (illustrator). 1998. *Snowflake Bentley*. Boston: Houghton Mifflin Harcourt.

McCann, Colum. 2015. *Thirteen Ways of Looking*. New York: Random House.

Medina, Jane. 1999. *My Name Is Jorge on Both Sides of the River: Poems in English and Spanish*. Honesdale, PA: WordSong.

Newman, Mark. 2015. *Polar Bears*. New York: Square Fish Publishers.

Palacio, R. J. 2012. *Wonder*. New York: Alfred A. Knopf.

_____ .2015. *Auggie and Me*. New York: Knopf Books for Young Readers.

Partridge, Elizabeth. 2002. *This Land Was Made for You and Me: The Life and Songs of Woody Guthrie*. New York: Viking.

Polacco, Patricia. 2012. *The Art of Miss Chew*. New York: G. P. Putnam's Sons.

Proimos, James. 2009. *Paulie Pastrami Achieves World Peace*. New York: Little, Brown Books for Young Readers.

Richardson, Trish. 2015. Editor for class-authored (grades two–three) *Polar Bears Are the King of the North*. sten.pub/literacyessentials.

Rowell, Rainbow. 2013. *Eleanor and Park*. New York: St. Martin's.

Ryan, Pam Muñoz. 2002. *When Marian Sang: The True Recital of Marian Anderson*. New York: Scholastic.

Saunders, George. 2013. *The Tenth of December*. New York: Random House.

Shoveler, Herb. 2008. *Ryan and Jimmy: And the Well in Africa That Brought Them Together*. Toronto: Kids Can Press.

Siegel, Siena Cherson. 2006. *To Dance: A Ballerina's Graphic Novel*. New York: Atheneum Books for Young Readers.

Solnit, Rebecca. 2016. *Hope in the Dark: Untold Histories, Wild Possibilities*. Chicago: Haymarket Books.

Spires, Ashley. 2014. *The Most Magnificent Thing*. Toronto, Ontario, Canada: Kids Can Press.

Stanley, Diane. 2016. *Ada Lovelace, Poet of Science: The First Computer Programmer*. New York: Simon & Schuster Books for Young Readers.

Steptoe, Javaka. 2016. *Radiant Child: The Story of Young Artist Jean-Michel Basquiat*. New York: Little, Brown.

Stone, Tanya Lee. 2008. *Sandy's Circus: A Story About Alexander Calder*. New York: Viking.

Strout, Elizabeth. 2014. *Olive Kitteridge*. New York: Random House.

Thimmesh, Catherine. 2011. *Friends: True Stories of Extraordinary Animal Friendships*. Boston: Houghton Mifflin Harcourt.

Waber, Bernard. 2002. *Courage*. Boston: Houghton Mifflin Harcourt.

Walters, Eric. 2013. *My Name Is Blessing*. Toronto, Ontario, Canada: Tundra Books.

Ward, Jesmyn, ed. 2016. *The Fire This Time: A New Generation Speaks About Race*. New York: Scribner.

Winter, Jeanette. 1998. *My Name Is Georgia: A Portrait*. San Diego, CA: Silver Whistle/Harcourt Brace.

Winter, Jonah (author), and Edel Rodriguez (illustrator). 2009. *Sonia Sotomayor: A Judge Grows in the Bronx*. New York: Atheneum Books for Young Readers. (A bilingual picture book in English and Spanish.)

Woodson, Jacqueline. 2012. *Each Kindness*. New York: Nancy Paulsen Books.

_____. 2014. *Brown Girl Dreaming*. New York: Nancy Paulsen Books.

_____. 2016. *Another Brooklyn*. New York: HarperCollins.

Yamada, Kobi. 2014. *What Do You Do with an Idea?* Seattle, WA: Compendium Inc.

Videos

Coates, Ta-Nehisi. 2015. "Advice on Writing." Three-minute video. *The Atlantic*, August. https://www.facebook.com/TheAtlantic/videos/10153577188343487/.

Freedom Road. 2016. By third and fourth graders in collaboration with their classroom teacher, Daria Orloff, and music teacher, Randal Bychuk, Strathmillan Elementary School, Winnipeg, Manitoba, Canada. https://www.youtube.com/watch?v=bsCDwWepjFU.

Global Goals for Sustainable Development. 2016. Brief video on girl power; appropriate and inspiring for high school students. https://www.youtube.com/watch?v=sZQ2RUFd54o.

Obama, Michelle. 2016. Speech to Democratic National Convention, Cleveland, Ohio, July 25. https://www.youtube.com/watch?v=4ZNWYqDU948.

Reed, Dwayne. 2016. "Welcome to the Fourth Grade." Video rap song. https://www.youtube.com/watch?v=XBLcuGunRxU&feature=youtube.

Richardson, Trish, and Regie Routman. 2016. Scaffolded conversation with third grader Liam. https://youtu.be/_6v8clz_Z9w.

Routman, Regie. 2005. Three-minute video on "Sharing Our Stories" with students, as part of "Setting up the classroom for independent readers and writers." *Transforming Our Teaching Through Reading/Writing Connections.* Portsmouth, NH: Heinemann. http://www.regieroutman.com/inresidence/cnctn/samples.aspx.

———.2008 and 2013. Video of 17-minute informal reading conference with a fourth-grade ELL student. *Transforming Our Teaching Through Reading to Understand.* Portsmouth, NH: Heinemann. http://www.regieroutman.com/inresidence/rdg/samples.aspx.

———.2016. "Ten Surefire Ideas to Remove Writing Roadblocks." Seven-minute video embedded within article. *Middleweb* (blog). http://www.middleweb.com/26954/10-surefire-ideas-to-remove-writing-roadblocks/.

———.N.d. Interview with Kathy, a reader, as a high school student. http://regieroutman.com/inresidence/overview.aspx.

Trudeau, Justin. 2016. "Justin Trudeau Explains the Power of Diversity." Video of talk in Davos, Switzerland, January 21. http://qz.com/602525/justin-trudeau-perfectly-articulates-the-value-of-diversity-in-childhood-not-just-in-the-workforce/.

INDEX